COLERIDGE.

THE WORKS

OF

THOMAS CARLYLE

(COMPLETE)

v.13

THE

LIFE OF JOHN STERLING

LATTER-DAY PAMPHLETS

ILLUSTRATED

Volume Thirteen

NEW YORK
PETER FENELON COLLIER, PUBLISHER
1897

0752

CONTENTS.

LIFE OF JOHN STERLING.

Part I.

Part II.

CONTENTS.

Part III.

LATTER–DAY PAMPHLETS.

LIFE OF JOHN STERLING.

PART I.

CHAPTER I.

INTRODUCTORY.

NEAR seven years ago, a short while before his death in 1844, John Sterling committed the care of his literary Character and printed Writings to two friends, Archdeacon Hare and myself. His estimate of the bequest was far from overweening; to few men could the small sum-total of his activities in this world seem more inconsiderable than, in those last solemn days, it did to him. He had burnt much; found much unworthy; looking steadfastly into the silent continents of Death and Eternity, a brave man's judgments about his own sorry work in the field of Time are not apt to be too lenient. But, in fine, here was some portion of his work which the world had already got hold of, and which he could not burn. This too, since it was not to be abolished and annihilated, but must still for some time live and act, he wished to be wisely settled, as the rest had been. And so it was left in charge to us, the survivors, to do for it what we judged fittest, if indeed doing nothing did not seem the fittest to us. This message, communicated after his decease, was naturally a sacred one to Mr. Hare and me.

After some consultation on it, and survey of the difficulties and delicate considerations involved in it, Archdeacon Hare

3

and I agreed that the whole task, of selecting what Writings
were to be reprinted, and of drawing up a Biography to introduce them, should be left to him alone; and done without
interference of mine: — as accordingly it was,[1] in a manner
surely far superior to the common, in every good quality of
editing; and visibly everywhere bearing testimony to the
friendliness, the piety, perspicacity and other gifts and virtues
of that eminent and amiable man.

In one respect, however, if in one only, the arrangement had
been unfortunate. Archdeacon Hare, both by natural tendency
and by his position as a Churchman, had been led, in editing
a Work not free from ecclesiastical heresies, and especially in
writing a Life very full of such, to dwell with preponderating
emphasis on that part of his subject; by no means extenuat-
ing the fact, nor yet passing lightly over it (which a layman
could have done) as needing no extenuation; but carefully
searching into it, with the view of excusing and explaining it;
dwelling on it, presenting all the documents of it, and as it
were spreading it over the whole field of his delineation; as if
religious heterodoxy had been the grand fact of Sterling's life,
which even to the Archdeacon's mind it could by no means
seem to be. *Hinc illæ lachrymæ.* For the Religious Newspapers, and Periodical Heresy-hunters, getting very lively in
those years, were prompt to seize the cue; and have prosecuted and perhaps still prosecute it, in their sad way, to all
lengths and breadths. John Sterling's character and writings,
which had little business to be spoken of in any Church-court,
have hereby been carried thither as if for an exclusive trial;
and the mournfulest set of pleadings, out of which nothing
but a misjudgment *can* be formed, prevail there ever since.
The noble Sterling, a radiant child of the empyrean, clad in
bright auroral hues in the memory of all that knew him, —
what is he doing here in inquisitorial *sanbenito*, with nothing
but ghastly spectralities prowling round him, and inarticulately screeching and gibbering what they call their judgment
on him!

---

[1] *John Sterling's Essays and Tales, with Life* by Archdeacon Hare.
Parker; London, 1848.

" The sin of Hare's Book," says one of my Correspondents in those years, " is easily defined, and not very condemnable, but it is nevertheless ruinous to his task as Biographer. He takes up Sterling as a clergyman merely. Sterling, I find, was a curate for exactly eight months; during eight months and no more had he any special relation to the Church. But he was a man, and had relation to the Universe, for eight-and-thirty years: and it is in this latter character, to which all the others were but features and transitory hues, that we wish to know him. His battle with hereditary Church formulas was severe; but it was by no means his one battle with things inherited, nor indeed his chief battle; neither, according to my observation of what it was, is it successfully delineated or summed up in this Book. The truth is, nobody that had known Sterling would recognize a feature of him here; you would never dream that this Book treated of *him* at all. A pale sickly shadow in torn surplice is presented to us here; weltering bewildered amid heaps of what you call 'Hebrew Old-clothes;' wrestling, with impotent impetuosity, to free itself from the baleful imbroglio, as if that had been its one function in life: who in this miserable figure would recognize the brilliant, beautiful and cheerful John Sterling, with his ever-flowing wealth of ideas, fancies, imaginations; with his frank affections, inexhaustible hopes, audacities, activities, and general radiant vivacity of heart and intelligence, which made the presence of him an illumination and inspiration wherever he went? It is too bad. Let a man be honestly forgotten when his life ends; but let him not be misremembered in this way. To be hung up as an ecclesiastical scarecrow, as a target for heterodox and orthodox to practise archery upon, is no fate that can be due to the memory of Sterling. It was not as a ghastly phantasm, choked in Thirty-nine-article controversies, or miserable Semitic, Anti-Semitic street-riots, — in scepticisms, agonized self-seekings, that this man appeared in life; nor as such, if the world still wishes to look at him, should you suffer the world's memory of him now to be. Once for all, it is unjust; emphatically untrue as an image of John Sterling: perhaps to few men that lived along with him could such an interpretation of their existence be more inapplicable."

Whatever truth there might be in these rather passionate representations, and to myself there wanted not a painful feeling of their truth, it by no means appeared what help or remedy any friend of Sterling's, and especially one so related to the matter as myself, could attempt in the interim. Perhaps endure in patience till the dust laid itself again, as all dust does if you leave it well alone? Much obscuration would thus of its own accord fall away; and, in Mr. Hare's narrative itself, apart from his commentary, many features of Sterling's true character would become decipherable to such as sought them. Censure, blame of this ·Work of Mr. Hare's was naturally far from my thoughts. A work which distinguishes itself ·by human piety and candid intelligence; which, in all details, is careful, lucid, exact; and which offers, as we say, to the observant reader that will interpret facts, many traits of Sterling besides his heterodoxy. Censure of it, from me especially, is not the thing due; from me a far other thing is due ! —

On the whole, my private thought was : First, How happy it comparatively is, for a man of any earnestness of life, to have no Biography written of him; but to return silently, with his small, sorely foiled bit of work, to the Supreme Silences, who alone can judge of it or him; and not to trouble the reviewers, and greater or lesser public, with attempting to judge it ! The idea of "fame," as they call it, posthumous or other, does not inspire one with much ecstasy in these points of view. — Secondly, That Sterling's performance and real or seeming importance in this world was actually not of a kind to demand an express Biography, even according to the world's usages. His character was not supremely original; neither was his fate in the world wonderful. What he did was inconsiderable enough; and as to what it lay in him to have done, this was but a problem, now beyond possibility of settlement. Why had a Biography been inflicted on this man; why had not No-biography, and the privilege of all the weary, been his lot? — Thirdly, That such lot, however, could now no longer be my good Sterling's; a tumult having risen around his name, enough to impress some pretended likeness of him (about as like as the Guy-Fauxes are, on Gunpowder-Day) upon the minds of many men: so that he could not be forgotten, and could only be misremembered, as matters now stood.

Whereupon, as practical conclusion to the whole, arose by degrees this final thought, That, at some calmer season, when the theological dust had well fallen, and both the matter itself, and my feelings on it, were in a suitabler condition, I ought to give my testimony about this friend whom I had known so well, and record clearly what my knowledge of him was. This has ever since seemed a kind of duty I had to do in the world before leaving it.

And so, having on my hands some leisure at this time, and being bound to it by evident considerations, one of which ought to be especially sacred to me, I decide to fling down on paper some outline of what my recollections and reflections contain in reference to this most friendly, bright and beautiful human soul; who walked with me for a season in this world, and remains to me very memorable while I continue in it. Gradually, if facts simple enough in themselves can be narrated as they came to pass, it will be seen what kind of man this was; to what extent condemnable for imaginary heresy and other crimes, to what extent laudable and lovable for noble manful *orthodoxy* and other virtues; — and whether the lesson his life had to teach us is not much the reverse of what the Religious Newspapers hitherto educe from it.

Certainly it was not as a "sceptic" that you could define him, whatever his definition might be. Belief, not doubt, attended him at all points of his progress; rather a tendency to too hasty and headlong belief. Of all men he was the least prone to what you could call scepticism: diseased self-listenings, self-questionings, impotently painful dubitations, all this fatal nosology of spiritual maladies, so rife in our day, was eminently foreign to him. Quite on the other side lay Sterling's faults, such as they were. In fact, you could observe, in spite of his sleepless intellectual vivacity, he was not properly a thinker at all; his faculties were of the active, not of the passive or contemplative sort. A brilliant *improvisatore;* rapid in thought, in word and in act; everywhere the promptest and least hesitating of men. I likened him often, in my banterings, to sheet-lightning; and reproachfully prayed that he would concentrate himself into a bolt, and rive the mountain-barriers for us, instead of merely playing on them and irradiating them.

True, he had his "religion" to seek, and painfully shape together for himself, out of the abysses of conflicting disbelief and sham-belief and bedlam delusion, now filling the world, as all men of reflection have; and in this respect too, — more especially as his lot in the battle appointed for us all was, if you can understand it, victory and not defeat, — he is an expressive emblem of his time, and an instruction and possession to his contemporaries. For, I say, it is by no means as a vanquished *doubter* that he figures in the memory of those who knew him; but rather as a victorious *believer,* and under great difficulties a victorious doer. An example to us all, not of lamed misery, helpless spiritual bewilderment and sprawling despair, or any kind of *drownage* in the foul welter of our so-called religious or other controversies and confusions; but of a swift and valiant vanquisher of all these; a noble asserter of himself, as worker and speaker, in spite of all these. Continually, so far as he went, he was a teacher, by act and word, of hope, clearness, activity, veracity, and human courage and nobleness : the preacher of a good gospel to all men, not of a bad to any man. The man, whether in priest's cassock or other costume of men, who is the enemy or hater of John Sterling, may assure himself that he does not yet know him, — that miserable differences of mere costume and dialect still divide him, whatsoever is worthy, catholic and perennial in him, from a brother soul who, more than most in his day, was his brother and not his adversary in regard to all that.

Nor shall the irremediable drawback that Sterling was not

current in the Newspapers, that he achieved neither what the world calls greatness nor what intrinsically is such, altogether discourage me. What his natural size, and natural and accidental limits were, will gradually appear, if my sketching be successful. And I have remarked that a true delineation of the smallest man, and his scene of pilgrimage through life, is capable of interesting the greatest man; that all men are to an unspeakable degree brothers, each man's life a strange emblem of every man's; and that Human Portraits, faithfully drawn, are of all pictures the welcomest on human walls. Monitions and moralities enough may lie in this small Work, if honestly written and honestly read; — and, in particular, if any image of John Sterling and his Pilgrimage through our poor Nineteenth Century be one day wanted by the world, and they can find some shadow of a true image here, my swift scribbling (which shall be very swift and immediate) may prove useful by and by.

CHAPTER II.

BIRTH AND PARENTAGE.

JOHN STERLING was born at Kaimes Castle, a kind of dilapidated baronial residence to which a small farm was then attached, rented by his Father, in the Isle of Bute, — on the 20th July, 1806. Both his parents were Irish by birth, Scotch by extraction; and became, as he himself did, essentially English by long residence and habit. Of John himself Scotland has little or nothing to claim except the birth and genealogy, for he left it almost before the years of memory; and in his mature days regarded it, if with a little more recognition and intelligence, yet without more participation in any of its accents outward or inward, than others natives of Middlesex or Surrey, where the scene of his chief education lay.

The climate of Bute is rainy, soft of temperature; with skies of unusual depth and brilliancy, while the weather is fair. In that soft rainy climate, on that wild-wooded rocky coast, with its gnarled mountains and green silent valleys, with its seething rain-storms and many-sounding seas, was young Sterling ushered into his first schooling in this world. I remember one little anecdote his Father told me of those first years: One of the cows had calved; young John, still in petticoats, was permitted to go, holding by his father's hand, and look at the newly arrived calf; a mystery which he surveyed with open intent eyes, and the silent exercise of all the scientific faculties he had; — very strange mystery indeed, this new arrival, and fresh denizen of our Universe: "Wull 't eat a-body?" said John in his first practical Scotch, inquiring into the tendencies this mystery might have to fall upon a little fellow and consume him as provision: "Will it eat one, Father?" — Poor little open-eyed John: the family long bantered him with this anecdote; and we, in far other years, laughed heartily on hearing it. — Simple peasant laborers, ploughers, house-servants, occasional fisher-people too; and the sight of ships, and crops, and Nature's doings where Art has little meddled with her: this was the kind of schooling our young friend had, first of all; on this bench of the grand world-school did he sit, for the first four years of his life.

Edward Sterling his Father, a man who subsequently came to considerable notice in the world, was originally of Waterford in Munster; son of the Episcopalian Clergyman there; and chief representative of a family of some standing in those parts. Family founded, it appears, by a Colonel Robert Sterling, called also Sir Robert Sterling; a Scottish Gustavus-Adolphus soldier, whom the breaking out of the Civil War had recalled from his German campaignings, and had before long, though not till after some waverings on his part, attached firmly to the Duke of Ormond and to the King's Party in that quarrel. A little bit of genealogy, since it lies ready to my hand, gathered long ago out of wider studies, and pleasantly connects things individual and present with the dim universal crowd of things past, — may as well be inserted here as thrown away.

This Colonel Robert designates himself Sterling "of Glorat;" I believe, a younger branch of the well-known Stirlings of Keir in Stirlingshire. It appears he prospered in his soldiering and other business, in those bad Ormond times; being a man of energy, ardor and intelligence, — probably prompt enough both with his word and with his stroke. There survives yet, in the Commons Journals,[1] dim notice of his controversies and adventures; especially of one controversy he had got into with certain victorious Parliamentary official parties, while his own party lay vanquished, during what was called the Ormond Cessation, or Temporary Peace made by Ormond with the Parliament in 1646 : — in which controversy Colonel Robert, after repeated applications, journeyings to London, attendances upon committees, and such like, finds himself worsted, declared to be in the wrong; and so vanishes from the Commons Journals.

What became of him when Cromwell got to Ireland, and to Munster, I have not heard: his knighthood, dating from the very year of Cromwell's Invasion (1649), indicates a man expected to do his best on the occasion : — as in all probability he did; had not Tredah Storm proved ruinous, and the neck of this Irish War been broken at once. Doubtless the Colonel Sir Robert followed or attended his Duke of Ormond into foreign parts, and gave up his management of Munster, while it was yet time : for after the Restoration we find him again, safe, and as was natural, flourishing with new splendor; gifted, recompensed with lands; — settled, in short, on fair revenues in those Munster regions. He appears to have had no children; but to have left his property to William, a younger brother who had followed him into Ireland. From this William descends the family which, in the years we treat of, had Edward Sterling, Father of our John, for its representative. And now enough of genealogy.

Of Edward Sterling, Captain Edward Sterling as his title was, who in the latter period of his life became well known in London political society, whom indeed all England, with a

[1] *Commons Journals*, iv. 15 (10th January, 1644–5); and again v. 307 &c., 498 (18th September, 1647–15th March, 1647–8).

curious mixture of mockery and respect and even fear, knew
well as "the Thunderer of the *Times* Newspaper," there were
much to be said, did the present task and its limits permit.
As perhaps it might, on certain terms ? What is indispensable
let us not omit to say. The history of a man's childhood is
the description of his parents and environment : this is his *in-*
articulate but highly important history, in those first times,
while of articulate he has yet none.

Edward Sterling had now just entered on his thirty-fourth
year ; and was already a man experienced in fortunes and
changes. A native of Waterford in Munster, as already mentioned ; born in the " Deanery House of Waterford, 27th February, 1773," say the registers. For his Father, as we learn,
resided in the Deanery House, though he was not himself Dean,
but only " Curate of the Cathedral " (whatever that may mean) ;
he was withal rector of two other livings, and the Dean's
friend, — friend indeed of the Dean's kinsmen the Beresfords
generally ; whose grand house of Curraghmore, near by Waterford, was a familiar haunt of his and his children's. This
reverend gentleman, along with his three livings and high
acquaintanceships, had inherited political connections ; — inherited especially a Government Pension, with survivorship
for still one life beyond his own ; his father having been Clerk
of the Irish House of Commons at the time of the Union, of
which office the lost salary was compensated in this way. The
Pension was of two hundred pounds ; and only expired with
the life of Edward, John's Father, in 1847. There were, and
still are, daughters of the family ; but Edward was the only
son ; — descended, too, from the Scottish hero Wallace, as the
old gentleman would sometimes admonish him ; his own wife,
Edward's mother, being of that name, and boasting herself, as
most Scotch Wallaces do, to have that blood in her veins.

This Edward had picked up, at Waterford, and among the
young Beresfords of Curraghmore and elsewhere, a thoroughly
Irish form of character : fire and fervor, vitality of all kinds,
in genial abundance ; but in a much more loquacious, ostentatious, much-*louder* style than is freely patronized on this side
of the Channel. Of Irish accent in speech he had entirely

divested himself, so as not to be traced by any vestige in that respect; but his Irish accent of character, in all manner of other more important respects, was very recognizable. An impetuous man, full of real energy, and immensely conscious of the same; who transacted everything not with the minimum of fuss and noise, but with the maximum: a very Captain Whirlwind, as one was tempted to call him.

In youth, he had studied at Trinity College, Dublin; visited the Inns of Court here, and trained himself for the Irish Bar. To the Bar he had been duly called, and was waiting for the results, — when, in his twenty-fifth year, the Irish Rebellion broke out; whereupon the Irish Barristers decided to raise a corps of loyal Volunteers, and a complete change introduced itself into Edward Sterling's way of life. For, naturally, he had joined the array of Volunteers; — fought, I have heard, " in three actions with the rebels" (Vinegar Hill, for one); and doubtless fought well: but in the mess-rooms, among the young military and civil officials, with all of whom he was a favorite, he had acquired a taste for soldier life, and perhaps high hopes of succeeding in it: at all events, having a commission in the Lancashire Militia offered him, he accepted that; altogether quitted the Bar, and became Captain Sterling thenceforth. From the Militia, it appears, he had volunteered with his Company into the Line; and, under some disappointments, and official delays of expected promotion, was continuing to serve as Captain there, "Captain of the Eighth Battalion of Reserve," say the Military Almanacs of 1803, — in which year the quarters happened to be Derry, where new events awaited him. At a ball in Derry he met with Miss Hester Coningham, the queen of the scene, and of the fair world in Derry at that time. The acquaintance, in spite of some opposition, grew with vigor, and rapidly ripened: and "at Fehan Church, Diocese of Derry," where the Bride's father had a country-house, "on Thursday 5th April, 1804, Hester Coningham, only daughter of John Coningham, Esquire, Merchant in Derry, and of Elizabeth Campbell his wife," was wedded to Captain Sterling; she happiest to him happiest, — as by Nature's kind law it is arranged.

Mrs. Sterling, even in her later days, had still traces of the old beauty : then and always she was a woman of delicate, pious, affectionate character; exemplary as a wife, a mother and a friend. A refined female nature ; something tremulous in it, timid, and with a certain rural freshness still unweakened by long converse with the world. The tall slim figure, always of a kind of quaker neatness ; the innocent anxious face, anxious bright hazel eyes; the timid, yet gracefully cordial ways, the natural intelligence, instinctive sense and worth, were very characteristic. Her voice too; with its something of soft querulousness, easily adapting itself to a light thin-flowing style of mirth on occasion, was characteristic : she had retained her Ulster intonations, and was withal somewhat copious in speech. A fine tremulously sensitive nature, strong chiefly on the side of the affections, and the graceful insights and activities that depend on these : — truly a beautiful, much-suffering, much-loving house-mother. From her chiefly, as one could discern, John Sterling had derived the delicate *aroma* of his nature, its piety, clearness, sincerity ; as from his Father, the ready practical gifts, the impetuosities and the audacities, were also (though in strange new form) visibly inherited. A man was lucky to have such a Mother ; to have such Parents as both his were.

Meanwhile the new Wife appears to have had, for the present, no marriage-portion; neither was Edward Sterling rich, — according to his own ideas and aims, far from it. Of course he soon found that the fluctuating barrack-life, especially with no outlooks of speedy promotion, was little suited to his new circumstances : but how change it ? His father was now dead; from whom he had inherited the Speaker Pension of two hundred pounds; but of available probably little or nothing more. The rents of the small family estate, I suppose, and other property, had gone to portion sisters. Two hundred pounds, and the pay of a marching captain: within the limits of that revenue all plans of his had to restrict themselves at present.

He continued for some time longer in the Army ; his wife undivided from him by the hardships of that way of life. Their first son Anthony (Captain Anthony Sterling, the only child who now survives) was born to them in this position, while lying at Dundalk, in January, 1805. Two months later, some eleven months after their marriage, the regiment was broken; and Captain Sterling, declining to serve elsewhere on the terms offered, and willingly accepting such decision of his doubts, was reduced to half-pay. This was the end of his soldiering: some five or six years in all; from which he had derived for life, among other things, a decided military bearing, whereof he was rather proud; an incapacity for practising law; — and considerable uncertainty as to what his next course of life was now to be.

For the present, his views lay towards farming: to establish himself, if not as country gentleman, which was an unattainable ambition, then at least as some kind of gentleman-farmer which had a flattering resemblance to that. Kaimes Castle with a reasonable extent of land, which, in his inquiries after farms, had turned up, was his first place of settlement in this new capacity; and here, for some few months, he had established himself when John his second child was born. This was Captain Sterling's first attempt towards a fixed course of life; not a very wise one, I have understood: — yet on the whole, who, then and there, could have pointed out to him a wiser?

A fixed course of life and activity he could never attain, or not till very late; and this doubtless was among the important points of his destiny, and acted both on his own character and that of those who had to attend him on his wayfarings.

CHAPTER III.

SCHOOLS: LLANBLETHIAN; PARIS; LONDON.

EDWARD STERLING never shone in farming; indeed I believe he never took heartily to it, or tried it except in fits. His Bute farm was, at best, a kind of apology for some far different ideal of a country establishment which could not be realized; practically a temporary landing-place from which he could make sallies and excursions in search of some more generous field of enterprise. Stormy brief efforts at energetic husbandry, at agricultural improvement and rapid field-labor, alternated with sudden flights to Dublin, to London, whithersoever any flush of bright outlook which he could denominate practical, or any gleam of hope which his impatient ennui could represent as such, allured him. This latter was often enough the case. In wet hay-times and harvest-times, the dripping outdoor world, and lounging indoor one, in the absence of the master, offered far from a satisfactory appearance! Here was, in fact, a man much imprisoned; haunted, I doubt not, by demons enough; though ever brisk and brave withal, — iracund, but cheerfully vigorous, opulent in wise or unwise hope. A fiery energetic soul consciously and unconsciously storming for deliverance into better arenas; and this in a restless, rapid, impetuous, rather than in a strong, silent and deliberate way.

In rainy Bute and the dilapidated Kaimes Castle, it was evident, there lay no Goshen for such a man. The lease, originally but for some three years and a half, drawing now to a close, he resolved to quit Bute; had heard, I know not where, of an eligible cottage without farm attached, in the pleasant little village of Llanblethian close by Cowbridge in Glamorganshire; of this he took a lease, and thither with his family he moved in search of new fortunes. Glamorganshire was at least a better climate than Bute; no groups of idle or of busy reapers could here stand waiting on the guidance of a master, for there was no farm here; — and among its other and probably its chief though secret advantages, Llanblethian was much more convenient both for Dublin and London than Kaimes Castle had been.

The removal thither took place in the autumn of 1809. Chief part of the journey (perhaps from Greenock to Swansea or Bristol) was by sea: John, just turned of three years, could in after-times remember nothing of this voyage; Anthony, some eighteen months older, has still a vivid recollection of the gray splashing tumult, and dim sorrow, uncertainty, regret and distress he underwent: to him a "dissolving-view" which not only left its effect on the *plate* (as all views and dissolving-views doubtless do on that kind of "plate"), but remained consciously present there. John, in the close of his twenty-first year, professes not to remember anything whatever of Bute; his whole existence, in that earliest scene of it, had faded away from him: Bute also, with its shaggy mountains, moaning woods, and summer and winter seas, had been wholly a dissolving-view for him, and had left no conscious impression, but only, like this voyage, an effect.

Llanblethian hangs pleasantly, with its white cottages, and orchard and other trees, on the western slope of a green hill; looking far and wide over green meadows and little or bigger hills, in the pleasant plain of Glamorgan; a short mile to the south of Cowbridge, to which smart little town it is properly a kind of suburb. Plain of Glamorgan, some ten miles wide and thirty or forty long, which they call the Vale of Glamorgan; — though properly it is not quite a Vale, there being only one range of mountains to it, if even one: certainly the central Mountains of Wales do gradually rise, in a miscellaneous manner, on the north side of it; but on the south are no mountains, not even land, only the Bristol Channel, and far off, the Hills of Devonshire, for boundary, — the "English Hills," as the natives call them, visible from every eminence in those parts. On such wide terms is it called Vale of Glamorgan. But called by whatever name, it is a most pleasant fruitful region: kind to the native, interesting to the visitor. A waving grassy region; cut with innumerable ragged lanes; dotted with sleepy unswept human hamlets, old ruinous castles with their ivy and their daws, gray sleepy churches with their ditto ditto: for ivy everywhere abounds; and generally a rank fragrant vegetation clothes all things; hanging, in rude many-colored festoons and fringed odoriferous tapestries, on your right and on your left, in every lane. A country kinder to the sluggard husbandman than any I have ever seen. For it lies all on limestone, needs no draining; the soil, everywhere of handsome depth and finest quality, will grow good crops for you with the most imperfect tilling. At a safe distance of a day's riding lie the tartarean copper-forges of Swansea, the tartarean iron-forges of Merthyr; their sooty battle far away, and not, at such safe distance, a defilement to the face of the earth and sky, but rather an encouragement to the earth at least; encouraging the husbandman to plough better, if he only would.

The peasantry seem indolent and stagnant, but peaceable and well-provided; much given to Methodism when they have any character; — for the rest, an innocent good-humored people, who all drink home-brewed beer, and have brown loaves of the most excellent home-baked bread. The native peasant village is not generally beautiful, though it might be, were it swept and trimmed; it gives one rather the idea of sluttish stagnancy, — an interesting peep into the Welsh Paradise of Sleepy Hollow. Stones, old kettles, naves of wheels, all kinds of broken litter, with live pigs and etceteras, lie about the street: for, as a rule, no rubbish is removed, but waits patiently the action of mere natural chemistry and accident; if even a house is burnt or falls, you will find it there after half a century, only cloaked by the ever-ready ivy. Sluggish man seems never to have struck a pick into it; his new hut is built close by on ground not encumbered, and the old stones are still left lying.

This is the ordinary Welsh village; but there are exceptions, where people of more cultivated tastes have been led to settle, and Llanblethian is one of the more signal of these. A decidedly cheerful group of human homes, the greater part of them indeed belonging to persons of refined habits; trimness, shady shelter, whitewash, neither conveniency nor decoration has been neglected here. Its effect from the distance on the eastward is very pretty: you see it like a little sleeping cataract of white houses, with trees overshadowing and fringing it; and there the cataract hangs, and does not rush away from you.

John Sterling spent his next five years in this locality. He did not again see it for a quarter of a century; but retained, all his life, a lively remembrance of it; and, just in the end of his twenty-first year, among his earliest printed pieces, we find an elaborate and diffuse description of it and its relations to him, — part of which piece, in spite of its otherwise insignificant quality, may find place here : —

"The fields on which I first looked, and the sands which were marked by my earliest footsteps, are completely lost to my memory ; and of those ancient walls among which I began to breathe, I retain no recollection more clear than the outlines of a cloud in a moonless sky. But of L——, the village where I afterwards lived, I persuade myself that every line and hue is more deeply and accurately fixed than those of any spot I have since beheld, even though borne in upon the heart by the association of the strongest feelings.

"My home was built upon the slope of a hill, with a little orchard stretching down before it, and a garden rising behind. At a considerable distance beyond and beneath the orchard, a rivulet flowed through meadows and turned a mill ; while, above the garden, the summit of the hill was crowned by a few gray rocks, from which a yew-tree grew, solitary and bare. Extending at each side of the orchard, toward the brook, two scattered patches of cottages lay nestled among their gardens ; and beyond this streamlet and the little mill and bridge, another slight eminence arose, divided into green fields, tufted and bordered with copsewood, and crested by a ruined castle, contemporary, as was said, with the Conquest. I know not whether these things in truth made up a prospect of much beauty. Since I was eight years old, I have never seen them ; but I well know that no landscape I have since beheld, no picture of Claude or Salvator, gave me half the impression of living, heartfelt, perfect beauty which fills my mind when I think of that green valley, that sparkling rivulet, that broken fortress of dark antiquity, and that hill with its aged yew and breezy summit, from which I have so often looked over the broad stretch of verdure beneath it, and the country-town, and church-tower, silent and white beyond.

"In that little town there was, and I believe is, a school where the elements of human knowledge were communicated to me, for some hours of every day, during a considerable time. The path to it lay across the rivulet and past the mill ;

from which point we could either journey through the fields
below the old castle, and the wood which surrounded it, or
along a road at the other side of the ruin, close to the gateway
of which it passed. The former track led through two or three
beautiful fields, the sylvan domain of the keep on one hand,
and the brook on the other; while an oak or two, like giant
warders advanced from the wood, broke the sunshine of the
green with a soft and graceful shadow. How often, on my
way to school, have I stopped beneath the tree to collect the
fallen acorns; how often run down to the stream to pluck a
branch of the hawthorn which hung over the water! The road
which passed the castle joined, beyond these fields, the path
which traversed them. It took, I well remember, a certain
solemn and mysterious interest from the ruin. The shadow of
the archway, the discolorizations of time on all the walls, the
dimness of the little thicket which encircled it, the traditions
of its immeasurable age, made St. Quentin's Castle a wonderful
and awful fabric in the imagination of a child; and long after
I last saw its mouldering roughness, I never read of fortresses,
or heights, or spectres, or banditti, without connecting them
with the one ruin of my childhood.

"It was close to this spot that one of the few adventures
occurred which marked, in my mind, my boyish days with importance. When loitering beyond the castle, on the way to
school, with a brother somewhat older than myself, who was
uniformly my champion and protector, we espied a round sloe
high up in the hedge-row. We determined to obtain it; and I
do not remember whether both of us, or only my brother,
climbed the tree. However, when the prize was all but
reached, — and no alchemist ever looked more eagerly for the
moment of projection which was to give him immortality and
omnipotence, — a gruff voice startled us with an oath, and an
order to desist; and I well recollect looking back, for long
after, with terror to the vision of an old and ill-tempered farmer, armed with a bill-hook, and vowing our decapitation; nor
did I subsequently remember without triumph the eloquence
whereby alone, in my firm belief, my brother and myself had
been rescued from instant death.

" At the entrance of the little town stood an old gateway,
with a pointed arch and decaying battlements. It gave admittance to the street which contained the church, and which
terminated in another street, the principal one in the town of
C——. In this was situated the school to which I daily
wended. I cannot now recall to mind the face of its good
conductor, nor of any of his scholars; but I have before me a
strong general image of the interior of his establishment. I
remember the reverence with which I was wont to carry to
his seat a well-thumbed duodecimo, the *History of Greece* by
Oliver Goldsmith. I remember the mental agonies I endured
in attempting to master the art and mystery of penmanship;
a craft in which, alas, I remained too short a time under Mr.
R—— to become as great a proficient as he made his other
scholars, and which my awkwardness has prevented me from
attaining in any considerable perfection under my various subsequent pedagogues. But that which has left behind it a
brilliant trait of light was the exhibition of what are called
'Christmas pieces;' things unknown in aristocratic seminaries, but constantly used at the comparatively humble academy
which supplied the best knowledge of reading, writing, and
arithmetic to be attained in that remote neighborhood.

" The long desks covered from end to end with those painted
masterpieces, the Life of Robinson Crusoe, the Hunting of
Chevy-Chase, the History of Jack the Giant-Killer, and all
the little eager faces and trembling hands bent over these, and
filling them up with some choice quotation, sacred or profane; — no, the galleries of art, the theatrical exhibitions, the
reviews and processions, — which are only not childish because
they are practised and admired by men instead of children, —
all the pomps and vanities of great cities, have shown me no
revelation of glory such as did that crowded school-room the
week before the Christmas holidays. But these were the
splendors of life. The truest and the strongest feelings do
not connect themselves with any scenes of gorgeous and gaudy
magnificence; they are bound up in the remembrances of
home.

" The narrow orchard, with its grove of old apple-trees,

against one of which I used to lean, and while I brandished a
beanstalk, roar out with Fitzjames, —

> 'Come one, come all; this rock shall fly
> From its firm base as soon as I!' —

while I was ready to squall at the sight of a cur, and run
valorously away from a casually approaching cow; the field
close beside it, where I rolled about in summer among the
hay; the brook in which, despite of maid and mother, I waded
by the hour; the garden where I sowed flower-seeds, and then
turned up the ground again and planted potatoes, and then
rooted out the potatoes to insert acorns and apple-pips, and
at last, as may be supposed, reaped neither roses, nor potatoes,
nor oak-trees, nor apples; the grass-plots on which I played
among those with whom I never can play nor work again: all
these are places and employments, — and, alas, playmates, —
such as, if it were worth while to weep at all, it would be
worth weeping that I enjoy no longer.

"I remember the house where I first grew familiar with
peacocks; and the mill-stream into which I once fell; and the
religious awe wherewith I heard, in the warm twilight, the
psalm-singing around the house of the Methodist miller; and
the door-post against which I discharged my brazen artillery;
I remember the window by which I sat while my mother
taught me French; and the patch of garden which I dug for —
But her name is best left blank; it was indeed writ in water.
These recollections are to me like the wealth of a departed
friend, a mournful treasure. But the public has heard enough
of them; to it they are worthless: they are a coin which only
circulates at its true value between the different periods of
an individual's existence, and good for nothing but to keep
up a commerce between boyhood and manhood. I have for
years looked forward to the possibility of visiting L——;
but I am told that it is a changed village; and not only has
man been at work, but the old yew on the hill has fallen,
and scarcely a low stump remains of the tree which I delighted in childhood to think might have furnished bows for
the Norman archers." [1]

[1] *Literary Chronicle*, New Series; London, Saturday, 21 June, 1828, Art. 11.

In Cowbridge is some kind of free school, or grammar-school, of a certain distinction; and this to Captain Sterling was probably a motive for settling in the neighborhood of it with his children. Of this however, as it turned out, there was no use made: the Sterling family, during its continuance in those parts, did not need more than a primary school. The worthy master who presided over these Christmas galas, and had the honor to teach John Sterling his reading and writing, was an elderly Mr. Reece of Cowbridge, who still (in 1851) survives, or lately did; and is still remembered by his old pupils as a worthy, ingenious and kindly man, "who wore drab breeches and white stockings." Beyond the Reece sphere of tuition John Sterling did not go in this locality.

In fact the Sterling household was still fluctuating; the problem of a task for Edward Sterling's powers, and of anchorage for his affairs in any sense, was restlessly struggling to solve itself, but was still a good way from being solved. Anthony, in revisiting these scenes with John in 1839, mentions going to the spot "where we used to stand with our Father, looking out for the arrival of the London mail:" a little chink through which is disclosed to us a big restless section of a human life. The Hill of Welsh Llanblethian, then, is like the mythic Caucasus in its degree (as indeed all hills and habitations where men sojourn are); and here too, on a small scale, is a Prometheus Chained! Edward Sterling, I can well understand, was a man to tug at the chains that held him idle in those the prime of his years; and to ask restlessly, yet not in anger and remorse, so much as in hope, locomotive speculation, and ever-new adventure and attempt, Is there no task nearer my own natural size, then? So he looks out from the Hill-side "for the arrival of the London mail;" thence hurries into Cowbridge to the Post-office; and has a wide web, of threads and gossamers, upon his loom, and many shuttles flying, in this world.

By the Marquis of Bute's appointment he had, very shortly after his arrival in that region, become Adjutant of the Glamorganshire Militia, "Local Militia," I suppose; and was, in this way, turning his military capabilities to some use. The office

involved pretty frequent absences, in Cardiff and elsewhere.
This doubtless was a welcome outlet, though a small one.   He
had also begun to try writing, especially on public subjects;
a much more copious outlet, — which indeed, gradually widening itself, became the final solution for him.   Of the year 1811
we have a Pamphlet of his, entitled *Military Reform;* this
is the second edition, "dedicated to the Duke of Kent;" the
first appears to have come out the year before, and had thus
attained a certain notice, which of course was encouraging.
He now furthermore opened a correspondence with the *Times*
Newspaper; wrote to it, in 1812, a series of Letters under
the signature *Vetus:* voluntary Letters I suppose, without
payment or pre-engagement, one successful Letter calling out
another; till *Vetus* and his doctrines came to be a distinguishable entity, and the business amounted to something.   Out of
my own earliest Newspaper reading, I can remember the name
Vetus, as a kind of editorial hacklog on which able-editors
were wont to chop straw now and then.   Nay the Letters
were collected and reprinted; both this first series, of 1812,
and then a second of next year: two very thin, very dim-
colored cheap octavos; stray copies of which still exist, and
may one day become distillable into a drop of History (should
such be wanted of our poor "Scavenger Age" in time coming),
though the reading of them has long ceased in this generation.[1]
The first series, we perceive, had even gone to a second edition.   The tone, wherever one timidly glances into this extinct cockpit, is trenchant and emphatic: the name of *Vetus,*
strenuously fighting there, had become considerable in the
talking political world; and, no doubt, was especially of mark,
as that of a writer who might otherwise be important, with
the proprietors of the *Times.*   The connection continued:
widened and deepened itself, — in a slow tentative manner;
passing naturally from voluntary into remunerated: and indeed proving more and more to be the true ultimate arena,
and battle-field and seed-field, for the exuberant impetuosities
and faculties of this man.

[1] "The Letters of Vetus from March 10th to May 10th, 1812" (second edition, London, 1812): Ditto, "Part III., with a Preface and Notes" (ibid. 1814).

What the *Letters of Vetus* treated of I do not know; doubtless they ran upon Napoleon, Catholic Emancipation, true
methods of national defence, of effective foreign Anti-galli-
cism, and of domestic ditto; which formed the staple of
editorial speculation at that time. I have heard in general
that Captain Sterling, then and afterwards, advocated "the
Marquis of Wellesley's policy;" but that also, what it was,
I have forgotten, and the world has been willing to forget.
Enough, the heads of the *Times* establishment, perhaps already the Marquis of Wellesley and other important persons,
had their eye on this writer; and it began to be surmised by
him that here at last was the career he had been seeking.

Accordingly, in 1814, when victorious Peace unexpectedly
arrived, and the gates of the Continent after five-and-twenty
years of fierce closure were suddenly thrown open; and the
hearts of all English and European men awoke staggering as
if from a nightmare suddenly removed, and ran hither and
thither, — Edward Sterling also determined on a new adventure, that of crossing to Paris, and trying what might lie in
store for him. For curiosity, in its idler sense, there was
evidently pabulum enough. But he had hopes moreover of
learning much that might perhaps avail him afterwards; —
hopes withal, I have understood, of getting to be Foreign
Correspondent of the *Times* Newspaper, and so adding to his
income in the mean while. He left Llanblethian in May;
dates from Dieppe the 27th of that month. He lived in occasional contact with Parisian notabilities (all of them except
Madame de Staël forgotten now), all summer, diligently sur-
veying his ground; — returned for his family, who were still
in Wales but ready to move, in the beginning of August; took
them immediately across with him; a house in the neighborhood of Paris, in the pleasant village of Passy at once town
and country, being now ready; and so, under foreign skies,
again set up his household there.

Here was a strange new "school" for our friend John now
in his eighth year! Out of which the little Anthony and he
drank doubtless at all pores, vigorously as they had done in no

school before. A change total and immediate. Somniferous
green Llanblethian has suddenly been blotted out; presto,
here are wakeful Passy and the noises of paved Paris instead.
Innocent ingenious Mr. Reece in drab breeches and white
stockings, he with his mild Christmas galas and peaceable rules
of Dilworth and Butterworth, has given place to such a satur-
nalia of panoramic, symbolic and other teachers and monitors, addressing all the five senses at once. Who John's
express tutors were, at Passy, I never heard; nor indeed,
especially in his case, was it much worth inquiring. To him
and to all of us, the expressly appointed schoolmasters and
schoolings we get are as nothing, compared with the unappointed incidental and continual ones, whose school-hours are
all the days and nights of our existence, and whose lessons,
noticed or unnoticed, stream in upon us with every breath we
draw. Anthony says they attended a French school, though
only for about three months; and he well remembers the last
scene of it, "the boys shouting *Vive l'Empereur* when Napoleon
came back."

Of John Sterling's express schooling, perhaps the most important feature, and by no means a favorable one to him, was
the excessive fluctuation that prevailed in it. Change of
scene, change of teacher, *both* express and implied, was incessant with him; and gave his young life a nomadic character, —
which surely, of all the adventitious tendencies that could
have been impressed upon him, so volatile, swift and airy a
being as him, was the one he needed least. His gentle pious-
hearted Mother, ever watching over him in all outward changes,
and assiduously keeping human pieties and good affections
alive in him, was probably the best counteracting element in
his lot. And on the whole, have we not all to run our chance
in that respect; and take, the most victoriously we can, such
schooling as pleases to be attainable in our year and place?
Not very victoriously, the most of us! A wise well-calculated
breeding of a young genial soul in this world, or alas of any
young soul in it, lies fatally over the horizon in these epochs!
— This French scene of things, a grand school of its sort, and
also a perpetual banquet for the young soul, naturally cap-

tivated John Sterling; he said afterwards, "New things and experiences here were poured upon his mind and sense, not in streams, but in a Niagara cataract." This too, however, was but a scene; lasted only some six or seven months; and in the spring of the next year terminated as abruptly as any of the rest could do.

For in the spring of the next year, Napoleon abruptly emerged from Elba; and set all the populations of the world in motion, in a strange manner;—set the Sterling household afloat, in particular; the big European tide rushing into all smallest creeks, at Passy and elsewhere. In brief, on the 20th of March, 1815, the family had to shift, almost to fly, towards home and the sea-coast; and for a day or two were under apprehension of being detained and not reaching home. Mrs. Sterling, with her children and effects, all in one big carriage with two horses, made the journey to Dieppe; in perfect safety, though in continual tremor: here they were joined by Captain Sterling, who had stayed behind at Paris to see the actual advent of Napoleon, and to report what the aspect of affairs was, "Downcast looks of citizens, with fierce saturnalian acclaim of soldiery:" after which they proceeded together to London without farther apprehension;—there to witness, in due time, the tar-barrels of Waterloo, and other phenomena that followed.

Captain Sterling never quitted London as a residence any more; and indeed was never absent from it, except on autumnal or other excursions of a few weeks, till the end of his life. Nevertheless his course there was as yet by no means clear; nor had his relations with the heads of the *Times,* or with other high heads, assumed a form which could be called definite, but were hanging as a cloudy maze of possibilities, firm substance not yet divided from shadow. It continued so for some years. The Sterling household shifted twice or thrice to new streets or localities,—Russell Square or Queen Square, Blackfriars Road, and longest at the Grove, Blackheath,—before the vapors of Wellesley promotions and such like slowly sank as useless precipitate, and the firm rock, which was definite employment, ending in lucrative co-proprietorship and

more and more important connection with the *Times* Newspaper, slowly disclosed itself.

These changes of place naturally brought changes in John
Sterling's schoolmasters : nor were domestic tragedies wanting,
still more important to him. New brothers and sisters had
been born ; two little brothers more, three little sisters he had
in all; some of whom came to their eleventh year beside him,
some passed away in their second or fourth : but from his
ninth to his sixteenth year they all died; and in 1821 only
Anthony and John were left.[1] How many tears, and passionate pangs, and soft infinite regrets; such as are appointed to
all mortals ! In one year, I find, indeed in one half-year, he
lost three little playmates, two of them within one month.
His own age was not yet quite twelve. For one of these three,
for little Edward, his next younger, who died now at the age
of nine, Mr. Hare records that John copied out, in large school-
hand, a *History of Valentine and Orson*, to beguile the poor
child's sickness, which ended in death soon, leaving a sad cloud
on John.

Of his grammar and other schools, which, as I said, are
hardly worth enumerating in comparison, the most important
seems to have been a Dr. Burney's at Greenwich; a large day-
school and boarding-school, where Anthony and John gave
their attendance for a year or two (1818–19) from Blackheath. "John frequently did themes for the boys," says Anthony, "and for myself when I was aground." His progress
in all school learning was certain to be rapid, if he even moderately took to it. A lean, tallish, loose-made boy of twelve;
strange alacrity, rapidity and joyous eagerness looking out of

[1] Here, in a Note, is the tragic little Register, with what indications for us
may lie in it : —

(1.) Robert Sterling died, 4th June, 1815, at Queen Square, in his fourth year
(John being now nine).

(2.) Elizabeth died, 12th March, 1818, at Blackfriars Road, in her second year.

(3.) Edward, 30th March, 1818 (same place, same month and year), in his
ninth.

(4.) Hester, 21st July, 1818 (three months later), at Blackheath, in her eleventh.

(5.) Catherine Hester Elizabeth, 16th January, 1821, in Seymour Street.

his eyes, and of all his ways and movements. I have a Picture
of him at this stage ; a little portrait, which carries its verifica-
tion with it. In manhood too, the chief expression of his eyes
and physiognomy was what I might call alacrity, cheerful
rapidity. You could see, here looked forth a soul which was
winged; which dwelt in hope and action, not in hesitation or
fear. Anthony says, he was "an affectionate and gallant kind
of boy, adventurous and generous, daring to a singular degree."
Apt enough withal to be "petulant now and then;" on the
whole, "very self-willed;" doubtless not a little discursive in
his thoughts and ways, and "difficult to manage."

I rather think Anthony, as the steadier, more substantial
boy, was the Mother's favorite; and that John, though the
quicker and cleverer, perhaps cost her many anxieties. Among
the Papers given me, is an old browned half-sheet in stiff
school hand, unpunctuated, occasionally ill spelt, — John Sterling's earliest remaining Letter, — which gives record of a
crowning escapade of his, the first and the last of its kind;
and so may be inserted here. A very headlong adventure on
the boy's part; so hasty and so futile, at once audacious and
impracticable; emblematic of much that befell in the history of
the man !

"*To Mrs. Sterling, Blackheath.*

"21st September, 1818.

"Dear Mamma, — I am now at Dover, where I arrived this
morning about seven o'clock. When you thought I was going
to church, I went down the Kent Road, and walked on till I
came to Gravesend, which is upwards of twenty miles from
Blackheath; at about seven o'clock in the evening, without
having eat anything the whole time. I applied to an in-
keeper (*sic*) there, pretending that I had served a haberdasher
in London, who left of (*sic*) business, and turned me away.
He believed me; and got me a passage in the coach here, for
I said that I had an Uncle here, and that my Father and
Mother were dead; — when I wandered about the quays for
some time, till I met Captain Keys, whom I asked to give me
a passage to Boulogne; which he promised to do, and took
me home to breakfast with him: but Mrs. Keys questioned

me a good deal; when I not being able to make my story good, I was obliged to confess to her that I had run away from you. Captain Keys says that he will keep me at his house till you answer my letter.

"J. STERLING."

Anthony remembers the business well; but can assign no origin to it, — some penalty, indignity or cross put suddenly on John, which the hasty John considered unbearable. His Mother's inconsolable weeping, and then his own astonishment at such a culprit's being forgiven, are all that remain with Anthony. The steady historical style of the young runaway of twelve, narrating merely, not in the least apologizing, is also noticeable.

This was some six months after his little brother Edward's death; three months after that of Hester, his little sister next in the family series to him: troubled days for the poor Mother in that small household on Blackheath, as there are for mothers in so many households in this world! I have heard that Mrs. Sterling passed much of her time alone, at this period. Her husband's pursuits, with his Wellesleys and the like, often carrying him into Town and detaining him late there, she would sit among her sleeping children, such of them as death had still spared, perhaps thriftily plying her needle, full of mournful affectionate night-thoughts, — apprehensive too, in her tremulous heart, that the head of the house might have fallen among robbers in his way homeward.

———◆———

CHAPTER IV.

UNIVERSITIES : GLASGOW ; CAMBRIDGE.

AT a later stage, John had some instruction from a Dr. Waite at Blackheath; and lastly, the family having now removed into Town, to Seymour Street in the fashionable region there, he "read for a while with Dr. Trollope, Master of Christ's Hospital;" which ended his school history.

In this his ever-changing course, from Reece at Cowbridge
to Trollope in Christ's, which was passed so nomadically,
under ferulas of various color, the boy had, on the whole,
snatched successfully a fair share of what was going. Competent skill in construing Latin, I think also an elementary
knowledge of Greek; add ciphering to a small extent, Euclid
perhaps in a rather imaginary condition; a swift but not
very legible or handsome penmanship, and the copious prompt
habit of employing it in all manner of unconscious English
prose composition, or even occasionally in verse itself: this,
or something like this, he had gained from his grammar-
schools: this is the most of what they offer to the poor young
soul in general, in these indigent times. The express schoolmaster is not equal to much at present, — while the un-
express, for good or for evil, is so busy with a poor little fellow! Other departments of schooling had been infinitely more
productive, for our young friend, than the gerund-grinding
one. A voracious reader I believe he all along was, — had
"read the whole Edinburgh Review" in these boyish years,
and out of the circulating libraries one knows not what cart-
loads; wading like Ulysses towards his palace "through infinite dung." A voracious observer and participator in all
things he likewise all along was; and had had his sights, and
reflections, and sorrows and adventures, from Kaimes Castle
onward, — and had gone at least to Dover on his own score.
Puer bonæ spei, as the school-albums say; a boy of whom
much may be hoped? Surely, in many senses, yes. A frank
veracity is in him, truth and courage, as the basis of all; and
of wild gifts and graces there is abundance. I figure him a
brilliant, swift, voluble, affectionate and pleasant creature;
out of whom, if it were not that symptoms of delicate health
already show themselves, great things might be made. Promotions at least, especially in this country and epoch of parliaments and eloquent palavers, are surely very possible for
such a one!

Being now turned of sixteen, and the family economics getting yearly more propitious and flourishing, he, as his brother

had already been, was sent to Glasgow University, in which
city their Mother had connections. His brother and he were
now all that remained of the young family; much attached to
one another in their College years as afterwards. Glasgow,
however, was not properly their College scene: here, except
that they had some tuition from Mr. Jacobson, then a senior
fellow-student, now (1851) the learned editor of St. Basil, and
Regius Professor of Divinity in Oxford, who continued ever
afterwards a valued intimate of John's, I find nothing special
recorded of them. The Glasgow curriculum, for John especially, lasted but one year; who, after some farther tutorage
from Mr. Jacobson or Dr. Trollope, was appointed for a more
ambitious sphere of education.

In the beginning of his nineteenth year, "in the autumn
of 1824," he went to Trinity College, Cambridge. His brother
Anthony, who had already been there a year, had just quitted
this Establishment, and entered on a military life under good
omens; I think, at Dublin under the Lord Lieutenant's patronage, to whose service he was, in some capacity, attached. The
two brothers, ever in company hitherto, parted roads at this
point; and, except on holiday visits and by frequent correspondence, did not again live together; but they continued in a
true fraternal attachment while life lasted, and I believe never
had any even temporary estrangement, or on either side a
cause for such. The family, as I said, was now, for the last
three years, reduced to these two; the rest of the young ones,
with their laughter and their sorrows, all gone. The parents
otherwise were prosperous in outward circumstances; the Father's position more and more developing itself into affluent
security, an agreeable circle of acquaintance, and a certain real
influence, though of a peculiar sort, according to his gifts for
work in this world.

Sterling's Tutor at Trinity College was Julius Hare, now
the distinguished Archdeacon of Lewes: — who soon conceived
a great esteem for him, and continued ever afterwards, in
looser or closer connection, his loved and loving friend. As
the Biographical and Editorial work above alluded to abun-

dantly evinces. Mr. Hare celebrates the wonderful and beautiful gifts, the sparkling ingenuity, ready logic, eloquent utterance, and noble generosities and pieties of his pupil; — records in particular how once, on a sudden alarm of fire in some neighboring College edifice while his lecture was proceeding, all hands rushed out to help; how the undergraduates instantly formed themselves in lines from the fire to the river, and in swift continuance kept passing buckets as was needful, ill the enemy was visibly fast yielding, — when Mr. Hare, going along the line, was astonished to find Sterling, at the river-end of it, standing up to his waist in water, deftly dealing with the buckets as they came and went. You in the river, Sterling; you with your coughs, and dangerous tendencies of health! — "Somebody must be in it," answered Sterling; "why not I, as well as another?" Sterling's friends may remember many traits of that kind. The swiftest in all things, he was apt to be found at the head of the column, whithersoever the march might be; if towards any brunt of danger, there was he surest to be at the head; and of himself and his peculiar risks or impediments he was negligent at all times, even to an excessive and plainly unreasonable degree.

Mr. Hare justly refuses him the character of an exact scholar, or technical proficient at any time in either of the ancient literatures. But he freely read in Greek and Latin, as in various modern languages; and in all fields, in the classical as well, his lively faculty of recognition and assimilation had given him large booty in proportion to his labor. One cannot under any circumstances conceive of Sterling as a steady dictionary philologue, historian, or archæologist; nor did he here, nor could he well, attempt that course. At the same time, Greek and the Greeks being here before him, he could not fail to gather somewhat from it, to take some hue and shape from it. Accordingly there is, to a singular extent, especially in his early writings, a certain tinge of Grecism and Heathen classicality traceable in him; — Classicality, indeed, which does not satisfy one's sense as real or truly living, but which glitters with a certain genial, if perhaps almost meretricious half-*japannish* splendor, — greatly distinguishable from mere gerund-grinding, and death in longs and shorts. If Classicality mean the practical conception, or attempt to conceive, what human life was in the epoch called classical, — perhaps few or none of Sterling's contemporaries in that Cambridge establishment carried away more of available Classicality than even he.

But here, as in his former schools, his studies and inquiries, diligently prosecuted I believe, were of the most discursive wide-flowing character; not steadily advancing along beaten roads towards College honors, but pulsing out with impetuous irregularity now on this tract, now on that, towards whatever spiritual Delphi might promise to unfold the mystery of this world, and announce to him what was, in our new day, the authentic message of the gods. His speculations, readings, inferences, glances and conclusions were doubtless sufficiently encyclopedic; his grand tutors the multifarious set of Books he devoured. And perhaps, — as is the singular case in most schools and educational establishments of this unexampled epoch, — it was not the express set of arrangements in this or any extant University that could essentially forward him, but only the implied and silent ones ; less in the prescribed "course of study," which seems to tend no-whither, than — if you will consider it — in the generous (not ungenerous) rebellion against said prescribed course, and the voluntary spirit of endeavor and adventure excited thereby, does help lie for a brave youth in such places. Curious to consider. The fagging, the illicit boating, and the things *forbidden* by the schoolmaster, — these, I often notice in my Eton acquaintances, are the things that have done them good; these, and not their inconsiderable or considerable knowledge of the Greek accidence almost at all! What is Greek accidence, compared to Spartan discipline, if it can be had ? That latter is a real and grand attainment. Certainly, if rebellion is unfortunately needful, and you can rebel in a generous manner, several things may be acquired in that operation, — rigorous mutual fidelity, reticence, steadfastness, mild stoicism, and other virtues far transcending your Greek accidence. Nor can the unwisest "prescribed course of study" be considered quite

useless, if it have incited you to try nobly on all sides for a
course of your own. A singular condition of Schools and
High-schools, which have come down, in their strange old
clothes and "courses of study," from the monkish ages into
this highly unmonkish one ; — tragical condition, at which the
intelligent observer makes deep pause !

One benefit, not to be dissevered from the most obsolete
University still frequented by young ingenuous living souls,
is that of manifold collision and communication with the said
young souls ; which, to every one of these coevals, is undoubtedly the most important branch of breeding for him. In this
point, as the learned Huber has insisted,[1] the two English
Universities, — their studies otherwise being granted to be
nearly useless, and even ill done of their kind, — far excel
all other Universities : so valuable are the rules of human
behavior which from of old have tacitly established themselves
there ; so manful, with all its sad drawbacks, is the style of
English character, " frank, simple, rugged and yet courteous,"
which has tacitly but imperatively got itself sanctioned and
prescribed there. Such, in full sight of Continental and other
Universities, is Huber's opinion. Alas, the question of University Reform goes deep at present ; deep as the world ; —
and the real University of these new epochs is yet a great
way from us ! Another judge in whom I have confidence
declares further, That of these two Universities, Cambridge is
decidedly the more catholic (not Roman catholic, but Human
catholic) in its tendencies and habitudes ; and that in fact, of
all the miserable Schools and High-schools in the England of
these years, he, if reduced to choose from them, would choose
Cambridge as a place of culture for the young idea. So that,
in these bad circumstances, Sterling had perhaps rather made
a hit than otherwise ?

Sterling at Cambridge had undoubtedly a wide and rather
genial circle of comrades ; and could not fail to be regarded
and beloved by many of them. Their life seems to have been
an ardently speculating and talking one ; by no means exces-

[1] *History of the English Universities.* (Translated from the German.)

sively restrained within limits; and, in the more adventurous heads like Sterling's, decidedly tending towards the latitudinarian in most things. They had among them a Debating Society called The Union; where on stated evenings was much logic, and other spiritual fencing and ingenuous collision, — probably of a really superior quality in that kind; for not a few of the then disputants have since proved themselves men of parts, and attained distinction in the intellectual walks of life. Fréderic Maurice, Richard Trench, John Kemble, Spedding, Venables, Charles Buller, Richard Milnes and others: — I have heard that in speaking and arguing, Sterling was the acknowledged chief in this Union Club; and that "none even came near him, except the late Charles Buller," whose distinction in this and higher respects was also already notable.

The questions agitated seem occasionally to have touched on the political department, and even on the ecclesiastical. I have heard one trait of Sterling's eloquence, which survived on the wings of grinning rumor, and had evidently borne upon Church Conservatism in some form: "Have they not," — or perhaps it was, Has she (the Church) not, — "a black dragoon in every parish, on good pay and rations, horse-meat and man's-meat, to patrol and battle for these things?" The "black dragoon," which naturally at the moment ruffled the general young imagination into stormy laughter, points towards important conclusions in respect to Sterling at this time. I conclude he had, with his usual alacrity and impetuous daring, frankly adopted the anti-superstitious side of things; and stood scornfully prepared to repel all aggressions or pretensions from the opposite quarter. In short, that he was already, what afterwards there is no doubt about his being, at all points a Radical, as the name or nickname then went. In other words, a young ardent soul looking with hope and joy into a world which was infinitely beautiful to him, though overhung with falsities and foul cobwebs as world never was before; overloaded, overclouded, to the zenith and the nadir of it, by incredible uncredited traditions, solemnly sordid hypocrisies, and beggarly deliriums old and new; which latter class of objects it was clearly the part of every noble

heart to expend all its lightnings and energies in burning up
without delay, and sweeping into their native Chaos out of
such a Cosmos as this.   Which process, it did not then seem
to him could be very difficult; or attended with much other
than heroic joy, and enthusiasm of victory or of battle, to the
gallant operator, in his part of it.   This was, with modifications such as might be, the humor and creed of College Radicalism five-and-twenty years ago.   Rather horrible at that
time; seen to be not so horrible now, at least to have grown
very universal, and to need no concealment now.   The natural
humor and attitude, we may well regret to say, — and honorable not dishonorable, for a brave young soul such as Sterling's,
in those years in those localities!

I do not find that Sterling had, at that stage, adopted the
then prevalent Utilitarian theory of human things.   But neither, apparently, had he rejected it; still less did he yet at all
denounce it with the damnatory vehemence we were used to
in him at a later period.   Probably he, so much occupied with
the negative side of things, had not yet thought seriously of
any positive basis for his world; or asked himself, too earnestly, What, then, *is* the noble rule of living for a man?   In
this world so eclipsed and scandalously overhung with fable
and hypocrisy, what *is* the eternal fact, on which a man may
front the Destinies and the Immensities?   The day for such
questions, sure enough to come in his case, was still but coming.   Sufficient for this day be the work thereof; that of
blasting into merited annihilation the innumerable and immeasurable recognized deliriums, and extirpating or coercing
to the due pitch those legions of "black dragoons," of all varieties and purposes, who patrol, with horse-meat and man's-
meat, this afflicted earth, so hugely to the detriment of it.

Sterling, it appears, after above a year of Trinity College,
followed his friend Maurice into Trinity Hall, with the intention of taking a degree in Law; which intention, like many
others with him, came to nothing; and in 1827 he left Trinity
Hall and Cambridge altogether; here ending, after two years,
his brief University life.

CHAPTER V.

A PROFESSION.

HERE, then, is a young soul, brought to the years of legal majority, furnished from his training-schools with such and such shining capabilities, and ushered on the scene of things, to inquire practically, What he will do there? Piety is in the man, noble human valor, bright intelligence, ardent proud veracity; light and fire, in none of their many senses, wanting for him, but abundantly bestowed: a kingly kind of man;— whose "kingdom," however, in this bewildered place and epoch of the world will probably be difficult to find and conquer!

For, alas, the world, as we said, already stands convicted to this young soul of being an untrue, unblessed world; its high dignitaries many of them phantasms and players'-masks; its worthships and worships unworshipful: from Dan to Beersheba, a mad world, my masters. And surely we may say, and none will now gainsay, this his idea of the world at that epoch was nearer to the fact than at most other epochs it has been. Truly, in all times and places, the young ardent soul that enters on this world with heroic purpose, with veracious insight, and the yet unclouded "inspiration of the Almighty" which has given us our intelligence, will find this world a very mad one: why else is *he*, with his little outfit of heroisms and inspirations, come hither into it, except to make it diligently a little saner? Of him there would have been no need, had it been quite sane. This is true; this will, in all centuries and countries, be true.

And yet perhaps of no time or country, for the last two thousand years, was it *so* true as here in this waste-weltering epoch of Sterling's and ours. A world all rocking and plunging, like that old Roman one when the measure of its iniquities was full; the abysses, and subterranean and supernal deluges, plainly broken loose; in the wild dim-lighted chaos all stars of Heaven gone out. No star of Heaven visible, hardly now to any man; the pestiferous fogs, and foul exhalations grown continual, have, except on the highest mountain-tops, blotted out all stars: will-o'-wisps, of various course and color, take the place of stars. Over the wild-surging chaos, in the leaden air, are only sudden glares of revolutionary lightning; then mere darkness, with philanthropistic phosphorescences, empty meteoric lights; here and there an ecclesiastical luminary still hovering, hanging on to its old quaking fixtures, pretending still to be a Moon or Sun, — though visibly it is but a Chinese Lantern made of *paper* mainly, with candle-end foully dying in the heart of it. Surely as mad a world as you could wish!

If you want to make sudden fortunes in it, and achieve the temporary hallelujah of flunkies for yourself, renouncing the perennial esteem of wise men; if you can believe that the chief end of man is to collect about him a bigger heap of gold than ever before, in a shorter time than ever before, you will find it a most handy and every way furthersome, blessed and felicitous world. But for any other human aim, I think you will find it not furthersome. If you in any way ask practically, How a noble life is to be led in it? you will be luckier than Sterling or I if you get any credible answer, or find any made road whatever. Alas, it is even so. Your heart's question, if it be of that sort, most things and persons will answer with a "Nonsense! Noble life is in Drury Lane, and wears yellow boots. You fool, compose yourself to your pudding!" — Surely, in these times, if ever in any, the young heroic soul entering on life, so opulent, full of sunny hope, of noble valor and divine intention, is tragical as well as beautiful to us.

Of the three learned Professions none offered any likelihood for Sterling. From the Church his notions of the "black dragoon," had there been no other obstacle, were sufficient to exclude him. Law he had just renounced, his own Radical philosophies disheartening him, in face of the ponderous impediments, continual up-hill struggles and formidable toils inherent in such a pursuit: with Medicine he had never been in any contiguity, that he should dream of it as a course for him. Clearly enough the professions were unsuitable; they to him, he to them. Professions, built so largely on speciosity instead of performance; clogged, in this bad epoch, and defaced under such suspicions of fatal imposture, were hateful not lovable to the young radical soul, scornful of gross profit, and intent on ideals and human noblenesses. Again, the professions, were they never so perfect and veracious, will require slow steady pulling, to which this individual young radical, with his swift, far-darting brilliancies, and nomadic desultory ways, is of all men the most averse and unfitted. No profession could, in any case, have well gained the early love of Sterling. And perhaps withal the most tragic element of his life is even this, That there now was none to which he could fitly, by those wiser than himself, have been bound and constrained, that he might learn to love it. So swift, light-limbed and fiery an Arab courser ought, for all manner of reasons, to have been trained to saddle and harness. Roaming at full gallop over the heaths, — especially when your heath was London, and English and European life, in the nineteenth century, — he suffered much, and did comparatively little. I have known few creatures whom it was more wasteful to send forth with the bridle thrown up, and to set to steeple-hunting instead of running on highways! But it is the lot of many such, in this dislocated time, — Heaven mend it! In a better time there will be other "professions" than those three extremely cramp, confused and indeed almost obsolete ones: professions, if possible, that are true, and do *not* require you at the threshold to constitute yourself an impostor. Human association, — which will mean discipline, vigorous wise subordination and co-ordination, — is so unspeakably important. Professions, "regimented human pursuits," how many of honorable and manful might be possible for men; and which should *not*, in their results to society, need to stumble along, in such an unwieldy futile manner, with legs swollen into such enormous elephantiasis and no *go* at all in them! Men will one day think of the force they squander in every generation, and the fatal damage they encounter, by this neglect.

The career likeliest for Sterling, in his and the world's circumstances, would have been what is called public life: some secretarial, diplomatic or other official training, to issue if possible in Parliament as the true field for him. And here, beyond question, had the gross material conditions been allowed, his spiritual capabilities were first-rate. In any arena where eloquence and argument was the point, this man was calculated to have borne the bell from all competitors. In lucid ingenious talk and logic, in all manner of brilliant utterance and tongue-fence, I have hardly known his fellow. So ready lay his store of knowledge round him, so perfect was his ready utterance of the same, — in coruscating wit, in jocund drollery, in compact articulated clearness or high poignant emphasis, as the case required, — he was a match for any man in argument before a crowd of men. One of the most supple-wristed, dexterous, graceful and successful fencers in that kind. A man, as Mr. Hare has said, " able to argue with four or five at once ;" could do the parrying all round, in a succession swift as light, and plant his hits wherever a chance offered. In Parliament, such a soul put into a body of the due toughness might have carried it far. If ours is to be called, as I hear some call it, the Talking Era, Sterling of all men had the talent to excel in it.

Probably it was with some vague view towards chances in this direction that Sterling's first engagement was entered upon; a brief connection as Secretary to some Club or Association into which certain public men, of the reforming sort, Mr. Crawford (the Oriental Diplomatist and Writer), Mr. Kirkman Finlay (then Member for Glasgow), and other political notabilities had now formed themselves, — with what specific objects I do not know, nor with what result if any. I have heard vaguely, it was "to open the trade to India." Of course they intended to stir up the public mind into co-operation, whatever their goal or object was : Mr. Crawford, an intimate in the Sterling household, recognized the fine literary

gift of John; and might think it a lucky hit that he had
caught such a Secretary for three hundred pounds a year.
That was the salary agreed upon; and for some months actually worked for and paid; Sterling becoming for the time an
intimate and almost an inmate in Mr. Crawford's circle, doubtless not without results to himself beyond the secretarial work
and pounds sterling: so much is certain. But neither the
Secretaryship nor the Association itself had any continuance;
nor can I now learn accurately more of it than what is here
stated; — in which vague state it must vanish from Sterling's
history again, as it in great measure did from his life. From
himself in after-years I never heard mention of it; nor were
his pursuits connected afterwards with those of Mr. Crawford,
though the mutual good-will continued unbroken.

In fact, however splendid and indubitable Sterling's qualifications for a parliamentary life, there was that in him withal
which flatly put a negative on any such project. He had not
the slow steady-pulling diligence which is indispensable in
that, as in all important pursuits and strenuous human com-
petitions whatsoever. In every sense, his momentum depended
on velocity of stroke, rather than on weight of metal; "beautifulest sheet-lightning," as I often said, "not to be condensed
into thunder-bolts." Add to this, — what indeed is perhaps
but the same phenomenon in another form, — his bodily frame
was thin, excitable, already manifesting pulmonary symptoms;
a body which the tear and wear of Parliament would infallibly
in few months have wrecked and ended. By this path there
was clearly no mounting. The far-darting, restlessly coruscating soul, equipt beyond all others to shine in the Talking
Era, and lead National Palavers with their *spolia opima* captive, is imprisoned in a fragile hectic body which quite forbids
the adventure. "*Es ist dafür gesorgt,*" says Goethe, "Provision has been made that the trees do not grow into the sky;" —
means are always there to stop them short of the sky.

CHAPTER VI.

LITERATURE: THE ATHENÆUM.

OF all forms of public life, in the Talking Era, it was clear that only one completely suited Sterling, — the anarchic, nomadic, entirely aerial and unconditional one, called Literature. To this all his tendencies, and fine gifts positive and negative, were evidently pointing; and here, after such brief attempting or thoughts to attempt at other posts, he already in this same year arrives. As many do, and ever more must do, in these our years and times. This is the chaotic haven of so many frustrate activities; where all manner of good gifts go up in far-seen smoke or conflagration; and whole fleets, that might have been war-fleets to conquer kingdoms, are *consumed* (too truly, often), amid "fame" enough, and the admiring shouts of the vulgar, which is always fond to see fire going on. The true Canaan and Mount Zion of a Talking Era must ever be Literature : the extraneous, miscellaneous, self-elected, indescribable *Parliamentum,* or Talking Apparatus, which talks by books and printed papers.

A literary Newspaper called *The Athenæum,* the same which still subsists, had been founded in those years by Mr. Buckingham; James Silk Buckingham, who has since continued notable under various figures. Mr. Buckingham's *Athenæum* had not as yet got into a flourishing condition; and he was willing to sell the copyright of it for a consideration. Perhaps Sterling and old Cambridge friends of his had been already writing for it. At all events, Sterling, who had already privately begun writing a Novel, and was clearly looking towards Literature, perceived that his gifted Cambridge friend, Frederic Maurice, was now also at large in a somewhat similar situation; and that here was an opening for both of them, and for other gifted friends. The copyright was purchased for I know

not what sum, nor with whose money, but guess it may have
been Sterling's, and no great sum; — and so, under free auspices, themselves their own captains, Maurice and he spread
sail for this new voyage of adventure into all the world.   It
was about the end of 1828 that readers of periodical literature,
and quidnuncs in those departments, began to report the appearance, in a Paper called the *Athenæum*, of writings showing
a superior brilliancy, and height of aim; one or perhaps two
slight specimens of which came into my own hands, in my
remote corner, about that time, and were duly recognized by
me, while the authors were still far off and hidden behind
deep veils.

Some of Sterling's best Papers from the *Athenæum* have
been published by Archdeacon Hare : first-fruits by a young
man of twenty-two; crude, imperfect, yet singularly beautiful and attractive; which will still testify what high literary
promise lay in him.   The ruddiest glow of young enthusiasm,
of noble incipient spiritual manhood reigns over them; once
more a divine Universe unveiling itself in gloom and splendor,
in auroral firelight and many-tinted shadow, full of hope and
full of awe, to a young melodious pious heart just arrived
upon it.   Often enough the delineation has a certain flowing
completeness, not to be expected from so young an artist;
here and there is a decided felicity of insight; everywhere the
point of view adopted is a high and noble one, and the result
worked out a result to be sympathized with, and accepted so
far as it will go.   Good reading still, those Papers, for the less-
furnished mind, — thrice-excellent reading compared with what
is usually going.   For the rest, a grand melancholy is the prevailing impression they leave; — partly as if, while the surface was so blooming and opulent, the heart of them was still
vacant, sad and cold.   Here is a beautiful mirage, in the dry
wilderness; but you cannot quench your thirst there!   The
writer's heart is indeed still too vacant, except of beautiful
shadows and reflexes and resonances; and is far from joyful,
though it wears commonly a smile.

In some of the Greek delineations (*The Lycian Painter*, for
example), we have already noticed a strange opulence of splen-

dor, characterizable as half-legitimate, half-meretricious, — a splendor hovering between the raffaelesque and the japannish. What other things Sterling wrote there, I never knew; nor would he in any mood, in those later days, have told you, had you asked. This period of his life he always rather accounted, as the Arabs do the idolatrous times before Mahomet's advent, the "period of darkness."

CHAPTER VII.

REGENT STREET.

On the commercial side the *Athenæum* still lacked success; nor was like to find it under the highly uncommercial management it had now got into. This, by and by, began to be a serious consideration. For money is the sinews of Periodical Literature almost as much as of war itself; without money, and under a constant drain of loss, Periodical Literature is one of the things that cannot be carried on. In no long time Sterling began to be practically sensible of this truth, and that an unpleasant resolution in accordance with it would be necessary. By him also, after a while, the *Athenæum* was transferred to other hands, better fitted in that respect; and under these it did take vigorous root, and still bears fruit according to its kind.

For the present, it brought him into the thick of London Literature, especially of young London Literature and speculation; in which turbid exciting element he swam and revelled, nothing loath, for certain months longer, — a period short of two years in all. He had lodgings in Regent Street: his Father's house, now a flourishing and stirring establishment, in South Place, Knightsbridge, where, under the warmth of increasing revenue and success, miscellaneous cheerful socialities and abundant speculations, chiefly political (and not John's kind, but that of the *Times* Newspaper and the Clubs), were rife, he could visit daily, and yet be master of his own

studies and pursuits. Maurice, Trench, John Mill, Charles
Buller: these, and some few others, among a wide circle of
a transitory phantasmal character, whom he speedily forgot
and cared not to remember, were much about him; with these
he in all ways employed and disported himself: a first favorite
with them all.

No pleasanter companion, I suppose, had any of them. So
frank, open, guileless, fearless, a brother to all worthy souls
whatsoever. Come when you might, here is he open-hearted,
rich in cheerful fancies, in grave logic, in all kinds of bright
activity. If perceptibly or imperceptibly there is a touch of
ostentation in him, blame it not; it is so innocent, so good
and childlike. He is still fonder of jingling publicly, and
spreading on the table, your big purse of opulences than his
own. Abrupt too he is, cares little for big-wigs and garnitures;
perhaps laughs more than the real fun he has would order;
but of arrogance there is no vestige, of insincerity or of ill-
nature none. These must have been pleasant evenings in Regent Street, when the circle chanced to be well adjusted there.
At other times, Philistines would enter, what we call bores,
dullards, Children of Darkness; and then, — except in a hunt
of dullards, and a *bore-baiting*, which might be permissible, —
the evening was dark. Sterling, of course, had innumerable
cares withal; and was toiling like a slave; his very recrea-
tions almost a kind of work. An enormous activity was in
the man; — sufficient, in a body that could have held it without breaking, to have gone far, even under the unstable guidance it was like to have!

Thus, too, an extensive, very variegated circle of connections
was forming round him. Besides his *Athenæum* work, and
evenings in Regent Street and elsewhere, he makes visits to
country-houses, the Bullers' and others; converses with established gentlemen, with honorable women not a few; is gay
and welcome with the young of his own age; knows also religious, witty, and other distinguished ladies, and is admiringly
known by them. On the whole, he is already locomotive;
visits hither and thither in a very rapid flying manner. Thus
I find he had made one flying visit to the Cumberland Lake-

region in 1828, and got sight of Wordsworth; and in the same
year another flying one to Paris, and seen with no undue enthusiasm the Saint-Simonian Portent just beginning to preach
for itself, and France in general simmering under a scum of
impieties, levities, Saint-Simonisms, and frothy fantasticalities
of all kinds, towards the boiling-over which soon made the
Three Days of July famous.   But by far the most important
foreign home he visited was that of Coleridge on the Hill of
Highgate, — if it were not rather a foreign shrine and Dodona-
Oracle, as he then reckoned, — to which (onwards from 1828,
as would appear) he was already an assiduous pilgrim.   Concerning whom, and Sterling's all-important connection with
him, there will be much to say anon.

Here, from this period, is a Letter of Sterling's, which the
glimpses it affords of bright scenes and figures now sunk, so
many of them, sorrowfully to the realm of shadows, will render interesting to some of my readers.   To me on the mere
Letter, not on its contents alone, there is accidentally a kind
of fateful stamp.   A few months after Charles Buller's death,
while his loss was mourned by many hearts, and to his poor
Mother all light except what hung upon his memory had gone
out in the world, a certain delicate and friendly hand, hoping
to give the poor bereaved lady a good moment, sought out this
Letter of Sterling's, one morning, and called, with intent to
read it to her: — alas, the poor lady had herself fallen suddenly into the languors of death, help of another grander sort
now close at hand; and to her this Letter was never read!

On "Fanny Kemble," it appears, there is an Essay by Sterling in the *Athenæum* of this year: "16th December, 1829."
Very laudatory, I conclude.   He much admired her genius,
nay was thought at one time to be vaguely on the edge of still
more chivalrous feelings.   As the Letter itself may perhaps
indicate.

" *To Anthony Sterling, Esq., 24th Regiment, Dublin.*

"Knightsbridge, 10th Nov., 1829.

"My dear Anthony, — Here in the Capital of England
and of Europe, there is less, so far as I hear. of movement and

variety than in your provincial Dublin, or among the Wicklow Mountains. We have the old prospect of bricks and smoke, the old crowd of busy stupid faces, the old occupations, the old sleepy amusements; and the latest news that reaches us daily has an air of tiresome, doting antiquity. The world has nothing for it but to exclaim with Faust, "Give me my youth again." And as for me, my month of Cornish amusement is over; and I must tie myself to my old employments. I have not much to tell you about these; but perhaps you may like to hear of my expedition to the West.

"I wrote to Polvellan (Mr. Buller's) to announce the day on which I intended to be there, so shortly before setting out, that there was no time to receive an answer; and when I reached Devonport, which is fifteen or sixteen miles from my place of destination, I found a letter from Mrs. Buller, saying that she was coming in two days to a Ball at Plymouth, and if I chose to stay in the mean while and look about me, she would take me back with her. She added an introduction to a relation of her husband's, a certain Captain Buller of the Rifles, who was with the Depôt there, — a pleasant person, who I believe had been acquainted with Charlotte,[1] or at least had seen her. Under his superintendence —. . .

"On leaving Devonport with Mrs. Buller, I went some of the way by water, up the harbor and river; and the prospects are certainly very beautiful; to say nothing of the large ships, which I admire almost as much as you, though without knowing so much about them. There is a great deal of fine scenery all along the road to Looe; and the House itself, a very unpretending Gothic cottage, stands beautifully among trees, hills and water, with the sea at the distance of a quarter of a mile.

"And here, among pleasant, good-natured, well-informed and clever people, I spent an idle month. I dined at one or two Corporation dinners; spent a few days at the old Mansion of Mr. Buller of Morval, the patron of West Looe; and during the rest of the time, read, wrote, played chess, lounged, and ate red mullet (he who has not done this has not begun to

---

[1] Mrs. Anthony Sterling, very lately Miss Charlotte Baird.

live) ; talked of cookery to the philosophers, and of metaphys-
ics to Mrs. Buller ; and altogether cultivated indolence, and
developed the faculty of nonsense with considerable pleasure
and unexampled success. Charles Buller you know : he has
just come to town, but I have not yet seen him. Arthur, his
younger brother, I take to be one of the handsomest men in
England ; and he too has considerable talent. Mr. Buller the
father is rather a clever man of sense, and particularly good-
natured and gentlemanly ; and his wife, who was a renowned
beauty and queen of Calcutta, has still many striking and delicate traces of what she was. Her conversation is more brilliant and pleasant than that of any one I know ; and, at all
events, I am bound to admire her for the kindness with which
she patronizes me. I hope that, some day or other, you may
be acquainted with her.

"I believe I have seen no one in London about whom you
would care to hear, — unless the fame of Fanny Kemble
has passed the Channel, and astonished the Irish Barbarians
in the midst of their bloody-minded politics. Young Kemble,
whom you have seen, is in Germany : but I have the happiness of being also acquainted with his sister, the divine Fanny ; and I have seen her twice on the stage, and three or four
times in private, since my return from Cornwall. I had seen
some beautiful verses of hers, long before she was an actress ;
and her conversation is full of spirit and talent. She never
was taught to act at all ; and though there are many faults
in her performance of Juliet, there is more power than in any
female playing I ever saw, except Pasta's Medea. She is not
handsome, rather short, and by no means delicately formed ;
but her face is marked, and the eyes are brilliant, dark, and
full of character. She has far more ability than she ever can
display on the stage ; but I have no doubt that, by practice
and self-culture, she will be a far finer actress at least than
any one since Mrs. Siddons. I was at Charles Kemble's a
few evenings ago, when a drawing of Miss Kemble, by Sir
Thomas Lawrence, was brought in ; and I have no doubt that
you will shortly see, even in Dublin, an engraving of her from
it, very unlike the caricatures that have hitherto appeared.

I hate the stage ; and but for her, should very likely never
have gone to a theatre again.   Even as it is, the annoyance is
much more than the pleasure ; but I suppose I must go to see
her in every character in which she acts.   If Charlotte cares
for plays, let me know, and I will write in more detail about
this new Melpomene.   I fear there are very few subjects on
which I can say anything that will in the least interest her.

"Ever affectionately yours,

"J. STERLING."

Sterling and his circle, as their ardent speculation and
activity fermented along, were in all things clear for progress,
liberalism ; their politics, and view of the Universe, decisively
of the Radical sort.   As indeed that of England then was,
more than ever ; the crust of old hide-bound Toryism being
now openly cracking towards some incurable disruption, which
accordingly ensued as the Reform Bill before long.   The Reform Bill already hung in the wind.   Old hide-bound Toryism,
long recognized by all the world, and now at last obliged to
recognize its very self, for an overgrown Imposture, supporting itself not by human reason, but by flunky blustering and
brazen lying, superadded to mere brute force, could be no creed
for young Sterling and his friends.   In all things he and they
were liberals, and, as was natural at this stage, democrats ;
contemplating root-and-branch innovation by aid of the hustings and ballot-box.   Hustings and ballot-box had speedily
to vanish out of Sterling's thoughts : but the character of
root-and-branch innovator, essentially of "Radical Reformer,"
was indelible with him, and under all forms could be traced
as his character through life.

For the present, his and those young people's aim was :
By democracy, or what means there are, be all impostures
put down.   Speedy end to Superstition, — a gentle one if
you can contrive it, but an end.   What can it profit any
mortal to adopt locutions and imaginations which do *not*
correspond to fact ; which no sane mortal can deliberately
adopt in his soul as true ; which the most orthodox of mortals
can only, and this after infinite essentially *impious* effort to

put out the eyes of his mind, persuade himself to "believe that he believes"?   Away with it; in the name of God, come out of it, all true men!

Piety of heart, a certain reality of religious faith, was always Sterling's, the gift of nature to him which he would not and could not throw away; but I find at this time his religion is as good as altogether Ethnic, Greekish, what Goethe calls the Heathen form of religion.   The Church, with her articles, is without relation to him.   And along with obsolete spiritualisms, he sees all manner of obsolete thrones and big-wigged temporalities; and for them also can prophesy, and wish, only a speedy doom.   Doom inevitable, registered in Heaven's Chancery from the beginning of days, doom unalterable as the pillars of the world; the gods are angry, and all nature groans, till this doom of eternal justice be fulfilled.

With gay audacity, with enthusiasm tempered by mockery, as is the manner of young gifted men, this faith, grounded for the present on democracy and hustings operations, and giving to all life the aspect of a chivalrous battle-field, or almost of a gay though perilous tournament, and bout of "A hundred knights against all comers," — was maintained by Sterling and his friends.   And in fine, after whatever loud remonstrances, and solemn considerations, and such shaking of our wigs as is undoubtedly natural in the case, let us be just to it and him.   We shall have to admit, nay it will behoove us to see and practically know, for ourselves and him and others, that the essence of this creed, in times like ours, was right and not wrong.   That, however the ground and form of it might change, essentially it was the monition of his natal genius to this as it is to every brave man; the behest of all his clear insight into this Universe, the message of Heaven through him, which he could not suppress, but was inspired and compelled to utter in this world by such methods as he had.   There for him lay the first commandment; *this* is what it would have been the unforgivable sin to swerve from and desert: the treason of treasons for him, it were there; compared with which all other sins are venial!

The message did not cease at all, as we shall see; the message was ardently, if fitfully, continued to the end: but the methods, the tone and dialect and all outer conditions of uttering it, underwent most important modifications!

CHAPTER VIII.

COLERIDGE.

COLERIDGE sat on the brow of Highgate Hill, in those years, looking down on London and its smoke-tumult, like a sage escaped from the inanity of life's battle; attracting towards him the thoughts of innumerable brave souls still engaged there.   His express contributions to poetry, philosophy, or any specific province of human literature or enlightenment, had been small and sadly intermittent; but he had, especially among young inquiring men, a higher than literary, a kind of prophetic or magician character.   He was thought to hold, he alone in England, the key of German and other Transcendentalisms; knew the sublime secret of believing by "the reason" what "the understanding" had been obliged to fling out as incredible; and could still, after Hume and Voltaire had done their best and worst with him, profess himself an orthodox Christian, and say and print to the Church of England, with its singular old rubrics and surplices at Allhallowtide, *Esto perpetua*.   A sublime man; who, alone in those dark days, had saved his crown of spiritual manhood; escaping from the black materialisms, and revolutionary deluges, with "God, Freedom, Immortality" still his : a king of men.   The practical intellects of the world did not much heed him, or carelessly reckoned him a metaphysical dreamer: but to the rising spirits of the young generation he had this dusky sublime character; and sat there as a kind of *Magus*, girt in mystery and enigma; his Dodona oak-grove (Mr. Gilman's house at Highgate) whispering strange things, uncertain whether oracles or jargon.

The Gilmans did not encourage much company, or excitation

of any sort, round their sage ; nevertheless access to him, if a youth did reverently wish it, was not difficult. He would stroll about the pleasant garden with you, sit in the pleasant rooms of the place, — perhaps take you to his own peculiar room, high up, with a rearward view, which was the chief view of all. A really charming outlook, in fine weather. Close at hand, wide sweep of flowery leafy gardens, their few houses mostly hidden, the very chimney-pots veiled under blossomy umbrage, flowed gloriously down hill ; gloriously issuing in wide-tufted undulating plain-country, rich in all charms of field and town. Waving blooming country of the brightest green ; dotted all over with handsome villas, handsome groves ; crossed by roads and human traffic, here inaudible or heard only as a musical hum : and behind all swam, under olive-tinted haze, the illimitable limitary ocean of London, with its domes and steeples definite in the sun, big Paul's and the many memories attached to it hanging high over all. Nowhere, of its kind, could you see a grander prospect on a bright summer day, with the set of the air going southward, — southward, and so draping with the city-smoke not *you* but the city. Here for hours would Coleridge talk, concerning all conceivable or in-conceivable things ; and liked nothing better than to have an intelligent, or failing that, even a silent and patient human listener. He distinguished himself to all that ever heard him as at least the most surprising talker extant in this world, — and to some small minority, by no means to all, as the most excellent.

The good man, he was now getting old, towards sixty per-haps ; and gave you the idea of a life that had been full of sufferings ; a life heavy-laden, half-vanquished, still swimming painfully in seas of manifold physical and other bewilderment. Brow and head were round, and of massive weight, but the face was flabby and irresolute. The deep eyes, of a light hazel, were as full of sorrow as of inspiration ; confused pain looked mildly from them, as in a kind of mild astonishment. The whole figure and air, good and amiable otherwise, might be called flabby and irresolute ; expressive of weakness under possibility of strength. He hung loosely on his limbs, with

knees bent, and stooping attitude; in walking, he rather
shuffled than decisively stept; and a lady once remarked, he
never could fix which side of the garden walk would suit him
best, but continually shifted, in corkscrew fashion, and kept
trying both. A heavy-laden, high-aspiring and surely much-
suffering man. His voice, naturally soft and good, had con-
tracted itself into a plaintive snuffle and singsong; he spoke
as if preaching, — you would have said, preaching earnestly
and also hopelessly the weightiest things. I still recollect his
" object " and " subject," terms of continual recurrence in the
Kantean province; and how he sang and snuffled them into
" om-m-mject " and " sum-m-mject," with a kind of solemn
shake or quaver, as he rolled along. No talk, in his century
or in any other, could be more surprising.

Sterling, who assiduously attended him, with profound reverence, and was often with him by himself, for a good many
months, gives a record of their first colloquy.[1] Their colloquies were numerous, and he had taken note of many; but
they are all gone to the fire, except this first, which Mr. Hare
has printed, — unluckily without date. It contains a number
of ingenious, true and half-true observations, and is of course
a faithful epitome of the things said; but it gives small idea of
Coleridge's way of talking; — this one feature is perhaps the
most recognizable, " Our interview lasted for three hours, during which he talked two hours and three quarters." Nothing
could be more copious than his talk; and furthermore it was
always, virtually or literally, of the nature of a monologue;
suffering no interruption, however reverent; hastily putting
aside all foreign additions, annotations, or most ingenuous
desires for elucidation, as well-meant superfluities which would
never do. Besides, it was talk not flowing any-whither like a
river, but spreading every-whither in inextricable currents and
regurgitations like a lake or sea; terribly deficient in definite
goal or aim, nay often in logical intelligibility; *what* you were
to believe or do, on any earthly or heavenly thing, obstinately
refusing to appear from it. So that, most times, you felt
logically lost; swamped near to drowning in this tide of

[1] *Biography*, by Hare, pp. xvi–xxvi.

ingenious vocables, spreading out boundless as if to submerge the world.

To sit as a passive bucket and be pumped into, whether you consent or not, can in the long-run be exhilarating to no creature; how eloquent soever the flood of utterance that is descending. But if it be withal a confused unintelligible flood of utterance, threatening to submerge all known landmarks of thought, and drown the world and you ! — I have heard Coleridge talk, with eager musical energy, two stricken hours, his face radiant and moist, and communicate no meaning whatsoever to any individual of his hearers, — certain of whom, I for one, still kept eagerly listening in hope; the most had long before given up, and formed (if the room were large enough) secondary humming groups of their own. He began anywhere: you put some question to him, made some suggestive observation : instead of answering this, or decidedly setting out towards answer of it, he would accumulate formidable apparatus, logical swim-bladders, transcendental life-preservers and other precautionary and vehiculatory gear, for setting out; perhaps did at last get under way, — but was swiftly solicited, turned aside by the glance of some radiant new game on this hand or that, into new courses; and ever into new ; and before long into all the Universe, where it was uncertain what game you would catch, or whether any.

His talk, alas, was distinguished, like himself, by irresolution : it disliked to be troubled with conditions, abstinences, definite fulfilments; — loved to wander at its own sweet will, and make its auditor and his claims and humble wishes a mere passive bucket for itself! He had knowledge about many things and topics, much curious reading; but generally all topics led him, after a pass or two, into the high seas of theosophic philosophy, the hazy infinitude of Kantean transcendentalism, with its "sum-m-mjects " and " om-m-mjects." Sad enough; for with such indolent impatience of the claims and ignorances of others, he had not the least talent for explaining this or anything unknown to them; and you swam and fluttered in the mistiest wide unintelligible deluge of things, for most part in a rather profitless uncomfortable manner.

Glorious islets, too, I have seen rise out of the haze; but they were few, and soon swallowed in the general element again. Balmy sunny islets, islets of the blest and the intelligible: — on which occasions those secondary humming groups would all cease humming, and hang breathless upon the eloquent words; till once your islet got wrapt in the mist again, and they could recommence humming. Eloquent artistically expressive words you always had; piercing radiances of a most subtle insight came at intervals; tones of noble pious sympathy, recognizable as pious though strangely colored, were never wanting long: but in general you could not call this aimless, cloud-capt, cloud-based, lawlessly meandering human discourse of reason by the name of "excellent talk," but only of "surprising;" and were reminded bitterly of Hazlitt's account of it: "Excellent talker, very, — if you let him start from no premises and come to no conclusion." Coleridge was not without what talkers call wit, and there were touches of prickly sarcasm in him, contemptuous enough of the world and its idols and popular dignitaries; he had traits even of poetic humor: but in general he seemed deficient in laughter; or indeed in sympathy for concrete human things either on the sunny or on the stormy side. One right peal of concrete laughter at some convicted flesh-and-blood absurdity, one burst of noble indignation at some injustice or depravity, rubbing elbows with us on this solid Earth, how strange would it have been in that Kantean haze-world, and how infinitely cheering amid its vacant air-castles and dim-melting ghosts and shadows! None such ever came. His life had been an abstract thinking and dreaming, idealistic, passed amid the ghosts of defunct bodies and of unborn ones. The moaning singsong of that theosophico-metaphysical monotony left on you, at last, a very dreary feeling.

In close colloquy, flowing within narrower banks, I suppose he was more definite and apprehensible; Sterling in after-times did not complain of his unintelligibility, or imputed it only to the abtruse high nature of the topics handled. Let us hope so, let us try to believe so! There is no doubt but Coleridge could speak plain words on things plain: his observations and

responses on the trivial matters that occurred were as simple
as the commonest man's, or were even distinguished by superior simplicity as well as pertinency. "Ah, your tea is too
cold, Mr. Coleridge!" mourned the good Mrs. Gilman once,
in her kind, reverential and yet protective manner, handing
him a very tolerable though belated cup. — "It 's better than
I deserve!" snuffled he, in a low hoarse murmur, partly courteous, chiefly pious, the tone of which still abides with me:
"It 's better than I deserve!"

But indeed, to the young ardent mind, instinct with pious
nobleness, yet driven to the grim deserts of Radicalism for a
faith, his speculations had a charm much more than literary,
a charm almost religious and prophetic. The constant gist of
his discourse was lamentation over the sunk condition of the
world; which he recognized to be given up to Atheism and
Materialism, full of mere sordid misbeliefs, mispursuits and
misresults. All Science had become mechanical; the science
not of men, but of a kind of human beavers. Churches themselves had died away into a godless mechanical condition; and
stood there as mere Cases of Articles, mere Forms of Churches;
like the dried carcasses of once swift camels, which you find
left withering in the thirst of the universal desert, — ghastly
portents for the present, beneficent ships of the desert no
more. Men's souls were blinded, hebetated; and sunk under
the influence of Atheism and Materialism, and Hume and
Voltaire : the world for the present was as an extinct world,
deserted of God, and incapable of well-doing till it changed its
heart and spirit. This, expressed I think with less of indignation and with more of long-drawn querulousness, was always
recognizable as the ground-tone : — in which truly a pious
young heart, driven into Radicalism and the opposition party,
could not but recognize a too sorrowful truth; and ask of the
Oracle, with all earnestness, What remedy, then ?

The remedy, though Coleridge himself professed to see it as
in sunbeams, could not, except by processes unspeakably difficult, be described to you at all. On the whole, those dead
Churches, this dead English Church especially, must be brought
to life again. Why not ? It was not dead; the soul of it, in

this parched-up body, was tragically asleep only. Atheistic Philosophy was true on its side, and Hume and Voltaire could on their own ground speak irrefragably for themselves against any Church: but lift the Church and them into a higher sphere of argument, *they* died into inanition, the Church revivified itself into pristine florid vigor, — became once more a living ship of the desert, and invincibly bore you over stock and stone. But how, but how! By attending to the "reason" of man, said Coleridge, and duly chaining up the "understanding" of man · the *Vernunft* (Reason) and *Verstand* (Understanding) of the Germans, it all turned upon these, if you could well understand them, — which you could n't. For the rest, Mr. Coleridge had on the anvil various Books, especially was about to write one grand Book *On the Logos*, which would help to bridge the chasm for us. So much appeared, however: Churches, though proved false (as you had imagined), were still true (as you were to imagine): here was an Artist who could burn you up an old Church, root and branch; and then as the Alchemists professed to do with organic substances in general, distil you an "Astral Spirit" from the ashes, which was the very image of the old burnt article, its air-drawn counterpart, — this you still had, or might get, and draw uses from, if you could. Wait till the Book on the Logos were done; — alas, till your own terrene eyes, blind with conceit and the dust of logic, were purged, subtilized and spiritualized into the sharpness of vision requisite for discerning such an "om-m-mject." — The ingenuous young English head, of those days, stood strangely puzzled by such revelations; uncertain whether it were getting inspired, or getting infatuated into flat imbecility; and strange effulgence, of new day or else of deeper meteoric night, colored the horizon of the future for it.

Let me not be unjust to this memorable man. Surely there was here, in his pious, ever-laboring, subtle mind, a precious truth, or prefigurement of truth; and yet a fatal delusion withal. Prefigurement that, in spite of beaver sciences and temporary spiritual hebetude and cecity, man and his Universe were eternally divine; and that no past nobleness, or revelation of the divine, could or would ever be lost to him.

Most true, surely, and worthy of all acceptance. Good also to do what you can with old Churches and practical Symbols of the Noble : nay quit not the burnt ruins of them while you find there is still gold to be dug there. But, on the whole, do not think you can, by logical alchemy, distil astral spirits from them; or if you could, that said astral spirits, or defunct logical phantasms, could serve you in anything. What the light of your mind, which is the direct inspiration of the Almighty, pronounces incredible, — that, in God's name, leave uncredited; at your peril do not try believing that. No subtlest hocus-pocus of "reason" *versus* "understanding" will avail for that feat; — and it is terribly perilous to try it in these provinces!

The truth is, I now see, Coleridge's talk and speculation was the emblem of himself: in it as in him, a ray of heavenly inspiration struggled, in a tragically ineffectual degree, with the weakness of flesh and blood. He says once, he "had skirted the howling deserts of Infidelity;" this was evident enough: but he had not had the courage, in defiance of pain and terror, to press resolutely across said deserts to the new firm lands of Faith beyond; he preferred to create logical fata-morganas for himself on this hither side, and laboriously solace himself with these.

To the man himself Nature had given, in high measure, the seeds of a noble endowment; and to unfold it had been forbidden him. A subtle lynx-eyed intellect, tremulous pious sensibility to all good and all beautiful; truly a ray of empyrean light; — but embedded in such weak laxity of character, in such indolences and esuriences as had made strange work with it. Once more, the tragic story of a high endowment with an insufficient will. An eye to discern the divineness of the Heaven's spendors and lightnings, the insatiable wish to revel in their godlike radiances and brilliances; but no heart to front the scathing terrors of them, which is the first condition of your conquering an abiding place there. The courage necessary for him, above all things, had been denied this man. His life, with such ray of the empyrean in it, was great and terrible to him; and he had not valiantly grappled

with it, he had fled from it; sought refuge in vague day-
dreams, hollow compromises, in opium, in theosophic meta-
physics. Harsh pain, danger, necessity, slavish harnessed
toil, were of all things abhorrent to him. And so the empyrean element, lying smothered under the terrene, and yet
inextinguishable there, made sad writhings. For pain, danger, difficulty, steady slaving toil, and other highly disagreeable behests of destiny, shall in nowise be shirked by any
brightest mortal that will approve himself loyal to his mission
in this world; nay precisely the higher he is, the deeper will
be the disagreeableness, and the detestability to flesh and
blood, of the tasks laid on him; and the heavier too, and more
tragic, his penalties if he neglect them.

For the old Eternal Powers do live forever; nor do their
laws know any change, however we in our poor wigs and
church-tippets may attempt to read their laws. To *steal* into
Heaven, — by the modern method, of sticking ostrich-like your
head into fallacies on Earth, equally as by the ancient and by
all conceivable methods, — is forever forbidden. High-treason
is the name of that attempt; and it continues to be punished
as such. Strange enough: here once more was a kind of
Heaven-scaling Ixion; and to him, as to the old one, the
just gods were very stern! The ever-revolving, never-advan-
cing Wheel (of a kind) was his, through life; and from his
Cloud-Juno did not he too procreate strange Centaurs, spec-
tral Puseyisms, monstrous illusory Hybrids, and ecclesiastical
Chimeras, — which now roam the earth in a very lamentable
manner!

CHAPTER IX.

SPANISH EXILES.

THIS magical ingredient thrown into the wild caldron of
such a mind, which we have seen occupied hitherto with mere
Ethnicism, Radicalism and revolutionary tumult, but hunger-
ing all along for something higher and better, was sure to be

eagerly welcomed and imbibed, and could not fail to produce important fermentations there. Fermentations; important new directions, and withal important new perversions, in the spiritual life of this man, as it has since done in the lives of so many. Here then is the new celestial manna we were all in quest of? This thrice-refined pabulum of transcendental moonshine? Whoso eateth thereof, — yes, what, on the whole, will *he* probably grow to?

Sterling never spoke much to me of his intercourse with Coleridge; and when we did compare notes about him, it was usually rather in the way of controversial discussion than of narrative. So that, from my own resources, I can give no details of the business, nor specify anything in it, except the general fact of an ardent attendance at Highgate continued for many months, which was impressively known to all Sterling's friends; and am unable to assign even the limitary dates, Sterling's own papers on the subject having all been destroyed by him. Inferences point to the end of 1828 as the beginning of this intercourse; perhaps in 1829 it was at the highest point; and already in 1830, when the intercourse itself was about to terminate, we have proof of the influences it was producing, — in the Novel of *Arthur Coningsby*, then on hand, the first and only Book that Sterling ever wrote. His writings hitherto had been sketches, criticisms, brief essays; he was now trying it on a wider scale; but not yet with satisfactory results, and it proved to be his only trial in that form.

He had already, as was intimated, given up his brief proprietorship of the *Athenæum;* the commercial indications, and state of sales and of costs, peremptorily ordering him to do so; the copyright went by sale or gift, I know not at what precise date, into other fitter hands; and with the copyright all connection on the part of Sterling. To *Athenæum* Sketches had now (in 1829–30) succeeded *Arthur Coningsby*, a Novel in three volumes; indicating (when it came to light, a year or two afterwards) equally hasty and much more ambitious aims in Literature; — giving strong evidence, too, of internal spiritual revulsions going painfully forward, and in particular of the impression Coleridge was producing on him. Without **and**

within, it was a wild tide of things this ardent light young
soul was afloat upon, at present; and his outlooks into the
future, whether for his spiritual or economic fortunes, were
confused enough.

Among his familiars in this period, I might have mentioned
one Charles Barton, formerly his fellow-student at Cambridge,
now an amiable, cheerful, rather idle young fellow about Town;
who led the way into certain new experiences, and lighter
fields, for Sterling.   His Father, Lieutenant-General Barton
of the Life-guards, an Irish landlord, I think in Fermanagh
County, and a man of connections about Court, lived in a certain figure here in Town; had a wife of fashionable habits,
with other sons, and also daughters, bred in this sphere.   These,
all of them, were amiable, elegant and pleasant people; — such
was especially an eldest daughter, Susannah Barton, a stately
blooming black-eyed young woman, attractive enough in form
and character; full of gay softness, of indolent sense and enthusiasm; about Sterling's own age, if not a little older.   In
this house, which opened to him, more decisively than his
Father's, a new stratum of society, and where his reception
for Charles's sake and his own was of the kindest, he liked
very well to be; and spent, I suppose, many of his vacant half-
hours, lightly chatting with the elders or the youngsters, —
doubtless with the young lady too, though as yet without particular intentions on either side.
     Nor, with all the Coleridge fermentation, was democratic
Radicalism by any means given up; — though how it was to
live if the Coleridgean moonshine took effect, might have been
an abtruse question.   Hitherto, while said moonshine was but
taking effect, and coloring the outer surface of things without
quite penetrating into the heart, democratic Liberalism, revolt
against superstition and oppression, and help to whosoever
would revolt, was still the grand element in Sterling's creed;
and practically he stood, not ready only, but full of alacrity
to fulfil all its behests.   We heard long since of the "black
dragoons," — whom doubtless the new moonshine had considerably silvered-over into new hues, by this time: — but here

now, while Radicalism is tottering for him and threatening to crumble, comes suddenly the grand consummation and explosion of Radicalism in his life; whereby, all at once, Radicalism exhausted and ended itself, and appeared no more there.

In those years a visible section of the London population, and conspicuous out of all proportion to its size or value, was a small knot of Spaniards, who had sought shelter here as Political Refugees. "Political Refugees:" a tragic succession of that class is one of the possessions of England in our time. Six-and-twenty years ago, when I first saw London, I remember those unfortunate Spaniards among the new phenomena. Daily in the cold spring air, under skies so unlike their own, you could see a group of fifty or a hundred stately tragic figures, in proud threadbare cloaks; perambulating, mostly with closed lips, the broad pavements of Euston Square and the regions about St. Pancras new Church. Their lodging was chiefly in Somers Town, as I understood: and those open pavements about St. Pancras Church were the general place of rendezvous. They spoke little or no English; knew nobody, could employ themselves on nothing, in this new scene. Old steel-gray heads, many of them; the shaggy, thick, blue-black hair of others struck you; their brown complexion, dusky look of suppressed fire, in general their tragic condition as of caged Numidian lions.

That particular Flight of Unfortunates has long since fled again, and vanished; and new have come and fled. In this convulsed revolutionary epoch, which already lasts above sixty years, what tragic flights of such have we not seen arrive on the one safe coast which is open to them, as they get successively vanquished, and chased into exile to avoid worse! Swarm after swarm, of ever-new complexion, from Spain as from other countries, is thrown off, in those ever-recurring paroxysms; and will continue to be thrown off. As there could be (suggests Linnæus) a "flower-clock," measuring the hours of the day, and the months of the year, by the kinds of flowers that go to sleep and awaken, that blow into beauty and fade into dust: so in the great Revolutionary Horologe, one might

mark the years and epochs by the successive kinds of exiles
that walk London streets, and, in grim silent manner, demand
pity from us and reflections from us. — This then extant group
of Spanish Exiles was the Trocadero swarm, thrown off in
1823, in the Riego and Quirogas quarrel. These were they
whom Charles Tenth had, by sheer force, driven from their
constitutionalisms and their Trocadero fortresses, — Charles
Tenth, who himself was soon driven out, manifoldly by sheer
force; and had to head his own swarm of fugitives; and has
now himself quite vanished, and given place to others. For
there is no end of them; propelling and propelled! —

Of these poor Spanish Exiles, now vegetating about Somers
Town, and painfully beating the pavement in Euston Square,
the acknowledged chief was General Torrijos, a man of high
qualities and fortunes, still in the vigor of his years, and in
these desperate circumstances refusing to despair; with whom
Sterling had, at this time, become intimate.

CHAPTER X.

TORRIJOS.

TORRIJOS, who had now in 1829 been here some four or
five years, having come over in 1824, had from the first enjoyed
a superior reception in England. Possessing not only a language to speak, which few of the others did, but manifold
experiences courtly, military, diplomatic, with fine natural
faculties, and high Spanish manners tempered into cosmo-
politan, he had been welcomed in various circles of society;
and found, perhaps he alone of those Spaniards, a certain
human companionship among persons of some standing in
this country. With the elder Sterlings, among others, he
had made acquaintance; became familiar in the social circle
at South Place, and was much esteemed there. With Madam
Torrijos, who also was a person of amiable and distinguished
qualities, an affectionate friendship grew up on the part of

Mrs. Sterling, which ended only with the death of these two ladies. John Sterling, on arriving in London from his University work, naturally inherited what he liked to take up of this relation: and in the lodgings in Regent Street, and the democratico-literary element there, Torrijos became a very prominent, and at length almost the central object.

The man himself, it is well known, was a valiant, gallant man; of lively intellect, of noble chivalrous character: fine talents, fine accomplishments, all grounding themselves on a certain rugged veracity, recommended him to the discerning. He had begun youth in the Court of Ferdinand; had gone on in Wellington and other arduous, victorious and unvictorious, soldierings; familiar in camps and council-rooms, in presence-chambers and in prisons. He knew romantic Spain; — he was himself, standing withal in the vanguard of Freedom's fight, a kind of living romance. Infinitely interesting to John Sterling, for one.

It was to Torrijos that the poor Spaniards of Somers Town looked mainly, in their helplessness, for every species of help. Torrijos, it was hoped, would yet lead them into Spain and glorious victory there; meanwhile here in England, under defeat, he was their captain and sovereign in another painfully inverse sense. To whom, in extremity, everybody might apply. When all present resources failed, and the exchequer was quite out, there still remained Torrijos. Torrijos has to find new resources for his destitute patriots, find loans, find Spanish lessons for them among his English friends: in all which charitable operations, it need not be said, John Sterling was his foremost man; zealous to empty his own purse for the object; impetuous in rushing hither or thither to enlist the aid of others, and find lessons or something that would do. His friends, of course, had to assist; the Bartons, among others, were wont to assist; — and I have heard that the fair Susan, stirring up her indolent enthusiasm into practicality, was very successful in finding Spanish lessons, and the like, for these distressed men. Sterling and his friends were yet new in this business; but Torrijos and the others were getting old in it, — and doubtless weary and almost desperate of it.

They had now been seven years in it, many of them; and were asking, When will the end be ?

Torrijos is described as a man of excellent discernment : who knows how long he' had repressed the unreasonable schemes of his followers, and turned a deaf ear to the temptings of fallacious hope ?   But there comes at length a sum-total of oppressive burdens which is intolerable, which tempts the wisest towards fallacies for relief.   These weary groups, pacing the Euston-Square pavements, had often said in their despair, "Were not death in battle better ?   Here are we slowly mouldering into nothingness; there we might reach it rapidly, in flaming splendor.   Flame, either of victory to Spain and us, or of a patriot death, the sure harbinger of victory to Spain.   Flame fit to kindle a fire which no Ferdinand, with all his Inquisitions and Charles Tenths, could put out."   Enough, in the end of 1829, Torrijos himself had yielded to this pressure; and hoping against hope, persuaded himself that if he could but land in the South of Spain with a small patriot band well armed and well resolved, a band carrying fire in its heart, — then Spain, all inflammable as touchwood, and groaning indignantly under its brutal tyrant, might blaze wholly into flame round him, and incalculable victory be won.   Such was his conclusion; not sudden, yet surely not deliberate either, — desperate rather, and forced on by circumstances.   He thought with himself that, considering Somers Town and considering Spain, the terrible chance was worth trying; that this big game of Fate, go how it might, was one which the omens credibly declared he and these poor Spaniards ought to play.

His whole industries and energies were thereupon bent towards starting the said game; and his thought and continual speech and song now was, That if he had a few thousand pounds to buy arms, to freight a ship and make the other preparations, he and these poor gentlemen, and Spain and the world, were made men and a saved Spain and world.   What talks and consultations in the apartment in Regent Street, during those winter days of 1829–30; setting into open conflagration the young democracy that was wont to assemble there! Of which there is now left next to no remembrance. For Sterling never spoke a word of this affair in after-days, nor was any of the actors much tempted to speak. We can understand too well that here were young fervid hearts in an explosive condition; young rash heads, sanctioned by a man's experienced head. Here at last shall enthusiasm and theory become practice and fact; fiery dreams are at last permitted to realize themselves; and now is the time or never!—How the Coleridge moonshine comported itself amid these hot telluric flames, or whether it had not yet begun to play there (which I rather doubt), must be left to conjecture.

Mr. Hare speaks of Sterling "sailing over to St. Valery in an open boat along with others," upon one occasion, in this enterprise;—in the *final* English scene of it, I suppose. Which is very possible. Unquestionably there was adventure enough of other kinds for it, and running to and fro with all his speed on behalf of it, during these months of his history! Money was subscribed, collected: the young Cambridge democrats were all ablaze to assist Torrijos; nay certain of them decided to go with him,—and went. Only, as yet, the funds were rather incomplete. And here, as I learn from a good hand, is the secret history of their becoming complete. Which, as we are upon the subject, I had better give. But for the following circumstance, they had perhaps never been completed; nor had the rash enterprise, or its catastrophe, so influential on the rest of Sterling's life, taken place at all.

A certain Lieutenant Robert Boyd, of the Indian Army, an Ulster Irishman, a cousin of Sterling's, had received some affront, or otherwise taken some disgust in that service; had thrown up his commission in consequence; and returned home, about this time, with intent to seek another course of life. Having only, for outfit, these impatient ardors, some experience in Indian drill exercise, and five thousand pounds of inheritance, he found the enterprise attended with difficulties; and was somewhat at a loss how to dispose of himself. Some young Ulster comrade, in a partly similar situation, had pointed out to him that there lay in a certain neighboring creek of the Irish coast, a worn-out royal gun-brig condemned to sale, to be had dog-cheap : this he proposed that they two, or in fact Boyd with his five thousand pounds, should buy; that they should refit and arm and man it; — and sail a-privateering "to the Eastern Archipelago," Philippine Isles, or I know not where; and *so* conquer the golden fleece.

Boyd naturally paused a little at this great proposal; did not quite reject it; came across, with it and other fine projects and impatiences fermenting in his head, to London, there to see and consider. It was in the months when the Torrijos enterprise was in the birth-throes; crying wildly for capital, of all things. Boyd naturally spoke of his projects to Sterling, — of his gun-brig lying in the Irish creek, among others. Sterling naturally said, "If you want an adventure of the Sea-king sort, and propose to lay your money and your life into such a game, here is Torrijos and Spain at his back; here is a golden fleece to conquer, worth twenty Eastern Archipelagoes." — Boyd and Torrijos quickly met; quickly bargained. Boyd's money was to go in purchasing, and storing with a certain stock of arms and etceteras, a small ship in the Thames, which should carry Boyd with Torrijos and the adventurers to the south coast of Spain; and there, the game once played and won, Boyd was to have promotion enough, — "the colonelcy of a Spanish cavalry regiment," for one express thing. What exact share Sterling had in this negotiation, or whether he did not even take the prudent side and caution Boyd to be wary, I know not; but it was he that brought the parties together; and all his friends knew, in silence, that to the end of his life he painfully remembered that fact.

And so a ship was hired, or purchased, in the Thames; due furnishings began to be executed in it; arms and stores were gradually got on board; Torrijos with his Fifty picked Spaniards, in the mean while, getting ready. This was in the spring of 1830. Boyd's £5000 was the grand nucleus of finance; but vigorous subscription was carried on likewise in Sterling's young democratic circle, or wherever a member of it could find access; not without considerable result, and with a zeal that may be imagined. Nay, as above hinted, certain of these young men decided, not to give their money only, but themselves along with it, as democratic volunteers and soldiers of progress; among whom, it need not be said, Sterling intended to be foremost. Busy weeks with him, those spring ones of the year 1830! Through this small Note, accidentally preserved to us, addressed to his friend Barton, we obtain a curious glance into the subterranean workshop : —

" *To Charles Barton, Esq., Dorset Sq., Regent's Park.*

[No date; apparently March or February, 1830.]

" My dear Charles, — I have wanted to see you to talk to you about my Foreign affairs. If you are going to be in London for a few days, I believe you can be very useful to me, at a considerable expense and trouble to yourself, in the way of buying accoutrements; *inter alia,* a sword and a saddle, — not, you will understand, for my own use.

" Things are going on very well, but are very, even frightfully near; only be quiet! Pray would you, in case of necessity, take a free passage to Holland, next week or the week after; stay two or three days, and come back, all expenses paid? If you write to B—— at Cambridge, tell him above all things to hold his tongue. If you are near Palace Yard to-morrow before two, pray come to see me. Do not come on purpose; especially as I may perhaps be away, and at all events shall not be there until eleven, nor perhaps till rather later.

" I fear I shall have alarmed your Mother by my irruption. Forgive me for that and all my exactions from you. If the next month were over, I should not have to trouble any one.

" Yours affectionately,

" J. Sterling."

Busy weeks indeed; and a glowing smithy-light coming through the chinks! — The romance of *Arthur Coningsby* lay written, or half-written, in his desk; and here, in his heart and among his hands, was an acted romance and unknown catastrophes keeping pace with that.

Doubts from the doctors, for his health was getting ominous, threw some shade over the adventure. Reproachful reminiscences of Coleridge and Theosophy were natural too; then fond regrets for Literature and its glories: if you act your romance, how can you also write it? Regrets, and reproachful reminiscences, from Art and Theosophy; perhaps some tenderer regrets withal. A crisis in life had come; when, of innumerable possibilities one possibility was to be elected king, and to swallow all the rest, the rest of course made noise enough, and swelled themselves to their biggest.

Meanwhile the ship was fast getting ready: on a certain day, it was to drop quietly down the Thames; then touch at Deal, and take on board Torrijos and his adventurers, who were to be in waiting and on the outlook for them there. Let every man lay in his accoutrements, then; let every man make his packages, his arrangements and farewells. Sterling went to take leave of Miss Barton. "You are going, then; to Spain? To rough it amid the storms of war and perilous insurrection; and with that weak health of yours; and — we shall never see you more, then!" Miss Barton, all her gayety gone, the dimpling softness become liquid sorrow, and the musical ringing voice one wail of woe, "burst into tears," — so I have it on authority : — here was one possibility about to be strangled that made unexpected noise! Sterling's interview ended in the offer of his hand, and the acceptance of it; — any sacrifice to get rid of this horrid Spanish business, and save the health and life of a gifted young man so precious to the world and to another!

" Ill-health," as often afterwards in Sterling's life, when the excuse was real enough but not the chief excuse; " ill-health, and insuperable obstacles and engagements," had to bear the chief brunt in apologizing: and, as Sterling's actual presence, or that of any Englishman except Boyd and his money, was not in the least vital to the adventure, his excuse was at once accepted. The English connections and subscriptions are a given fact, to be presided over by what English volunteers there are: and as for Englishmen, the fewer Englishmen that go, the larger will be the share of influence for each. The other adventurers, Torrijos among them in due readiness, moved silently one by one down to Deal; Sterling, superintending the naval hands, on board their ship in the Thames, was to see the last finish given to everything in that department; then, on the set evening, to drop down quietly to Deal, and there say *Andad con Dios*, and return.

Behold! Just before the set evening came, the Spanish Envoy at this Court has got notice of what is going on; the Spanish Envoy, and of course the British Foreign Secretary, and of course also the Thames Police. Armed men spring suddenly on board, one day, while Sterling is there; declare the ship seized and embargoed in the King's name; nobody on board to stir till he has given some account of himself in due time and place! Huge consternation, naturally, from stem to stern. Sterling, whose presence of mind seldom forsook him, casts his eye over the River and its craft; sees a wherry, privately signals it, drops rapidly on board of it: "Stop!" fiercely interjects the marine policeman from the ship's deck. — "Why stop? What use have you for me, or I for you?" and the oars begin playing. — "Stop, or I'll shoot you!" cries the marine policeman, drawing a pistol. — "No, you won't." — "I will!" — "If you do you'll be hanged at the next Maidstone assizes, then; that's all," — and Sterling's wherry shot rapidly ashore; and out of this perilous adventure.

That same night he posted down to Deal; disclosed to the Torrijos party what catastrophe had come. No passage Spainward from the Thames; well if arrestment do not suddenly come from the Thames! It was on this occasion, I suppose, that the passage in the open boat to St. Valery occurred; — speedy flight in what boat or boats, open or shut, could be got at Deal on the sudden. Sterling himself, according to Hare's authority, actually went with them so far. Enough, they got shipping, as private passengers in one craft or the other; and, by degrees or at once, arrived all at Gibraltar, — Boyd, one or two young democrats of Regent Street, the fifty picked Spaniards, and Torrijos, — safe, though without arms; still in the early part of the year.

CHAPTER XI.

MARRIAGE: ILL-HEALTH; WEST-INDIES.

STERLING'S outlooks and occupations, now that his Spanish
friends were gone, must have been of a rather miscellaneous
confused description. He had the enterprise of a married life
close before him; and as yet no profession, no fixed pursuit
whatever. His health was already very threatening; often
such as to disable him from present activity, and occasion the
gravest apprehensions; practically blocking up all important
courses whatsoever, and rendering the future, if even life were
lengthened and he had any future, an insolubility for him.
Parliament was shut, public life was shut: Literature, — if,
alas, any solid fruit could lie in Literature!

Or perhaps one's health would mend, after all; and many
things be better than was hoped! Sterling was not of a de-
spondent temper, or given in any measure to lie down and
indolently moan: I fancy he walked briskly enough into this
tempestuous-looking future; not heeding too much its thun-
derous aspects; doing swiftly, for the day, what his hand
found to do. *Arthur Coningsby*, I suppose, lay on the anvil
at present; visits to Coleridge were now again more possible;
grand news from Torrijos might be looked for, though only
small yet came: — nay here, in the hot July, is France, at
least, all thrown into volcano again! Here are the miraculous
Three Days; heralding, in thunder, great things to Torrijos
and others; filling with babblement and vaticination the
mouths and hearts of all democratic men.

So rolled along, in tumult of chaotic remembrance and uncertain hope, in manifold emotion, and the confused struggle
(for Sterling as for the world) to extricate the New from the
falling ruins of the Old, the summer and autumn of 1830.
From Gibraltar and Torrijos the tidings were vague, unim-

portant and discouraging: attempt on Cadiz, attempt on the
lines of St. Roch, those attempts, or rather resolutions to
attempt, had died in the birth, or almost before it. Men
blamed Torrijos, little knowing his impediments. Boyd was
still patient at his post: others of the young English (on the
strength of the subscribed moneys) were said to be thinking
of tours, — perhaps in the Sierra Morena and neighboring
Quixote regions. From that Torrijos enterprise it did not
seem that anything considerable would come.

On the edge of winter, here at home, Sterling was married:
"at Christchurch, Marylebone, 2d November, 1830," say the
records. His blooming, kindly and true-hearted Wife had not
much money, nor had he as yet any: but friends on both
sides were bountiful and hopeful; had made up, for the young
couple, the foundations of a modestly effective household;
and in the future there lay more substantial prospects. On
the finance side Sterling never had anything to suffer. His
Wife, though somewhat languid, and of indolent humor, was
a graceful, pious-minded, honorable and affectionate woman;
she could not much support him in the ever-shifting struggles
of his life, but she faithfully attended him in them, and loyally marched by his side through the changes and nomadic
pilgrimings, of which many were appointed him in his short
course.

Unhappily a few weeks after his marriage, and before any
household was yet set up, he fell dangerously ill; worse in
health than he had ever yet been: so many agitations crowded
into the last few months had been too much for him. He fell
into dangerous pulmonary illness, sank ever deeper; lay for
many weeks in his Father's house utterly prostrate, his young
Wife and his Mother watching over him; friends, sparingly
admitted, long despairing of his life. All prospects in this
world were now apparently shut upon him.

After a while, came hope again, and kindlier symptoms:
but the doctors intimated that there lay consumption in the
question, and that perfect recovery was not to be looked for.
For weeks he had been confined to bed; it was several months

before he could leave his sick-room, where the visits of a few
friends had much cheered him. And now when delivered,
readmitted to the air of day again, — weak as he was, and
with such a liability still lurking in him, — what his young
partner and he were to do, or whitherward to turn for a good
course of life, was by no means too apparent.

One of his Mother Mrs. Edward Sterling's Uncles, a Coningham from Derry, had, in the course of his industrious and
adventurous life, realized large property in the West Indies, —
a valuable Sugar-estate, with its equipments, in the Island of
St. Vincent; — from which Mrs. Sterling and her family were
now, and had been for some years before her Uncle's decease,
deriving important benefits. I have heard, it was then worth
some ten thousand pounds a year to the parties interested.
Anthony Sterling, John, and another a cousin of theirs were
ultimately to be heirs, in equal proportions. The old gentleman, always kind to his kindred, and a brave and solid
man though somewhat abrupt in his ways, had lately died;
leaving a settlement to this effect, not without some intrica-
cies, and almost caprices, in the conditions attached.

This property, which is still a valuable one, was Sterling's
chief pecuniary outlook for the distant future. Of course it
well deserved taking care of; and if the eye of the master
were upon it, of course too (according to the adage) the cattle
would fatten better. As the warm climate was favorable to
pulmonary complaints, and Sterling's occupations were so
shattered to pieces and his outlooks here so waste and vague,
why should not he undertake this duty for himself and
others ?

It was fixed upon as the eligiblest course. A visit to St.
Vincent, perhaps a permanent residence there : he went into
the project with his customary impetuosity; his young Wife
cheerfully consenting, and all manner of new hopes clustering
round it. There are the rich tropical sceneries, the romance
of the torrid zone with its new skies and seas and lands ;
there are Blacks, and the Slavery question to be investigated :
there are the bronzed Whites and Yellows, and their strange

new way of life: by all means let us go and try! — Arrangements being completed, so soon as his strength had sufficiently recovered, and the harsh spring winds had sufficiently abated, Sterling with his small household set sail for St. Vincent; and arrived without accident. His first child, a son Edward, now living and grown to manhood, was born there, " at Brighton in the Island of St. Vincent," in the fall of that year 1831.

———◆———

CHAPTER XII.

ISLAND OF ST. VINCENT.

STERLING found a pleasant residence, with all its adjuncts, ready for him, at Colonarie, in this "volcanic Isle" under the hot sun. An interesting Isle: a place of rugged chasms, precipitous gnarled heights, and the most fruitful hollows; shaggy everywhere with luxuriant vegetation; set under magnificent skies, in the mirror of the summer seas; offering everywhere the grandest sudden outlooks and contrasts. His Letters represent a placidly cheerful riding life: a pensive humor, but the thunder-clouds all sleeping in the distance. Good relations with a few neighboring planters; indifference to the noisy political and other agitations of the rest: friendly, by no means romantic appreciation of the Blacks; quiet prosperity economic and domestic: on the whole a healthy and recommendable way of life, with Literature very much in abeyance in it.

He writes to Mr. Hare (date not given): "The landscapes around me here are noble and lovely as any that can be conceived on Earth. How indeed could it be otherwise, in a small Island of volcanic mountains, far within the Tropics, and perpetually covered with the richest vegetation?" The moral aspect of things is by no means so good; but neither is that without its fair features. "So far as I see, the Slaves here are cunning, deceitful and idle; without any great aptitude for ferocious crimes, and with very little scruple at committing others. But I have seen them much only in very favorable circumstances. They are, as a body, decidedly unfit for freedom; and if left, as at present, completely in the hands of their masters, will never become so, unless through the agency of the Methodists." [1]

In the Autumn came an immense hurricane; with new and indeed quite perilous experiences of West-Indian life. This hasty Letter, addressed to his Mother, is not intrinsically his remarkablest from St. Vincent : but the body of fact delineated in it being so much the greatest, we will quote it in preference. A West-Indian tornado, as John Sterling witnesses it, and with vivid authenticity describes it, may be considered worth looking at.

" To Mrs. Sterling, South Place, Knightsbridge, London.

"BRIGHTON, ST. VINCENT, 28th August, 1831.

" MY DEAR MOTHER, — The packet came in yesterday; bringing me some Newspapers, a Letter from my Father, and one from Anthony, with a few lines from you. I wrote, some days ago, a hasty Note to my Father, on the chance of its reaching you through Grenada sooner than any communication by the packet; and in it I spoke of the great misfortune which had befallen this Island and Barbadoes, but from which all those you take an interest in have happily escaped unhurt.

" From the day of our arrival in the West Indies until Thursday the 11th instant, which will long be a memorable day with us, I had been doing my best to get ourselves established comfortably ; and I had at last bought the materials for making some additions to the house. But on the morning I have mentioned, all that I had exerted myself to do, nearly all the property both of Susan and myself, and the very house we lived in, were suddenly destroyed by a visitation of Providence far more terrible than any I have ever witnessed.

" When Susan came from her room, to breakfast, at eight

[1] *Biography*, by Mr. Hare, p. xli.

o'clock, I pointed out to her the extraordinary height and violence of the surf, and the singular appearance of the clouds of heavy rain sweeping down the valleys before us. At this time I had so little apprehension of what was coming, that I talked of riding down to the shore when the storm should abate, as I had never seen so fierce a sea. In about a quarter of an hour the House-Negroes came in, to close the outside shutters of the windows. They knew that the plantain-trees about the Negro houses had been blown down in the night; and had told the maid-servant Tyrrell, but I had heard nothing of it. A very few minutes after the closing of the windows, I found that the shutters of Tyrrell's room, at the south and commonly the most sheltered end of the House, were giving way. I tried to tie them; but the silk handkerchief which I used soon gave way; and as I had neither hammer, boards nor nails in the house, I could do nothing more to keep out the tempest. I found, in pushing at the leaf of the shutter, that the wind resisted, more as if it had been a stone wall or a mass of iron, than a mere current of air. There were one or two people outside trying to fasten the windows, and I went out to help; but we had no tools at hand: one man was blown down the hill in front of the house, before my face; and the other and myself had great difficulty in getting back again inside the door. The rain on my face and hands felt like so much small shot from a gun. There was great exertion necessary to shut the door of the house.

"The windows at the end of the large room were now giving way; and I suppose it was about nine o'clock, when the hurricane burst them in, as if it had been a discharge from a battery of heavy cannon. The shutters were first forced open, and the wind fastened them back to the wall; and then the panes of glass were smashed by the mere force of the gale, without anything having touched them. Even now I was not at all sure the house would go. My books, I saw, were lost; for the rain poured past the bookcases, as if it had been the Colonarie River. But we carried a good deal of furniture into the passage at the entrance; we set Susan there on a sofa, and the Black Housekeeper was even attempt-

ing to get her some breakfast. The house, however, began to
shake so violently, and the rain was so searching, that she
could not stay there long. She went into her own room;
and I stayed to see what could be done.

"Under the forepart of the house, there are cellars built
of stone, but not arched. To these, however, there was no
access except on the outside; and I knew from my own experience that Susan could not have gone a step beyond the
door, without being carried away by the storm, and probably
killed on the spot. The only chance seemed to be that of
breaking through the floor. But when the old Cook and
myself resolved on this, we found that we had no instrument
with which it would be possible to do it. It was now clear
that we had only God to trust in. The front windows were
giving way with successive crashes, and the floor shook as you
may have seen a carpet on a gusty day in London. I went
into our bedroom; where I found Susan, Tyrrell, and a little
Colored girl of seven or eight years old; and told them that
we should probably not be alive in half an hour. I could have
escaped, if I had chosen to go alone, by crawling on the ground
either into the kitchen, a separate stone building at no great
distance, or into the open fields away from trees or houses;
but Susan could not have gone a yard. She became quite
calm when she knew the worst; and she sat on my knee in
what seemed the safest corner of the room, while every blast
was bringing nearer and nearer the moment of our seemingly
certain destruction. —

"The house was under two parallel roofs; and the one next
the sea, which sheltered the other, and us who were under the
other, went off, I suppose about ten o'clock. After my old
plan, I will give you a sketch, from which you may perceive
how we were situated : —

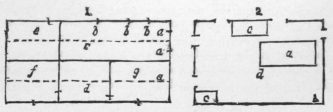

The *a, a* are the windows that were first destroyed : *b* went next; my books were between the windows *b*, and on the wall opposite to them.   The lines *c* and *d* mark the directions of the two roofs ; *e* is the room in which we were, and 2 is a plan of it on a larger scale.   Look now at 2 : *a* is the bed ; *c, c* the two wardrobes ; *b* the corner in which we were.   I was sitting in an arm-chair, holding my Wife; and Tyrrell and the little Black child were close to us.   We had given up all notion of surviving; and only waited for the fall of the roof to perish together.

"Before long the roof went.   Most of the materials, however, were carried clear away : one of the large couples was caught on the bedpost marked *d*, and held fast by the iron spike; while the end of it hung over our heads : had the beam fallen an inch on either side of the bedpost, it must necessarily have crushed us.   The walls did not go with the roof ; and we remained for half an hour, alternately praying to God, and watching them as they bent, creaked, and shivered before the storm.

"Tyrrell and the child, when the roof was off, made their way through the remains of the partition, to the outer door ; and with the help of the people who were looking for us, got into the kitchen.   A good while after they were gone, and before we knew anything of their fate, a Negro suddenly came upon us ; and the sight of him gave us a hope of safety. When the people learned that we were in danger, and while their own huts were flying about their ears, they crowded to help us; and the old Cook urged them on to our rescue.   He made five attempts, after saving Tyrrell, to get to us ; and four times he was blown down.   The fifth time he, and the Negro we first saw, reached the house.   The space they had to traverse was not above twenty yards of level ground, if so much.   In another minute or two, the Overseers and a crowd of Negroes, most of whom had come on their hands and knees, were surrounding us; and with their help Susan was carried round to the end of the house ; where they broke open the cellar window, and placed her in comparative safety. The force of the hurricane was, by this time, a good deal

diminished, or it would have been impossible to stand before it.

"But the wind was still terrific; and the rain poured into
the cellars through the floor above. Susan, Tyrrell, and a
crowd of Negroes remained under it, for more than two hours:
and I was long afraid that the wet and cold would kill her, if
she did not perish more violently. Happily we had wine and
spirits at hand, and she was much nerved by a tumbler of
claret. As soon as I saw her in comparative security, I went
off with one of the Overseers down to the Works, where the
greater number of the Negroes were collected, that we might
see what could be done for them. They were wretched
enough, but no one was hurt; and I ordered them a dram
apiece, which seemed to give them a good deal of consolation.

"Before I could make my way back, the hurricane became
as bad as at first; and I was obliged to take shelter for half an
hour in a ruined Negro house. This, however, was the last
of its extreme violence. By one o'clock, even the rain had in
a great degree ceased; and as only one room of the house, the
one marked *f,* was standing, and that rickety, — I had Susan
carried in a chair down the hill, to the Hospital; where, in
a small paved unlighted room, she spent the next twenty-four
hours. She was far less injured than might have been expected from such a catastrophe.

"Next day, I had the passage at the entrance of the house
repaired and roofed; and we returned to the ruins of our habitation, still encumbered as they were with the wreck of almost
all we were possessed of. The walls of the part of the house
next the sea were carried away, in less I think than half an
hour after we reached the cellar: when I had leisure to examine the remains of the house, I found the floor strewn with
fragments of the building, and with broken furniture; and
our books all soaked as completely as if they had been for
several hours in the sea.

"In the course of a few days I had the other room, *g,* which
is under the same roof as the one saved, rebuilt; and Susan
stayed in this temporary abode for a week, — when we left
Colonarie, and came to Brighton. Mr. Munro's kindness

exceeds all precedent. We shall certainly remain here till my Wife is recovered from her confinement. In the mean while we shall have a new house built, in which we hope to be well settled before Christmas.

" The roof was half blown off the kitchen, but I have had it mended already; the other offices were all swept away. The gig is much injured; and my horse received a wound in the fall of the stable, from which he will not be recovered for some weeks : in the mean time I have no choice but to buy another, as I must go at least once or twice a week to Colonarie, besides business in Town. As to our own comforts, we can scarcely expect ever to recover from the blow that has now stricken us. No money would repay me for the loss of my books, of which a large proportion had been in my hands for so many years that they were like old and faithful friends, and of which many had been given me at different times by the persons in the world whom I most value.

" But against all this I have to set the preservation of our lives, in a way the most awfully providential ; and the safety of every one on the Estate. And I have also the great satis- faction of reflecting that all the Negroes from whom any as- sistance could reasonably be expected, behaved like so many Heroes of Antiquity ; risking their lives and limbs for us and our property, while their own poor houses were flying like chaff before the hurricane. There are few White people here who can say as much for their Black dependents ; and the force and value of the relation between Master and Slave has been tried by the late calamity on a large scale.

" Great part of both sides of this Island has been laid com- pletely waste. The beautiful wide and fertile Plain called the Charib Country, extending for many miles to the north of Colonarie, and formerly containing the finest sets of works and best dwelling-houses in the Island, is, I am told, completely desolate : on several estates not a roof even of a Negro hut standing. In the embarrassed circumstances of many of the proprietors, the ruin is, I fear, irreparable. — At Colonarie the damage is serious, but by no means desperate. The crop is perhaps injured ten or fifteen per cent. The roofs of several

large buildings are destroyed, but these we are already supplying; and the injuries done to the cottages of the Negroes
are, by this time, nearly if not quite remedied.

"Indeed, all that has been suffered in St. Vincent appears
nothing when compared with the appalling loss of property
and of human lives at Barbadoes. There the Town is little
but a heap of ruins, and the corpses are reckoned by thousands; while throughout the Island there are not, I believe,
ten estates on which the buildings are standing. The Elliotts,
from whom we have heard, are living with all their family in
a tent; and may think themselves wonderfully saved, when
whole families round them were crushed at once beneath their
houses. Hugh Barton, the only officer of the Garrison hurt,
has broken his arm, and we know nothing of his prospects
of recovery. The more horrible misfortune of Barbadoes is
partly to be accounted for by the fact of the hurricane having
begun there during the night. The flatness of the surface in
that Island presented no obstacle to the wind, which must,
however, I think have been in itself more furious than with
us. No other island has suffered considerably.

"I have told both my Uncle and Anthony that I have given
you the details of our recent history; — which are not so
pleasant that I should wish to write them again. Perhaps
you will be good enough to let them see this, as soon as you
and my Father can spare it. . . . I am ever, dearest Mother,

"Your grateful and affectionate
"JOHN STERLING."

This Letter, I observe, is dated 28th August, 1831; which
is otherwise a day of mark to the world and me, — the Poet
Goethe's last birthday. While Sterling sat in the Tropical
solitudes, penning this history, little European Weimar had
its carriages and state-carriages busy on the streets, and was
astir with compliments and visiting-cards, doing its best, as
heretofore, on behalf of a remarkable day; and was not, for
centuries or tens of centuries, to see the like of it again! —

At Brighton, the hospitable home of those Munros, our
friends continued for above two months. Their first child,

Edward, as above noticed, was born here, "14th October, 1831;" — and now the poor lady, safe from all her various perils, could return to Colonarie under good auspices.

It was in this year that I first heard definitely of Sterling as a contemporary existence; and laid up some note and outline of him in my memory, as of one whom I might yet hope to know. John Mill, Mrs. Austin and perhaps other friends, spoke of him with great affection and much pitying admiration; and hoped to see him home again, under better omens, from over the seas. As a gifted amiable being, of a certain radiant tenuity and velocity, too thin and rapid and diffusive, in danger of dissipating himself into the vague, or alas into death itself: it was so that, like a spot of bright colors, rather than a portrait with features, he hung occasionally visible in my imagination.

CHAPTER XIII.

A CATASTROPHE.

The ruin of his house had hardly been repaired, when there arrived out of Europe tidings which smote as with a still more fatal hurricane on the four corners of his inner world, and awoke all the old thunders that lay asleep on his horizon there. Tidings, at last of a decisive nature, from Gibraltar and the Spanish democrat adventure. This is what the Newspapers had to report — the catastrophe at once, the details by degrees — from Spain concerning that affair, in the beginning of the new year 1832.

Torrijos, as we have seen, had hitherto accomplished as good as nothing, except disappointment to his impatient followers, and sorrow and regret to himself. Poor Torrijos, on arriving at Gibraltar with his wild band, and coming into contact with the rough fact, had found painfully how much his imagination had deceived him. The fact lay round him haggard and iron-bound; flatly refusing to be handled accord-

ing to his scheme of it. No Spanish soldiery nor citizenry
showed the least disposition to join him; on the contrary
the official Spaniards of that coast seemed to have the watch-
fulest eye on all his movements, nay it was conjectured they
had spies in Gibraltar who gathered his very intentions and
betrayed them. This small project of attack, and then that
other, proved futile, or was abandoned before the attempt.
Torrijos had to lie painfully within the lines of Gibraltar, —
his poor followers reduced to extremity of impatience and
distress; the British Governor too, though not unfriendly to
him, obliged to frown. As for the young Cantabs, they, as
was said, had wandered a little over the South border of
romantic Spain; had perhaps seen Seville, Cadiz, with picturesque views, since not with belligerent ones; and their
money being done, had now returned home. So had it lasted
for eighteen months.

The French Three Days breaking out had armed the
Guerrillero Mina, armed all manner of democratic guerrieros
and guerrilleros; and considerable clouds of Invasion, from
Spanish exiles, hung minatory over the North and North-
East of Spain, supported by the new-born French Democracy,
so far as privately possible. These Torrijos had to look upon
with inexpressible feelings, and take no hand in supporting
from the South; these also he had to see brushed away,
successively abolished by official generalship; and to sit within
his lines, in the painfulest manner, unable to do anything.
The fated, gallant-minded, but too headlong man. At length
the British Governor himself was obliged, in official decency,
and as is thought on repeated remonstrance from his Spanish
official neighbors, to signify how indecorous, improper and
impossible it was to harbor within one's lines such explosive
preparations, once they were discovered, against allies in full
peace with us, — the necessity, in fact, there was for the
matter ending. It is said, he offered Torrijos and his people
passports, and British protection, to any country of the world
except Spain: Torrijos did not accept the passports; spoke of
going peaceably to this place or to that; promised at least,
what he saw and felt to be clearly necessary, that he would

soon leave Gibraltar. And he did soon leave it; he and his, Boyd alone of the Englishmen being now with him.

It was on the last night of November, 1831, that they all set forth; Torrijos with Fifty-five companions; and in two small vessels committed themselves to their nigh-desperate fortune. No sentry or official person had noticed them; it was from the Spanish Consul, next morning, that the British Governor first heard they were gone. The British Governor knew nothing of them; but apparently the Spanish officials were much better informed. Spanish guardships, instantly awake, gave chase to the two small vessels, which were making all sail towards Malaga; and, on shore, all manner of troops and detached parties were in motion, to render a retreat to Gibraltar by land impossible.

Crowd all sail for Malaga, then; there perhaps a regiment will join us; there, — or if not, we are but lost! Fancy need not paint a more tragic situation than that of Torrijos, the unfortunate gallant man, in the gray of this morning, first of December, 1831, — his last free morning. Noble game is afoot, afoot at last; and all the hunters have him in their toils. — The guardships gain upon Torrijos; he cannot even reach Malaga; has to run ashore at a place called Fuengirola, not far from that city; — the guardships seizing his vessels, so soon as he is disembarked. The country is all up; troops scouring the coast everywhere: no possibility of getting into Malaga with a party of Fifty-five. He takes possession of a farmstead (Ingles, the place is called); barricades himself there, but is speedily beleaguered with forces hopelessly superior. He demands to treat; is refused all treaty; is granted six hours to consider, shall then either surrender at discretion, or be forced to do it. Of course he *does* it, having no alternative; and enters Malaga a prisoner, all his followers prisoners. Here had the Torrijos Enterprise, and all that was embarked upon it, finally arrived.

Express is sent to Madrid; express instantly returns; "Military execution on the instant; give them shriving if they want it; that done, fusillade them all." So poor Torrijos and his followers, the whole Fifty-six of them, Robert Boyd

included, meet swift death in Malaga. In such manner rushes
down the curtain on them and their affair; they vanish thus
on a sudden; rapt away as in black clouds of fate. Poor
Boyd, Sterling's cousin, pleaded his British citizenship; to no
purpose: it availed only to his dead body, this was delivered
to the British Consul for interment, and only this. Poor
Madam Torrijos, hearing, at Paris where she now was, of her
husband's capture, hurries towards Madrid to solicit mercy;
whither also messengers from Lafayette and the French Government were hurrying, on the like errand: at Bayonne, news
met the poor lady that it was already all over, that she was
now a widow, and her husband hidden from her forever. —
Such was the handsel of the new year 1832 for Sterling in his
West-Indian solitudes.

Sterling's friends never heard of these affairs; indeed we
were all secretly warned not to mention the name of Torrijos
in his hearing, which accordingly remained strictly a forbidden
subject. His misery over this catastrophe was known, in his
own family, to have been immense. He wrote to his Brother
Anthony: "I hear the sound of that musketry; it is as if the
bullets were tearing my own brain." To figure in one's sick
and excited imagination such a scene of fatal man-hunting,
lost valor hopelessly captured and massacred; and to add to
it, that the victims are not men merely, that they are noble
and dear forms known lately as individual friends: what a
Dance of the Furies and wild-pealing Dead-march is this, for
the mind of a loving, generous and vivid man! Torrijos getting ashore at Fuengirola; Robert Boyd and others ranked to
die on the esplanade at Malaga — Nay had not Sterling, too,
been the innocent yet heedless means of Boyd's embarking
in this enterprise? By his own kinsman poor Boyd had
been witlessly guided into the pitfalls. "I hear the sound
of that musketry; it is as if the bullets were tearing my own
brain!"

CHAPTER XIV.

PAUSE.

THESE thoughts dwelt long with Sterling; and for a good while, I fancy, kept possession of the proscenium of his mind; madly parading there, to the exclusion of all else, — coloring all else with their own black hues. He was young, rich in the power to be miserable or otherwise; and this was his first grand sorrow which had now fallen upon him.

An important spiritual crisis, coming at any rate in some form, had hereby suddenly in a very sad form come. No doubt, as youth was passing into manhood in these Tropical seclusions, and higher wants were awakening in his mind, and years and reflection were adding new insight and admonition, much in his young way of thought and action lay already under ban with him, and repentances enough over many things were not wanting. But here on a sudden had all repentances, as it were, dashed themselves together into one grand whirlwind of repentance; and his past life was fallen wholly as into a state of reprobation. A great remorseful misery had come upon him. Suddenly, as with a sudden lightning-stroke, it had kindled into conflagration all the ruined structure of his past life; such ruin had to blaze and flame round him, in the painfulest manner, till it went out in black ashes. His democratic philosophies, and mutinous radicalisms, already falling doomed in his thoughts, had reached their consummation and final condemnation here. It was all so rash, imprudent, arrogant, all that; false, or but half true; inapplicable wholly as a rule of noble conduct; — and it has ended *thus*. Woe on it! Another guidance must be found in life, or life is impossible! —

It is evident, Sterling's thoughts had already, since the old days of the "black dragoon," much modified themselves. We perceive that, by mere increase of experience and length of time, the opposite and much deeper side of the question, which also has its adamantine basis of truth, was in turn coming into play; and in fine that a Philosophy of Denial, and world illuminated merely by the flames of Destruction, could never have permanently been the resting-place of such a man. Those pilgrimings to Coleridge, years ago, indicate deeper wants beginning to be felt, and important ulterior resolutions becoming inevitable for him. If in your own soul there is any tone of the "Eternal Melodies," you cannot live forever in those poor outer, transitory grindings and discords; you will have to struggle inwards and upwards, in search of some diviner home for yourself!—Coleridge's prophetic moonshine, Torrijos's sad tragedy: those were important occurrences in Sterling's life. But, on the whole, there was a big Ocean for him, with impetuous Gulf-streams, and a doomed voyage in quest of the Atlantis, *before* either of those arose as lights on the horizon. As important beacon-lights let us count them nevertheless;—signal-dates they form to us, at lowest. We may reckon this Torrijos tragedy the crisis of Sterling's history; the turning-point, which modified, in the most important and by no means wholly in the most favorable manner, all the subsequent stages of it.

Old Radicalism and mutinous audacious Ethnicism having thus fallen to wreck, and a mere black world of misery and remorse now disclosing itself, whatsoever of natural piety to God and man, whatsoever of pity and reverence, of awe and devout hope was in Sterling's heart now awoke into new activity; and strove for some due utterance and predominance. His Letters, in these months, speak of earnest religious studies and efforts;—of attempts by prayer and longing endeavor of all kinds, to struggle his way into the temple, if temple there were, and there find sanctuary.[1] The realities were grown so haggard; life a field of black ashes, if there rose no temple anywhere on it! Why, like a fated Orestes, is man so whipt by the Furies, and driven madly hither and thither, if it is not

even that he may seek some shrine, and there make expiation
and find deliverance ?

In these circumstances, what a scope for Coleridge's philosophy, above all! "If the bottled moonshine *be* actually
substance ? Ah, could one but believe in a Church while finding it incredible! What is faith; what is conviction, credibility, insight ? Can a thing be at once known for true, and
known for false ? 'Reason,' 'Understanding:' is there, then,
such an internecine war between these two ? It was so Coleridge imagined it, the wisest of existing men!" — No, it is
not an easy matter (according to Sir Kenelm Digby), this of
getting up your "astral spirit" of a thing, and setting it in
action, when the thing itself is well burnt to ashes. Poor
Sterling ; poor sons of Adam in general, in this sad age of
cobwebs, worn-out symbolisms, reminiscences and simulacra!
Who can tell the struggles of poor Sterling, and his pathless
wanderings through these things! Long afterwards, in speech
with his Brother, he compared his case in this time to that
of "a young lady who has tragically lost her lover, and is willing to be half-hoodwinked into a convent, or in any noble
or quasi-noble way to escape from a world which has become
intolerable."

During the summer of 1832, I find traces of attempts towards
Anti-Slavery Philanthropy; shadows of extensive schemes in
that direction. Half-desperate outlooks, it is likely, towards
the refuge of Philanthropism, as a new chivalry of life. These
took no serious hold of so clear an intellect; but they hovered
now and afterwards as day-dreams, when life otherwise was
shorn of aim ; — mirages in the desert, which are found not to
be lakes when you put your bucket into them. One thing was
clear, the sojourn in St. Vincent was not to last much longer.

Perhaps one might get some scheme raised into life, in
Downing Street, for universal Education to the Blacks, pre-
paratory to emancipating them ? There were a noble work
for a man! Then again poor Mrs. Sterling's health, contrary
to his own, did not agree with warm moist climates. And
again, &c. &c. These were the outer surfaces of the measure;

the unconscious pretexts under which it showed itself to
Sterling and was shown by him: but the inner heart and
determining cause of it (as frequently in Sterling's life, and in
all our lives) was not these. In brief, he had had enough of
St. Vincent. The strangling oppressions of his soul were too
heavy for him there. Solution lay in Europe, or might lie;
not in these remote solitudes of the sea, — where no shrine or
saint's well is to be looked for, no communing of pious pilgrims
journeying together towards a shrine.

CHAPTER XV.

BONN; HERSTMONCEUX.

AFTER a residence of perhaps fifteen months Sterling
quitted St. Vincent, and never returned. He reappeared at his
Father's house, to the joy of English friends, in August, 1832;
well improved in health, and eager for English news; but,
beyond vague schemes and possibilities, considerably uncertain
what was next to be done.

After no long stay in this scene, — finding Downing Street
dead as stone to the Slave-Education and to all other schemes,
— he went across, with his wife and child, to Germany; pur-
posing to make not so much a tour as some loose ramble, or
desultory residence in that country, in the Rhineland first of
all. Here was to be hoped the picturesque in scenery, which
he much affected; here the new and true in speculation, which
he inwardly longed for and wanted greatly more; at all events,
here as readily as elsewhere might a temporary household be
struck up, under interesting circumstances. — I conclude he
went across in the Spring of 1833; perhaps directly after
Arthur Coningsby had got through the press. This Novel,
which, as we have said, was begun two or three years ago,
probably on his cessation from the *Athenæum*, and was mainly
finished, I think, before the removal to St. Vincent, had by
this time fallen as good as obsolete to his own mind; and its

destination now, whether to the press or to the fire, was in some sort a matter at once of difficulty and of insignificance to him.   At length deciding for the milder alternative, he had thrown in some completing touches here and there, — especially, as I conjecture, a proportion of Coleridgean moonshine at the end; and so sent it forth.

It was in the sunny days, perhaps in May or June of this year, that *Arthur Coningsby* reached my own hand, far off amid the heathy wildernesses; sent by John Mill: and I can still recollect the pleasant little episode it made in my solitude there.   The general impression it left on me, which has never since been renewed by a second reading in whole or in part, was the certain prefigurement to myself, more or less distinct, of an opulent, genial and sunny mind, but misdirected, disappointed, experienced in misery; — nay crude and hasty; mistaking for a solid outcome from its woes what was only to me a gilded vacuity.   The hero an ardent youth, representing Sterling himself, plunges into life such as we now have it in these anarchic times, with the radical, utilitarian, or mutinous heathen theory, which is the readiest for inquiring souls; finds, by various courses of adventure, utter shipwreck in this; lies broken, very wretched : that is the tragic nodus, or apogee of his life-course.   In this mood of mind, he clutches desperately towards some new method (recognizable as Coleridge's) of laying hand again on the old Church, which has hitherto been extraneous and as if non-extant to his way of thought; makes out, by some Coleridgean legedermain, that there actually is still a Church for him; that this extant Church, which he long took for an extinct shadow, is not such, but a substance; upon which he can anchor himself amid the storms of fate; — and he does so, even taking orders in it, I think.   Such could by no means seem to me the true or tenable solution.   Here clearly, struggling amid the tumults, was a lovable young fellow-soul; who had by no means yet got to land; but of whom much might be hoped, if he ever did.   Some of the delineations are highly pictorial, flooded with a deep ruddy effulgence; betokening much wealth, in the crude or the ripe state.   The hope of perhaps, one day, knowing Sterling, was welcome and interesting to me. *Arthur Coningsby,* struggling imperfectly in a sphere high above circulating-library novels, gained no notice whatever in that quarter; gained, I suppose in a few scattered heads, some such recognition as the above; and there rested. Sterling never mentioned the name of it in my hearing, or would hear it mentioned.

In those very days while *Arthur Coningsby* was getting read amid the Scottish moors, "in June, 1833," Sterling, at Bonn in the Rhine-country, fell in with his old tutor and friend, the Reverend Julius Hare; one with whom he always delighted to communicate, especially on such topics as then altogether occupied him. A man of cheerful serious character, of much approved accomplishment, of perfect courtesy; surely of much piety, in all senses of that word. Mr. Hare had quitted his scholastic labors and distinctions, some time ago; the call or opportunity for taking orders having come; and as Rector of Herstmonceux in Sussex, a place patrimonially and otherwise endeared to him, was about entering, under the best omens, on a new course of life. He was now on his return from Rome, and a visit of some length to Italy. Such a meeting could not but be welcome and important to Sterling in such a mood. They had much earnest conversation, freely communing on the highest matters; especially of Sterling's purpose to undertake the clerical profession, in which course his reverend friend could not but bid him good speed.

It appears, Sterling already intimated his intention to become a clergyman: He would study theology, biblicalities, perfect himself in the knowledge seemly or essential for his new course; — read diligently "for a year or two in some good German University," then seek to obtain orders: that was his plan. To which Mr. Hare gave his hearty *Euge;* adding that if his own curacy happened then to be vacant, he should be well pleased to have Sterling in that office. So they parted.

"A year or two" of serious reflection "in some good German University," or anywhere in the world, might have thrown much elucidation upon these confused strugglings and purposings of Sterling's, and probably have spared him some confusion in his subsequent life. But the talent of waiting was, of all others, the one he wanted most. Impetuous velocity, all-hoping headlong alacrity, what we must call rashness and impatience, characterized him in most of his important and unimportant procedures; from the purpose to the execution there was usually but one big leap with him. A few months after Mr. Hare was gone, Sterling wrote that his purposes were a little changed by the late meeting at Bonn; that he now longed to enter the Church straightway: that if the Herstmonceux Curacy was still vacant, and the Rector's kind thought towards him still held, he would instantly endeavor to qualify himself for that office.

Answer being in the affirmative on both heads, Sterling returned to England; took orders, — "ordained deacon at Chichester on Trinity Sunday in 1834" (he never became technically priest) : — and so, having fitted himself and family with a reasonable house, in one of those leafy lanes in quiet Herstmonceux, on the edge of Pevensey Level, he commenced the duties of his Curacy.

The bereaved young lady has *taken* the veil, then! Even so. "Life is growing all so dark and brutal; must be redeemed into human, if it will continue life. Some pious heroism, to give a human color to life again, on any terms," — even on impossible ones !

To such length can transcendental moonshine, cast by some morbidly radiating Coleridge into the chaos of a fermenting life, act magically there, and produce divulsions and convulsions and diseased developments. So dark and abstruse, without lamp or authentic finger-post, is the course of pious genius towards the Eternal Kingdoms grown. No fixed highway more; the old spiritual highways and recognized paths to the Eternal, now all torn up and flung in heaps, submerged in unutterable boiling mud-oceans of Hypocrisy and Unbelievability, of brutal living Atheism and damnable dead putrescent Cant: surely a tragic pilgrimage for all mortals; Darkness, and the mere shadow of Death, enveloping all things from pole to pole; and in the raging gulf-currents, offering us will-o'-wisps for loadstars, — intimating that there are no stars, nor ever were, except certain Old-Jew ones which have now gone out. Once more, a tragic pilgrimage for all mortals; and for the young pious soul, winged with genius, and passionately seeking land, and passionately abhorrent of floating carrion withal, more tragical than for any! — A pilgrimage we must all undertake nevertheless, and make the best of with our respective means. Some arrive; a glorious few: many must be lost, — go down upon the floating wreck which they took for land. Nay, courage! These also, so far as there was any heroism in them, have bequeathed their life as a contribution to us, have valiantly laid their bodies in the chasm for us: of these also there is no ray of heroism *lost*, — and, on the whole, what else of them could or should be "saved" at any time? Courage, and ever Forward!

Concerning this attempt of Sterling's to find sanctuary in the old Church, and desperately grasp the hem of her garment in such manner, there will at present be many opinions: and mine must be recorded here in flat reproval of it, in mere pitying condemnation of it, as a rash, false, unwise and unpermitted step. Nay, among the evil lessons of his Time to poor Sterling, I cannot but account this the worst; properly indeed, as we may say, the apotheosis, the solemn apology and consecration, of all the evil lessons that were in it to him. Alas, if we did remember the divine and awful nature of God's Truth, and had not so forgotten it as poor doomed creatures never did before, — should we, durst we in our most audacious moments, think of wedding *it* to the World's Untruth, which is also, like all untruths, the Devil's? Only in the world's last lethargy can such things be done, and accounted safe and pious! Fools! "Do you think the Living God is a buzzard idol," sternly asks Milton, that you dare address Him in this manner? — Such darkness, thick sluggish clouds of cowardice and oblivious baseness, have accumulated on us: thickening as if towards the eternal sleep! It is not now known, what never needed proof or statement before, that Religion is not a doubt; that it is a certainty, — or else a mockery and horror. That none

or all of the many things we are in doubt about, and need to
have demonstrated and rendered probable, can by any alchemy
be made a "Religion" for us; but are and must continue
a baleful, quiet or unquiet, Hypocrisy for us; and bring —
salvation, do we fancy? I think, it is another thing they
will bring, and are, on all hands, visibly bringing this good
while! —

The time, then, with its deliriums, has done its worst for
poor Sterling. Into deeper aberration it cannot lead him;
this is the crowning error. Happily, as beseems the superlative of errors, it was a very brief, almost a momentary one.
In June, 1834, Sterling dates as installed at Herstmonceux;
and is flinging, as usual, his whole soul into the business;
successfully so far as outward results could show: but already
in September, he begins to have misgivings; and in February
following, quits it altogether, — the rest of his life being, in
great part, a laborious effort of detail to pick the fragments
of it off him, and be free of it in soul as well as in title.

At this the extreme point of spiritual deflexion and depres-
sion, when the world's madness, unusually impressive on such
a man, has done its very worst with him, and in all future errors
whatsoever he will be a little less mistaken, we may close the
First Part of Sterling's Life.

PART II.

CHAPTER I.

CURATE.

By Mr. Hare's account, no priest of any Church could more fervently address himself to his functions than Sterling now did. He went about among the poor, the ignorant, and those that had need of help; zealously forwarded schools and beneficences; strove, with his whole might, to instruct and aid whosoever suffered consciously in body, or still worse unconsciously in mind. He had charged himself to make the Apostle Paul his model; the perils and voyagings and ultimate martyrdom of Christian Paul, in those old ages, on the great scale, were to be translated into detail, and become the practical emblem of Christian Sterling on the coast of Sussex in this new age. "It would be no longer from Jerusalem to Damascus," writes Sterling, "to Arabia, to Derbe, Lystra, Ephesus, that he would travel: but each house of his appointed Parish would be to him what each of those great cities was, — a place where he would bend his whole being, and spend his heart for the conversion, purification, elevation of those under his influence. The whole man would be forever at work for this purpose; head, heart, knowledge, time, body, possessions, all would be directed to this end." A high enough model set before one : — how to be realized ! — Sterling hoped to realize it, to struggle towards realizing it, in some small degree. This is Mr. Hare's report of him : —

"He was continually devising some fresh scheme for improving the condition of the Parish. His aim was to awaken

the minds of the people, to arouse their conscience, to call
forth their sense of moral responsibility, to make them feel
their own sinfulness, their need of redemption, and thus lead
them to a recognition of the Divine Love by which that redemption is offered to us. In visiting them he was diligent
in all weathers, to the risk of his own health, which was
greatly impaired thereby; and his gentleness and considerate
care for the sick won their affection; so that, though his stay
was very short, his name is still, after a dozen years, cherished
by many."

How beautiful would Sterling be in all this; rushing forward like a host towards victory; playing and pulsing like
sunshine or soft lightning; busy at all hours to perform his
part in abundant and superabundant measure! "Of that
which it was to me personally," continues Mr. Hare, "to have
such a fellow-laborer, to live constantly in the freest communion with such a friend, I cannot speak. He came to me at a
time of heavy affliction, just after I had heard that the Brother,
who had been the sharer of all my thoughts and feelings from
childhood, had bid farewell to his earthly life at Rome; and
thus he seemed given to me to make up in some sort for him
whom I had lost. Almost daily did I look out for his usual
hour of coming to me, and watch his tall slender form walking
rapidly across the hill in front of my window; with the assurance that he was coming to cheer and brighten, to rouse and
stir me, to call me up to some height of feeling, or down to
some depth of thought. His lively spirit, responding instan-
taneously to every impulse of Nature and Art; his generous
ardor in behalf of whatever is noble and true; his scorn of
all meanness, of all false pretenses and conventional beliefs,
softened as it was by compassion for the victims of those beset-
ting sins of a cultivated age; his never-flagging impetuosity in
pushing onward to some unattained point of duty or of knowledge: all this, along with his gentle, almost reverential affec-
tionateness towards his former tutor, rendered my intercourse
with him an unspeakable blessing; and time after time has it
seemed to me that his visit had been like a shower of rain,
bringing down freshness and brightness on a dusty roadside

hedge. By him too the recollection of these our daily meetings was cherished till the last." [1]

There are many poor people still at Herstmonceux who affectionately remember him : Mr. Hare especially makes mention of one good man there, in his young days "a poor cobbler," and now advanced to a much better position, who gratefully ascribes this outward and the other improvements in his life to Sterling's generous encouragement and charitable care for him. Such was the curate life at Herstmonceux. So, in those actual leafy lanes, on the edge of Pevensey Level, in this new age, did our poor New Paul (on hest of certain oracles) diligently study to comport himself, — and struggle with all his might *not* to be a moonshine shadow of the First Paul.

It was in this summer of 1834, — month of May, shortly after arriving in London, — that I first saw Sterling's Father. A stout broad gentleman of sixty, perpendicular in attitude, rather showily dressed, and of gracious, ingenious and slightly elaborate manners. It was at Mrs. Austin's in Bayswater ; he was just taking leave as I entered, so our interview lasted only a moment : but the figure of the man, as Sterling's father, had already an interest for me, and I remember the time well. Captain Edward Sterling, as we formerly called him, had now quite dropt the military title, nobody even of his friends now remembering it ; and was known, according to his wish, in political and other circles, as Mr. Sterling, a private gentleman of some figure. Over whom hung, moreover, a kind of mysterious nimbus as the principal or one of the principal writers in the *Times*, which gave an interesting chiaroscuro to his character in society. A potent, profitable, but somewhat questionable position ; of which, though he affected, and sometimes with anger, altogether to disown it, and rigorously insisted on the rights of anonymity, he was not unwilling to take the honors too : the private pecuniary advantages were very undeniable ; and his reception in the Clubs, and occasionally in higher quarters, was a good deal modelled on the universal belief in it.

[1] Hare, xlviii, liv, lv.

John Sterling at Herstmonceux that afternoon, and his
Father here in London, would have offered strange contrasts
to an eye that had seen them both. Contrasts, and yet con-
cordances. They were two very different-looking men, and
were following two very different modes of activity that afternoon. And yet with a strange family likeness, too, both in
the men and their activities; the central impulse in each, the
faculties applied to fulfil said impulse, not at all dissimilar, —
as grew visible to me on farther knowledge.

———◆———

CHAPTER II.

NOT CURATE.

Thus it went on for some months at Herstmonceux; but
thus it could not last. We said there were already misgivings
as to health, &c. in September:[1] that was but the fourth
month, for it had begun only in June. The like clouds of
misgiving, flights of dark vapor, chequering more and more
the bright sky of this promised land, rose heavier and rifer
month after month; till in February following, that is in the
eighth month from starting, the sky had grown quite over-
shaded; and poor Sterling had to think practically of departure from his promised land again, finding that the goal of his
pilgrimage was *not* there. Not there, wherever it may be!
March again, therefore; the abiding city, and post at which
we can live and die, is still ahead of us, it would appear!

"Ill-health" was the external cause; and, to all parties concerned, to Sterling himself I have no doubt as completely as to
any, the one determining cause. Nor was the ill-health wanting; it was there in too sad reality. And yet properly it was
not there as the burden; it was there as the last ounce which
broke the camel's back. I take it, in this as in other cases
known to me, ill-health was not the primary cause but rather

[1] Hare, p. lvi.

the ultimate one, the summing-up of innumerable far deeper
conscious and unconscious causes, — the cause which *could*
boldly show itself on the surface, and give the casting vote.
Such was often Sterling's way, as one could observe in such
cases : though the most guileless, undeceptive and transparent
of men, he had a noticeable, almost childlike faculty of self-
deception, and usually substituted for the primary determining
motive and set of motives, some ultimate ostensible one, and
gave that out to himself and others as the ruling impulse for
important changes in life.　As is the way with much more
ponderous and deliberate men; — as is the way, in a degree,
with all men !

Enough, in February, 1835, Sterling came up to London, to
consult with his physicians, — and in fact in all ways to consider with himself and friends, — what was to be done in
regard to this Herstmonceux business.　The oracle of the
physicians, like that of Delphi, was not exceedingly deter-
minate : but it did bear, what was a sufficiently undeniable
fact, that Sterling's constitution, with a tendency to pulmonary
ailments, was ill-suited for the office of a preacher; that total
abstinence from preaching for a year or two would clearly be
the safer course.　To which effect he writes to Mr. Hare with
a tone of sorrowful agitation ; gives up his clerical duties at
Herstmonceux ; — and never resumed them there or elsewhere.
He had been in the Church eight months in all : a brief section
of his life, but an important one, which colored several of his
subsequent years, and now strangely colors all his years in the
memory of some.

This we may account the second grand crisis of his History.
Radicalism, not long since, had come to its consummation, and
vanished from him in a tragic manner.　"Not by Radicalism
is the path to Human Nobleness for me ! "　And here now had
English Priesthood risen like a sun, over the waste ruins and
extinct volcanoes of his dead Radical world, with promise of
new blessedness and healing under its wings ; and this too
has soon found itself an illusion : " Not by Priesthood either
lies the way, then.　Once more, where does the way lie ! " —
To follow illusions till they burst and vanish is the lot of all

new souls who, luckily or lucklessly, are left to their own choice in starting on this Earth. The roads are many ; the authentic finger-posts are few, — never fewer than in this era, when in so many senses the waters are out. Sterling of all men had the quickest sense for nobleness, heroism and the human *summum bonum ;* the liveliest headlong spirit of adventure and audacity ; few gifted living men less stubbornness of persever-ance. Illusions, in his chase of the *summum bonum,* were not likely to be wanting ; aberrations, and wasteful changes of course, were likely to be many ! It is in the history of such vehement, trenchant, far-shining and yet intrinsically light and volatile souls, missioned into this epoch to seek their way there, that we best see what a confused epoch it is.

This clerical aberration, — for such it undoubtedly was in Sterling, — we have ascribed to Coleridge ; and do clearly think that had there been no Coleridge, neither had this been, — nor had English Puseyism or some other strange enough universal portents been. Nevertheless, let us say farther that it lay partly in the general bearing of the world for such a man. This battle, universal in our sad epoch of " all old things pass-ing away " against " all things becoming new," has its summary and animating heart in that of Radicalism against Church ; there, as in its flaming core, and point of focal splendor, does the heroic worth that lies in each side of the quarrel most clearly disclose itself ; and Sterling was the man, above many, to recognize such worth on both sides. Natural enough, in such a one, that the light of Radicalism having gone out in darkness for him, the opposite splendor should next rise as the chief, and invite his loyalty till it also failed. In one form or the other, such an aberration was not unlikely for him. But an aberration, especially in this form, we may certainly call it. No man of Sterling's veracity, had he clearly consulted his own heart, or had his own heart been capable of clearly re-sponding, and not been dazzled and bewildered by transient fantasies and theosophic moonshine, could have undertaken this function. His heart would have answered: "No, thou canst not. What is incredible to thee, thou shalt not, at thy soul's peril, attempt to believe ! — Elsewhither for a refuge,

or die here. Go to Perdition if thou must, — but not with a
lie in thy mouth; by the Eternal Maker, no!"

Alas, once more! How are poor mortals whirled hither and
thither in the tumultuous chaos of our era; and, under the
thick smoke-canopy which has eclipsed all stars, how do
they fly now after this poor meteor, now after that! — Sterling abandoned his clerical office in February, 1835; having
held it, and ardently followed it, so long as we say, — eight
calendar months in all.

It was on this his February expedition to London that I first
saw Sterling, — at the India House incidentally, one afternoon,
where I found him in company with John Mill, whom I happened like himself to be visiting for a few minutes. The sight
of one whose fine qualities I had often heard of lately, was interesting enough; and, on the whole, proved not disappointing,
though it was the translation of dream into fact, that is of
poetry into prose, and showed its unrhymed side withal. A
loose, careless-looking, thin figure, in careless dim costume,
sat, in a lounging posture, carelessly and copiously talking.
I was struck with the kindly but restless swift-glancing eyes,
which looked as if the spirits were all out coursing like a pack
of merry eager beagles, beating every bush. The brow, rather
sloping in form, was not of imposing character, though again
the head was longish, which is always the best sign of intellect; the physiognomy in general indicated animation rather
than strength.

We talked rapidly of various unmemorable things: I remember coming on the Negroes, and noticing that Sterling's notions
on the Slavery Question had not advanced into the stage of
mine. In reference to the question whether an "engagement
for life," on just terms, between parties who are fixed in the
character of master and servant, as the Whites and the Negroes
are, is not really better than one from day to day, — he said
with a kindly jeer, "I would have the Negroes themselves
consulted as to that!" — and would not in the least believe
that the Negroes were by no means final or perfect judges
of it. — His address, I perceived, was abrupt, unceremonious;

probably not at all disinclined to logic, and capable of dashing
in upon you like a charge of Cossacks, on occasion : but it was
also eminently ingenious, social, guileless. We did all very
well together : and Sterling and I walked westward in company, choosing whatever lanes or quietest streets there were,
as far as Knightsbridge where our roads parted; talking on
moralities, theological philosophies ; arguing copiously, but
except in opinion not disagreeing.

In his notions on such subjects, the expected Coleridge cast
of thought was very visible ; and he seemed to express it even
with exaggeration, and in a fearless dogmatic manner. Identity of sentiment, difference of opinion : these are the known
elements of a pleasant dialogue. We parted with the mutual
wish to meet again ; — which accordingly, at his Father's house
and at mine, we soon repeatedly did ; and already, in the few
days before his return to Herstmonceux, had laid the foundations of a frank intercourse, pointing towards pleasant intima-
cies both with himself and with his circle, which in the future
were abundantly fulfilled. His Mother, essentially and even
professedly "Scotch," took to my Wife gradually with a most
kind maternal relation; his Father, a gallant showy stirring
gentleman, the Magus of the *Times,* had talk and argument
ever ready, was an interesting figure, and more and more took
interest in us. We had unconsciously made an acquisition,
which grew richer and wholesomer with every new year ; and
ranks now, seen in the pale moonlight of memory, and must
ever rank, among the precious possessions of life.

Sterling's bright ingenuity, and also his audacity, velocity
and alacrity, struck me more and more. It was, I think, on
the occasion of a party given one of these evenings at his
Father's, where I remember John Mill, John Crawford, Mrs.
Crawford, and a number of young and elderly figures of distinction, — that a group having formed on the younger side of
the room, and transcendentalisms and theologies forming the
topic, a number of deep things were said in abrupt conversational style, Sterling in the thick of it. For example, one
sceptical figure praised the Church of England, in Hume's
phrase, " as a Church tending to keep down fanaticism," and

recommendable for its very indifferency; whereupon a transcendental figure urges him: "You are afraid of the horse's
kicking: but will you sacrifice all qualities to being safe from
that? Then get a dead horse. None comparable to that for
not kicking in your stable!" Upon which, a laugh; with
new laughs on other the like occasions; — and at last, in the
fire of some discussion, Sterling, who was unusually eloquent
and animated, broke out with this wild phrase, "I could plunge
into the bottom of Hell, if I were sure of finding the Devil
there and getting him strangled!" Which produced the loudest laugh of all; and had to be repeated, on Mrs. Crawford's
inquiry, to the house at large; and, creating among the elders
a kind of silent shudder, — though we urged that the feat
would really be a good investment of human industry, —
checked or stopt these theologic thunders for the evening. I
still remember Sterling as in one of his most animated moods
that evening. He probably returned to Herstmonceux next
day, where he proposed yet to reside for some indefinite time.

Arrived at Herstmonceux, he had not forgotten us. One of
his Letters written there soon after was the following, which
much entertained me, in various ways. It turns on a poor
Book of mine, called *Sartor Resartus;* which was not then
even a Book, but was still hanging desolately under biblio-
polic difficulties, now in its fourth or fifth year, on the wrong
side of the river, as a mere aggregate of Magazine Articles;
having at last been slit into that form, and lately completed
so, and put together into legibility. I suppose Sterling had
borrowed it of me. The adventurous hunter spirit which
had started such a bemired *Auerochs,* or Urus of the German
woods, and decided on chasing that as game, struck me not a
little; — and the poor Wood-Ox, so bemired in the forests,
took it as a compliment rather: —

> "*To Thomas Carlyle, Esq., Chelsea, London.*
>
> "Herstmonceux near Battle, 29th May, 1835.

"My dear Carlyle, — I have now read twice, with care,
the wondrous account of Teufelsdröckh and his Opinions;
and I need not say that it has given me much to think of. It

falls in with the feelings and tastes which were, for years, the
ruling ones of my life ; but which you will not be angry with
me when I say that I am infinitely and hourly thankful for
having escaped from. Not that I think of this state of mind
as one with which I have no longer any concern. The sense
of a oneness of life and power in all existence ; and of a
boundless exuberance of beauty around us, to which most men
are well-nigh dead, is a possession which no one that has ever
enjoyed it would wish to lose. When to this we add the deep
feeling of the difference between the actual and the ideal in
Nature, and still more in Man ; and bring in, to explain this,
the principle of duty, as that which connects us with a possible Higher State, and sets us in progress towards it, — we
have a cycle of thoughts which was the whole spiritual empire
of the wisest Pagans, and which might well supply food for
the wide speculations and richly creative fancy of Teufelsdröckh, or his prototype Jean Paul.

" How then comes it, we cannot but ask, that these ideas,
displayed assuredly with no want of eloquence, vivacity or
earnestness, have found, unless I am much mistaken, so little
acceptance among the best and most energetic minds in this
country ? In a country where millions read the Bible, and
thousands Shakspeare ; where Wordsworth circulates through
book-clubs and drawing-rooms ; where there are innumerable
admirers of your favorite Burns ; and where Coleridge, by
sending from his solitude the voice of earnest spiritual instruction, came to be beloved, studied and mourned for, by no
small or careless school of disciples ? — To answer this question would, of course, require more thought and knowledge
than I can pretend to bring to it. But there are some points
on which I will venture to say a few words.

" In the first place, as to the form of composition, — which
may be called, I think, the Rhapsodico-Reflective. In this
the *Sartor Resartus* resembles some of the master-works of
human invention, which have been acknowledged as such by
many generations ; and especially the works of Rabelais,
Montaigne, Sterne and Swift. There is nothing I know of
in Antiquity like it. That which comes nearest is perhaps

the Platonic Dialogue. But of this, although there is something of the playful and fanciful on the surface, there is in
reality neither in the language (which is austerely determined
to its end), nor in the method and progression of .the work,
any of that headlong self-asserting capriciousness, which, if
not discernible in the plan of Teufelsdröckh's Memoirs, is
yet plainly to be seen in the structure of the sentences, the
lawless oddity, and strange heterogeneous combination and
allusion. The principle of this difference, observable often
elsewhere in modern literature (for the same thing is to be
found, more or less, in many of our most genial works of
imagination, — *Don Quixote*, for instance, and the writings
of Jeremy Taylor), seems to be that well-known one of the
predominant objectivity of the Pagan mind ; while among us
the subjective has risen into superiority, and brought with it
in each individual a multitude of peculiar associations and
relations. These, as not explicable from any one *external*
principle assumed as a premiss by the ancient philosopher,
were rejected from the sphere of his æsthetic creation : but
to us they all have a value and meaning; being connected by
the bond of our own personality, and all alike existing in that
infinity which is its arena.

"But however this may be, and comparing the Teufels-
dröckhean Epopee only with those other modern works, — it is
noticeable that Rabelais, Montaigne and Sterne have trusted
for the currency of their writings, in a great degree, to the use
of obscene and sensual stimulants. Rabelais, besides, was full
of contemporary and personal satire ; and seems to have been
a champion in the great cause of his time, — as was Montaigne
also, — that of the right of thought in all competent minds,
unrestrained by any outward authority. Montaigne, moreover, contains more pleasant and lively gossip, and more distinct good-humored painting of his own character and daily
habits, than any other writer I know. Sterne is never obscure, and never moral ; and the costume of his subjects is
drawn from the familiar experience of his own time and country : and Swift, again, has the same merit of the clearest per-
spicuity, joined to that of the most homely, unaffected, forcible

English. These points of difference seem to me the chief ones which bear against the success of the *Sartor*. On the other hand, there is in Teufelsdröckh a depth and fervor of feeling, and a power of serious eloquence, far beyond that of any of these four writers ; and to which indeed there is nothing at all comparable in any of them, except perhaps now and then, and very imperfectly, in Montaigne.

" Of the other points of comparison there are two which I would chiefly dwell on : and first as to the language. A good deal of this is positively barbarous. 'Environment,' 'vestural,' 'stertorous,' 'visualized,' 'complected,' and others to be found I think in the first twenty pages, — are words, so far as I know, without any authority ; some of them contrary to analogy : and none repaying by their value the disadvantage of novelty. To these must be added new and erroneous locutions ; 'whole other tissues' for *all the other*, and similar uses of the word *whole ;* 'orients' for *pearls ;* 'lucid' and 'lucent' employed as if they were different in meaning ; 'hulls' perpetually for *coverings*, it being a word hardly used, and then only for the husk of a nut ; 'to insure a man of misapprehension ;' 'talented,' a mere newspaper and hustings word, invented, I believe, by O'Connell.

" I must also mention the constant recurrence of some words in a quaint and queer connection, which gives a grotesque and somewhat repulsive mannerism to many sentences. Of these the commonest offender is 'quite;' which appears in almost every page, and gives at first a droll kind of emphasis ; but soon becomes wearisome. 'Nay,' 'manifold,' 'cunning enough significance,' 'faculty' (meaning a man's rational or moral *power*), 'special,' 'not without,' haunt the reader as if in some uneasy dream which does not rise to the dignity of nightmare. Some of these strange mannerisms fall under the general head of a singularity peculiar, so far as I know, to Teufelsdröckh. For instance, that of the incessant use of a sort of odd superfluous qualification of his assertions ; which seems to give the character of deliberateness and caution to the style, but in time sounds like mere trick or involuntary habit. 'Almost' does more than yeoman's, *almost* slave's

service in this way. Something similar may be remarked of
the use of the double negative by way of affirmation.

"Under this head, of language, may be mentioned, though
not with strict grammatical accuracy, two standing characteristics of the Professor's style, — at least as rendered into
English: *First*, the composition of words, such as 'snow-and-
rosebloom maiden:' an attractive damsel doubtless in Germany, but, with all her charms, somewhat uncouth here.
'Life-vision' is another example; and many more might be
found. To say nothing of the innumerable cases in which
the words are only intelligible as a compound term, though
not distinguished by hyphens. Of course the composition of
words is sometimes allowable even in English: but the habit
of dealing with German seems to have produced, in the pages
before us, a prodigious superabundance of this form of expression; which gives harshness and strangeness, where the
matter would at all events have been surprising enough.
Secondly, I object, with the same qualification, to the frequent use of *inversion;* which generally appears as a trans-
position of the two members of a clause, in a way which
would not have been practised in conversation. It certainly
gives emphasis and force, and often serves to point the meaning. But a style may be fatiguing and faulty precisely by
being too emphatic, forcible and pointed; and so straining the
attention to find its meaning, or the admiration to appreciate
its beauty.

"Another class of considerations connects itself with the
heightened and plethoric fulness of the style: its accumulation and contrast of imagery; its occasional jerking and
almost spasmodic violence; — and above all, the painful subjective excitement, which seems the element and groundwork
even of every description of Nature; often taking the shape of
sarcasm or broad jest, but never subsiding into calm. There
is also a point which I should think worth attending to, were
I planning any similar book: I mean the importance, in a
work of imagination, of not too much disturbing in the reader's mind the balance of the New and Old. The former ad
dresses itself to his active, the latter to his passive faculty;

and these are mutually dependent, and must coexist in certain proportion, if you wish to combine his sympathy and progressive exertion with willingness and ease of attention. This should be taken into account in forming a style; for of course it cannot be consciously thought of in composing each sentence.

"But chiefly it seems important in determining the plan of a work. If the tone of feeling, the line of speculation are out of the common way, and sure to present some difficulty to the average reader, then it would probably be desirable to select, for the circumstances, drapery and accessories of all kinds, those most familiar, or at least most attractive. A fable of the homeliest purport, and commonest every-day application, derives an interest and charm from its turning on the characters and acts of gods and genii, lions and foxes, Arabs and Affghauns. On the contrary, for philosophic inquiry and truths of awful preciousness, I would select as my personages and interlocutors beings with whose language and 'whereabouts' my readers would be familiar. Thus did Plato in his Dialogues, Christ in his Parables. Therefore it seems doubtful whether it was judicious to make a German Professor the hero of *Sartor*. Berkeley began his *Siris* with tar-water; but what can English readers be expected to make of *Gukguk* by way of prelibation to your nectar and tokay? The circumstances and details do not flash with living reality on the minds of your readers, but, on the contrary, themselves require some of that attention and minute speculation, the whole original stock of which, in the minds of most of them, would not be too much to enable them to follow your views of Man and Nature. In short, there is not a sufficient basis of the common to justify the amount of peculiarity in the work. In a book of science, these considerations would of course be inapplicable; but then the whole shape and coloring of the book must be altered to make it such; and a man who wishes merely to get at the philosophical result, or summary of the whole, will regard the details and illustrations as so much unprofitable surplusage.

"The sense of strangeness is also awakened by the marvellous combinations, in which the work abounds to a degree that the common reader must find perfectly bewildering. This can hardly, however, be treated as a consequence of the *style ;* for the style in this respect coheres with, and springs from, the whole turn and tendency of thought. The noblest images are objects of a humorous smile, in a mind which sees itself above all Nature and throned in the arms of an Almighty Necessity ; while the meanest have a dignity, inasmuch as they are trivial symbols of the same one life to which the great whole belongs. And hence, as I divine, the startling whirl of incongruous juxtaposition, which of a truth must to many readers seem as amazing as if the Pythia on the tripod should have struck up a drinking-song, or Thersites had caught the prophetic strain of Cassandra.

" All this, of course, appears to me true and relevant; but I cannot help feeling that it is, after all, but a poor piece of quackery to comment on a multitude of phenomena without adverting to the principle which lies at the root, and gives the true meaning to them all. Now this principle I seem to myself to find in the state of mind which is attributed to Teufelsdröckh ; in his state of mind, I say, not in his opinions, though these are, in him as in all men, most important, — being one of the best indices to his state of mind. Now what distinguishes him, not merely from the greatest and best men who have been on earth for eighteen hundred years, but from the whole body of those who have been working forwards towards the good, and have been the salt and light of the world, is this : That he does not believe in a God. Do not be indignant, I am blaming no one ; — but if I write my thoughts, I must write them honestly.

" Teufelsdröckh does not belong to the herd of sensual and thoughtless men ; because he does perceive in all Existence a unity of power ; because he does believe that this is a real power external to him and dominant to a certain extent over him, and does not think that he is himself a shadow in a world of shadows. He had a deep feeling of the beautiful, the good and the true ; and a faith in their final victory.

"At the same time, how evident is the strong inward unrest, the Titanic heaving of mountain on mountain; the storm-like rushing over land and sea in search of peace. He writhes and roars under his consciousness of the difference in himself between the possible and the actual, the hoped-for and the existent. He feels that duty is the highest law of his own being; and knowing how it bids the waves be stilled into an icy fixedness and grandeur, he trusts (but with a boundless inward misgiving) that there is a principle of order which will reduce all confusion to shape and clearness. But wanting peace himself, his fierce dissatisfaction fixes on all that is weak, corrupt and imperfect around him; and instead of a calm and steady co-operation with all those who are endeavoring to apply the highest ideas as remedies for the worst evils, he holds himself aloof in savage isolation; and cherishes (though he dare not own) a stern joy at the prospect of that Catastrophe which is to turn loose again the elements of man's social life, and give for a time the victory to evil; — in hopes that each new convulsion of the world must bring us nearer to the ultimate restoration of all things; fancying that each may be the last. Wanting the calm and cheerful reliance, which would be the spring of active exertion, he flatters his own distemper by persuading himself that his own age and generation are peculiarly feeble and decayed; and would even perhaps be willing to exchange the restless immaturity of our self-consciousness, and the promise of its long throe-pangs, for the unawakened undoubting simplicity of the world's childhood; of the times in which there was all the evil and horror of our day, only with the difference that conscience had not arisen to try and condemn it. In these longings, if they are Teufels-dröckh's, he seems to forget that, could we go back five thousand years, we should only have the prospect of travelling them again, and arriving at last at the same point at which we stand now.

"Something of this state of mind I may say that I understand; for I have myself experienced it. And the root of the matter appears to me: A want of sympathy with the great body of those who are now endeavoring to guide and help

onward their fellow-men. And in what is this alienation
grounded? It is, as I believe, simply in the difference on
that point: viz. the clear, deep, habitual recognition of a one
Living *Personal* God, essentially good, wise, true and holy, the
Author of all that exists; and a reunion with whom is the
only end of all rational beings. This belief . . . [*There follow
now several pages on "Personal God," and other abstruse or indeed properly unspeakable matters; these, and a general Post-
script of qualifying purport, I will suppress; extracting only the
following fractions, as luminous or slightly significant to us:*]

"Now see the difference of Teufelsdröckh's feelings. At the
end of book iii. chap. 8, I find these words: 'But whence? O
Heaven, whither? Sense knows not; Faith knows not; only
that it is through mystery to mystery, from God to God.

> " We *are such stuff*
> As dreams are made of, and our little life
> Is rounded with a sleep." '

And this tallies with the whole strain of his character. What
we find everywhere, with an abundant use of the name of God,
is the conception of a formless Infinite whether in time or
space; of a high inscrutable Necessity, which it is the chief
wisdom and virtue to submit to, which is the mysterious imper-
sonal base of all Existence, — shows itself in the laws of every
separate being's nature; and for man in the shape of duty.
On the other hand, I affirm, we do know whence we come and
whither we go! —

. . . "And in this state of mind, as there is no true sympathy with others, just as little is there any true peace for
ourselves. There is indeed possible the unsympathizing fac-
titious calm of Art, which we find in Goethe. But at what
expense is it bought? Simply, by abandoning altogether the
idea of duty, which is the great witness of our personality.
And he attains his inhuman ghastly calmness by reducing the
Universe to a heap of material for the idea of beauty to work
on! —

. . . "The sum of all I have been writing as to the connection of our faith in God with our feeling towards men and

our mode of action, may of course be quite erroneous : but
granting its truth, it would supply the one principle which I
have been seeking for, in order to explain the peculiarities of
style in your account of Teufelsdröckh and his writings. . . .
The life and works of Luther are the best comment I know of
on this doctrine of mine.

"Reading over what I have written, I find I have not nearly
done justice to my own sense of the genius and moral energy
of the book; but this is what you will best excuse. — Believe
me most sincerely and faithfully yours,

"JOHN STERLING."

Here are sufficient points of "discrepancy with agreement,"
here is material for talk and argument enough; and an expanse
of free discussion open, which requires rather to be speedily
restricted for convenience' sake, than allowed to widen itself
into the boundless, as it tends to do! —

In all Sterling's Letters to myself and others, a large collection of which now lies before me, duly copied and indexed,
there is, to one that knew his speech as well, a perhaps unusual likeness between the speech and the Letters; and yet,
for most part, with a great inferiority on the part of these.
These, thrown off, one and all of them, without premeditation,
and with most rapid-flowing pen, are naturally as like his
speech as writing can well be; this is their grand merit to
us : but on the other hand, the want of the living tones, swift
looks and motions, and manifold dramatic accompaniments,
tells heavily, more heavily than common.   What can be done
with champagne itself, much more with soda-water, when the
gaseous spirit is fled !   The reader, in any specimens he may
see, must bear this in mind.

Meanwhile these Letters do excel in honesty, in candor and
transparency; their very carelessness secures their excellence
in this respect.   And in another much deeper and more essential respect I must likewise call them excellent, — in their
childlike goodness, in the purity of heart, the noble affection
and fidelity they everywhere manifest in the writer.   This
often touchingly strikes a familiar friend in reading them;

and will awaken reminiscences (when you have the commentary in your own memory) which are sad and beautiful, and
not without reproach to you on occasion.   To all friends, and
all good causes, this man is true; behind their back as before
their face, the same man! — Such traits of the autobiographic
sort, from these Letters, as can serve to paint him or his life,
and promise not to weary the reader, I must endeavor to select,
in the sequel.

CHAPTER III.

BAYSWATER.

STERLING continued to reside at Herstmonceux through the
spring and summer; holding by the peaceable retired house
he still had there, till the vague future might more definitely
shape itself, and better point out what place of abode would
suit him in his new circumstances.   He made frequent brief
visits to London; in which I, among other friends, frequently
saw him, our acquaintance at each visit improving in all
ways.   Like a swift dashing meteor he came into our circle;
coruscated among us, for a day or two, with sudden pleasant
illumination; then again suddenly withdrew, — we hoped,
not for long.

I suppose, he was full of uncertainties; but undoubtedly
was gravitating towards London.   Yet, on the whole, on the
surface of him, you saw no uncertainties; far from that: it
seemed always rather with peremptory resolutions, and swift
express businesses, that he was charged.   Sickly in body, the
testimony said: but here always was a mind that gave you the
impression of peremptory alertness, cheery swift decision, —
of a *health* which you might have called exuberant.   I remember dialogues with him, of that year; one pleasant dialogue
under the trees of the Park (where now, in 1851, is the thing
called "Crystal Palace"), with the June sunset flinging long
shadows for us; the last of the Quality just vanishing for

dinner, and the great night beginning to prophesy of itself. Our talk (like that of the foregoing Letter) was of the faults of my style, of my way of thinking, of my &c. &c.; all which admonitions and remonstrances, so friendly and innocent, from this young junior-senior, I was willing to listen to, though unable, as usual, to get almost any practical hold of them. As usual, the garments do not fit you, you are lost in the garments, or you cannot get into them at all; this is not your suit of clothes, it must be another's : — alas, these are not your dimensions, these are only the optical angles you subtend; on the whole, you will never get measured in that way ! —

Another time, of date probably very contiguous, I remember hearing Sterling preach. It was in some new college-chapel in Somerset-house (I suppose, what is now called King's College); a very quiet small place, the audience student-looking youths, with a few elder people, perhaps mostly friends of the preacher's. The discourse, delivered with a grave sonorous composure, and far surpassing in talent the usual run of sermons, had withal an air of human veracity as I still recollect, and bespoke dignity and piety of mind : but gave me the impression rather of artistic excellence than of unction or inspiration in that kind. Sterling returned with us to Chelsea that day ; — and in the afternoon we went on the Thames Putney-ward together, we two with my Wife ; under the sunny skies, on the quiet water, and with copious cheery talk, the remembrance of which is still present enough to me.

This was properly my only specimen of Sterling's preaching. Another time, late in the same autumn, I did indeed attend him one evening to some Church in the City, — a big Church behind Cheapside, "built by Wren" as he carefully informed me ; — but there, in my wearied mood, the chief subject of reflection was the almost total vacancy of the place, and how an eloquent soul was preaching to mere lamps and prayer-books ; and of the sermon I retain no image. It came up in the way of banter, if he ever urged the duty of "Church extension," which already he very seldom did and at length never, what a specimen we once had of bright lamps, gilt prayer-books, baize-lined pews, Wren-built architecture ; and

how, in almost all directions, you might have fired a musket
through the church, and hit no Christian life. A terrible
outlook indeed for the Apostolic laborer in the brick-and-
mortar line ! —

In the Autumn of this same 1835, he removed permanently
to London, whither all summer he had been evidently tending;
took a house in Bayswater, an airy suburb, half town, half
country, near his Father's, and within fair distance of his
other friends and objects ; and decided to await there what
the ultimate developments of his course might be. His house
was in Orme Square, close by the corner of that little place
(which has only *three* sides of houses); its windows looking
to the east : the Number was, and I believe still is, No. 5. A
sufficiently commodious, by no means sumptuous, small mansion; where, with the means sure to him, he could calculate on
finding adequate shelter for his family, his books and himself,
and live in a decent manner, in no terror of debt, for one thing.
His income, I suppose, was not large; but he lived generally
a safe distance within it; and showed himself always as a man
bountiful in money matters, and taking no thought that way.

His study-room in this house was perhaps mainly the
drawing-room ; looking out safe, over the little dingy grass-
plot in front, and the quiet little row of houses opposite,
with the huge dust-whirl of Oxford Street and London far
enough ahead of you as background, — as back-curtain,
blotting out only *half* your blue hemisphere with dust and
smoke. On the right, you had the continuous growl of the
Uxbridge Road and its wheels, coming as lullaby not interruption. Leftward and rearward, after some thin belt of
houses, lay mere country ; bright sweeping green expanses,
crowned by pleasant Hampstead, pleasant Harrow, with their
rustic steeples rising against the sky. Here on winter evenings, the bustle of removal being all well ended, and family
and books got planted in their new places, friends could find
Sterling, as they often did, who was delighted to be found
by them, and would give and take, vividly as few others, an
hour's good talk at any time.

His outlooks, it must be admitted, were sufficiently vague and overshadowed; neither the past nor the future of a too joyful kind. Public life, in any professional form, is quite forbidden; to work with his fellows anywhere appears to be forbidden: nor can the humblest solitary endeavor to work worthily as yet find an arena. How unfold one's little bit of talent; and live, and not lie sleeping, while it is called To-day? As Radical, as Reforming Politician in any public or private form, — not only has this, in Sterling's case, received tragical sentence and execution; but the opposite extreme, the Church whither he had fled, likewise proves abortive: the Church also is not the haven for him at all. What is to be done? Something must be done, and soon, — under penalties. Whoever has received, on him there is an inexorable behest to give. "*Fais ton fait,* Do thy little stroke of work:" this is Nature's voice, and the sum of all the commandments, to each man!

A shepherd of the people, some small Agamemnon after his sort, doing what little sovereignty and guidance he can in his day and generation: such every gifted soul longs, and should long, to be. But how, in any measure, is the small kingdom necessary for Sterling to be attained? Not through newspapers and parliaments, not by rubrics and reading-desks: none of the sceptres offered in the world's market-place, nor none of the crosiers there, it seems, can be the shepherd's-crook for this man. A most cheerful, hoping man; and full of swift faculty, though much lamed, — considerably bewildered too; and tending rather towards the wastes and solitary places for a home; the paved world not being friendly to him hitherto! The paved world, in fact, both on its practical and spiritual side, slams to its doors against him; indicates that he cannot enter, and even must not, — that it will prove a choke-vault, deadly to soul and to body, if he enter. Sceptre, crosier, sheep-crook is none there for him.

There remains one other implement, the resource of all Adam's posterity that are otherwise foiled, — the Pen. It was evident from this point that Sterling, however otherwise beaten about, and set fluctuating, would gravitate steadily with all his real weight towards Literature. That he would gradually try with consciousness to get into Literature; and, on the whole, never quit Literature, which was now all the world for him. Such is accordingly the sum of his history henceforth :· such small sum, so terribly obstructed and diminished by circumstances, is all we have realized from him.

Sterling had by no means as yet consciously quitted the clerical profession, far less the Church as a creed. We have seen, he occasionally officiated still in these months, when a friend requested or an opportunity invited. Nay it turned out afterwards, he had, unknown even to his own family, during a good many weeks in the coldest period of next spring, when it was really dangerous for his health and did prove hurtful to it, — been constantly performing the morning service in some Chapel in Bayswater for a young clerical neighbor, a slight acquaintance of his, who was sickly at the time. So far as I know, this of the Bayswater Chapel in the spring of 1836, a feat severely rebuked by his Doctor withal, was his last actual service as a churchman. But the conscious life ecclesiastical still hung visibly about his inner unconscious and real life, for years to come; and not till by slow degrees he had unwinded from him the wrappages of it, could he become clear about himself, and so much as try heartily what his now sole course was. Alas, and he had to live all the rest of his days, as in continual flight for his very existence; " ducking under like a poor unfledged partridge-bird," as one described it, " before the mower; darting continually from nook to nook, and there crouching, to escape the scythe of Death." For Literature Proper there was but little left in such a life. Only the smallest broken fractions of his last and heaviest-laden years can poor Sterling be said to have completely lived. His purpose had risen before him slowly in noble clearness; clear at last, — and even then the inevitable hour was at hand.

In those first London months, as always afterwards while it remained physically possible, I saw much of him; loved him, as was natural, more and more; found in him, many ways, a beautiful acquisition to my existence here. He was full of bright speech and argument; radiant with arrowy vitalities, vivacities and ingenuities. Less than any man he gave you the idea of ill-health. Hopeful, sanguine; nay he did not even seem to need definite hope, or much to form any; projecting himself in aerial pulses like an aurora borealis, like a summer dawn, and filling all the world with present brightness for himself and others. Ill-health? Nay you found at last, it was the very excess of *life* in him that brought on disease. This restless play of being, fit to conquer the world, could it have been held and guided, could not be held. It had worn *holes* in the outer case of it, and there found vent for itself, — there, since not otherwise.

In our many promenades and colloquies, which were of the freest, most copious and pleasant nature, religion often formed a topic, and perhaps towards the beginning of our intercourse was the prevailing topic. Sterling seemed much engrossed in matters theological, and led the conversation towards such; talked often about Church, Christianity Anglican and other, how essential the belief in it to man; then, on the other side, about Pantheism and such like; — all in the Coleridge dialect, and with eloquence and volubility to all lengths. I remember his insisting often and with emphasis on what he called a "personal God," and other high topics, of which it was not always pleasant to give account in the argumentative form, in a loud hurried voice, walking and arguing through the fields or streets. Though of warm quick feelings, very positive in his opinions, and vehemently eager to convince and conquer in such discussions, I seldom or never saw the least anger in him against me or any friend. When the blows of contradiction came too thick, he could with consummate dexterity whisk aside out of their way; prick into his adversary on some new quarter; or gracefully flourishing his weapon, end the duel in some handsome manner. One angry glance I remember in him, and it was but a glance, and gone in a moment. "Flat Pantheism!" urged he once (which he would often enough do about this time), as if triumphantly, of something or other, in the fire of a debate, in my hearing: "It is mere Pantheism, that!" — "And suppose it were Pot-theism?" cried the other:

"If the thing is true!" — Sterling did look hurt at such flippant heterodoxy, for a moment. The soul of his own creed, in those days, was far other than this indifference to Pot or Pan in such departments of inquiry.

To me his sentiments for most part were lovable and admirable, though in the logical outcome there was everywhere room for opposition. I admired the temper, the longing towards antique heroism, in this young man of the nineteenth century; but saw not how, except in some German-English empire of the air, he was ever to realize it on those terms. In fact, it became clear to me more and more that here was nobleness of heart striving towards all nobleness; here was ardent recognition of the worth of Christianity, for one thing; but no belief in it at all, in my sense of the word belief, — no belief but one definable as mere theoretic moonshine, which would never stand the wind and weather of fact. Nay it struck me farther that Sterling's was not intrinsically, nor had ever been in the highest or chief degree, a devotional mind. Of course all excellence in man, and worship as the supreme excellence, was part of the inheritance of this gifted man: but if called to define him, I should say, Artist not Saint was the real bent of his being. He had endless admiration, but intrinsically rather a deficiency of reverence in comparison. Fear, with its corollaries, on the religious side, he appeared to have none, nor ever to have had any.

In short, it was a strange enough symptom to me of the bewildered condition of the world, to behold a man of this temper, and of this veracity and nobleness, self-consecrated here, by free volition and deliberate selection, to be a Christian Priest; and zealously struggling to fancy himself such in very truth. Undoubtedly a singular present fact; — from which, as from their point of intersection, great perplexities and aberrations in the past, and considerable confusions in the future might be seen ominously radiating. Happily our friend, as I said, needed little hope. To-day with its activities was always bright and rich to him. His unmanageable, dislocated, devastated world, spiritual or economical, lay all illuminated in living sunshine, making it almost beautiful to his eyes, and gave him no hypochondria. A richer soul, in the way of natural outfit for felicity, for joyful activity in this world, so far as his strength would go, was nowhere to be met with.

The Letters which Mr. Hare has printed, Letters addressed, I imagine, mostly to himself, in this and the following year or two, give record of abundant changeful plannings and laborings, on the part of Sterling; still chiefly in the theological department. Translation from Tholuck, from Schleiermacher; treatise on this thing, then on that, are on the anvil: it is a life of abstruse vague speculations, singularly cheerful and hopeful withal, about Will, Morals, Jonathan Edwards, Jewhood, Manhood, and of Books to be written on these topics. Part of which adventurous vague plans, as the Translation from Tholuck, he actually performed; other greater part, merging always into wider undertakings, remained plan merely. I remember he talked often about Tholuck, Schleiermacher, and others of that stamp; and looked disappointed, though full of good nature, at my obstinate indifference to them and their affairs.

His knowledge of German Literature, very slight at this time, limited itself altogether to writers on Church matters, — Evidences, Counter-Evidences, Theologies and Rumors of Theologies; by the Tholucks, Schleiermachers, Neanders, and I know not whom. Of the true sovereign souls of that Literature, the Goethes, Richters, Schillers, Lessings, he had as good as no knowledge; and of Goethe in particular an obstinate misconception, with proper abhorrence appended, — which did not abate for several years, nor quite abolish itself till a very late period. Till, in a word, he got Goethe's works fairly read and studied for himself! This was often enough the course with Sterling in such cases. He had a most swift glance of recognition for the worthy and for the unworthy; and was prone, in his ardent decisive way, to put much faith in it. "Such a one is a worthless idol; not excellent, only sham-excellent:" here, on this negative side especially, you often had to admire how right he was; — often, but not quite always. And he would maintain, with endless ingenuity, confidence and persistence, his fallacious spectrum to be a real image. However, it was sure to come all right in the end. Whatever real excellence he might misknow, you had but to let it stand before him, soliciting new examination from him: none surer than he to recognize it at last, and to pay it all his dues, with the arrears and interest on them. Goethe, who figures as some absurd high-stalking hollow play-actor, or empty ornamental clock-case of an "Artist" so-called, in the Tale of the *Onyx Ring*, was in the throne of Sterling's intellectual world before all was done; and the theory of "Goethe's want of feeling," want of &c. &c. appeared to him also abundantly contemptible and forgettable.

Sterling's days, during this time as always, were full of occupation, cheerfully interesting to himself and others; though, the wrecks of theology so encumbering him, little fruit on the positive side could come of these labors. On the negative side they were productive; and there also, so much of encumbrance requiring removal, before fruit could grow, there was plenty of labor needed. He looked happy as well as busy; roamed extensively among his friends, and loved to have them about him, — chiefly old Cambridge comrades now settling into occupations in the world; — and was felt by all friends, by myself as by few, to be a welcome illumination in the dim whirl of things. A man of altogether social and human ways; his address everywhere pleasant and enlivening. A certain smile of thin but genuine laughter, we might say, hung gracefully over all he said and did; — expressing gracefully, according to the model of this epoch, the stoical pococurantism which is required of the cultivated Englishman. Such laughter in him was not deep, but neither was it false (as lamentably happens often); and the cheerfulness it went to symbolize was hearty and beautiful, — visible in the silent *un*symbolized state in a still gracefuler fashion.

Of wit, so far as rapid lively intellect produces wit, he had plenty, and did not abuse his endowment that way, being always fundamentally serious in the purport of his speech: of what we call humor, he had some, though little; nay of

real sense for the ludicrous, in any form, he had not much
for a man of his vivacity; and you remarked that his laugh
was limited in compass, and of a clear but not rich quality.
To the like effect shone something, a kind of childlike half-
embarrassed shimmer of expression, on his fine vivid countenance; curiously mingling with its ardors and audacities. A
beautiful childlike soul! He was naturally a favorite in conversation, especially with all who had any funds for conversing : frank and direct, yet polite and delicate withal, — though
at times too he could crackle with his dexterous petulancies,
making the air all like needles round you; and there was no
end to his logic when you excited it ; no end, unless in some
form of silence on your part. Elderly men of reputation I
have sometimes known offended by him : for he took a frank
way in the matter of talk; spoke freely out of him, freely listening to what others spoke, with a kind of " hail-fellow well
met " feeling; and carelessly measured a man much less by
his reputed account in the bank of wit, or in any other bank,
than by what the man had to show for himself in the shape
of real spiritual cash on the occasion. But withal there was
ever a fine element of natural courtesy in Sterling; his deliberate demeanor to acknowledged superiors was fine and graceful;
his apologies and the like, when in a fit of repentance he felt
commanded to apologize, were full of naïveté, and very pretty
and ingenuous.

His circle of friends was wide enough; chiefly men of his
own standing, old College friends many of them; some of
whom have now become universally known. Among whom
the most important to him was Frederic Maurice, who had not
long before removed to the Chaplaincy of Guy's Hospital here,
and was still, as he had long been, his intimate and counsellor.
Their views and articulate opinions, I suppose, were now fast
beginning to diverge; and these went on diverging far enough :
but in their kindly union, in their perfect trustful familiarity,
precious to both parties, there never was the least break,
but a steady, equable and duly increasing current to the end.
One of Sterling's commonest expeditions, in this time, was a
sally to the other side of London Bridge: " Going to Guy's

to-day." Maurice, in a year or two, became Sterling's brother-
in-law; wedded Mrs. Sterling's younger sister, — a gentle excellent female soul; by whom the relation was, in many ways,
strengthened and beautified for Sterling and all friends of the
parties.   With the Literary notabilities I think he had no acquaintance; his thoughts indeed still tended rather towards
a certain class of the Clerical; but neither had he much to do
with these; for he was at no time the least of a tuft-hunter,
but rather had a marked natural indifference to *tufts*.

The Rev. Mr. Dunn, a venerable and amiable Irish gentleman, "distinguished," we were told, "by having refused a
bishopric:" and who was now living, in an opulent enough
retirement, amid his books and philosophies and friends, in
London, — is memorable to me among this clerical class: one
of the mildest, beautifulest old men I have ever seen, — "like
Fénelon," Sterling said: his very face, with its kind true smile,
with its look of suffering cheerfulness and pious wisdom, was
a sort of benediction.   It is of him that Sterling writes, in the
Extract which Mr. Hare, modestly reducing the name to an
initial "Mr. D.," has given us:[1] "Mr. Dunn, for instance;
the defect of whose Theology, compounded as it is of the doctrine of the Greek Fathers, of the Mystics and of Ethical
Philosophers, consists, — if I may hint a fault in one whose
holiness, meekness and fervor would have made him the beloved disciple of him whom Jesus loved, — in an insufficient
apprehension of the reality and depth of Sin."   A characteristic "defect" of this fine gentle soul.   On Mr. Dunn's death,
which occurred two or three years later, Stirling gave, in some
veiled yet transparent form, in *Blackwood's Magazine,* an affectionate and eloquent notice of him; which, stript of the veil,
was excerpted into the Newspapers also.[2]

Of Coleridge there was little said.   Coleridge was now dead,
not long since; nor was his name henceforth much heard in
Sterling's circle; though on occasion, for a year or two to come,
he would still assert his transcendent admiration, especially
if Maurice were by to help.   But he was getting into German,
into various inquiries and sources of knowledge new to him,

---

[1] P. lxxviii.   [2] Given in Hare (ii. 188–193).

and his admirations and notions on many things were silently
and rapidly modifying themselves.

So, amid interesting human realities, and wide cloud-canopies
of uncertain speculation, which also had their interests and
their rainbow-colors to him, and could not fail in his life just
now, did Sterling pass his year and half at Bayswater. Such
vaporous speculations were inevitable for him at present; but
it was to be hoped they would subside by and by, and leave
the sky clear. All this was but the preliminary to whatever
work might lie in him: — and, alas, much other interruption
lay between him and that.

CHAPTER IV.

TO BORDEAUX.

AMONG the quondam Cambridge acquaintances I have seen
with Sterling about this time, one struck me, less from his
qualities than from his name and genealogy: Frank Edgeworth, youngest son of the well-known Lovell Edgeworth,
youngest brother of the celebrated Maria Edgeworth, the Irish
Novelist. Frank was a short neat man; of sleek, square,
colorless face (resembling the Portraits of his Father), with
small blue eyes in which twinkled curiously a joyless smile;
his voice was croaky and shrill, with a tone of shrewish obstinacy in it, and perhaps of sarcasm withal. A composed,
dogmatic, speculative, exact, and not melodious man. He was
learned in Plato and likewise in Kant; well-read in philosophies and literatures; entertained not creeds, but the Platonic
or Kantean *ghosts* of creeds; coldly sneering away from him,
in the joyless twinkle of those eyes, in the inexorable jingle
of that shrill voice, all manner of Toryisms, superstitions; for
the rest, a man of perfect veracity, of great diligence, and
other worth; — notable to see alongside of Sterling.

He is the "E." quoted by Mr. Hare from one of Sterling's
letters; — and I will incidentally confess that the discreet

"B." of the next leaf in that Volume must, if need be, convert himself into "C.," my recognizable self namely. Sterling has written there: "I find in all my conversations with Carlyle that his fundamental position is, the good of evil: he is for-ever quoting Goethe's Epigram about the idleness of wishing to jump off one's own shadow." — Even so : —

> *Was lehr' ich dich vor allen Dingen ? —*
> *Könntest mich lehren von meiner Schatte zu springen !*

— indicating conversations on the Origin of Evil, or rather resolution on my part to suppress such, as wholly fruitless and worthless; which are now all grown dark to me! The passage about Frank is as follows, — likewise elucidative of Sterling and his cloud-compellings, and duels with the shadows, about this time : —

"Edgeworth seems to me not to have yet gone beyond a mere notional life. It is manifest that he has no knowledge of the necessity of a progress from *Wissen* to *Wesen* [say, *Knowing* to *Being*]; and one therefore is not surprised that he should think Kant a sufficient hierarch. I know very little of Kant's doctrine; but I made out from Edgeworth what seems to me a fundamental unsoundness in his moral scheme : namely, the assertion of the certainty of a heavenly Futurity for man, because the idea of duty involves that of merit or reward. Now duty seems rather to exclude merit; and at all events, the notion of external reward is a mere empirical appendage, and has none but an arbitrary connection with ethics. — I regard it as a very happy thing for Edgeworth that he has come to England. In Italy he probably would never have gained any intuition into the reality of Being as different from a mere power of Speculating and Perceiving; and of course without this, he can never reach to more than the merest Gnosis; which taken alone is a poor inheritance, a box of title-deeds to an estate which is covered with lava, or sunk under the sea." [1]

This good little Edgeworth had roved extensively about the Continent; had married a young Spanish wife, whom by a

[1] Hare, pp. lxxiv, lxxii.

romantic accident he came upon in London; having really good scholarship, and consciousness of faculty and fidelity, he now hoped to find support in preparing young men for the University, in taking pupils to board; and with this view, was endeavoring to form an establishment somewhere in the environs; — ignorant that it is mainly the Clergy whom simple persons trust with that trade at present; that his want of a patent of orthodoxy, not to say his inexorable secret heterodoxy of mind, would far override all other qualifications in the estimate of simple persons, who are afraid of many things, and are *not* afraid of hypocrisy which is the worst and one irremediably bad thing. Poor Edgeworth tried this business for a while, but found no success at all; went across, after a year or two, to native Edgeworthstown, in Longford, to take the management of his brother's estate; in which function it was said he shone, and had quite given up philosophies and speculations, and become a taciturn grim land-manager and county magistrate, likely to do much good in that department; when we learned next that he was dead, that we should see him no more. The good little Frank!

One day in the spring of 1836, I can still recollect, Sterling had proposed to me, by way of wide ramble, useful for various ends, that I should walk with him to Eltham and back, to see this Edgeworth, whom I also knew a little. We went accordingly together; walking rapidly, as was Sterling's wont, and no doubt talking extensively. It probably was in the end of February: I can remember leafless hedges, gray driving clouds; — procession of boarding-school girls in some quiet part of the route. I very well recollect the big Edgeworth house at Eltham; the big old Palace now a barn; — in general, that the day was full of action; and likewise that rain came upon us in our return, and that the closing phasis was a march along Piccadilly, still full of talk, but now under decided wet, and in altogether muddy circumstances. This was the last walk that poor Sterling took for a great many months.

He had been ailing for some time, little known to me, and

too disregardful himself of minatory symptoms, as his wont
was, so long as strength remained; and this rainy walk of
ours had now brought the matter to a crisis. He was shut
up from all visitors whatsoever; the doctors and his family
in great alarm about him, he himself coldly professing that
death at no great distance was very likely. So it lasted for a
long anxious while. I remember tender messages to and from
him; loan of books, particularly some of Goethe's which he
then read, — still without recognition of much worth in them.
At length some select friends were occasionally admitted;
signs of improvement began to appear; — and in the bright
twilight, Kensington Gardens were green, and sky and earth
were hopeful, as one went to make inquiry. The summer
brilliancy was abroad over the world before we fairly saw
Sterling again *sub dio.* — Here was a fatal hand on the wall;
checking tragically whatsoever wide-drawn schemes might be
maturing themselves in such a life; sternly admonitory that
all schemes must be narrow, and admitted problematic.

Sterling, by the doctor's order, took to daily riding in
summer; scouring far and wide on a swift strong horse, and
was allowed no other exercise; so that my walks with him
had, to my sorrow, ended. We saw him otherwise pretty
often; but it was only for moments in comparison. His life,
at any rate, in these circumstances was naturally devoid of
composure. The little Bayswater establishment, with all its
schemes of peaceable activity on the small or on the great
scale, was evidently set adrift; the anchor lifted, and Sterling
and his family again at sea, for farther uncertain voyaging.
Here is not thy rest; not here: — where, then! The question, What to do even for next autumn? had become the
pressing one.

A rich Bordeaux merchant, an Uncle of his Wife's, of the
name of Mr. Johnston, possessed a sumptuous mansion and
grounds, which he did not occupy, in the environs of that
southern City: it was judged that the climate might be favorable; to the house and its copious accommodation there was
welcome ingress, if Sterling chose to occupy it. Servants
were not needed, servants and conveniences enough, in the

big solitary mansion with its marble terraces, were already there. Conveniences enough within, and curiosities without. It is the "South of France," with its Gascon ways; the Garonne, *Garumna* river, the Gironde and Montaigne's country: here truly are invitations.

In short, it was decided that he and his family should move thither; there, under warmer skies, begin a new residence. The doctors promised improvement, if the place suited for a permanency; there at least, much more commodiously than elsewhere, he might put over the rigorous period of this present year. Sterling left us, I find noted, "on the first of August, 1836." The name of his fine foreign mansion is Belsito; in the village of Floirac, within short distance of Bordeaux.

Counting in his voyage to the West Indies, this is the second of some five health-journeys which, sometimes with his family, sometimes without, he had to make in all. "Five forced peregrinities;" which, in their sad and barren alternation, are the main incidents of his much-obstructed life henceforth. Five swift flights, not for any high or low object in life, but for life itself; swift jerkings aside from whatever path or object you might be following, to escape the scythe of Death. On such terms had poor Sterling henceforth to live; and surely with less complaint, with whatever result otherwise, no man could do it.

His health prospered at Bordeaux. He had, of course, new interests and objects of curiosity; but when once the household was settled in its new moorings, and the first dazzle of strangeness fairly over, he returned to his employments and pursuits, — which were, in good part, essentially the old ones. His chosen books, favorite instructors of the period, were with him; at least the world of his own thoughts was with him, and the grand ever-recurring question: What to do with that; How best to regulate that?

I remember kind and happy-looking Letters from him at Bordeaux, rich enough in interests and projects, in activities and emotions. He looked abroad over the Gironde country, over the towers and quays of Bordeaux at least with a painter's eye, which he rather eminently had, and very eminently loved to exercise. Of human acquaintances he found not many to attract him, nor could he well go much into deeper than picto-rial connection with the scene around him; but on this side too, he was, as usual, open and willing. A learned young German, tutor in some family of the neighborhood, was admitted frequently to see him; probably the only scholar in those parts with whom he could converse of an evening. One of my Letters contained notice of a pilgrimage he had made to the old Château of Montaigne; a highly interesting sight to a reading man. He wrote to me also about the Caves of St. Emilion or Libourne, hiding-place of Barbaroux, Petion and other Girondins, concerning whom I was then writing. Nay here is the Letter itself still left; and I may as well insert it, as a relic of that time. The projected "walking expedition" into France; the vision of Montaigne's old House, Barbaroux's death-scene; the Chinese *Iu-Kiao-Li* or *Two Fair Cousins:* all these things are long since asleep, as if dead; and affect one's own mind with a sense of strangeness when resuscitated: —

" *To Thomas Carlyle, Esq., Chelsea, London.*

"Belsito, near Bordeaux, 26th October, 1836.

"My dear Carlyle, — I have to thank you for two Letters, which, unlike other people's, have the writer's signature in every word as well as at the end. Your assurances of remem-brance and kindness were by no means necessary, but are not at all less pleasant. The patronage you bestow on my old stick requires the acknowledgment from me which my care of its education had not succeeded in teaching it to express for itself. May your more genial and more masculine treatment be more effectual! I remember that I used to fling it along the broad walk in Kensington Gardens, for Edward to run after it; and I suspect you will find the scars resulting from the process, on the top of the hook.

"If the purveyors of religion and its implements to this department of France supplied such commodities as waxen hecatombs, I would sacrifice one for the accomplishment of your pedestrian design; and am already meditating an appropriate invocation, *sermone pedestri*. Pray come, in the first fine days of spring; or rather let us look forward to your coming, for as to the fact, where may both or either of us be before this day six months? I am not, however, resolute as to any plan of my own that would take me either along the finite or the infinite sea. I still bear up, and do my best here; and have no distinct schemes of departure: for I am well, and well situated at present, and enjoy my books, my leisure, and the size and comfort of the house I live in. I shall go, if go I must; and not otherwise. I have sometimes thought that, if driven away later in the year, I might try Italy, — probably at first Pisa; and if so, should hope, in spite of cholera, to see your Brother, who would be helpful both to mind and body. When you write to him, pray just touch with your pen the long cobweb thread that connects me with him, and which is more visible and palpable about eighteen inches above your writing-table than anywhere else in this much becobwebbed world.

" Your account of the particular net you occupy in the great reticulation is not very consolatory; — I should be sorry if it were from thinking of it as a sort of *paries proximus*. When you slip the collar of the *French Revolution,* and the fine weather comes round again, and my life becomes insurable at less than fifty per cent, I hope to see you as merry as Philina or her husband, in spite of your having somewhat more wisdom. — And all these good things *may* be, in some twenty-six weeks or less; a space of time for which the paltriest Dutch clock would be warranted to go, without more than an hour or two of daily variation. I trust we have, both of us, souls above those that tick in country kitchens! — Of your Wife I think you say nothing in your last. Why does she not write to me? Is it because she will not stoop to nonsense, and that would be the only proper answer to an uncanonical epistle I sent her while in Scotland? Tell her she is, at all events, sure of being constantly remembered; for I play backgammon with Charles Barton for *want* of any one to play chess with.

"Of my expedition to Montaigne's old House I cannot say much: for I indited Notes thereof for my own use, and also wrote something about it to Mr. Dunn; which is as much as the old walls would well bear. It is truly an interesting place; for it does not seem as if a stone had been touched since Montaigne's time; though his house is still inhabited, and the apartment that he describes in the *Essai des Trois Commerces* might, barring the evident antiquity, have been built yesterday to realize his account. The rafters of the room which was his library have still his inscriptions on their lower faces: all very characteristic; many from *Ecclesiastes*. The view is open all round; over a rather flat, elevated country, apparently clayey ploughed lands, with little wood, no look of great population, and here and there a small stone windmill with a conical roof. The village church close by is much older than Montaigne's day. His house looks just as he describes it: a considerable building that never was at all fortified.

"St. Emilion I had not time to see or learn much of; but the place looks all very old. A very small town, built of stone; jostled into a sort of ravine, or large quarry, in the slope from the higher table-land towards the Dordogne. Quite on the ridge, at the top of the town, is an immense Gothic steeple, that would suit a cathedral, but has under it only a church (now abandoned) cut out in the sandstone rock, and of great height and size. There is a large church above ground close by, and several monastic buildings. Of the Caves I only saw some entrances. I fancy they are all artificial, but am not sure. The Dordogne is in sight below in the plain. I cannot lay my hands on any Book for you which gives an account of the time the Girondins spent here; or who precisely those were that made this their hiding-place.

"I was prepared for what you say of *Mirabeau* and its postponement, from an advertisement of the Articles, in the *Times:* — but this I only saw the day *after* I had written to Paris to order the new Number [of the *London-and-Westminster*] by mail; so I consider the Editor in my debt for ten or twelve francs of postage, which I hope to recover when we get our equitable adjustment of all things in this world.

"I have now read through Saint Simon's twenty volumes; which have well repaid me. The picture of the daily detail of a despotic court is something quite startling from its vividness and reality; and there is perhaps a much deeper interest in his innumerable portraits and biographies, — many of which, told in the quietest way, are appalling tragedies; and the best, I think, have something painful and delirious about them. I have also lounged a good deal over the *Biographie Universelle* and *Bayle*. The last I never looked into before. One would think he had spent his whole life in the Younger Pliny's windowless study; had never seen, except by candlelight; and thought the Universe a very good raw-material for books. But he is an amiable honest man; and more good material than enough was spent in making the case for that logical wheel-work of his. As to the *Biographie Universelle*, you know it better than I. I wish Craik, or some such man, could be employed on an English edition, in which the British lives should be better done. — I sent for the *Chinese Cousins* as soon as I received your Letter; but the answer was, that the book is out of print.

"Have you seen the last Number of the *Foreign Review;* where there is an article on Eckermann's *Conversations of Goethe*, written by a stupid man, but giving extracts of much interest? Goethe's talk has been running in my head for the last fortnight; and I find I am more inclined than I was to value the flowers that grow (as on the Alps) on the margin of his glaciers. I shall read his *Dichtung und Wahrheit*, and *Italian Tour*, when the books come in my way. But I have still little hope of finding in him what I should look for in Jean Paul, and what I possess in some others: a ground prolonging and encircling that on which I myself rest.

"I suppose the dramatic projects of Henry Taylor (to whom remember me cordially) are mainly *Thomas à Becket*. I too have been scheming Tragedies and Novels; — but with little notion of doing more than play the cloud-compeller, for want of more substantial work on earth. I do not know why, but my thoughts have, since I reached this, been running more on History and Poetry than on Theology and Philosophy, more

indeed than for years past. I suppose it is a providential arrangement, that I may find out I am good for as little in the
one way as the other. — In the mean time do not let my mo-
nopoly of your correspondence be only a nominal privilege.
Accept my Wife's kindest remembrances; give my love to
yours. Tell me if I can do anything for you. Do not let the
ides of March go by without starting for the Garonne: — and
believe me,

> "Yours *jusqu'à la mort sans phrase,*
>
> "JOHN STERLING."

"*La mort sans phrase*" was Sieyès's vote in the Trial of
Louis. Sterling's "Notes for his own use," which are here
mentioned in reference to that Montaigne pilgrimage of his,
were employed not long after, in an Essay on Montaigne.[1]
He also read the *Chinese Cousins,* and loved it, — as I had
expected. Of which take this memorandum : " *Iu-Kiao-Li, ou
les Deux Cousines ;* translated by Rémusat; — well translated
into English also, from his version ; and one of the notablest
Chinese Books. A book in fact by a Chinese *man of genius ;*
most strangely but recognizably such, — man of genius made
on the dragon pattern ! Recommended to me by Carlyle ; to
him by Leigh Hunt." The other points need no explanation.

By this time, I conclude, as indeed this Letter indicates, the
theological tumult was decidedly abating in him ; to which result this still hermit-life in the Gironde would undoubtedly
contribute. Tholuck, Schleiermacher, and the war of articles
and rubrics, were left in the far distance ; Nature's blue skies,
and awful eternal verities, were once more around one, and
small still voices, admonitory of many things, could in the
beautiful solitude freely reach the heart. Theologies, rubrics,
surplices, church-articles, and this enormous ever-repeated
thrashing of the straw ? A world of rotten straw ; thrashed
all into powder ; filling the Universe and blotting out the stars
and worlds : — Heaven pity you with such a thrashing-floor for
world, and its draggled dirty farthing-candle for sun ! There

[1] *London and Westminster Review;* Hare, i. 129.

is surely other worship possible for the heart of man; there should be other work, or none at all, for the intellect and creative faculty of man! —

It was here, I find, that Literature first again decisively began to dawn on Sterling as the goal he ought to aim at. To this, with his poor broken opportunities and such inward faculties as were given him, it became gradually clearer that he ought altogether to apply himself. Such result was now decisively beginning for him ; the original bent of his mind, the dim mandate of all the facts in his outward and inward condition; evidently the one wholesome tendency for him, which grew ever clearer to the end of his course, and gave at least one steady element, and that the central one, in his fluctuating existence henceforth. It was years still before he got the inky tints of that Coleridgean adventure completely bleached from his mind; but here the process had begun, — and I doubt not, we have to thank the solitude of Floirac for it a little ; which is some consolation for the illness that sent him thither.

His best hours here were occupied in purely literary occupations ; in attempts at composition on his own footing again. Unluckily in this too the road for him was now far away, after so many years of aberration ; true road not to be found all at once. But at least he was seeking it again. The *Sexton's Daughter*, which he composed here this season, did by no means altogether please us as a Poem ; but it was, or deserved to be, very welcome as a symptom of spiritual return to the open air. Adieu ye thrashing-floors of rotten straw, with bleared tallow-light for sun ; to you adieu ! The angry sordid dust-whirlwinds begin to allay themselves ; settle into soil underfoot, where their place is: glimpses, call them distant intimations still much veiled, of the everlasting azure, and a much higher and wider priesthood than that under copes and mitres, and wretched dead mediæval monkeries and extinct traditions. This was perhaps the chief intellectual result of Sterling's residence at Bordeaux, and flight to the Gironde in pursuit of health ; which does not otherwise deserve to count as an epoch or chapter with him.

In the course of the summer and autumn of 1837, I do not now find at what exact dates, he made two journeys from Bordeaux to England; the first by himself, on various small specific businesses, and uncertain outlooks; the second with his family, having at last, after hesitation, decided on removal from those parts. "The cholera had come to France;" — add to which, I suppose, his solitude at Belsito was growing irksome, and home and merry England, in comparison with the monotony of the Gironde, had again grown inviting. He had vaguely purposed to make for Nice in the coming winter; but that also the cholera or other causes prevented. His Brother Anthony, a gallant young soldier, was now in England, home from the Ionian Islands on a visit to old friends and scenes; and that doubtless was a new and strong inducement hitherward. It was this summer, I think, that the two Brothers revisited together the scene of their early boyhood at Llanblethian; a touching pilgrimage, of which John gave me account in reference to something similar of my own in Scotland, where I then was.

Here, in a Letter to his Mother, is notice of his return from the first of these sallies into England; and how doubtful all at Bordeaux still was, and how pleasant some little certainties at home. The "Annie" of whose "engagement" there is mention, was Miss Anna Barton, Mrs. John Sterling's younger sister, who, to the joy of more than one party, as appears, had accepted his friend Maurice while Sterling was in England:

"*To Mrs. Sterling, Knightsbridge, London.*

"FLOIRAC, 7th August, 1837.

"MY DEAR MOTHER, — I am now beginning to feel a little less dizzy and tired, and will try to write you a few lines to tell you of my fortunes.

"I found my things all right at the Albion. Unluckily, the steamer could not start from Brighton, and I was obliged to go over to Shoreham; but the weather cleared up, and we had rather a smooth passage into France. The wind was off the French coast, so that we were in calm water at last. We got in about ten o'clock; — too late for the Custom-house. Next morning I settled all my business early ; but was detained for horses till nine, — owing to the nearness of the Duke of Orleans, which had caused a great stir on the roads. I was for the same reason stopped at Rouen ; and I was once again stopped, on Saturday for an hour, waiting for horses ; otherwise I travelled without any delay, and in the finest weather, from Dieppe to this place, which I reached on Sunday morning at five. I took the shortest road, by Alençon, Saumur and Niort ; and was very well satisfied with my progress, — at least, till about Blaye, on the Garonne, where there was a good deal of deep sand, which, instead of running merrily through the hour-glass of Time, on the contrary clogged the wheels of my carriage. At last, however, I reached home ; and found everybody well, and glad to see me. — I felt tired and stupid, and not at all disposed to write. But I am now sorry I did not overcome my laziness, and send you a line to announce my safe arrival ; for I know that at a distance people naturally grow anxious, even without any reason.

"It seems now almost like a dream, that I have ever been away from hence. But Annie's engagement to Maurice is, I trust, a lasting memorial of my journey. I find Susan quite as much pleased as I expected with her Sister's prospects ; and satisfied that nothing could have so well secured her happiness, and mental (or rather cordial) advancement as her union to such a man. On the whole, it is a great happiness to me to look back both to this matter, and on the kindness and affection of the relatives and friends whom I saw in England. It will be a very painful disappointment to me if I should be obliged to pass the next summer without taking my Wife and Children to our own country : — we will, at all events, enjoy the hope of my doing so. In the mean time I trust you will enjoy your Tour, and on your return spend a quiet and cheerful winter. Love to my Father, and kindest regards to Mrs. Carlyle.

"Your affectionate son,

"John Sterling."

CHAPTER V.

TO MADEIRA.

STERLING'S dubieties as to continuing at Bordeaux were quickly decided. The cholera in France, the cholera in Nice, the — In fact his moorings were now loose ; and having been fairly at sea, he never could anchor himself here again. Very shortly after this Letter, he left Belsito again (for good, as it proved) ; and returned to England with his household, there to consider what should next be done.

On my return from Scotland, that year, perhaps late in September, I remember finding him lodged straitly but cheerfully, and in happy humor, in a little cottage on Blackheath ; whither his Father one day persuaded me to drive out with him for dinner. Our welcome, I can still recollect, was conspicuously cordial ; the place of dinner a kind of upper room, half garret and full of books, which seemed to be John's place of study. From a shelf, I remember also, the good soul took down a book modestly enough bound in three volumes, lettered on the back *Carlyle's French Revolution*, which had been published lately ; this he with friendly banter bade me look at as a first symptom, small but significant, that the book was not to die all at once. "One copy of it at least might hope to last the date of sheep-leather," I admitted, — and in my then mood the little fact was welcome. Our dinner, frank and happy on the part of Sterling, was peppered with abundant jolly satire from his Father : before tea, I took myself away ; towards Woolwich, I remember, where probably there was another call to make, and passage homeward by steamer : Sterling strode along with me a good bit of road in the bright sunny evening, full of lively friendly talk, and altogether kind and amiable ; and beautifully sympathetic with the loads he thought he saw on *me*, forgetful

of his own. We shook hands on the road near the foot of
Shooter's ;Hill: — at which point dim oblivious clouds rush
down; and of small or great I remember nothing more in my
history or his for some time.

Besides running much about among friends, and holding
counsels for the management of the coming winter, Sterling
was now considerably occupied with Literature again; and
indeed may be said to have already definitely taken it up as
the one practical pursuit left for him. Some correspondence
with *Blackwood's Magazine* was opening itself, under promising omens: now, and more and more henceforth, he began to
look on Literature as his real employment, after all; and was
prosecuting it with his accustomed loyalty and ardor. And
he continued ever afterwards, in spite of such fitful circumstances and uncertain outward fluctuations as his were sure of
being, to prosecute it steadily with all the strength he had.

One evening about this time, he came down to us, to
Chelsea, most likely by appointment and with stipulation for
privacy; and read, for our opinion, his Poem of the *Sexton's
Daughter*, which we now first heard of. The judgment in this
house was friendly, but not the most encouraging. We found
the piece monotonous, cast in the mould of Wordsworth, deficient in real human fervor or depth of melody, dallying on the
borders of the infantile and "goody-good;" — in fact, involved
still in the shadows of the surplice, and inculcating (on
hearsay mainly) a weak morality, which he would one day
find not to be moral at all, but in good part maudlin-hypocriti-
cal and immoral. As indeed was to be said still of most of his
performances, especially the poetical; a sickly *shadow* of the
parish-church still hanging over them, which he could by no
means recognize for sickly. *Imprimatur* nevertheless was the
concluding word, — with these grave abatements, and rhada-
manthine admonitions. To all which Sterling listened seriously and in the mildest humor. His reading, it might have
been added, had much hurt the effect of the piece: a dreary
pulpit or even conventicle manner; that flattest moaning hoo-
hoo of predetermined pathos, with a kind of rocking canter
introduced by way of intonation, each stanza the exact fellow

of the other, and the dull swing of the rocking-horse duly in
each; — no reading could be more unfavorable to Sterling's
poetry than his own. Such a mode of reading, and indeed
generally in a man of such vivacity the total absence of all
gifts for play-acting or artistic mimicry in any kind, was a
noticeable point.

After much consultation, it was settled at last that Sterling
should go to Madeira for the winter. One gray dull autumn
afternoon, towards the middle of October, I remember walking
with him to the eastern Dock region, to see his ship, and how
the final preparations in his own little cabin were proceeding
there. A dingy little ship, the deck crowded with packages,
and bustling sailors within eight-and-forty hours of lifting
anchor; a dingy chill smoky day, as I have said withal, and
a chaotic element and outlook, enough to make a friend's
heart sad. I admired the cheerful careless humor and brisk
activity of Sterling, who took the matter all on the sunny
side, as he was wont in such cases. We came home together
in manifold talk: he accepted with the due smile my last contribution to his sea-equipment, a sixpenny box of German luci-
fers purchased on the sudden in St. James's Street, fit to be
offered with laughter or with tears or with both; he was to
leave for Portsmouth almost immediately, and there go on
board. Our next news was of his safe arrival in the temperate
Isle. Mrs. Sterling and the children were left at Knightsbridge; to pass this winter with his Father and Mother.

At Madeira Sterling did well: improved in health; was
busy with much Literature; and fell in with society which
he could reckon pleasant. He was much delighted with the
scenery of the place; found the climate wholesome to him in
a marked degree; and, with good news from home, and kindly
interests here abroad, passed no disagreeable winter in that
exile. There was talking, there was writing, there was hope
of better health; he rode almost daily, in cheerful busy humor,
along those fringed shore-roads: — beautiful leafy roads and
horse-paths; with here and there a wild cataract and bridge

to look at; and always with the soft sky overhead, the dead
volcanic mountain on one hand, and broad illimitable sea
spread out on the other. Here are two Letters which give
reasonably good account of him: —

"*To Thomas Carlyle, Esq., Chelsea, London.*

"Funchal, Madeira, 16th November, 1837.

"My dear Carlyle, — I have been writing a good many
letters all in a batch, to go by the same opportunity; and I
am thoroughly weary of writing the same things over and
over again to different people. My letter to you therefore, I
fear, must have much of the character of remainder-biscuit.
But you will receive it as a proof that I do not wish you to
forget me, though it may be useless for any other purpose.

"I reached this on the 2d, after a tolerably prosperous voyage, deformed by some days of sea-sickness, but otherwise not
to be complained of. I liked my twenty fellow-passengers far
better than I expected ; — three or four of them I like much,
and continue to see frequently. The Island too is better than
I expected : so that my Barataria at least does not disappoint
me. The bold rough mountains, with mist about their summits, verdure below, and a bright sun over all, please me much ;
and I ride daily on the steep and narrow paved roads, which
no wheels ever journeyed on. The Town is clean, and there
its merits end: but I am comfortably lodged ; with a large
and pleasant sitting-room to myself. I have met with much
kindness; and see all the society I want, — though it is not
quite equal to that of London, even excluding Chelsea.

"I have got about me what Books I brought out; and have
read a little, and done some writing for *Blackwood*, — all, I
have the pleasure to inform you, prose, nay extremely prose.
I shall now be more at leisure ; and hope to get more steadily
to work; though I do not know what I shall begin upon.
As to reading, I have been looking at *Goethe*, especially the
Life, — much as a shying horse looks at a post. In truth, I
am afraid of him. I enjoy and admire him so much, and feel
I could so easily be tempted to go along with him. And yet
I have a deeply rooted and old persuasion that he was the

most splendid of anachronisms. A thoroughly, nay intensely
Pagan Life, in an age when it is men's duty to be Christian.
I therefore never take him up without a kind of inward check,
as if I were trying some forbidden spell; while, on the other
hand, there is so infinitely much to be learnt from him, and it
is so needful to understand the world we live in, and our own
age, and especially its greatest minds, that I cannot bring
myself to burn my books as the converted Magicians did, or
sink them as did Prospero. There must, as I think, have been
some prodigious defect in his mind, to let him hold such views
as his about women and some other things; and in another
respect, I find so much coldness and hollowness as to the highest truths, and feel so strongly that the Heaven he looks up
to is but a vault of ice, — that these two indications, leading
to the same conclusion, go far to convince me he was a profoundly immoral and irreligious spirit, with as rare faculties
of intelligence as ever belonged to any one. All this may be
mere *goody* weakness and twaddle, on my part: but it is a persuasion that I cannot escape from; though I should feel the
doing so to be a deliverance from a most painful load. If you
could help me, I heartily wish you would. I never take him
up without high admiration, or lay him down without real
sorrow for what he chose to be.

"I have been reading nothing else that you would much
care for. Southey's *Amadis* has amused me; and Lyell's
Geology interested me. The latter gives one the same sort of
bewildering view of the abysmal extent of Time that Astron-
omy does of Space. I do not think I shall take your advice as
to learning Portuguese. It is said to be very ill spoken here;
and assuredly it is the most direful series of nasal twangs I
ever heard. One gets on quite well with English.

" The people here are, I believe, in a very low condition;
but they do not appear miserable. I am told that the influence
of the priests makes the peasantry all Miguelites; but it is said
that nobody wants any more revolutions. There is no appearance of riot or crime; and they are all extremely civil. I was
much interested by learning that Columbus once lived here,
before he found America and fame. I have been to see a

deserted *quinta* (country-house), where there is a great deal
of curious old sculpture, in relief, upon the masonry ; many of
the figures, which are nearly as large as life, representing soldiers clad and armed much as I should suppose those of Cortez
were.   There are no buildings about the Town, of the smallest
pretensions to beauty or charm of any kind.   On the whole, if
Madeira were one's world, life would certainly rather tend to
stagnate ; but as a temporary refuge, a niche in an old ruin
where one is sheltered from the shower, it has great merit.
I am more comfortable and contented than I expected to be,
so far from home and from everybody I am closely connected
with : but, of course, it is at best a tolerable exile.

"Tell Mrs. Carlyle that I have written, since I have been
here, and am going to send to *Blackwood,* a humble imitation
of her *Watch and Canary-Bird,* entitled *The Suit of Armor
and the Skeleton.*[1]   I am conscious that I am far from having
reached the depth and fulness of despair and mockery which
distinguish the original!   But in truth there is a lightness
of tone about her style, which I hold to be invaluable: where
she makes hairstrokes, I make blotches.   I have a vehement
suspicion that my Dialogue is an entire failure ; but I cannot
be plagued with it any longer.   Tell her I will not send her
messages, but will write to her soon. — Meanwhile I am affectionately hers and yours,

"JOHN STERLING."

The next is to his Brother-in-law ; and in a still hopefuler
tone : —

"*To Charles Barton, Esq.*[2]

"FUNCHAL, MADEIRA, 3d March, 1838.

"MY DEAR CHARLES, — I have often been thinking of you
and your whereabouts in Germany, and wishing I knew more
about you ; and at last it occurred to me that you might perhaps have the same wish about me, and that therefore I should
do well to write to you.

---

[1] Came out, as will soon appear, in *Blackwood* (February, 1838).
[2] "*Hôtel de l'Europe, Berlin,*" added in Mrs. Sterling's hand.

"I have been here exactly four months, having arrived on the 2d of November, — my wedding-day; and though you perhaps may not think it a compliment to Susan, I have seldom passed four months more cheerfully and agreeably. I have of course felt my absence from my family, and missed the society of my friends; for there is not a person here whom I knew before I left England. But, on the whole, I have been in good health, and actively employed. I have a good many agreeable and valuable acquaintances, one or two of whom I hope I may hereafter reckon as friends. The weather has generally been fine, and never cold; and the scenery of the Island is of a beauty which you unhappy Northern people can have little conception of.

"It consists of a great mass of volcanic mountains, covered in their lower parts with cottages, vines and patches of vegetables. When you pass through, or over the central ridge, and get towards the North, there are woods of trees, of the laurel kind, covering the wild steep slopes, and forming some of the strangest and most beautiful prospects I have ever seen. Towards the interior, the forms of the hills become more abrupt, and loftier; and give the notion of very recent volcanic disturbances, though in fact there has been nothing of the kind since the discovery of the Island by Europeans. Among these mountains, the dark deep precipices, and narrow ravines with small streams at the bottom; the basaltic knobs and ridges on the summits; and the perpetual play of mist and cloud around them, under this bright sun and clear sky, — form landscapes which you would thoroughly enjoy, and which I much wish I could give you a notion of. The Town is on the south, and of course the sheltered side of the Island; perfectly protected from the North and East; although we have seen sometimes patches of bright snow on the dark peaks in the distance. It is a neat cheerful place; all built of gray stone, but having many of the houses colored white or red. There is not a really handsome building in it, but there is a general aspect of comfort and solidity. The shops are very poor. The English do not mix at all with the Portuguese. The Bay is a very bad anchorage; but is wide, bright and cheerful; and there are some picturesque points — one a small black island — scattered about it.

" I lived till a fortnight ago in lodgings, having two rooms, one a very good one; and paying for everything fifty-six dollars a month, the dollar being four shillings and twopence. This you will see is dear; but I could make no better arrangement, for there is an unusual affluence of strangers this year. I have now come to live with a friend, a Dr. Calvert, in a small house of our own, where I am much more comfortable, and live greatly cheaper. He is a friend of Mrs. Percival's; about my age, an Oriel man, and a very superior person. I think the chances are, we shall go home together. . . . I cannot tell you of all the other people I have become familiar with; and shall only mention in addition Bingham Baring, eldest son of Lord Ashburton, who was here for some weeks on account of a dying brother, and whom I saw a great deal of. He is a pleasant, very good-natured and rather clever man; Conservative Member for North Staffordshire.

" During the first two months I was here, I rode a great deal about the Island, having a horse regularly; and was much in agreeable company, seeing a great deal of beautiful scenery. Since then, the weather has been much more unsettled, though not cold; and I have gone about less, as I cannot risk the being wet. But I have spent my time pleasantly, reading and writing. I have written a good many things for *Blackwood;* one of which, the *Armor and the Skeleton*, I see is printed in the February Number. I have just sent them a long Tale, called the *Onyx Ring*, which cost me a good deal of trouble; and the extravagance of which, I think, would amuse you; but its length may prevent its appearance in *Blackwood.* If so, I think I should make a volume of it. I have also written some poems, and shall probably publish the *Sexton's Daughter* when I return.

" My health goes on most favorably. I have had no attack of the chest this spring; which has not happened to me since the spring before we went to Bonn; and I am told, if I take care, I may roll along for years. But I have little hope of being allowed to spend the four first months of any year in

England; and the question will be, Whether to go at once to
Italy, by way of Germany and Switzerland, with my family,
or to settle with them in England, perhaps at Hastings, and go
abroad myself when it may be necessary. I cannot decide till
I return; but I think the latter the most probable.

" To my dear Charles I do not like to use the ordinary forms
of ending a letter, for they are very inadequate to express
my sense of your long and most unvarying kindness; but be
assured no one living could say with more sincerity that he is
ever affectionately yours,

" JOHN STERLING."

Other Letters give occasionally views of the shadier side of
things : dark broken weather, in the sky and in the mind; ugly
clouds covering one's poor fitful transitory prospect, for a time,
as they might well do in Sterling's case. Meanwhile we perceive his literary business is fast developing itself; amid all
his confusions, he is never idle long. Some of his best Pieces
— the *Onyx Ring*, for one, as we perceive — were written here
this winter. Out of the turbid whirlpool of the days he strives
assiduously to snatch what he can.

Sterling's communications with *Blackwood's Magazine* had
now issued in some open sanction of him by Professor Wilson, the distinguished presiding spirit of that Periodical; a
fact naturally of high importance to him under the literary
point of view. For Wilson, with his clear flashing eye and
great genial heart, had at once recognized Sterling; and lav-
ished stormily, in his wild generous way, torrents of praise on
him in the editorial comments : which undoubtedly was one
of the gratefulest literary baptisms, by fire or by water, that
could befall a soul like Sterling's. He bore it very gently,
being indeed past the age to have his head turned by anybody's praises : nor do I think the exaggeration that was in
these eulogies did him any ill whatever; while surely their
generous encouragement did him much good, in his solitary
struggle towards new activity under such impediments as his.
Laudari a laudato ; to be called noble by one whom you and
the world recognize as noble: this great satisfaction, never

perhaps in such a degree before or after, had now been vouch-safed to Sterling; and was, as I compute, an important fact for him. He proceeded on his pilgrimage with new energy, and felt more and more as if authentically consecrated to the same.

The *Onyx Ring*, a curious Tale, with wild improbable basis, but with a noble glow of coloring and with other high merits in it, a Tale still worth reading, in which, among the imaginary characters, various friends of Sterling's are shadowed forth, not always in the truest manner, came out in *Blackwood* in the winter of this year. Surely a very high talent for paint-ing, both of scenery and persons, is visible in this Fiction; the promise of a Novel such as we have few. But there wants maturing, wants purifying of clear from unclear; — properly there want patience and steady depth. The basis, as we said, is wild and loose; and in the details, lucent often with fine color, and dipt in beautiful sunshine, there are several things mis*seen*, untrue, which is the worst species of mispainting. Witness, as Sterling himself would have by and by admitted, the "empty clockcase" (so we called it) which he has labelled Goethe, — which puts all other untruths in the Piece to silence.

One of the great alleviations of his exile at Madeira he has already celebrated to us: the pleasant circle of society he fell into there. Great luck, thinks Sterling in this voyage; as in-deed there was: but he himself, moreover, was readier than most men to fall into pleasant circles everywhere, being singu-larly prompt to make the most of any circle. Some of his Madeira acquaintanceships were really good; and one of them, if not more, ripened into comradeship and friendship for him. He says, as we saw, "The chances are, Calvert and I will come home together."

Among the English in pursuit of health, or in flight from fatal disease, that winter, was this Dr. Calvert; an excellent ingenious cheery Cumberland gentleman, about Sterling's age, and in a deeper stage of ailment, this not being his first visit to Madeira: he, warmly joining himself to Sterling, as we have

seen, was warmly received by him; so that there soon grew a
close and free intimacy between them; which for the next
three years, till poor Calvert ended his course, was a leading
element in the history of both.   Companionship in incurable
malady, a touching bond of union, was by no means purely or
chiefly a companionship in misery in their case.   The sunniest
inextinguishable cheerfulness shone, through all manner of
clouds, in both. Calvert had been travelling physician in some
family of rank, who had rewarded him with a pension, shield-
ing his own ill-health from one sad evil.   Being hopelessly
gone in pulmonary disorder, he now moved about among
friendly climates and places, seeking what alleviation there
might be; often spending his summers in the house of a sister
in the environs of London; an insatiable rider on his little
brown pony; always, wherever you might meet him, one of
the cheeriest of men.   He had plenty of speculation too, clear
glances of all kinds into religious, social, moral concerns; and
pleasantly incited Sterling's outpourings on such subjects.   He
could report of fashionable persons and manners, in a fine
human Cumberland manner; loved art, a great collector of
drawings; he had endless help and ingenuity; and was in short
every way a very human, lovable, good and nimble man, —
the laughing blue eyes of him, the clear cheery soul of him,
still redolent of the fresh Northern breezes and transparent
Mountain streams.   With this Calvert, Sterling formed a
natural intimacy; and they were to each other a great possession, mutually enlivening many a dark day during the next
three years.   They did come home together this spring; and
subsequently made several of these health-journeys in partnership.

CHAPTER VI.

LITERATURE: THE STERLING CLUB.

In spite of these wanderings, Sterling's course in life, so far as his poor life could have any course or aim beyond that of screening itself from swift death, was getting more and more clear to him; and he pursued it diligently, in the only way permitted him, by hasty snatches, in the intervals of continual fluctuation, change of place and other interruption.

Such, once for all, were the conditions appointed him. And it must be owned he had, with a most kindly temper, adjusted himself to these; nay you would have said, he loved them; it was almost as if he would have chosen them as the suitablest. Such an adaptation was there in him of volition to necessity: — for indeed they both, if well seen into, proceeded from one source. Sterling's bodily disease was the expression, under physical conditions, of the too vehement life which, under the moral, the intellectual and other aspects, incessantly struggled within him. Too vehement; — which would have required a frame of oak and iron to contain it: in a thin though most wiry body of flesh and bone, it incessantly "wore holes," and so found outlet for itself. He could take no rest, he had never learned that art; he was, as we often reproached him, fatally incapable of sitting still. Rapidity, as of pulsing auroras, as of dancing lightnings: rapidity in all forms characterized him. This, which was his bane, in many senses, being the real origin of his disorder, and of such continual necessity to move and change, — was also his antidote, so far as antidote there might be; enabling him to love change, and to snatch, as few others could have done, from the waste chaotic years, all tumbled into ruin by incessant change, what hours and minutes of available turned up. He had an incredible facility of labor.

He flashed with most piercing glance into a subject; gathered it up into organic utterability, with truly wonderful despatch, considering the success and truth attained; and threw it on paper with a swift felicity, ingenuity, brilliancy and general excellence, of which, under such conditions of swiftness, I have never seen a parallel. Essentially an *improviser* genius; as his Father too was, and of admirable completeness he too, though under a very different form.

If Sterling has done little in Literature, we may ask, What other man than he, in such circumstances, could have done anything? In virtue of these rapid faculties, which otherwise cost him so dear, he has built together, out of those wavering boiling quicksands of his few later years, a result which may justly surprise us. There is actually some result in those poor Two Volumes gathered from him, such as they are; he that reads there will not wholly lose his time, nor rise with a malison instead of a blessing on the writer. Here actually is a real seer-glance, of some compass, into the world of our day; blessed glance, once more, of an eye that is human; truer than one of a thousand, and beautifully capable of making others see with it. I have known considerable temporary reputations gained, considerable piles of temporary guineas, with loud reviewing and the like to match, on a far less basis than lies in those two volumes. Those also, I expect, will be held in memory by the world, one way or other, till the world has extracted all its benefit from them. Graceful, ingenious and illuminative reading, of their sort, for all manner of inquiring souls. A little verdant flowery island of poetic intellect, of melodious human verity; sunlit island founded on the rocks; — which the enormous circumambient continents of mown reed-grass and floating lumber, with *their* mountain-ranges of ejected stable-litter however alpine, cannot by any means or chance submerge: nay, I expect, they will not even quite hide it, this modest little island, from the well-discerning; but will float past it towards the place appointed for them, and leave said island standing. *Allah kereem,* say the Arabs! And of the English also some still know that there is a difference in the material of mountains! —

As it is this last little result, the amount of his poor and ever-interrupted literary labor, that henceforth forms the essential history of Sterling, we need not dwell at too much length on the foreign journeys, disanchorings, and nomadic vicissitudes of household, which occupy his few remaining years, and which are only the disastrous and accidental arena of this. He had now, excluding his early and more deliberate residence in the West Indies, made two flights abroad, once with his family, once without, in search of health. He had two more, in rapid succession, to make, and many more to meditate; and in the whole from Bayswater to the end, his family made no fewer than five complete changes of abode, for his sake. But these cannot be accepted as in any sense epochs in his life: the one last epoch of his life was that of his internal change towards Literature as his work in the world; and we need not linger much on these, which are the mere outer accidents of that, and had no distinguished influence in modifying that.

Friends still hoped the unrest of that brilliant too rapid soul would abate with years. Nay the doctors sometimes promised, on the physical side, a like result; prophesying that, at forty-five or some mature age, the stress of disease might quit the lungs, and direct itself to other quarters of the system. But no such result was appointed for us; neither forty-five itself, nor the ameliorations promised then, were ever to be reached. Four voyages abroad, three of them without his family, in flight from death; and at home, for a like reason, five complete shiftings of abode: in such wandering manner, and not otherwise, had Sterling to continue his pilgrimage till it ended.

Once more I must say, his cheerfulness throughout was wonderful. A certain grimmer shade, coming gradually over him, might perhaps be noticed in the concluding years; not impatience properly, yet the consciousness how much he needed patience; something more caustic in his tone of wit, more trenchant and indignant occasionally in his tone of speech: but at no moment was his activity bewildered or abated, nor did his composure ever give way. No; both his activity and

his composure he bore with him, through all weathers, to the
final close; and on the whole, right manfully he walked his
wild stern way towards the goal, and like a Roman wrapt his
mantle round him when he fell. — Let us glance, with brevity,
at what he saw and suffered in his remaining pilgrimings and
changings; and count up what fractions of spiritual fruit he
realized to us from them.

Calvert and he returned from Madeira in the spring of 1838.
Mrs. Sterling and the family had lived in Knightsbridge with
his Father's people through the winter: they now changed to
Blackheath, or ultimately Hastings, and he with them, coming
up to London pretty often; uncertain what was to be done for
next winter. Literature went on briskly here: *Blackwood* had
from him, besides the *Onyx Ring* which soon came out with
due honor, assiduous almost monthly contributions in prose
and verse. The series called *Hymns of a Hermit* was now
going on; eloquent melodies, tainted to me with something of
the same disease as the *Sexton's Daughter*, though perhaps in
a less degree, considering that the strain was in a so much
higher pitch. Still better, in clear eloquent prose, the series
of detached thoughts, entitled *Crystals from a Cavern;* of which
the set of fragments, generally a little larger in compass, called
Thoughts and Images, and again those called *Sayings and Es-
sayings*,[1] are properly continuations. Add to which, his friend
John Mill had now charge of a Review, *The London and
Westminster* its name; wherein Sterling's assistance, ardently
desired, was freely afforded, with satisfaction to both parties,
in this and the following years. An Essay on *Montaigne*, with
the notes and reminiscences already spoken of, was Sterling's
first contribution here; then one on *Simonides:*[2] both of the
present season.

On these and other businesses, slight or important, he was
often running up to London; and gave us almost the feeling
of his being resident among us. In order to meet the most
or a good many of his friends at once on such occasions, he
now furthermore contrived the scheme of a little Club, where

[1] Hare, ii. 95–167.   [2] Ib. i. 129, 188.

monthly over a frugal dinner some reunion might take place; that is, where friends of his, and withal such friends of theirs as suited, — and in fine, where a small select company definable as persons to whom it was pleasant to talk together, — might have a little opportunity of talking. The scheme was approved by the persons concerned: I have a copy of the Original Regulations, probably drawn up by Sterling, a very solid lucid piece of economics; and the List of the proposed Members, signed "James Spedding, Secretary," and dated "8th August, 1838."[1] The Club grew; was at first called the *Anonymous Club*; then, after some months of success, in compliment to the founder who had now left us again, the *Sterling Club*;— under which latter name, it once lately, for a time, owing to the Religious Newspapers, became rather famous in the world! In which strange circumstances the name was again altered, to suit weak brethren; and the Club still subsists, in a sufficiently

---

[1] Here in a Note they are, if they can be important to anybody. The marks of interrogation, attached to some Names as not yet consulted or otherwise questionable, are in the Secretary's hand: —

J. D. Acland, Esq.	H. Malden, Esq.
Hon. W. B. Baring.	J. S. Mill, Esq.
Rev. J. W. Blakesley.	R. M. Milnes, Esq.
W. Boxall, Esq.	R. Monteith, Esq.
T. Carlyle, Esq.	S. A. O'Brien, Esq.
Hon. R. Cavendish (?)	Sir F. Palgrave (?)
H. N. Coleridge, Esq. (?)	W. F. Pollok, Esq.
J. W. Colville, Esq.	Philip Pusey, Esq.
Allan Cunningham, Esq. (?)	A. Rio, Esq.
Rev. H. Donn.	C. Romilly, Esq.
F. H. Doyle, Esq.	James Spedding, Esq.
C. L. Eastlake, Esq.	Rev. John Sterling.
Alex. Ellice, Esq.	Alfred Tennyson, Esq.
J. F. Elliott, Esq.	Rev. Connop Thirlwall.
Copley Fielding, Esq.	Rev. W. Hepworth Thompson.
Rev. J. C. Hare.	Edward Twisleton, Esq.
Sir Edmund Head (?)	G. S. Venables, Esq.
D. D. Heath, Esq.	Samuel Wood, Esq.
G. C. Lewis, Esq.	Rev. T. Worsley.
H. L. Lushington, Esq.	
The Lord Lyttleton.	James Spedding, *Secretary.*
C. Macarthy, Esq.	8th August, 1838.

flourishing though happily once more a private condition.
That is the origin and genesis of poor Sterling's Club; which,
having honestly paid the shot for itself at Will's Coffee-house
or elsewhere, rashly fancied its bits of affairs were quite settled; and once little thought of getting into Books of History
with them! —

But now, Autumn approaching, Sterling had to quit Clubs,
for matters of sadder consideration. A new removal, what we
call "his third peregrinity," had to be decided on; and it was
resolved that Rome should be the goal of it, the journey to be
done in company with Calvert, whom also the Italian climate
might be made to serve instead of Madeira. One of the liveliest recollections I have, connected with the *Anonymous Club,*
is that of once escorting Sterling, after a certain meeting there,
which I had seen only towards the end, and now remember
nothing of, — except that, on breaking up, he proved to be
encumbered with a carpet-bag, and could not at once find a
cab for Knightsbridge. Some small bantering hereupon, during the instants of embargo. But we carried his carpet-bag,
slinging it on my stick, two or three of us alternately, through
dusty vacant streets, under the gaslights and the stars, towards
the surest cab-stand; still jesting, or pretending to jest, he
and we, not in the mirthfulest manner; and had (I suppose)
our own feelings about the poor Pilgrim, who was to go on the
morrow, and had hurried to meet us in this way, as the last
thing before leaving England.

CHAPTER VII.

ITALY.

THE journey to Italy was undertaken by advice of Sir James
Clark, reckoned the chief authority in pulmonary therapeu-
tics; who prophesied important improvements from it, and
perhaps even the possibility henceforth of living all the year

PALACE OF THE CÆSARS.

Vol. 13. p. 162.

in some English home. Mrs. Sterling and the children continued in a house avowedly temporary, a furnished house at
Hastings, through the winter. The two friends had set off
for Belgium, while the due warmth was still in the air. They
traversed Belgium, looking well at pictures and such objects;
ascended the Rhine; rapidly traversed Switzerland and the
Alps; issuing upon Italy and Milan, with immense appetite
for pictures, and time still to gratify themselves in that pursuit, and be deliberate in their approach to Rome. We will
take this free-flowing sketch of their passage over the Alps;
written amid "the rocks of Arona," — Santo Borromeo's country, and poor little Mignon's! The "elder Perdonnets" are
opulent Lausanne people, to whose late son Sterling had been
very kind in Madeira the year before: —

"*To Mrs. Sterling, Knightsbridge, London.*

"ARONA on the LAGO MAGGIORE, 8th Oct., 1838.

"MY DEAR MOTHER, — I bring down the story of my proceedings to the present time since the 29th of September.
I think it must have been after that day that I was at a great
breakfast at the elder Perdonnets', with whom I had declined
to dine, not choosing to go out at night. . . . I was taken by
my hostess to see several pretty pleasure-grounds and points
of view in the neighborhood; and latterly Calvert was better,
and able to go with us. He was in force again, and our passports were all settled so as to enable us to start on the morning of the 2d, after taking leave of our kind entertainer with
thanks for her infinite kindness.

"We reached St. Maurice early that evening; having had
the Dent du Midi close to us for several hours; glittering like
the top of a silver teapot, far up in the sky. Our course lay
along the Valley of the Rhone; which is considered one of
the least beautiful parts of Switzerland, and perhaps for this
reason pleased us, as we had not been prepared to expect much.
We saw, before reaching the foot of the Alpine pass at Brieg,
two rather celebrated Waterfalls; the one the Pissevache,
which has no more beauty than any waterfall one hundred
or two hundred feet high must necessarily have: the other,

near Tourtemagne, is much more pleasing, having foliage
round it, and being in a secluded dell. If you buy a Swiss
Waterfall, choose this one.

"Our second day took us through Martigny to Sion, celebrated for its picturesque towers upon detached hills, for its
strong Romanism and its population of *crétins*, — that is,
maimed idiots having the *goître*. It looked to us a more
thriving place than we expected. They are building a great
deal; among other things, a new Bishop's Palace and a new
Nunnery, — to inhabit either of which *ex officio* I feel myself
very unsuitable. From Sion we came to Brieg; a little village in a nook, close under an enormous mountain and glacier,
where it lies like a molehill, or something smaller, at the foot
of a haystack. Here also we slept; and the next day our
voiturier, who had brought us from Lausanne, started with us
up the Simplon Pass; helped on by two extra horses.

"The beginning of the road was rather cheerful; having
a good deal of green pasturage, and some mountain villages;
but it soon becomes dreary and savage in aspect, and but for
our bright sky and warm air, would have been truly dismal.
However, we gained gradually a distinct and near view of
several large glaciers; and reached at last the high and melancholy valleys of the Upper Alps; where even the pines
become scanty, and no sound is heard but the wheels of one's
carriage, except when there happens to be a storm or an avalanche, neither of which entertained us. There is, here and
there, a small stream of water pouring from the snow; but
this is rather a monotonous accompaniment to the general
desolation than an interruption of it. The road itself is
certainly very good, and impresses one with a strong notion
of human power. But the common descriptions are much
exaggerated; and many of what the Guide-Books call 'galleries' are merely parts of the road supported by a wall built
against the rock, and have nothing like a roof above them.
The 'stupendous bridges,' as they are called, might be
packed, a dozen together, into one arch of London Bridge;
and they are seldom even very striking from the depth below.
The roadway is excellent, and kept in the best order. On

the whole, I am very glad to have travelled the most famous road in Europe, and to have had delightful weather for doing so, as indeed we have had ever since we left Lausanne. The Italian descent is greatly more remarkable than the other side.

"We slept near the top, at the Village of Simplon, in a very fair and well-warmed inn, close to a mountain stream, which is one of the great ornaments of this side of the road. We have here passed into a region of granite, from that of limestone, and what is called gneiss. The valleys are sharper and closer, — like cracks in a hard and solid mass; — and there is much more of the startling contrast of light and shade, as well as more angular boldness of outline; to all which the more abundant waters add a fresh and vivacious interest. Looking back through one of these abysmal gorges, one sees two torrents dashing together, the precipice and ridge on one side, pitch-black with shade; and that on the other all flaming gold; while behind rises, in a huge cone, one of the glacier summits of the chain. The stream at one's feet rushes at a leap some two hundred feet down, and is bordered with pines and beeches, struggling through a ruined world of clefts and boulders. I never saw anything so much resembling some of the *Circles* described by Dante. From Simplon we made for Duomo d'Ossola; having broken out, as through the mouth of a mine, into green and fertile valleys full of vines and chestnuts, and white villages, — in short, into sunshine and Italy.

"At this place we dismissed our Swiss voiturier, and took an Italian one; who conveyed us to Omegna on the Lake of Orta; a place little visited by English travellers, but which fully repaid us the trouble of going there. We were lodged in a simple and even rude Italian inn; where they cannot speak a word of French; where we occupied a barn-like room, with a huge chimney fit to lodge a hundred ghosts, whom we expelled by dint of a hot woodfire. There were two beds, and as it happened good ones, in this strange old apartment; which was adorned by pictures of Architecture, and by Heads of Saints, better than many at the Royal Academy Exhibition,

and which one paid nothing for looking at. The thorough
Italian character of the whole scene amused us, much more
than Meurice's at Paris would have done; for we had voluble,
commonplace good-humor, with the aspect and accessories of
a den of banditti.

"To-day we have seen the Lake of Orta, have walked for
some miles among its vineyards and chestnuts; and thence
have come, by Baveno, to this place;—having seen by the
way, I believe, the most beautiful part of the Lago Maggiore,
and certainly the most cheerful, complete and extended example of fine scenery I have ever fallen in with. Here we are,
much to my wonder,—for it seems too good to be true,—
fairly in Italy; and as yet my journey has been a pleasanter
and more instructive, and in point of health a more successful
one, than I at all imagined possible. Calvert and I go on as
well as can be. I let him have his way about natural science,
and he only laughs benignly when he thinks me absurd in my
moral speculations. My only regrets are caused by my sepa-
ration from my family and friends, and by the hurry I have
been living in, which has prevented me doing any work,—
and compelled me to write to you at a good deal faster rate
than the *vapore* moves on the Lago Maggiore. It will take me
to-morrow to Sesto Calende, whence we go to Varese. We
shall not be at Milan for some days. Write thither, if you
are kind enough to write at all, till I give you another address.
Love to my Father.

"Your affectionate son,
"JOHN STERLING."

Omitting Milan, Florence nearly all, and much about " Art,"
Michael Angelo, and other aerial matters, here are some select terrestrial glimpses, the fittest I can find, of his progress
towards Rome:—

To his Mother.

"*Lucca, Nov. 27th,* 1838.—I had dreams, like other people,
before I came here, of what the Lombard Lakes must be;
and the week I spent among them has left me an image,
not only more distinct, but far more warm, shining and

various, and more deeply attractive in innumerable respects,
than all I had before conceived of them. And so also it has
been with Florence; where I spent three weeks: enough for
the first hazy radiant dawn of sympathy to pass away; yet
constantly adding an increase of knowledge and of love, while
I examined, and tried to understand, the wonderful minds that
have left behind them there such abundant traces of their
presence. . . . On Sunday, the day before I left Florence,
I went to the highest part of the Grand Duke's Garden of
Boboli, which commands a view of most of the City, and of
the vale of the Arno to the westward; where, as we had been
visited by several rainy days, and now at last had a very fine
one, the whole prospect was in its highest beauty. The mass
of buildings, chiefly on the other side of the River, is sufficient
to fill the eye, without perplexing the mind by vastness like
that of London; and its name and history, its outline and
large and picturesque buildings, give it grandeur of a higher
order than that of mere multitudinous extent. The Hills that
border the Valley of the Arno are also very pleasing and striking to look upon; and the view of the rich Plain, glimmering
away into blue distance, covered with an endless web of villages and country-houses, is one of the most delightful images
of human well-being I have ever seen. . . .

"Very shortly before leaving Florence, I went through the
house of Michael Angelo; which is still possessed by persons
of the same family, descendants, I believe, of his Nephew.
There is in it his 'first work in marble,' as it is called; and
a few drawings, — all with the stamp of his enginery upon
them, which was more powerful than all the steam in London. . . . On the whole, though I have done no work in Florence that can be of any use or pleasure to others, except my
Letters to my Wife, — I leave it with the certainty of much
valuable knowledge gained there, and with a most pleasant
remembrance of the busy and thoughtful days I owe to it.

"We left Florence before seven yesterday morning [26th
November] for this place; travelling on the northern side of
the Arno, by Prato, Pistoia, Pescia. We tried to see some

old frescos in a Church at Prato; but found the Priests all about, saying mass; and of course did not venture to put our hands into a hive where the bees were buzzing and on the wing. Pistoia we only coasted. A little on one side of it, there is a Hill, the first on the road from Florence; which we walked up, and had a very lively and brilliant prospect over the road we had just travelled, and the town of Pistoia. Thence to this place the whole land is beautiful, and in the highest degree prosperous, — in short, to speak metaphorically, all dotted with Leghorn bonnets, and streaming with olive-oil. The girls here are said to employ themselves chiefly in platting straw, which is a profitable employment; and the slightness and quiet of the work are said to be much more favorable to beauty than the coarser kinds of labor performed by the country-women elsewhere. Certain it is that I saw more pretty women in Pescia, in the hour I spent there, than I ever before met with among the same numbers of the 'phare sect.' Wherefore, as a memorial of them, I bought there several Legends of Female Saints and Martyrs, and of other Ladies quite the reverse, and held up as warnings; all of which are written in *ottava rima*, and sold for three halfpence apiece. But unhappily I have not yet had time to read them. This Town has 30,000 inhabitants, and is surrounded by Walls, laid out as walks, and evidently not at present intended to be besieged, — for which reason, this morning, I merely walked on them round the Town, and did not besiege them. . . .

"The Cathedral [of Lucca] contains some Relics; which have undoubtedly worked miracles on the imagination of the people hereabouts. The Grandfather of all Relics (as the Arabs would say) in the place is the *Volto Santo*, which is a Face of the Saviour appertaining to a wooden Crucifix. Now you must know that, after the ascension of Christ, Nicodemus was ordered by an Angel to carve an image of him; and went accordingly with a hatchet, and cut down a cedar for that purpose. He then proceeded to carve the figure; and being tired, fell asleep before he had done the face; which however, on awaking, he found completed by celestial aid. This image was brought to Lucca, from Leghorn, I think, where it had

arrived in a ship, 'more than a thousand years ago,' and has
ever since been kept, in purple and fine linen and gold and
diamonds, quietly working miracles. I saw the gilt Shrine
of it; and also a Hatchet which refused to cut off the head
of an innocent man, who had been condemned to death, and
who prayed to the *Volto Santo*. I suppose it is by way of
economy (they being a frugal people) that the Italians have
their Book of Common Prayer and their Arabian Nights'
Entertainments condensed into one."

To the Same.

" *Pisa, December 2d,* 1838. — Pisa is very unfairly treated
in all the Books I have read. It seems to me a quiet, but
very agreeable place ; with wide clean streets, and a look of
stability and comfort ; and I admire the Cathedral and its
appendages more, the more I see them. The leaning of the
Tower is to my eye decidedly unpleasant ; but it is a beautiful building nevertheless, and the view from the top is,
under a bright sky, remarkably lively and satisfactory. The
Lucchese Hills form a fine mass, and the sea must in clear
weather be very distinct. There was some haze over it when
I was up, though the land was all clear. I could just see the
Leghorn Light-house. Leghorn itself I shall not be able to
visit. . . .

"The quiet gracefulness of Italian life, and the mental
maturity and vigor of Germany, have a great charm when
compared with the restless whirl of England, and the chorus
of mingled yells and groans sent up by our parties and sects,
and by the suffering and bewildered crowds of the laboring
people. Our politics make my heart ache, whenever I think
of them. The base selfish frenzies of factions seem to me, at
this distance, half diabolic ; and I am out of the way of knowing anything that may be quietly a-doing to elevate the standard of wise and temperate manhood in the country, and to
diffuse the means of physical and moral well-being among all
the people. . . . I will write to my Father as soon as I can
after reaching the capital of his friend the Pope, — who, if he
had happened to be born an English gentleman, would no

doubt by this time be a respectable old-gentlemanly gouty
member of the Carlton. I have often amused myself by
thinking what a mere accident it is that Phillpotts is not
Archbishop of Tuam, and M'Hale Bishop of Exeter; and how
slight a change of dress, and of a few catchwords, would even
now enable them to fill those respective posts with all the pro-
priety and discretion they display in their present positions."

At Rome he found the Crawfords, known to him long since;
and at different dates other English friends old and new; and
was altogether in the liveliest humor, no end to his activities
and speculations. Of all which, during the next four months,
the Letters now before me give abundant record, — far too
abundant for our objects here. His grand pursuit, as natural
at Rome, was Art; into which metaphysical domain we shall
not follow him; preferring to pick out, here and there, something of concrete and human. Of his interests, researches,
speculations and descriptions on this subject of Art, there is
always rather a superabundance, especially in the Italian Tour.
Unfortunately, in the hard weather, poor Calvert fell ill; and
Sterling, along with his Art-studies, distinguished himself as
a sick-nurse till his poor comrade got afoot again. His general impressions of the scene and what it held for him may
be read in the following excerpts. The Letters are all dated
Rome, and addressed to his Father or Mother : —

" *December 21st*, 1838. — Of Rome itself, as a whole, there
are infinite things to be said, well worth saying; but I shall
confine myself to two remarks : first, that while the Monuments and works of Art gain in wondrousness and significance
by familiarity with them, the actual life of Rome, the Papacy
and its pride, lose; and though one gets accustomed to Cardinals and Friars and Swiss Guards, and ragged beggars and
the finery of London and Paris, all rolling on together, and sees
how it is that they subsist in a sort of spurious unity, one
loses all tendency to idealize the Metropolis and System of
the Hierarchy into anything higher than a piece of showy
stage-declamation, at bottom, in our day, thoroughly mean
and prosaic. My other remark is, that Rome, seen from the

tower of the Capitol, from the Pincian or the Janiculum, is at this day one of the most beautiful spectacles which eyes ever beheld. The company of great domes rising from a mass of large and solid buildings, with a few stone-pines and scattered edifices on the outskirts; the broken bare Campagna all around; the Alban Hills not far, and the purple range of Sabine Mountains in the distance with a cope of snow; — this seen in the clear air, and the whole spiritualized by endless recollections, and a sense of the grave and lofty reality of human existence which has had this place for a main theatre, fills at once the eyes and heart more forcibly, and to me delightfully, than I can find words to say."

"*January 22d*, 1839. — The Modern Rome, Pope and all inclusive, are a shabby attempt at something adequate to fill the place of the old Commonwealth. It is easy enough to live among them, and there is much to amuse and even interest a spectator; but the native existence of the place is now thin and hollow, and there is a stamp of littleness, and childish poverty of taste, upon all the great Christian buildings I have seen here, — not excepting St. Peter's; which is crammed with bits of colored marble and gilding, and Gog-and-Magog colossal statues of saints (looking prodigiously small), and mosaics from the worst pictures in Rome; and has altogether, with most imposing size and lavish splendor, a tang of Guildhall finery about it that contrasts oddly with the melancholy vastness and simplicity of the Ancient Monuments, though these have not the Athenian elegance. I recur perpetually to the galleries of Sculpture in the Vatican, and to the Frescos of Raffael and Michael Angelo, of inexhaustible beauty and greatness, and to the general aspect of the City and the Country round it, as the most impressive scene on earth. But the Modern City, with its churches, palaces, priests and beggars, is far from sublime."

Of about the same date, here is another paragraph worth inserting: "Gladstone has three little agate crosses which he will give you for my little girls. Calvert bought them, as a present, for 'the bodies,' at Martigny in Switzerland, and I have had no earlier opportunity of sending them. Will you

despatch them to Hastings when you have an opportunity ?
I have not yet seen Gladstone's *Church and State ;* but as
there is a copy in Rome, I hope soon to lay hands on it. I saw
yesterday in the *Times* a furious, and I am sorry to say, most
absurd attack on him and it, and the new Oxonian school."

"*February 28th,* 1839. — There is among the people plenty
of squalid misery ; though not nearly so much as, they say,
exists in Ireland ; and here there is a certain freedom and
freshness of manners, a dash of Southern enjoyment in the
condition of the meanest and most miserable. There is, I
suppose, as little as well can be of conscience or artificial
cultivation of any kind ; but there is not the affectation of a
virtue which they do not possess, nor any feeling of being
despised for the want of it ; and where life generally is so
inert, except as to its passions and material wants, there is
not the bitter consciousness of having been beaten by the more
prosperous, in a race which the greater number have never
thought of running. Among the laboring poor of Rome, a
bribe will buy a crime ; but if common work procures enough
for a day's food or idleness, ten times the sum will not induce
them to toil on, as an English workman would, for the sake
of rising in the world. Sixpence any day will put any of
them at the top of the only tree they care for, — that on
which grows the fruit of idleness. It is striking to see the
way in which, in magnificent churches, the most ragged beggars kneel on the pavement before some favorite altar in the
midst of well-dressed women and of gazing foreigners. Or
sometimes you will see one with a child come in from the
street where she has been begging, put herself in a corner,
say a prayer (probably for the success of her petitions), and
then return to beg again. There is wonderfully little of any
moral strength connected with this devotion ; but still it is
better than nothing, and more than is often found among the
men of the upper classes in Rome. I believe the Clergy to be
generally profligate, and the state of domestic morals as bad
as it has ever been represented." —

Or, in sudden contrast, take this other glance homeward ; a
Letter to his eldest child ; in which kind of Letters, more than

in any other, Sterling seems to me to excel. Readers recollect the hurricane in St. Vincent; the hasty removal to a neighbor's house, and the birth of a son there, soon after. The boy has grown to some articulation, during these seven years; and his Father, from the new foreign scene of Priests and Dilettanti, thus addresses him : —

"*To Master Edward C. Sterling, Hastings.*

"ROME, 21st January, 1839.

"MY DEAR EDWARD, — I was very glad to receive your Letter, which showed me that you have learned something since I left home. If you knew how much pleasure it gave me to see your handwriting, I am sure you would take pains to be able to write well, that you might often send me letters, and tell me a great many things which I should like to know about Mamma and your Sisters as well as yourself.

"If I go to Vesuvius, I will try to carry away a bit of the lava, which you wish for. There has lately been a great eruption, as it is called, of that Mountain; which means a great breaking-out of hot ashes and fire, and of melted stones which is called lava.

"Miss Clark is very kind to take so much pains with you; and I trust you will show that you are obliged to her, by paying attention to all she tells you. When you see how much more grown people know than you, you ought to be anxious to learn all you can from those who teach you; and as there are so many wise and good things written in Books, you ought to try to read early and carefully ; that you may learn something of what God has made you able to know. There are Libraries containing very many thousands of Volumes; and all that is written in these is, — accounts of some part or other of the World which God has made, or of the Thoughts which he has enabled men to have in their minds. Some Books are descriptions of the earth itself, with its rocks and ground and water, and of the air and clouds, and the stars and moon and sun, which shine so beautifully in the sky. Some tell you about the things that grow upon the ground ; the many millions of plants, from little mosses and threads of grass up to great trees

and forests. Some also contain accounts of living things :
flies, worms, fishes, birds and four-legged beasts. And some,
which are the most, are about men and their thoughts and
doings. These are the most important of all; for men are the
best and most wonderful creatures of God in the world; being
the only ones able to know him and love him, and to try of
their own accord to do his will.

"These Books about men are also the most important to us,
because we ourselves are human beings, and may learn from
such Books what we ought to think and to do and to try to be.
Some of them describe what sort of people have lived in old
times and in other countries. By reading them, we know what
is the difference between ourselves in England now, and the
famous nations which lived in former days. Such were the
Egyptians who built the Pyramids, which are the greatest
heaps of stone upon the face of the earth : and the Babylo-
nians, who had a city with huge walls, built of bricks, having
writing on them that no one in our time has been able to make
out. There were also the Jews, who were the only ancient
people that knew how wonderful and how good God is : and
the Greeks, who were the wisest of all in thinking about men's
lives and hearts, and who knew best how to make fine statues
and buildings, and to write wise books. By Books also we
may learn what sort. of people the old Romans were, whose
chief city was Rome, where I am now ; and how brave and
skilful they were in war ; and how well they could govern and
teach many nations which they had conquered. It is from
Books, too, that you must learn what kind of men were our
Ancestors in the Northern part of Europe, who belonged to
the tribes that did the most towards pulling down the power
of the Romans : and you will see in the same way how Christianity was sent among them by God, to make them wiser and
more peaceful, and more noble in their minds; and how all
the nations that now are in Europe, and especially the Italians
and the Germans, and the French and the English, came to be
what they now are. — It is well worth knowing (and it can be
known only by reading) how the Germans found out the Print-
ing of Books, and what great changes this has made in the.

world. And everybody in England ought to try to understand how the English came to have their Parliaments and Laws; and to have fleets that sail over all seas of the world.

"Besides learning all these things, and a great many more about different times and countries, you may learn from Books, what is the truth of God's will, and what are the best and wisest thoughts, and the most beautiful words; and how men are able to lead very right lives, and to do a great deal to better the world. I have spent a great part of my life in reading; and I hope you will come to like it as much as I do, and to learn in this way all that I know.

"But it is a still more serious matter that you should try to be obedient and gentle; and to command your temper; and to think of other people's pleasure rather than your own, and of what you *ought* to do rather than what you *like*. If you try to be better for all you read, as well as wiser, you will find Books a great help towards goodness as well as knowledge, — and above all other Books, the Bible; which tells us of the will of God, and of the love of Jesus Christ towards God and men.

"I had a Letter from Mamma to-day, which left Hastings on the 10th of this month. I was very glad to find in it that you were all well and happy; but I know Mamma is not well, — and is likely to be more uncomfortable every day for some time. So I hope you will all take care to give her as little trouble as possible. After sending you so much advice, I shall write a little Story to divert you. — I am, my dear Boy,

"Your affectionate Father,

"JOHN STERLING."

The "Story" is lost, destroyed, as are many such which Sterling wrote, with great felicity, I am told, and much to the satisfaction of the young folk, when the humor took him.

Besides these plentiful communications still left, I remember long Letters, not now extant, principally addressed to his Wife, of which we and the circle at Knightsbridge had due perusal, treating with animated copiousness about all manner of picture-galleries, pictures, statues and objects of Art at Rome, and on the road to Rome and from it, wheresoever his course led him into neighborhood of such objects. That was Sterling's habit. It is expected in this Nineteenth Century that a man of culture shall understand and worship Art: among the windy gospels addressed to our poor Century there are few louder than this of Art; — and if the Century expects that every man shall do his duty, surely Sterling was not the man to balk it! Various extracts from these picture-surveys are given in Hare; the others, I suppose, Sterling himself subsequently destroyed, not valuing them much.

Certainly no stranger could address himself more eagerly to reap what artistic harvest Rome offers, which is reckoned the peculiar produce of Rome among cities under the sun; to all galleries, churches, sistine chapels, ruins, coliseums, and artistic or dilettante shrines he zealously pilgrimed; and had much to say then and afterwards, and with real technical and historical knowledge I believe, about the objects of devotion there. But it often struck me as a question, Whether all this even to himself was not, more or less, a nebulous kind of element; prescribed not by Nature and her verities, but by the Century expecting every man to do his duty? Whether not perhaps, in good part, temporary dilettante cloudland of our poor Century; — or can it be the real diviner Pisgah height, and everlasting mount of vision, for man's soul in any Century? And I think Sterling himself bent towards a negative conclusion, in the course of years. Certainly, of all subjects this was the one I cared least to hear even Sterling talk of: indeed it is a subject on which earnest men, abhorrent of hypocrisy and speech that has no meaning, are admonished to silence in this sad time, and had better, in such a Babel as we have got into for the present, "perambulate their picture-gallery with little or no speech."

Here is another and to me much more earnest kind of "Art," which renders Rome unique among the cities of the world; of this we will, in preference, take a glance through Sterling's eyes: —

"*January 22d*, 1839. — On Friday last there was a great

Festival at St. Peter's; the only one I have seen. The Church
was decorated with crimson hangings, and the choir fitted up
with seats and galleries, and a throne for the Pope. There
were perhaps a couple of hundred guards of different kinds;
and three or four hundred English ladies, and not so many
foreign male spectators; so that the place looked empty. The
Cardinals in scarlet, and Monsignori in purple, were there;
and a body of officiating Clergy. The Pope was carried in
in his chair on men's shoulders, wearing the Triple Crown;
which I have thus actually seen: it is something like a gigantic Egg, and of the same color, with three little bands of
gold, — very large Egg-shell with three streaks of the yolk
smeared round it. He was dressed in white silk robes, with
gold trimmings.

" It was a fine piece of state-show; though, as there are three
or four such Festivals yearly, of course there is none of the
eager interest which breaks out at coronations and similar rare
events; no explosion of unwonted velvets, jewels, carriages
and footmen, such as London and Milan have lately enjoyed.
I guessed all the people in St. Peter's, including performers
and spectators, at 2,000; where 20,000 would hardly have been
a crushing crowd. Mass was performed, and a stupid but short
Latin sermon delivered by a lad, in honor of St. Peter, who
would have been much astonished if he could have heard it.
The genuflections, and train-bearings, and folding up the tails
of silk petticoats while the Pontiff knelt, and the train of Cardinals going up to kiss his Ring, and so forth, — made on me
the impression of something immeasurably old and sepulchral,
such as might suit the Grand Lama's court, or the inside of an
Egyptian Pyramid; or as if the Hieroglyphics on one of the
Obelisks here should begin to pace and gesticulate, and nod
their bestial heads upon the granite tablets. The careless by-
standers, the London ladies with their eye-glasses and look of
an Opera-box, the yawning young gentlemen of the *Guarda
Nobile,* and the laugh of one of the file of vermilion Priests
round the steps of the altar at the whispered good thing of
his neighbor, brought one back to nothing indeed of a very
lofty kind, but still to the Nineteenth Century." —

"At the great Benediction of the City and the World on Easter Sunday by the Pope," he writes afterwards, "there was a large crowd both native and foreign, hundreds of carriages, and thousands of the lower orders of people from the country; but even of the poor hardly one in twenty took off his hat, and a still smaller number knelt down. A few years ago, not a head was covered, nor was there a knee which did not bow." — A very decadent "Holiness of our Lord the Pope," it would appear! —

Sterling's view of the Pope, as seen in these his gala days, doing his big play-actorism under God's earnest sky, was much more substantial to me than his studies in the picture-galleries. To Mr. Hare also he writes: "I have seen the Pope in all his pomp at St. Peter's; and he looked to me a mere lie in livery. The Romish Controversy is doubtless a much more difficult one than the managers of the Religious-Tract Society fancy, because it is a theoretical dispute; and in dealing with notions and authorities, I can quite understand how a mere student in a library, with no eye for facts, should take either one side or other. But how any man with clear head and honest heart, and capable of seeing realities, and distinguishing them from scenic falsehoods, should, after living in a Romanist country, and especially at Rome, be inclined to side with Leo against Luther, I cannot understand."[1]

It is fit surely to recognize with admiring joy any glimpse of the Beautiful and the Eternal that is hung out for us, in color, in form or tone, in canvas, stone, or atmospheric air, and made accessible by any sense, in this world: but it is greatly fitter still (little as we are used that way) to shudder in pity and abhorrence over the scandalous tragedy, transcendent nadir of human ugliness and contemptibility, which under the daring title of religious worship, and practical recognition of the Highest God, daily and hourly everywhere transacts itself there. And, alas, not there only, but elsewhere, everywhere more or less; whereby our sense is so blunted to it; — whence, in all provinces of human life, these tears! —

But let us take a glance at the Carnival, since we are here.

Hare, p. cxviii.

The Letters, as before, are addressed to Knightsbridge; the date *Rome :* —

"*February 5th,* 1839. — The Carnival began yesterday. It is a curious example of the trifling things which will heartily amuse tens of thousands of grown people, precisely because they are trifling, and therefore a relief from serious business, cares and labors. The Corso is a street about a mile long, and about as broad as Jermyn Street; but bordered by much loftier houses, with many palaces and churches, and has two or three small squares opening into it. Carriages, mostly open, drove up and down it for two or three hours; and the contents were shot at with handfuls of comfits from the windows, — in the hope of making them as non-content as possible, — while they returned the fire to the best of their inferior ability. The populace, among whom was I, walked about; perhaps one in fifty were masked in character; but there was little in the masquerade either of splendor of costume or liveliness of mimicry. However, the whole scene was very gay; there were a good many troops about, and some of them heavy dragoons, who flourished their swords with the magnanimity of our Life-Guards, to repel the encroachments of too ambitious little boys. Most of the windows and balconies were hung with colored drapery; and there were flags, trumpets, nosegays and flirtations of all shapes and sizes. The best of all was, that there was laughter enough to have frightened Cassius out of his thin carcass, could the lean old homicide have been present, otherwise than as a fleshless ghost; — in which capacity I thought I had a glimpse of him looking over the shoulder of a parti-colored clown, in a carriage full of London Cockneys driving towards the Capitol. This good-humored foolery will go on for several days to come, ending always with the celebrated Horse-race, of horses without riders. The long street is cleared in the centre by troops, and half a dozen quadrupeds, ornamented like Grimaldi in a London pantomime, scamper away, with the mob closing and roaring at their heels."

"*February 9th,* 1839. — The usual state of Rome is quiet and sober. One could almost fancy the actual generation held their breath, and stole by on tiptoe, in presence of so memorable a past. But during the Carnival all mankind, womankind and childkind think it unbecoming not to play the fool. The modern donkey pokes its head out of the lion's skin of old Rome, and brays out the absurdest of asinine roundelays. Conceive twenty thousand grown people in a long street, at the windows, on the footways, and in carriages, amused day after day for several hours in pelting and being pelted with handfuls of mock or real sugar-plums; and this no name or pretence, but real downright showers of plaster comfits, from which people guard their eyes with meshes of wire. As sure as a carriage passes under a window or balcony where are acquaintances of theirs, down comes a shower of hail, ineffectually returned from below. The parties in two crossing carriages similarly assault each other; and there are long balconies hung the whole way with a deep canvas pocket full of this mortal shot. One Russian Grand Duke goes with a troop of youngsters in a wagon, all dressed in brown linen frocks and masked, and pelts among the most furious, also being pelted. The children are of course preeminently vigorous, and there is a considerable circulation of real sugar-plums, which supply consolation for all disappointments."

The whole to conclude, as is proper, with a display, with two displays, of fireworks; in which art, as in some others, Rome is unrivalled: —

"*February 9th*, 1839. — It seems to be the ambition of all the lower classes to wear a mask and showy grotesque disguise of some kind; and I believe many of the upper ranks do the same. They even put St. Peter's into masquerade; and make it a Cathedral of Lamplight instead of a stone one. Two evenings ago this feat was performed; and I was able to see it from the rooms of a friend near this, which command an excellent view of it. I never saw so beautiful an effect of artificial light. The evening was perfectly serene and clear; the principal lines of the building, the columns, architrave and pediment of the front, the two inferior cupolas, the curves of the dome from which the dome rises, the ribs of the dome itself, the small oriel windows between them, and the lantern

and ball and cross, — all were delineated in the clear vault
of air by lines of pale yellow fire. The dome of another
great Church, much nearer to the eye, stood up as a great
black mass,.— a funereal contrast to the luminous taber-
nacle.

" While I was looking at this latter, a red blaze burst from
the summit, and at the same moment seemed to flash over
the whole building, filling up the pale outline with a simulta-
neous burst of fire. This is a celebrated display; and is done,
I believe, by the employment of a very great number of men
to light, at the same instant, the torches which are fixed for
the purpose all over the building. After the first glare of
fire, I did not think the second aspect of the building so
beautiful as the first; it wanted both softness and distinctness. The two most animated days of the Carnival are still
to come."

" *April 4th*, 1839. — We have just come to the termination
of all the Easter spectacles here. On Sunday evening St.
Peter's was a second time illuminated; I was in the Piazza,
and admired the sight from a nearer point than when I had
seen it before at the time of the Carnival.

" On Monday evening the celebrated fire-works were let off
from the Castle of St. Angelo ; they were said to be, in some
respects more brilliant than usual. I certainly never saw any
fire-works comparable to them for beauty. The Girandola
is a discharge of many thousands of rockets at once, which
of course fall back, like the leaves of a lily, and form for a
minute a very beautiful picture. There was also in silvery
light a very long Façade of a Palace, which looked a·residence
for Oberon and Titania, and beat Aladdin's into darkness. Afterwards a series of cascades of red fire poured down the faces
of the Castle and of the scaffoldings round it, and seemed
a burning Niagara. Of course there were abundance of ser-
pents, wheels and cannon-shot ; there was also a display of
dazzling white light, which made a strange appearance on
the houses, the river, the bridge, and the faces of the multitude. The whole ended with a second and a more splendid
Girandola."

Take finally, to people the scene a little for us, if our imagination be at all lively, these three small entries, of different dates, and so wind up : —

"*December 30th*, 1838. — I received on Christmas-day a packet from Dr. Carlyle, containing Letters from the Maurices ; which were a very pleasant arrival. The Dr. wrote a few lines with them, mentioning that he was only at Civita Vecchia while the steamer baited on its way to Naples. I have written to thank him for his despatches."

"*March 16th*, 1839. — I have seen a good deal of John Mill, whose society I like much. He enters heartily into the interest of the things which I most care for here, and I have seldom had more pleasure than in taking him to see Raffael's Loggie, where are he Frescos called his Bible, and to the Sixtine Chapel, which I admire and love more and more. He is in very weak health, but as fresh and clear in mind as possible. . . . English politics seem in a queer state, the Conservatives creeping on, the Whigs losing ground ; like combatants on the top of a breach, while there is a social mine below which will probe ly blow both parties into the air."

"*April 4th*, 1839. — I walked out on Tuesday on the Ancona Road, and about noon met a travelling carriage, which from a distance looked very suspicious, and on nearer approach was found really to contain Captain Sterling and an Albanian manservant on the front, and behind under the hood Mrs. A. Sterling and the she portion of the tail. They seemed very well ; and, having turned the Albanian back to the rear of the whole machine, I sat by Anthony, and entered Rome in triumph." — Here is indeed a conquest ! Captain A. Sterling, now on his return from service in Corfu, meets his Brother in this manner ; and the remaining Roman days are of a brighter complexion. As these suddenly ended, I believe he turned southward, and found at Naples the Dr. Carlyle above mentioned (an extremely intimate acquaintance of mine), who was still there. For we are a most travelling people, we of this Island in this time ; and, as the Prophet threatened, see ourselves, in so many senses, made "like unto a wheel !" —

Sterling returned from Italy filled with much cheerful imagery and reminiscence, and great store of artistic, serious, dilettante and other speculation for the time ; improved in health, too ; but probably little enriched in real culture or spiritual strength ; and indeed not permanently altered by his tour in any respect to a sensible extent, that one could notice. He returned rather in haste, and before the expected time ; summoned, about the middle of April, by his Wife's domestic situation at Hastings ; who, poor lady, had been brought to bed before her calculation, and had in few days lost her infant ; and now saw a household round her much needing the master's presence. He hurried off to Malta, dreading the Alps at that season ; and came home, by steamer, with all speed, early in May, 1839.

PART III.

⸺◆⸺

CHAPTER I.

CLIFTON.

MATTERS once readjusted at Hastings, it was thought Sterling's health had so improved, and his activities towards Literature so developed themselves into congruity, that a permanent English place of abode might now again be selected, — on the Southwest coast somewhere, — and the family once more have the blessing of a home, and see its *lares* and *penates* and household furniture unlocked from the Pantechnicon repositories, where they had so long been lying.

Clifton, by Bristol, with its soft Southern winds and high cheerful situation, recommended too by the presence of one or more valuable acquaintances there, was found to be the eligible place ; and thither in this summer of 1839, having found a tolerable lodging, with the prospect by and by of an agreeable house, he and his removed. This was the end of what I call his " third peregrinity ; " — or reckoning the West Indies one, his fourth. This also is, since Bayswater, the fourth time his family has had to shift on his account. Bayswater ; then to Bordeaux, to Blackheath and Knightsbridge (during the Madeira time), to Hastings (Roman time) ; and now to Clifton, not to stay there either : a sadly nomadic life to be prescribed to a civilized man !

At Clifton his habitation was speedily enough set up ; household conveniences, methods of work, daily promenades on foot or horseback, and before long even a circle of friends, or of
176

kindly neighborhoods ripening into intimacy, were established round him. In all this no man could be more expert or expeditious, in such cases. It was with singular facility, in a loving, hoping manner, that he threw himself open to the new interests and capabilities of the new place; snatched out of it whatsoever of human or material would suit him; and in brief, in all senses had pitched his tent-habitation, and grew to look on it as a house. It was beautiful too, as well as pathetic. This man saw himself reduced to be a dweller in tents, his house is but a stone tent; and he can so kindly accommodate himself to that arrangement; — healthy faculty and diseased necessity, nature and habit, and all manner of things primary and secondary, original and incidental, conspiring now to make it easy for him. With the evils of nomadism, he participated to the full in whatever benefits lie in it for a man.

He had friends enough, old and new, at Clifton, whose intercourse made the place human for him. Perhaps among the most valued of the former sort may be mentioned Mrs. Edward Strachey, Widow of the late Indian Judge, who now resided here; a cultivated, graceful, most devout and high-minded lady; whom he had known in old years, first probably as Charles Buller's Aunt, and whose esteem was constant for him, and always precious to him. She was some ten or twelve years older than he; she survived him some years, but is now also gone from us. Of new friends acquired here, besides a skilful and ingenious Dr. Symonds, physician as well as friend, the principal was Francis Newman, then and still an ardently inquiring soul, of fine University and other attainments, of sharp-cutting, restlessly advancing intellect, and the mildest pious enthusiasm; whose worth, since better known to all the world, Sterling highly estimated; — and indeed practically testified the same; having by will appointed him, some years hence, guardian to his eldest Son; which pious function Mr. Newman now successfully discharges.

Sterling was not long in certainty as to his abode at Clifton: alas, where could he long be so? Hardly six months were gone when his old enemy again overtook him; again admon-

ished him how frail his hopes of permanency were. Each
winter, it turned out, he had to fly; and after the second of
these, he quitted the place altogether. Here, meanwhile, in
a Letter to myself, and in Excerpts from others, are some
glimpses of his advent and first summer there: —

To his Mother.

" *Clifton, June* 11*th*, 1839. — As yet I am personally very
uncomfortable from the general confusion of this house, which
deprives me of my room to sit and read and write in; all being
more or less lumbered by boxes, and invaded by servile domes-
ticities aproned, handled, bristled, and of nondescript varieties.
We have very fine warm weather, with occasional showers;
and the verdure of the woods and fields is very beautiful.
Bristol seems as busy as need be; and the shops and all kinds
of practical conveniences are excellent; but those of Clifton
have the usual sentimental, not to say meretricious fraudu-
lence of commercial establishments in Watering-places.

"The bag which Hannah forgot reached us safely at Bath
on Friday morning; but I cannot quite unriddle the mystery
of the change of padlocks, for I left the right one in care of
the Head Steam-engine at Paddington, which seemed a very
decent person with a good black coat on, and a pen behind its
ear. I have been meditating much on the story of Palarea's
'box of papers;' which does not appear to be in my possession,
and I have a strong impression that I gave it to young Florez
Calderon. I will write to say so to Madam Torrijos speedily."
Palarea, Dr. Palarea, I understand, was "an old guerilla
leader whom they called *El Medico.*" Of him and of the vanished shadows, now gone to Paris, to Madrid, or out of the
world, let us say nothing!

To Mr. Carlyle.

" *June* 15*th*, 1839. — We have a room now occupied by
Robert Barton [a brother-in-law]; to which Anthony may
perhaps succeed; but which after him, or in lieu of him,
would expand itself to receive you. Is there no hope of your

coming? I would undertake to ride with you at all possible paces, and in all existing directions.

"As yet my books are lying as ghost books, in a limbo on the banks of a certain Bristolian Styx, humanly speaking, a *Canal;* but the other apparatus of life is gathered about me, and performs its diurnal functions. The place pleases me better than I expected: a far lookout on all sides, over green country; a sufficient old City lying in the hollow near; and civilization, in no tumultuous state, rather indeed stagnant, visible in the Rows of Houses and Gardens which call themselves Clifton. I hope soon to take a lease of a house, where I may arrange myself more methodically; keep myself equably boiling in my own kitchen; and spread myself over a series of book-shelves. . . . I have just been interrupted by a visit from Mrs. Strachey; with whom I dined yesterday. She seems a very good and thoroughly kind-hearted woman; and it is pleasant to have her for a neighbor. . . . I have read Emerson's Pamphlets. I should find it more difficult than ever to write to him."

To his Father.

"*June 30th,* 1839. — Of Books I shall have no lack, though no plethora; and the Reading-room supplies all one can want in the way of Papers and Reviews. I go there three or four times a week, and inquire how the human race goes on. I suppose this Turco-Egyptian War will throw several diplomatists into a state of great excitement, and massacre a good many thousands of Africans and Asiatics? — For the present, it appears, the English Education Question is settled. I wish the Government had said that, in their inspection and superintendence, they would look only to secular matters, and leave religious ones to the persons who set up the schools, whoever these might be. It seems to me monstrous that the State should be prevented taking any efficient measures for teaching Roman Catholic children to read, write and cipher, merely because they believe in the Pope, and the Pope is an impostor, — which I candidly confess he is! There is no question which I can so ill endure to see made a party one as that of Education." — The following is of the same day: —

" To Thomas Carlyle, Esq., Chelsea, London.

"Manor House, Clifton Place, Clifton,
"30th June, 1839.

"My dear Carlyle,—I have heard, this morning, from my Father, that you are to set out on Tuesday for Scotland : so I have determined to fillip away some spurt of ink in your direction, which may reach you before you move towards Thule.

" Writing to you, in fact, is considerably easier than writing about you; which has been my employment of late, at leisure moments,—that is, moments of leisure from idleness, not work. As you partly guessed, I took in hand a Review of *Teufelsdröckh*—for want of a better Heuschrecke to do the work; and when I have been well enough, and alert enough, during the last fortnight, have tried to set down some notions about Tobacco, Radicalism, Christianity, Assafœtida and so forth. But a few abortive pages are all the result as yet. If my speculations should ever see daylight, they may chance to get you into scrapes, but will certainly get me into worse. . . . But one must work; *sic itur ad astra,*—and the *astra* are always there to befriend one, at least as asterisks, filling up the gaps which yawn in vain for words.

"Except my unsuccessful efforts to discuss you and your offences, I have done nothing that leaves a trace behind ;—unless the endeavor to teach my little boy the Latin declensions shall be found, at some time short of the Last Day, to have done so. I have—rather I think from dyspepsia than dyspneumony—been often and for days disabled from doing anything but read. In this way I have gone through a good deal of Strauss's Book ; which is exceedingly clever and clear-headed; with more of insight, and less of destructive rage than I expected. It will work deep and far, in such a time as ours. When so many minds are distracted about the history, or rather genesis of the Gospel, it is a great thing for partisans on the one side to have, what the other never have wanted, a Book of which they can say, This is our Creed and Code,—or rather Anti-creed and Anti-code. And Strauss seems perfectly secure against the sort of answer to which Voltaire's critical and historical shallowness perpetually exposed him. I mean to read the Book through. It seems admitted that the orthodox theologians have failed to give any sufficient answer. — I have also looked through Michelet's *Luther,* with great delight; and have read the fourth volume of Coleridge's *Literary Remains,* in which there are things that would interest you. He has a great hankering after Cromwell, and explicitly defends the execution of Charles.

"Of Mrs. Strachey we have seen a great deal; and might have seen more, had I had time and spirits for it. She is a warm-hearted, enthusiastic creature, whom one cannot but like. She seems always excited by the wish for more excitement than her life affords. And such a person is always in danger of doing something less wise than his best knowledge and aspirations; because he must do something, and circumstances do not allow him to do what he desires. Thence, after the first glow of novelty, endless self-tormenting comes from the contrast between aims and acts. She sets out, with her daughter and two boys, for a Tour in Wales to-morrow morning. Her talk of you is always most affectionate; and few, I guess, will read *Sartor* with more interest than she.

"I am still in a very extempore condition as to house, books, &c. One which I have hired for three years will be given up to me in the middle of August; and then I may hope to have something like a house, — so far as that is possible for any one to whom Time itself is often but a worse or a better kind of cave in the desert. We have had rainy and cheerless weather almost since the day of our arrival. But the sun now shines more lovingly, and the skies seem less disdainful of man and his perplexities. The earth is green, abundant and beautiful. But human life, so far as I can learn, is mean and meagre enough in its purposes, however striking to the speculative or sentimental bystander. Pray be assured that whatever you may say of the 'landlord at Clifton,'[1] the more I know of him, the less I shall like him. Well with me if I can put up with him for the present, and

---

[1] Of Sterling himself, I suppose.

make use of him, till at last I can joyfully turn him off forever!

"Love to you Wife and self. My little Charlotte desires
me to tell you that she has new shoes for her Doll, which she
will show you when you come.

"Yours,

"JOHN STERLING."

The visit to Clifton never took effect; nor to any of Sterling's subsequent homes; which now is matter of regret to me.
Concerning the "Review of *Teufelsdröckh*" there will be more
to say anon. As to "little Charlotte and her Doll," I remember well enough and was more than once reminded, this bright
little creature, on one of my first visits to Bayswater, had earnestly applied to me to put her Doll's shoes on for her; which
feat was performed. — The next fragment indicates a household settled, fallen into wholesome routine again; and may
close the series here: —

To his Mother.

"*July* 22d, 1839. — A few evenings ago we went to Mr.
Griffin's, and met there Dr. Prichard, the author of a well-
known Book on the *Races of Mankind,* to which it stands in
the same relation among English books as the Racing Calendar
does to those of Horsekind. He is a very intelligent, accomplished person. We had also there the Dean; a certain
Dr. —— of Corpus College, Cambridge (a booby); and a clever
fellow, a Mr. Fisher, one of the Tutors of Trinity in my days.
We had a very pleasant evening." —

At London we were in the habit of expecting Sterling pretty
often; his presence, in this house as in others, was looked for,
once in the month or two, and came always as sunshine in
the gray weather to me and mine. My daily walks with him
had long since been cut short without renewal; that walk to
Eltham and Edgeworth's perhaps the last of the kind he and
I had: but our intimacy, deepening and widening year after
year, knew no interruption or abatement of increase; an honest, frank and truly human mutual relation, valuable or even

invaluable to both parties, and a lasting loss, hardly to be re-placed in this world, to the survivor of the two.

His visits, which were usually of two or three days, were always full of business, rapid in movement as all his life was. To me, if possible, he would come in the evening; a whole cornucopia of talk and speculation was to be discharged. If the evening would not do, and my affairs otherwise permitted, I had to mount into cabs with him; fly far and wide, shuttling athwart the big Babel, wherever his calls and pauses had to be. This was his way to husband time! Our talk, in such straitened circumstances, was loud or low as the circum-ambient groaning rage of wheels and sound prescribed, — very loud it had to be in such thoroughfares as London Bridge and Cheapside; but except while he was absent, off for minutes into some banker's office, lawyer's, stationer's, haberdasher's or what office there might be, it never paused. In this way extensive strange dialogues were carried on : to me also very strange, — private friendly colloquies, on all manner of rich subjects, held thus amid the chaotic roar of things. Sterling was full of speculations, observations and bright sallies; viv-idly awake to what was passing in the world ; glanced perti-nently with victorious clearness, without spleen, though often enough with a dash of mockery, into its Puseyisms, Liberal-isms, literary Lionisms, or what else the mad hour might be producing, — always prompt to recognize what grain of sanity might be in the same. He was opulent in talk, and the rapid movement and vicissitude on such occasions seemed to give him new excitement.

Once, I still remember, — it was some years before, proba-bly in May, on his return from Madeira, — he undertook a day's riding with me ; once and never again. We coursed ex-tensively over the Hampstead and Highgate regions, and the country beyond, sauntering or galloping through many leafy lanes and pleasant places, in ever-flowing, ever-changing talk ; and returned down Regent Street at nightfall : one of the cheerfulest days I ever had; — not to be repeated, said the Fates. Sterling was charming on such occasions : at once a child and a gifted man. A serious fund of thought he always

had, a serious drift you never missed in him : nor indeed had
he much depth of real laughter or sense of the ludicrous, as I
have elsewhere said; but what he had was genuine, free and
continual : his sparkling sallies bubbled up as from aerated
natural fountains; a mild dash of gayety was native to the
man, and had moulded his physiognomy in a very graceful
way. We got once into a cab, about Charing Cross; I know
not now whence or well whitherward, nor that our haste was
at all special; however, the cabman, sensible that his pace was
slowish, took to whipping, with a steady, passionless, business-
like assiduity which, though the horse seemed lazy rather
than weak, became afflictive; and I urged remonstrance with
the savage fellow: " Let him alone," answered Sterling ; " he
is kindling the enthusiasm of his horse, you perceive ; that is
the first thing, then we shall do very well ! " — as accordingly
we did.

At Clifton, though his thoughts began to turn more on
poetic forms of composition, he was diligent in prose elabora-
tions too, — doing Criticism, for one thing, as we incidentally
observed. He wrote there, and sent forth in this autumn of
1839, his most important contribution to John Mill's Review,
the article on *Carlyle*, which stands also in Mr. Hare's collection.[1] What its effect on the public was I knew not, and
know not; but remember well, and may here be permitted
to acknowledge, the deep silent joy, not of a weak or ignoble
nature, which it gave to myself in my then mood and situation; as it well might. The first generous human recognition,
expressed with heroic emphasis, and clear conviction visible
amid its fiery exaggeration, that one's poor battle in this
world is not quite a mad and futile, that it is perhaps a
worthy and manful one, which will come to something yet :
this fact is a memorable one in every history; and for me
Sterling, often enough the stiff gainsayer in our private com-
munings, was the doer of this. The thought burnt in me like
a lamp, for several days; lighting up into a kind of heroic
splendor the sad volcanic wrecks, abysses, and convulsions of

[1] Hare, ii. p. 252.

said poor battle, and secretly I was very grateful to my daring friend, and am still, and ought to be. What the public might be thinking about him and his audacities, and me in consequence, or whether it thought at all, I never learned, or much heeded to learn.

Sterling's gainsaying had given way on many points; but on others it continued stiff as ever, as may be seen in that article; indeed he fought Parthian-like in such cases, holding out his last position as doggedly as the first: and to some of my notions he seemed to grow in stubbornness of opposition, with the growing inevitability, and never would surrender. Especially that doctrine of the "greatness and fruitfulness of Silence," remained afflictive and incomprehensible: "Silence?" he would say: "Yes, truly; if they give you leave to proclaim silence by cannon-salvos! My Harpocrates-Stentor!" In like manner, "Intellect and Virtue," how they are proportional, or are indeed one gift in us, the same great summary of gifts; and again, "Might and Right," the identity of these two, if a man will understand this God's-Universe, and that only he who conforms to the law of *it* can in the long-run have any "might:" all this, at the first blush, often awakened Sterling's musketry upon me, and many volleys I have had to stand, — the thing not being decidable by that kind of weapon or strategy.

In such cases your one method was to leave our friend in peace. By small-arms practice no mortal could dislodge him: but if you were in the right, the silent hours would work continually for you; and Sterling, more certainly than any man, would and must at length swear fealty to the right, and passionately adopt it, burying all hostilities under foot. A more candid soul, once let the stormful velocities of it expend themselves, was nowhere to be met with. A son of light, if I have ever seen one; recognizing the truth, if truth there were; hurling overboard his vanities, petulances, big and small interests, in ready loyalty to truth: very beautiful; at once a loyal child, as I said, and a gifted man! — Here is a very pertinent passage from one of his Letters, which, though the name continues blank, I will insert: —

To his Father.

" *October* 15*th*, 1839. — As to my 'over-estimate of ——,'
your expressions rather puzzle me. I suppose there may be,
at the outside, a hundred persons in England whose opinions
on such a matter are worth as much as mine. If by 'the
public' you and my Mother mean the other ninety-nine, I
submit. I have no doubt that, on any matter not relating
peculiarly to myself, the judgment of the ninety-nine most
philosophical heads in the country, if unanimous, would be
right, and mine, if opposed to them, wrong. But then I am
at a loss to make out, How the decision of the very few really
competent persons has been ascertained to be thus in contradiction to me? And on the other hand, I conceive myself,
from my opportunities, knowledge and attention to the subject, to be alone quite entitled to outvote tens of thousands
of gentlemen, however much my superiors as men of business,
men of the world, or men of merely dry or merely frivolous
literature.

"I do not remember ever before to have heard the saying,
whether of Talleyrand or of any one else, That *all* the world
is a wiser man than any man in the world. Had it been said
even by the Devil, it would nevertheless be false. I have
often indeed heard the saying, *On peut être plus* FIN *qu'un
autre, mais pas plus* FIN *que tous les autres*. But observe that
'*fin*' means *cunning*, not *wise*. The difference between this
assertion and the one you refer to is curious and worth ex-
amining. It is quite certain, there is always some one man in
the world wiser than all the rest; as Socrates was declared
by the oracle to be; and as, I suppose, Bacon was in his day,
and perhaps Burke in his. There is also some one, whose
opinion would be probably true, if opposed to that of all
around him; and it is always indubitable that the wise men
are the scores, and the unwise the millions. The millions
indeed come round, in the course of a generation or two, to
the opinions of the wise; but by that time a new race of wise
men have again shot ahead of their contemporaries: so it has
always been, and so, in the nature of things, it always must

be. But with cunning, the matter is quite different. Cunning is not *dishonest wisdom*, which would be a contradiction in terms; it is *dishonest prudence*, acuteness in practice, not in thought: and though there must always be some one the most cunning in the world, as well as some one the most wise, these two superlatives will fare very differently in the world. In the case of cunning, the shrewdness of a whole people, of a whole generation, may doubtless be combined against that of the one, and so triumph over it; which was pretty much the case with Napoleon. But although a man of the greatest cunning can hardly conceal his designs and true character from millions of unfriendly eyes, it is quite impossible thus to club the eyes of the mind, and to constitute by the union of ten thousand follies an equivalent for a single wisdom. A hundred school-boys can easily unite and thrash their one master; but a hundred thousand school-boys would not be nearer than a score to knowing as much Greek among them as Bentley or Scaliger. To all which, I believe, you will assent as readily as I; — and I have written it down only because I have nothing more important to say." —

Besides his prose labors, Sterling had by this time written, publishing chiefly in *Blackwood*, a large assortment of verses, *Sexton's Daughter, Hymns of a Hermit*, and I know not what other extensive stock of pieces; concerning which he was now somewhat at a loss as to his true course. He could write verses with astonishing facility, in any given form of metre; and to various readers they seemed excellent, and high judges had freely called them so, but he himself had grave misgivings on that latter essential point. In fact here once more was a parting of the ways, "Write in Poetry; write in Prose?" upon which, before all else, it much concerned him to come to a settlement.

My own advice was, as it had always been, steady against Poetry; and we had colloquies upon it, which must have tried his patience, for in him there was a strong leaning the other way. But, as I remarked and urged: Had he not already gained superior excellence in delivering, by way of *speech* or

prose, what thoughts were in him, which is the grand and only
intrinsic function of a writing man, call him by what title
you will ?   Cultivate that superior excellence till it become a
perfect and superlative one.   Why *sing* your bits of thoughts,
if you *can* contrive to speak them ?   By your thought, not by
your mode of delivering it, you must live or die. — Besides I
had to observe there was in Sterling intrinsically no depth of
tune; which surely is the real test of a Poet or Singer, as distinguished from a Speaker ?   In music proper he had not the
slightest ear; all music was mere impertinent noise to him,
nothing in it perceptible but the mere march or time.   Nor in
his way of conception and utterance, in the verses he wrote,
was there any contradiction, but a constant confirmation to me,
of that fatal prognostic; — as indeed the whole man, in ear
and heart and tongue, is one; and he whose soul does not sing,
need not try to do it with his throat.   Sterling's verses had a
monotonous rub-a-dub, instead of tune; no trace of music
deeper than that of a well-beaten drum; to which limited
range of excellence the substance also corresponded; being
intrinsically always a rhymed and slightly rhythmical *speech,*
not a *song.*

   In short, all seemed to me to say, in his case : "You can
speak with supreme excellence; sing with considerable excellence you never can.   And the Age itself, does it not, beyond
most ages, demand and require clear speech; an Age incapable
of being sung to, in any but a trivial manner, till these con-
vulsive agonies and wild revolutionary overturnings readjust
themselves ?   Intelligible word of command, not musical
psalmody and fiddling, is possible in this fell storm of battle.
Beyond all ages, our Age admonishes whatsoever thinking or
writing man it has : Oh, speak to me some wise intelligible
speech; your wise meaning in the shortest and clearest way ;
behold I am dying for want of wise meaning, and insight into
the devouring fact: speak, if you have any wisdom !   As to
song so called, and your fiddling talent, — even if you have one,
much more if you have none, — we will talk of that a couple
of centuries hence, when things are calmer again.   Homer
shall be thrice welcome; but only when Troy is *taken:* alas,

while the siege lasts, and battle's fury rages everywhere, what can I do with the Homer? I want Achilleus and Odysseus, and am enraged to see them trying to be Homers!" —

Sterling, who respected my sincerity, and always was amenable enough to counsel, was doubtless much confused by such contradictory diagnosis of his case. The question, Poetry or Prose? became more and more pressing, more and more insoluble. He decided, at last, to appeal to the public upon it; — got ready, in the late autumn, a small select Volume of his verses; and was now busy pushing it through the press. Unfortunately, in the mean while, a grave illness, of the old pulmonary sort, overtook him, which at one time threatened to be dangerous. This is a glance again into his interior household in these circumstances: —

To his Mother.

"*December 21st*, 1839. — The Tin box came quite safe, with all its miscellaneous contents. I suppose we are to thank you for the *Comic Almanac*, which, as usual, is very amusing; and for the Book on *Watt*, which disappointed me. The scientific part is no doubt very good, and particularly clear and simple; but there is nothing remarkable in the account of Watt's character; and it is an absurd piece of French impertinence in Arago to say, that England has not yet learnt to appreciate men like Watt, because he was not made a peer; which, were our peerage an institution like that of France, would have been very proper.

"I have now finished correcting the proofs of my little Volume of Poems. It has been a great plague to me, and one that I would not have incurred, had I expected to be laid up as I have been; but the matter was begun before I had any notion of being disabled by such an illness, — the severest I have suffered since I went to the West Indies. The Book will, after all, be a botched business in many respects; and I much doubt whether it will pay its expenses: but I try to consider it as out of my hands, and not to fret myself about it. I shall be very curious to see Carlyle's Tractate on *Chartism;* which" — But we need not enter upon that.

Sterling's little Book was printed at his own expense;[1] published by Moxon in the very end of this year. It carries an appropriate and pretty Epigraph: —

> " Feeling, Thought, and Fancy be
> Gentle sister Graces three :
> If these prove averse to me,
> They will punish, — pardon Ye!"

He had dedicated the little Volume to Mr. Hare ; — and he submitted very patiently to the discouraging neglect with which it was received by the world; for indeed the " Ye " said nothing audible, in the way of pardon or other doom; so that whether the " sister Graces " were averse or not, remained as doubtful as ever.

CHAPTER II.

TWO WINTERS.

As we said above, it had been hoped by Sterling's friends, not very confidently by himself, that in the gentler air of Clifton his health might so far recover as to enable him to dispense with autumnal voyages, and to spend the year all round in a house of his own. These hopes, favorable while the warm season lasted, broke down when winter came. In November of this same year, while his little Volume was passing through the press, bad and worse symptoms, spitting of blood to crown the sad list, reappeared ; and Sterling had to equip himself again, at this late season, for a new flight to Madeira ; wherein the good Calvert, himself suffering, and ready on all grounds for such an adventure, offered to accompany him. Sterling went by land to Falmouth, meaning there to wait for Calvert, who was to come by the Madeira Packet, and there take him on board.

Calvert and the Packet did arrive, in stormy January weather ; which continued wildly blowing for weeks ; forbid-

---

[1] *Poems by John Sterling.* London (Moxon), 1839.

ding all egress Westward, especially for invalids. These elemental tumults, and blustering wars of sea and sky, with
nothing but the misty solitude of Madeira in the distance,
formed a very discouraging outlook. In the mean while Falmouth itself had offered so many resources, and seemed so
tolerable in climate and otherwise, while this wintry ocean
looked so inhospitable for invalids, it was resolved our voyagers should stay where they were till spring returned. Which
accordingly was done; with good effect for that season, and
also with results for the coming seasons. Here again, from
Letters to Knightsbridge, are some glimpses of his winter-
life : —

"*Falmouth, February 5th,* 1840. — I have been to-day to see
a new tin-mine, two or three miles off, which is expected to
turn into a copper-mine by and by, so they will have the
two constituents of bronze close together. This, by the way,
was the 'brass' of Homer and the Ancients generally, who
do not seem to have known our brass made of copper and zinc.
Achilles in his armor must have looked like a bronze statue.
— I took Sheridan's advice, and did not go down the mine."

"*February 15th.* — To some iron-works the other day ; where
I saw half the beam of a great steam-engine, a piece of iron
forty feet long and seven broad, cast in about five minutes.
It was a very striking spectacle. I hope to go to Penzance
before I leave this country, and will not fail to tell you about
it." He did make trial of Penzance, among other places, next
year; but only of Falmouth this.

"*February 20th.* — I am going on *asy* here, in spite of a
great change of weather. The East-winds are come at last,
bringing with them snow, which has been driving about for
the last twenty-four hours; not falling heavily, nor lying long
when fallen. Neither is it as yet very cold, but I suppose
there will be some six weeks of unpleasant temperature. The
marine climate of this part of England will, no doubt, modify
and mollify the air into a happier sort of substance than that
you breathe in London.

"The large vessels that had been lying here for weeks, waiting for a wind, have now sailed; two of them for the East

Indies, and having three hundred soldiers on board. It is a curious thing that the long-continued westerly winds had so prevented the coasters arriving, that the Town was almost on the point of a famine as to bread. The change has brought in abundance of flour. — The people in general seem extremely comfortable; their houses are excellent, almost all of stone. Their habits are very little agricultural, but mining and fishing seem to prosper with them. There are hardly any gentry here; I have not seen more than two gentlemen's carriages in the Town; indeed I think the nearest one comes from five miles off. . . .

"I have been obliged to try to occupy myself with Natural Science, in order to give some interest to my walks; and have begun to feel my way in Geology. I have now learnt to recognize three or four of the common kinds of stone about here, when I see them; but I find it stupid work compared with Poetry and Philosophy. In the mornings, however, for an hour or so before I get up, I generally light my candle, and try to write some verses; and since I have been here, I have put together short poems, almost enough for another small volume. In the evenings I have gone on translating some of Goethe. But six or seven hours spent on my legs, in the open air, do not leave my brain much energy for thinking. Thus my life is a dull and unprofitable one, but still better than it would have been in Madeira or on board ship. I hear from Susan every day, and write to her by return of post."

At Falmouth Sterling had been warmly welcomed by the well-known Quaker family of the Foxes, principal people in that place, persons of cultivated opulent habits, and joining to the fine purities and pieties of their sect a reverence for human intelligence in all kinds; to whom such a visitor as Sterling was naturally a welcome windfall. The family had grave elders, bright cheery younger branches, men and women; truly amiable all, after their sort: they made a pleasant image of home for Sterling in his winter exile. "Most worthy, respectable and highly cultivated people, with a great deal of money among them," writes Sterling in the end of February; "who make the place pleasant to me. They are connected with all the large Quaker circle, the Gurneys, Frys, &c., and also with Buxton the Abolitionist. It is droll to hear them talking of all the common topics of science, literature, and life, and in the midst of it : 'Does thou know Wordsworth ?' or, 'Did thou see the Coronation ?' or 'Will thou take some refreshment ?' They are very kind and pleasant people to know."

"Calvert," continues our Diarist, "is better than he lately was, though he has not been at all laid up. He shoots little birds, and dissects and stuffs them ; while I carry a hammer, and break flints and slates, to look for diamonds and rubies inside ; and admire my success in the evening, when I empty my great-coat pocket of its specimens. On the whole, I doubt whether my physical proceedings will set the Thames on fire. Give my love to Anthony's Charlotte ; also remember me affectionately to the Carlyles." —

At this time, too, John Mill, probably encouraged by Sterling, arrived in Falmouth, seeking refuge of climate for a sickly younger Brother, to whom also, while he continued there, and to his poor patient, the doors and hearts of this kind family were thrown wide open. Falmouth, during these winter weeks, especially while Mill continued, was an unexpectedly engaging place to Sterling ; and he left it in spring, for Clifton, with a very kindly image of it in his thoughts. So ended, better than it might have done, his first year's flight from the Clifton winter.

In April, 1840, he was at his own hearth again ; cheerily pursuing his old labors, — struggling to redeem, as he did with a gallant constancy, the available months and days, out of the wreck of so many that were unavailable, for the business allotted him in this world. His swift, decisive energy of character ; the valiant rally he made again and ever again, starting up fresh from amid the wounded, and cheerily storming in anew, was admirable, and showed a noble fund of natural health amid such an element of disease. Somehow one could never rightly fancy that he was diseased ; that those fatal ever-recurring downbreaks were not almost rather the penalties paid for exuberance of health, and of faculty for living and work-

ing; criminal forfeitures, incurred by excess of self-exertion
and such irrepressible over-rapidity of movement: and the
vague hope was habitual with us, that increase of years, as it
deadened this over-energy, would first make the man secure of
life, and a sober prosperous worker among his fellows. It was
always as if with a kind of blame that one heard of his being
ill again! Poor Sterling; — no man knows another's burden:
these things were not, and were not to be, in the way we had
fancied them!

Summer went along in its usual quiet tenor at Clifton;
health good, as usual while the warm weather lasted, and
activity abundant; the scene as still as the busiest could wish.
"You metropolitan signors," writes Sterling to his Father, " cannot conceive the dulness and scantiness of our provincial chronicle." Here is a little excursion to the seaside; the lady of the
family being again, — for good reasons, — in a weakly state : —

" To Edward Sterling, Esq., Knightsbridge, London.

"Portshead, Bristol, 1st Sept., 1840.

" My dear Father, — This place is a southern headland
at the mouth of the Avon. Susan, and the Children too, were
all suffering from languor; and as she is quite unfit to travel
in a carriage, we were obliged to move, if at all, to some place
accessible by water; and this is the nearest where we could
get the fresher air of the Bristol Channel. We sent to take a
house, for a week; and came down here in a steamer yesterday morning. It seems likely to do every one good. We have
a comfortable house, with eight rather small bedrooms, for
which we pay four guineas and a half for the week. We have
brought three of our own maids, and leave one to take care of
the house at Clifton.

" A week ago my horse fell with me, but did not hurt seriously either himself or me : it was, however, rather hard that,
as there were six legs to be damaged, the one that did scratch
itself should belong to the part of the machine possessing only
two, instead of the quadrupedal portion. I grazed about the
size of a halfpenny on my left knee; and for a couple of days
walked about as if nothing had happened. I found, however,

that the skin was not returning correctly; and so sent for a
doctor : he treated the thing as quite insignificant, but said I
must keep my leg quiet for a few days. It is still not quite
healed; and I lie all day on a sofa, much to my discomposure;
but the thing is now rapidly disappearing; and I hope, in
a day or two more, I shall be free again. I find I can do no
work, while thus crippled in my leg. The man in Horace who
made verses *stans pede in uno* had the advantage of me.

"The Great Western came in last night about eleven, and
has just been making a flourish past our windows; looking
very grand, with four streamers of bunting, and one of smoke.
Of course I do not yet know whether I have Letters by her,
as if so they will have gone to Clifton first. This place is
quiet, green and pleasant; and will suit us very well, if we
have good weather, of which there seems every appearance.

"Milnes spent last Sunday with me at Clifton; and was
very amusing and cordial. It is impossible for those who
know him well not to like him. — I send this to Knightsbridge, not knowing where else to hit you. Love to my
Mother.

"Your affectionate,

"JOHN STERLING."

The expected "Letters by the Great Western" are from
Anthony, now in Canada, doing military duties there. The
"Milnes" is our excellent Richard, whom all men know, and
truly whom none can know well without even doing as Sterling says. — In a week the family had returned to Clifton;
and Sterling was at his poetizings and equitations again. His
grand business was now Poetry; all effort, outlook and aim
exclusively directed thither, this good while.

Of the published Volume Moxon gave the worst tidings;
no man had hailed it with welcome; unsold it lay, under the
leaden seal of general neglect; the public when asked what
it thought, had answered hitherto by a lazy stare. It shall
answer otherwise, thought Sterling; by no means taking that
as the final response. It was in this same September that he
announced to me and other friends, under seal of secrecy as

usual, the completion, or complete first-draught, of "a new Poem reaching to two thousand verses." By working "three hours every morning" he had brought it so far. This Piece, entitled *The Election*, of which in due time we obtained perusal, and had to give some judgment, proved to be in a new vein, — what might be called the mock-heroic, or sentimental Hudibrastic, reminding one a little, too, of Wieland's *Oberon;* — it had touches of true drollery combined not ill with grave clear insight; showed spirit everywhere, and a plainly improved power of execution. Our stingy verdict was to the effect, "Better, but still not good enough: — why follow that sad 'metrical' course, climbing the loose sandhills, when you have a firm path along the plain?" To Sterling himself it remained dubious whether so slight a strain, new though it were, would suffice to awaken the sleeping public; and the Piece was thrown away and taken up again, at intervals; and the question, Publish or not publish? lay many months undecided.

Meanwhile his own feeling was now set more and more towards Poetry; and in spite of symptoms and dissuasions, and perverse prognostics of outward wind and weather, he was rallying all his force for a downright struggle with it; resolute to see which *was* the stronger. It must be owned, he takes his failures in the kindliest manner; and goes along, bating no jot of heart or hope. Perhaps I should have more admired this than I did! My dissuasions, in that case, might have been fainter. But then my sincerity, which was all the use of my poor counsel in assent or dissent, would have been less. He was now furthermore busy with a *Tragedy of Strafford*, the theme of many failures in Tragedy; planning it industriously in his head; eagerly reading in *Whitlocke, Rushworth* and the Puritan Books, to attain a vesture and local habitation for it. Faithful assiduous studies I do believe; — of which, knowing my stubborn realism, and savage humor towards singing by the Thespian or other methods, he told me little, during his visits that summer.

The advance of the dark weather sent him adrift again; to Torquay, for this winter: there, in his old Falmouth climate, he hoped to do well; — and did, so far as well-doing was readily possible, in that sad wandering way of life. However, be where he may, he tries to work "two or three hours in the morning," were it even " with a lamp," in bed, before the fires are lit; and so makes something of it. From abundant Letters of his now before me, I glean these two or three small glimpses; sufficient for our purpose at present. The general date is "Tor, near Torquay : " —

To Mrs. Charles Fox, Falmouth.

" *Tor, November 30th,* 1840. — I reached this place on Thursday ; having, after much hesitation, resolved to come here, at least for the next three weeks, — with some obscure purpose of embarking, at the New Year, from Falmouth for Malta, and so reaching Naples, which I have not seen. There was also a doubt whether I should not, after Christmas, bring my family here for the first four months of the year. All this, however, is still doubtful. But for certain inhabitants of Falmouth and its neighborhood, this place would be far more attractive than it. But I have here also friends, whose kindness, like much that I met with last winter, perpetually makes me wonder at the stock of benignity in human nature. A brother of my friend Julius Hare, Marcus by name, a Naval man, and though not a man of letters, full of sense and knowledge, lives here in a beautiful place, with a most agreeable and excellent wife, a daughter of Lord Stanley of Alderley. I had hardly seen them before; but they are fraternizing with me, in a much better than the Jacobin fashion ; and one only feels ashamed at the enormity of some people's good-nature. I am in a little rural sort of lodging ; and as comfortable as a solitary oyster can expect to be. " —

To C. Barton.

" *December 5th.* — This place is extremely small, much more so than Falmouth even ; but pretty, cheerful, and very mild in climate. There are a great many villas in and about the little Town, having three or four reception-rooms, eight or ten bedrooms ; and costing about fifteen hundred or two thousand

pounds each, and occupied by persons spending a thousand or
more pounds a year. If the Country would acknowledge my
merits by the gift of one of these, I could prevail on myself
to come and live here; which would be the best move for
my health I could make in England; but, in the absence of
any such expression of public feeling, it would come rather
dear." —

To Mrs. Fox again.

"*December 22d.* — By the way, did you ever read a Novel?
If you ever mean to do so hereafter, let it be Miss Martineau's
Deerbrook. It is really very striking; and parts of it are very
true and very beautiful. It is not so true, or so thoroughly
clear and harmonious, among delineations of English middle-
class gentility, as Miss Austen's books, especially as *Pride and
Prejudice*, which I think exquisite; but it is worth reading.
The Hour and the Man is eloquent, but an absurd exaggeration. — I hold out so valorously against this Scandinavian
weather, that I deserve to be ranked with Odin and Thor, and
fancy I may go to live at Clifton or Drontheim. Have you had
the same icy desolation as prevails here?"

To W. Coningham, Esq.

"*December 28th.* — Looking back to him [a deceased Uncle,
father of his correspondent], as I now very often do, I feel
strongly, what the loss of other friends has also impressed on
me, how much Death deepens our affection; and sharpens our
regret for whatever has been even slightly amiss in our conduct towards those who are gone. What trifles then swell
into painful importance; how we believe that, could the past
be recalled, life would present no worthier, happier task, than
that of so bearing ourselves towards those we love, that we
might ever after find nothing but melodious tranquillity breathing about their graves! Yet, too often, I feel the difficulty of
always practising such mild wisdom towards those who are
still left me. — You will wonder less at my rambling off in
this way, when I tell you that my little lodging is close to a
picturesque old Church and Churchyard, where, every day, I

brush past a tombstone, recording that an Italian, of Manferrato, has buried there a girl of sixteen, his only daughter: '*L' unica speranza di mia vita.*' — No doubt, as you say, our Mechanical Age is necessary as a passage to something better; but, at least, do not let us go back." —

At the New-year time, feeling unusually well, he returns to Clifton. His plans, of course, were ever fluctuating; his movements were swift and uncertain. Alas, his whole life, especially his winter-life, had to be built as if on wavering drift-sand; nothing certain in it, except if possible the "two or three hours of work" snatched from the general whirlpool of the dubious four-and-twenty!

To Dr. Carlyle.

"*Clifton, January* 10*th,* 1841. — I stood the sharp frost at Torquay with such entire impunity, that at last I took courage, and resolved to return home. I have been here a week, in extreme cold; and have suffered not at all; so that I hope, with care I may prosper in spite of medical prognostics, — if you permit such profane language. I am even able to work a good deal; and write for some hours every morning, by dint of getting up early, which an Arnott stove in my study enables me to do." — But at Clifton he cannot continue. Again, before long, the rude weather has driven him Southward; the spring finds him in his former haunts; doubtful as ever what to decide upon for the future; but tending evidently towards a new change of residence for household and self: —

To W. Coningham, Esq.

"*Penzance, April* 19*th,* 1841. — My little Boy and I have been wandering about between Torquay and this place; and latterly have had my Father for a few days with us, — he left us yesterday. In all probability I shall endeavor to settle either at Torquay, at Falmouth, or here; as it is pretty clear that I cannot stand the sharp air of Clifton, and still less the London east-winds. Penzance is, on the whole, a pleasant-looking, cheerful place; with a delightful mildness of air, and a great appearance of comfort among the people: the view of

Mount's Bay is certainly a very noble one. Torquay would suit the health of my Wife and Children better; or else I should be glad to live here always, London and its neighborhood being impracticable." — Such was his second wandering winter; enough to render the prospect of a third at Clifton very uninviting.

With the Falmouth friends, young and old, his intercourse had meanwhile continued cordial and frequent. The omens were pointing towards that region at his next place of abode. Accordingly, in few weeks hence, in the June of this Summer, 1841, his dubitations and inquirings are again ended for a time; he has fixed upon a house in Falmouth, and removed thither; bidding Clifton, and the regretful Clifton friends, a kind farewell. This was the *fifth* change of place for his family since Bayswater; the fifth, and to one chief member of it the last. Mrs. Sterling had brought him a new child in October last; and went hopefully to Falmouth, dreading *other* than what befell there.

CHAPTER III.

FALMOUTH : POEMS.

At Falmouth, as usual, he was soon at home in his new environment; resumed his labors; had his new small circle of acquaintance, the ready and constant centre of which was the Fox family, with whom he lived on an altogether intimate, honored and beloved footing; realizing his best anticipations in that respect, which doubtless were among his first inducements to settle in this new place. Open cheery heights, rather bare of wood: fresh southwestern breezes; a brisk laughing sea, swept by industrious sails, and the nets of a most stalwart, wholesome, frank and interesting population: the clean little fishing, trading and packet Town; hanging on its slope towards the Eastern sun, close on the waters of its

basin and intricate bay, — with the miniature Pendennis
Castle seaward on the right, the miniature St. Mawes land-
ward to left, and the mining world and the farming world
open boundlessly to the rear : — all this made a pleasant outlook and environment. And in all this, as in the other new
elements of his position, Sterling, open beyond most men to
the worth of things about him, took his frank share. From
the first, he had liked the general aspect of the population,
and their healthy, lively ways ; not to speak of the special
friendships he had formed there, which shed a charm over
them all. " Men of strong character, clear heads and genuine
goodness," writes he, " are by no means wanting." And long
after : " The common people here dress better than in most
parts of England ; and on Sundays, if the weather be at all
fine, their appearance is very pleasant. One sees them all
round the Town, especially towards Pendennis Castle, streaming in a succession of little groups, and seeming for the most
part really and quietly happy." On the whole he reckoned
himself lucky ; and, so far as locality went, found this a handsome shelter for the next two years of his life. Two years,
and not without an interruption ; that was all. Here we have
no continuing city ; he less than any of us ! One other flight
for shelter ; and then it is ended, and he has found an in-
expugnable refuge. Let us trace his remote footsteps, as we
have opportunity : —

To Dr. Symonds, Clifton.

" *Falmouth, June 28th*, 1841. — Newman writes to me that
he is gone to the Rhine. I wish I were ! And yet the only
' wish ' at the bottom of my heart, is to be able to work vigorously in my own way anywhere, were it in some Circle of
Dante's Inferno. This, however, is the secret of my soul,
which I disclose only to a few."

To his Mother.

" *Falmouth, July 6th*, 1841. — I have at last my own study
made comfortable ; the carpet being now laid down, and most
of my appurtenances in tolerable order. By and by I shall,

unless stopped by illness, get myself together, and begin living an orderly life and doing my daily task. I have swung a cot in my dressing-room ; partly as a convenience for myself, partly as a sort of memorial of my poor Uncle, in whose cot in his dressing-room at Lisworney I remember to have slept when a child. I have put a good large bookcase in my drawing-room, and all the rest of my books fit very well into the study."

To Mr. Carlyle.

"*July 6th.* — No books have come in my way but Emerson's, which I value full as much as you, though as yet I have read only some corners of it. We have had an Election here, of the usual stamp; to me a droll 'realized Ideal,' after my late metrical adventures in that line. But the oddest sign of the Times I know, is a cheap Translation of Strauss's *Leben Jesu*, now publishing in numbers, and said to be circulating far and wide. What does — or rather, what does not — this portend ? " —

With the Poem called *The Election*, here alluded to, which had been more than once revised and reconsidered, he was still under some hesitations ; but at last had well-nigh resolved, as from the first it was clear he would do, on publishing it. This occupied some occasional portion of his thoughts. But his grand private affair, I believe, was now *Strafford ;* to which, or to its adjuncts, all working hours were devoted. Sterling's notions of Tragedy are high enough. This is what he writes once, in reference to his own task in these weeks : "Few, I fancy, know how much harder it is to write a Tragedy than to realize or be one. Every man has in his heart and lot, if he pleases, and too many whether they please or no, all the woes of Œdipus and Antigone. But it takes the One, the Sophocles of a thousand years, to utter these in the full depth and harmony of creative song. Curious, by the way, how that Dramatic Form of the old Greek, with only some superficial changes, remains a law not only for the stage, but for the thoughts of all Poets ; and what a charm it has even for the reader who never saw a theatre. The Greek Plays and Shakspeare have interested a hundred as books, for one who has seen their writings acted. How lightly does the mere clown, the idle school-girl, build a private theatre in the fancy, and laugh or weep with Falstaff and Macbeth: with how entire an oblivion of the artificial nature of the whole contrivance, which thus compels them to be their own architects, machinists, scene-painters, and actors! In fact, the artifice succeeds, — becomes grounded in the substance of the soul: and every one loves to feel how he is thus brought face to face with the brave, the fair, the woful and the great of all past ages; looks into their eyes, and feels the beatings of their hearts; and reads, over the shoulder, the secret written tablets of the busiest and the largest brains; while the Juggler, by whose cunning the whole strange beautiful absurdity is set in motion, keeps himself hidden; sings loud with a mouth unmoving as that of a statue, and makes the human race cheat itself unanimously and delightfully by the illusion that he preordains; while as an obscure Fate, he sits invisible, and hardly lets his being be divined by those who cannot flee him. The Lyric Art is childish, and the Epic barbarous, compared to this. But of the true and perfect Drama it may be said, as of even higher mysteries, Who is sufficient for these things?" — On this *Tragedy of Strafford,* writing it and again writing it, studying for it, and bending himself with his whole strength to do his best on it, he expended many strenuous months, — "above a year of his life," he computes, in all.

For the rest, what Falmouth has to give him he is willing to take, and mingles freely in it. In Hare's Collection there is given a *Lecture* which he read in Autumn, 1841 (Mr. Hare says "1842," by mistake), to a certain Public Institution in the place, — of which more anon; — a piece interesting in this, if not much in any other respect. Doubtless his friends the Foxes were at the heart of that lecturing enterprise, and had urged and solicited him. Something like proficiency in certain branches of science, as I have understood, characterized one or more of this estimable family; love of knowledge, taste for art, wish to consort with wisdom and wise men, were the tendencies of all; to opulent means superadd the Quaker beneficence, Quaker purity and reverence, there is a circle in which wise men also may love to be. Sterling made acquaintance here with whatever of notable in worthy persons or things might be afoot in those parts; and was led thereby, now and then, into pleasant reunions, in new circles of activity, which might otherwise have continued foreign to him. The good Calvert, too, was now here; and intended to remain; — which he mostly did henceforth, lodging in Sterling's neighborhood, so long as lodging in this world was permitted him. Still good and clear and cheerful; still a lively comrade, within doors or without, — a diligent rider always, — though now wearing visibly weaker, and less able to exert himself.

Among those accidental Falmouth reunions, perhaps the notablest for Sterling occurred in this his first season. There is in Falmouth an Association called the *Cornwall Polytechnic Society*, established about twenty years ago, and supported by the wealthy people of the Town and neighborhood, for the encouragement of the arts in that region; it has its Library, its Museum, some kind of Annual Exhibition withal; gives prizes, publishes reports: the main patrons, I believe, are Sir Charles Lemon, a well-known country gentleman of those parts, and the Messrs. Fox. To this, so far as he liked to go in it, Sterling was sure to be introduced and solicited. The Polytechnic meeting of 1841 was unusually distinguished; and Sterling's part in it formed one of the pleasant occurrences for him in Falmouth. It was here that, among other profitable as well as pleasant things, he made acquaintance with Professor Owen (an event of which I too had my benefit in due time, and still have): the bigger assemblage called *British Association*, which met at Plymouth this year, having now just finished its affairs there, Owen and other distinguished persons had taken Falmouth in their route from it. Sterling's account of this Polytechnic gala still remains, — in three Letters to his Father, which, omitting the extraneous portions, I will give in one, — as a piece worth reading among those still-life pictures: —

" *To Edward Sterling, Esq., Knightsbridge, London.*

"FALMOUTH, 10th August, 1841.

" MY DEAR FATHER, — I was not well for a day or two
after you went; and since, I have been busy about an annual
show of the Polytechnic Society here, in which my friends
take much interest, and for which I have been acting as one
of the judges in the department of the Fine Arts, and have
written a little Report for them. As I have not said that
Falmouth is as eminent as Athens or Florence, perhaps the
Committee will not adopt my statement. But if they do, it
will be of some use; for I have hinted, as delicately as possible, that people should not paint historical pictures before
they have the power of drawing a decent outline of a pig or a
cabbage. I saw Sir Charles Lemon yesterday, who was kind
as well as civil in his manner; and promises to be a pleasant
neighbor. There are several of the British Association heroes
here; but not Whewell, or any one whom I know."

"*August* 17*th*. — At the Polytechnic Meeting here we had
several very eminent men; among others, Professor Owen,
said to be the first of comparative anatomists, and Conybeare
the geologist. Both of these gave evening Lectures; and
after Conybeare's, at which I happened to be present, I said
I would, if they chose, make some remarks on the Busts which
happened to be standing there, intended for prizes in the
department of the Fine Arts. They agreed gladly. The
heads were Homer, Pericles, Augustus, Dante and Michael
Angelo. I got into the box-like platform, with these on a shelf
before me; and began a talk which must have lasted some
three quarters of an hour; describing partly the characters
and circumstances of the men, illustrated by anecdotes and
compared with their physiognomies, and partly the several
styles of sculpture exhibited in the Casts, referring these to
what I considered the true principles of the Art. The subject
was one that interests me, and I got on in famous style; and
had both pit and galleries all applauding, in a way that had had
no precedent during any other part of the meeting. Conybeare
paid me high compliments; Owen looked much pleased, — an

honor well purchased by a year's hard work; — and everybody, in short, seemed delighted. Susan was not there, and I had nothing to make me nervous; so that I worked away freely, and got vigorously over the ground. After so many years' disuse of rhetoric, it was a pleasant surprise to myself to find that I could still handle the old weapons without awkwardness. More by good luck than good guidance, it has done my health no harm. I have been at Sir Charles Lemon's, though only to pay a morning visit, having declined to stay there or dine, the hours not suiting me. They were very civil. The person I saw most of was his sister, Lady Dunstanville; a pleasant, well-informed and well-bred woman. He seems a most amiable, kindly man, of fair good sense and cultivated tastes. — I had a letter to-day from my Mother [in Scotland]; who says she sent you one which you were to forward me; which I hope soon to have."

"*August 29th.* — I returned yesterday from Carclew, Sir C. Lemon's fine place about five miles off; where I had been staying a couple of days, with apparently the heartiest welcome. Susan was asked; but wanting a Governess, could not leave home.

"Sir Charles is a widower (his Wife was sister to Lord Ilchester) without children; but had a niece staying with him, and his sister Lady Dunstanville, a pleasant and very civil woman. There were also Mr. Bunbury, eldest son of Sir Henry Bunbury, a man of much cultivation and strong talents; Mr. Fox Talbot, son, I think, of another Ilchester lady, and brother of *the* Talbot of Wales, but himself a man of large fortune, and known for photogenic and other scientific plans of extracting sunbeams from cucumbers. He also is a man of known ability, but chiefly employed in that peculiar department. *Item* Professors Lloyd and Owen: the former, of Dublin, son of the late Provost, I had seen before and knew; a great mathematician and optician, and a discoverer in those matters; with a clever little Wife, who has a great deal of knowledge, quite free from pretension. Owen is a first-rate comparative anatomist, they say the greatest since Cuvier; lives in London, and lectures there. On the whole, he interested me more than any of them, — by an apparent force and downrightness of mind, combined with much simplicity and frankness.

"Nothing could be pleasanter and easier than the habits of life, with what to me was a very unusual degree of luxury, though probably nothing but what is common among people of large fortune. The library and pictures are nothing extraordinary. The general tone of good nature, good sense and quiet freedom, was what struck me most; and I think besides this there was a disposition to be cordially courteous towards me. . . .

"I took Edward a ride of two hours yesterday on Calvert's pony, and he is improving fast in horsemanship. The school appears to answer very well. We shall have the Governess in a day or two, which will be a great satisfaction. Will you send my Mother this scribble with my love; and believe me,

"Your affectionate son,

"JOHN STERLING."

One other little event dwells with me, out of those Falmouth times, exact date now forgotten; a pleasant little matter, in which Sterling, and principally the Misses Fox, bright cheery young creatures, were concerned; which, for the sake of its human interest, is worth mention. In a certain Cornish mine, said the Newspapers duly specifying it, two miners deep down in the shaft were engaged putting in a shot for blasting: they had completed their affair, and were about to give the signal for being hoisted up, — one at a time was all their coadjutor at the top could manage, and the second was to kindle the match, and then mount with all speed. Now it chanced while they were both still below, one of them thought the match too long; tried to break it shorter, took a couple of stones, a flat and a sharp, to cut it shorter; did cut it of the due length, but, horrible to relate, kindled it at the same time, and both were still below! Both shouted vehemently to the coadjutor at the windlass, both sprang at the basket; the windlass man could not move it with them both. Here was a moment for poor miner Jack and miner Will! Instant horrible death hangs

over both, — when Will generously resigns himself : " Go aloft,
Jack," and sits down; "away; in one minute I shall be in
Heaven!" Jack bounds aloft, the explosion instantly follows,
bruises his face as he looks over; he is safe above ground: and
poor Will? Descending eagerly they find Will too, as if by
miracle, buried under rocks which had arched themselves over
him, and little injured: he too is brought up safe, and all ends
joyfully, say the Newspapers.

Such a piece of manful promptitude, and salutary human
heroism, was worth investigating. It was investigated; found
to be accurate to the letter, — with this addition and explanation, that Will, an honest, ignorant good man, entirely given
up to Methodism, had been perfect in the "faith of assurance,"
certain that *he* should get to Heaven if he died, certain that
Jack would not, which had been the ground of his decision in
that great moment;—for the rest, that he much wished to
learn readin and writing, and find some way of life above
ground instead of below. By aid of the Misses Fox and the
rest of that family, a subscription (modest *Anti*-Hudson testi-
monial) was raised to this Methodist hero: he emerged into
daylight with fifty pounds in his pocket; did strenuously try,
for certain months, to learn reading and writing; found he
could not learn those arts or either of them; took his money
and bought cows with it, wedding at the same time some religious likely milkmaid; and is, last time I heard of him, a prosperous modest dairyman, thankful for the upper light and
safety from the wrath to come. Sterling had some hand in
this affair: but, as I said, it was the two young ladies of the
family that mainly did it.

In the end of 1841, after many hesitations and revisals, *The
Election* came out; a tiny Duodecimo without name attached;[1]
again inquiring of the public what its suffrage was; again to
little purpose. My vote had never been loud for this step, but
neither was it quite adverse; and now, in reading the poor
little Poem over again, after ten years' space, I find it, with a
touching mixture of pleasure and repentance, considerably
better than it then seemed to me. My encouragement, if not

---

[1] *The Election: a Poem, in Seven Books.* London, Murray, 1841.

to print this poem, yet to proceed with Poetry, since there was such a resolution for it, might have been a little more decided!

This is a small Piece, but aims at containing great things; a *multum in parvo* after its sort; and is executed here and there with undeniable success. The style is free and flowing, the rhyme dances along with a certain joyful triumph; everything of due brevity withal. That mixture of mockery on the surface, which finely relieves the real earnestness within, and flavors even what is not very earnest and might even be insipid otherwise, is not ill managed: an amalgam difficult to effect well in writing; nay, impossible in writing, — unless it stand already done and effected, as a general fact, in the writer's mind and character; which will betoken a certain ripeness there.

As I said, great things are intended in this little Piece; the motto itself foreshadowing them: —

> "*Fluellen*. Ancient Pistol, I do partly understand your meaning.
> *Pistol*. Why, then, rejoice therefor."

A stupid commonplace English Borough has lost its Member suddenly, by apoplexy or otherwise; resolves, in the usual explosive temper of mind, to replace him by one of two others; whereupon strange stirring-up of rival-attorney and other human interests and catastrophes. "Frank Vane" (Sterling himself), and "Peter Mogg," the pattern English blockhead of elections: these are the candidates. There are, of course, fierce rival attorneys; electors of all creeds and complexions to be canvassed: a poor stupid Borough thrown all into red or white heat; into blazing paroxysms of activity and enthusiasm, which render the inner life of it (and of England and the world through it) luminously transparent, so to speak; — of which opportunity our friend and his "Muse" take dexterous advantage, to delineate the same. His pictures are uncommonly good; brief, joyous, sometimes conclusively true: in rigorously compressed shape; all is merry freshness and exuberance: we have leafy summer embowering red bricks and small human interests, presented as in

glowing miniature; a mock-heroic action fitly interwoven; —
and many a clear glance is carelessly given into the deepest
things by the way.   Very happy also is the little love-episode;
and the absorption of all the interest into that, on the part of
Frank Vane and of us, when once this gallant Frank, — having
fairly from his barrel-head stated his own (and John Sterling's)
views on the aspects of the world, and of course having quite
broken down with his attorney and his public,·— handsomely,
by stratagem, gallops off with the fair Anne; and leaves free
field to Mogg, free field to the Hippopotamus if it like.   This
portrait of Mogg may be considered to have merit: —

> "Though short of days, how large the mind of man;
> A godlike force enclosed within a span!
> To climb the skies we spurn our nature's clog,
> And toil as Titans to elect a Mogg.
>   "And who was Mogg?   O Muse! the man declare,
> How excellent his worth, his parts how rare.
> A younger son, he learnt in Oxford's halls
> The spheral harmonies of billiard-balls,
> Drank, hunted, drove, and hid from Virtue's frown
> His venial follies in Decorum's gown.
> Too wise to doubt on insufficient cause,
> He signed old Cranmer's lore without a pause;
> And knew that logic's cunning rules are taught
> To guard our creed, and not invigorate thought, —
> As those bronze steeds at Venice, kept for pride,
> Adorn a Town where not one man can ride.
>   "From Isis sent with all her loud acclaims,
> The Laws he studied on the banks of Thames.
> Park, race and play, in his capacious plan,
> Combined with Coke to form the finished man,
> Until the wig's ambrosial influence shed
> Its last full glories on the lawyer's head.
>   "But vain are mortal schemes.   The eldest son
> At Harrier Hall had scarce his stud begun,
> When Death's pale courser took the Squire away
> To lands where never dawns a hunting-day:
> And so, while Thomas vanished 'mid the fog,
> Bright rose the morning-star of Peter Mogg." [1]

And this little picture, in a quite opposite way: —

[1] Pp. 7, 8.

"Now, in her chamber all alone, the maid
Her polished limbs and shoulders disarrayed;
One little taper gave the only light,
One little mirror caught so dear a sight;
'Mid hangings dusk and shadows wide she stood,
Like some pale Nymph in dark-leafed solitude
Of rocks and gloomy waters all alone,
Where sunshine scarcely breaks on stump or stone
To scare the dreamy vision. Thus did she,
A star in deepest night, intent but free,
Gleam through the eyeless darkness, heeding not
Her beauty's praise, but musing o'er her lot.

"Her garments one by one she laid aside,
And then her knotted hair's long locks untied
With careless hand, and down her cheeks they fell,
And o'er her maiden bosom's blue-veined swell.
The right-hand fingers played amidst her hair,
And with her reverie wandered here and there:
The other hand sustained the only dress
That now but half concealed her loveliness;
And pausing, aimlessly she stood and thought,
In virgin beauty by no fear distraught."

Manifold, and beautiful of their sort, are Anne's musings, in this interesting attitude, in the summer midnight, in the crisis of her destiny now near;—at last:—

"But Anne, at last her mute devotions o'er,
Perceived the fact she had forgot before
Of her too shocking nudity; and shame
Flushed from her heart o'er all the snowy frame:
And, struck from top to toe with burning dread,
She blew the light out, and escaped to bed." [1]

—which also is a very pretty movement.

It must be owned withal, the Piece is crude in parts, and far enough from perfect. Our good painter has yet several things to learn, and to unlearn. His brush is not always of the finest; and dashes about, sometimes, in a recognizably sprawling way: but it hits many a feature with decisive accuracy and felicity; and on the palette, as usual, lie the richest colors. A grand merit, too, is the brevity of everything; by no means a spontaneous, or quite common merit with Sterling.

[1] Pp. 89–93.

This new poetic Duodecimo, as the last had done and as the next also did, met with little or no recognition from the world: which was not very inexcusable on the world's part; though many a poem with far less proof of merit than this offers, has run, when the accidents favored it, through its tens of editions, and raised the writer to the demigods for a year or two, if not longer.　Such as it is, we may take it as marking, in its small way, in a noticed or unnoticed manner, a new height arrived at by Sterling in his Poetic course; and almost as vindicating the determination he had formed to keep climbing by that method.　Poor Poem, or rather Promise of a Poem!　In Sterling's brave struggle, this little *Election* is the highest point he fairly lived to see attained, and openly demonstrated in print. His next public adventure in this kind was of inferior worth; and a third, which had perhaps intrinsically gone much higher than any of its antecessors, was cut off as a fragment, and has not hitherto been published.　Steady courage is needed on the Poetic course, as on all courses! —

Shortly after this Publication, in the beginning of 1842, poor Calvert, long a hopeless sufferer, was delivered by death: Sterling's faithful fellow-pilgrim could no more attend him in his wayfarings through this world.　The weary and heavy-laden man had borne his burden well.　Sterling says of him to Hare: "Since I wrote last, I have lost Calvert; the man with whom, of all others, I have been during late years the most intimate.　Simplicity, benevolence, practical good sense and moral earnestness were his great unfailing characteristics; and no man, I believe, ever possessed them more entirely.　His illness had latterly so prostrated him, both in mind and body, that those who most loved him were most anxious for his departure."　There was something touching in this exit; in the quenching of so kind and bright a little life under the dark billows of death.　To me he left a curious old Print of James Nayler the Quaker, which I still affectionately preserve.

Sterling, from this greater distance, came perhaps rather seldomer to London; but we saw him still at moderate intervals; and, through his family here and other direct and indirect channels, were kept in lively communication with him. Literature was still his constant pursuit; and, with encouragement or without, Poetic composition his chosen department therein. On the ill success of *The Election*, or any ill success with the world, nobody ever heard him utter the least murmur; condolence upon that or any such subject might have been a questionable operation, by no means called for! Nay, my own approval, higher than this of the world, had been languid, by no means enthusiastic. But our valiant friend took all quietly; and was not to be repulsed from his Poetics either by the world's coldness or by mine; he labored at his *Strafford;* — determined to labor, in all ways, till he felt the end of his tether in this direction.

He sometimes spoke, with a certain zeal, of my starting a Periodical: Why not lift up some kind of war-flag against the obese platitudes, and sickly superstitious aperies and impostures of the time? But I had to answer, "Who will join it, my friend?" He seemed to say, "I, for one;" and there was occasionally a transient temptation in the thought, but transient only. No fighting regiment, with the smallest attempt towards drill, co-operation, commissariat, or the like unspeakable advantages, could be raised in Sterling's time or mine; which truly, to honest fighters, is a rather grievous want. A grievous, but not quite a fatal one. For, failing this, failing all things and all men, there remains the solitary battle (and were it by the poorest weapon, the tongue only, or were it even by wise abstinence and silence and without any weapon), such as each man for himself can wage while he has life: an indubitable and infinitely comfortable fact for every man! Said battle shaped itself for Sterling, as we have long since seen, chiefly in the poetic form, in the singing or hymning rather than the speaking form; and in that he was cheerfully assiduous according to his light. The unfortunate *Strafford* is far on towards completion; a *Cœur-de-Lion*, of which we shall hear farther, " *Cœur-de-Lion*, greatly the best of all his Poems," unluckily not completed, and still unpublished, already hangs in the wind.

His Letters to friends continue copious; and he has, as

always, a loyally interested eye on whatsoever of notable is
passing in the world. Especially on whatsoever indicates to
him the spiritual condition of the world. Of "Strauss," in
English or in German, we now hear nothing more; of Church
matters, and that only to special correspondents, less and less.
Strauss, whom he used to mention, had interested him only as
a sign of the times; in which sense alone do we find, for a
year or two back, any notice of the Church, or its affairs by
Sterling; and at last even this as good as ceases : "Adieu,
O Church ; thy road is that way, mine is this : in God's name,
adieu!" "What we are going *to*," says he once, "is abundantly obscure; but what all men are going *from*, is very
plain." — Sifted out of many pages, not of sufficient interest,
here are one or two miscellaneous sentences, about the date
we are now arrived at : —

To Dr. Symonds.

"*Falmouth, 3d November,* 1841. — Yesterday was my Wedding-day : eleven years of marriage; and on the whole my
verdict is clear for matrimony. I solemnized the day by reading *John Gilpin* to the children, who with their Mother are
all pretty well. . . . There is a trick of sham Elizabethan
writing now prevalent, that looks plausible, but in most
cases means nothing at all. Darley has real (lyrical) genius;
Taylor, wonderful sense, clearness and weight of purpose;
Tennyson, a rich and exquisite fancy. All the other men of
our tiny generation that I know of are, in Poetry, either feeble or fraudulent. I know nothing of the Reviewer you ask
about."

To his Mother.

"*December* 11*th*. — I have seen no new books ; but am reading your last. I got hold of the two first Numbers of the
Hoggarty Diamond ; and read them with extreme delight.
What is there better in Fielding or Goldsmith ? The man is
a true genius; and, with quiet and comfort, might produce
masterpieces that would last as long as any we have, and delight millions of unborn readers. There is more truth and

nature in one of these papers than in all —— 's Novels together." — Thackeray, always a close friend of the Sterling
house, will observe that this is dated 1841, not 1851, and have
his own reflections on the matter!

To the Same.

" *December* 17*th*. — I am not much surprised at Lady —— 's
views of Coleridge's little Book on *Inspiration*. — Great part
of the obscurity of the Letters arises from his anxiety to avoid
the difficulties and absurdities of the common views, and his
panic terror of saying anything that bishops and good people would disapprove. He paid a heavy price, viz. all his
own candor and simplicity, in hope of gaining the favor of persons like Lady ——; and you see what his reward is! A good
lesson for us all."

To the Same.

" *February* 1*st*, 1842. — English Toryism has, even in my
eyes, about as much to say for itself as any other form of doctrine; but Irish Toryism is the downright proclamation of
brutal injustice, and all in the name of God and the Bible! It
is almost enough to make one turn Mahometan, but for the
fear of the four wives."

To his Father.

" *March* 12*th*, 1842. — . . . Important to me as these matters are, it almost seems as if there were something unfeeling
in writing of them, under the pressure of such news as ours
from India. If the Cabool Troops have perished, England
has not received such a blow from an enemy, nor anything
approaching it, since Buckingham's Expedition to the Isle of
Rhé. Walcheren destroyed us by climate; and Corunna, with
all its losses, had much of glory. But here we are dismally
injured by mere Barbarians, in a War on our part shamefully
unjust as well as foolish: a combination of disgrace and calamity that would have shocked Augustus even more than the
defeat of Varus. One of the four officers with Macnaghten
was George Lawrence, a brother-in-law of Nat Barton; a dis-

tinguished man, and the father of five totally unprovided
children. He is a prisoner, if not since murdered. Macnaghten I do not pity; he was the prime author of the whole
mad War. But Burnes; and the women; and our regiments!
India, however, I feel sure, is safe."

So roll the months at Falmouth; such is the ticking of the
great World-Horologe as heard there by a good ear. "I willingly add," so ends he, once, "that I lately found somewhere
this fragment of an Arab's love-song: 'O Ghalia! If my
father were a jackass, I would sell him to purchase Ghalia!'
A beautiful parallel to the French '*Avec cette sauce on man-
gerait son père.*'"

CHAPTER IV.

NAPLES: POEMS.

IN the bleak weather of this spring, 1842, he was again
abroad for a little while; partly from necessity, or at least
utility; and partly, as I guess, because these circumstances
favored, and he could with a good countenance indulge a
little wish he had long had. In the Italian Tour, which
ended suddenly by Mrs. Sterling's illness recalling him, he
had missed Naples; a loss which he always thought to be
considerable; and which, from time to time, he had formed
little projects, failures hitherto, for supplying. The rigors
of spring were always dangerous to him in England, and it
was always of advantage to get out of them: and then the
sight of Naples, too; this, always a thing to be done some
day, was now possible. Enough, with the real or imaginary
hope of bettering himself in health, and the certain one of
seeing Naples, and catching a glance of Italy again, he now
made a run thither. It was not long after Calvert's death.
The Tragedy of *Strafford* lay finished in his desk. Several
things, sad and bright, were finished. A little intermezzo of
ramble was not unadvisable.

His tour by water and by land was brief and rapid enough; hardly above two months in all. Of which the following Letters will, with some abridgment, give us what details are needful : —

    " *To Charles Barton, Esq., Leamington.*

                       "FALMOUTH, 25th March, 1842.

"MY DEAR CHARLES, — My attempts to shoot you flying with my paper pellets turned out very ill. I hope young ladies succeed better when they happen to make appointments with you. Even now, I hardly know whether you have received a Letter I wrote on Sunday last, and addressed to The Cavendish. I sent it thither by Susan's advice.

"In this missive, — happily for us both, it did not contain a hundred-pound note or any trifle of that kind, — I informed you that I was compelled to plan an expedition towards the South Pole; stopping, however, in the Mediterranean; and that I designed leaving this on Monday next for Cadiz or Gibraltar, and then going on to Malta, whence Italy and Sicily would be accessible. Of course your company would be a great pleasure, if it were possible for you to join me. The delay in hearing from you, through no fault of yours, has naturally put me out a little; but, on the whole, my plan still holds, and I shall leave this on Monday for Gibraltar, where the *Great Liverpool* will catch me, and carry me to Malta. The *Great Liverpool* leaves Southampton on the 1st of April, and Falmouth on the 2d; and will reach Gibraltar in from four to five days.

"Now, if you *should* be able and disposed to join me, you have only to embark in that sumptuous tea-kettle, and pick me up under the guns of the Rock. We could then cruise on to Malta, Sicily, Naples, Rome, &c., *à discrétion*. It is just *possible*, though extremely improbable, that my steamer of Monday (most likely the *Montrose*) may not reach Gibraltar so soon as the *Liverpool*. If so, and if you should actually be on board, you must stop at Gibraltar. But there are ninety-nine chances to one against this. Write at all events to Susan, to let her know what you propose.

"I do not wait till the *Great Liverpool* goes, because the object for me is to get into a warm climate as soon as possible. I am decidedly better.

"Your affectionate Brother,

"JOHN STERLING."

Barton did not go with him, none went; but he arrives safe, and not *hurt* in health, which is something.

"*To Mrs. Sterling, Knightsbridge, London.*

"MALTA, 14th April, 1842.

"DEAREST MOTHER,—I am writing to Susan through France, by to-morrow's mail; and will also send you a line, instead of waiting for the longer English conveyance.

"We reached this the day before yesterday, in the evening; having had a strong breeze against us for a day or two before; which made me extremely uncomfortable, — and indeed my headache is hardly gone yet. From about the 4th to the 9th of the month, we had beautiful weather, and I was happy enough. You will see by the map that the straightest line from Gibraltar to this place goes close along the African coast; which accordingly we saw with the utmost clearness; and found it generally a line of mountains, the higher peaks and ridges covered with snow. We went close in to Algiers; which looks strong, but entirely from art. The town lies on the slope of a straight coast; and is not at all embayed, though there is some little shelter for shipping within the mole. It is a square patch of white buildings huddled together; fringed with batteries; and commanded by large forts on the ridge above: a most uncomfortable-looking place; though, no doubt, there are *cafés* and billiard-rooms and a theatre within, — for the French like to have their Houris, &c., on *this* side of Paradise, if possible.

"Our party of fifty people (we had taken some on board at Gibraltar) broke up, on reaching this; never, of course, to meet again. The greater part do not proceed to Alexandria. Considering that there was a bundle of midshipmen, ensigns, &c., we had as much reason among us as could perhaps be looked for ; and from several I gained bits of information and traits of character, though nothing very remarkable. . . .

"I have established myself in an inn, rather than go to Lady Louis's ;[1] not feeling quite equal to company, except in moderate doses. I have, however, seen her a good deal ; and dine there to-day, very privately, for Sir John is not quite well, and they will have no guests. The place, however, is full of official banqueting, for various unimportant reasons. When here before, I was in much distress and anxiety, on my way from Rome ; and I suppose this it was that prevented its making the same impression on me as now, when it seems really the stateliest town I have ever seen. The architecture is generally of a corrupt Roman kind ; with something of the varied and picturesque look, though much more massive, of our Elizabethan buildings. We have the finest English summer and a pellucid sky. . . . Your affectionate

" JOHN STERLING."

At Naples next, for three weeks, was due admiration of the sceneries and antiquities, Bay and Mountain, by no means forgetting Art and the Museum : " to Pozzuoli, to Baiæ, round the Promontory of Sorrento ; " — above all, " twice to Pompeii," where the elegance and classic simplicity of Ancient Housekeeping strikes us much ; and again to Pæstum, where " the Temple of Neptune is far the noblest building I have ever seen ; and makes both Greek and Revived Roman seem quite barbaric. . . . Lord Ponsonby lodges in the same house with me ; — but, of course, I do not countenance an adherent of a beaten Party ! "[2] — Or let us take this more compendious account, which has much more of human in it, from an onward stage, ten days later : —

" *To Thomas Carlyle, Esq., Chelsea, London.*

" ROME, 13th May, 1842.

" MY DEAR CARLYLE, — I hope I wrote to you before leaving England, to tell you of the necessity for my doing so. Though

---

[1] Sister of Mrs. Strachey and Mrs. Buller : Sir John Louis was now in a high Naval post at Malta.

[2] Long Letter to his Father : Naples, 3d May, 1842.

coming to Italy, there was little comfort in the prospect of being divided from my family, and pursuits which grew on me every day. However, I tried to make the best of it, and have gained both health and pleasure.

"In spite of scanty communications from England (owing to the uncertainty of my position), a word or two concerning you and your dear Wife have reached me. Lately it has often occurred to me, that the sight of the Bay of Naples, of the beautiful coast from that to this place, and of Rome itself, all bathed in summer sunshine, and green with spring foliage, would be some consolation to her.[1] Pray give her my love.

"I have been two days here; and almost the first thing I did was to visit the Protestant burial-ground, and the graves of those I knew when here before. But much as being now alone here, I feel the difference, there is no scene where Death seems so little dreadful and miserable as in the lonelier neighborhoods of this old place. All one's impressions, however, as to that and everything else, appear to me, on reflection, more affected than I had for a long time any notion of, by one's own isolation. All the feelings and activities which family, friends and occupation commonly engage, are turned, here in one's solitude, with strange force into the channels of mere observation and contemplation; and the objects one is conversant with seem to gain a tenfold significance from the abundance of spare interest one now has to bestow on them. This explains to me a good deal of the peculiar effect that Italy has always had on me: and something of that artistic enthusiasm which I remember you used to think so singular in Goethe's *Travels*. Darley, who is as much a brooding hermit in England as here, felt nothing but disappointment from a country which fills me with childish wonder and delight.

"Of you I have received some slight notice from Mrs. Strachey; who is on her way hither; and will (she writes) be at Florence on the 15th, and here before the end of the month. She notices having received a Letter of yours which had pleased her much. She now proposes spending the sum-

[1] Death of her Mother, four months before. (*Note of* 1870.)

mer at Sorrento, or thereabouts ; and if mere delight of land-scape and climate were enough, Adam and Eve, had their courier taken them to that region, might have done well enough without Paradise, — and not been tempted, either, by any Tree of Knowledge ; a kind that does not flourish in the Two Sicilies.

" The ignorance of the Neapolitans, from the highest to the lowest, is very eminent; and excites the admiration of all the rest of Italy. In the great building containing all the Works of Art, and a Library of 150,000 volumes, I asked for the best existing Book (a German one published ten years ago) on the Statues in that very Collection; and, after a rabble of clerks and custodes, got up to a dirty priest, who bowing to the ground regretted ' they did not possess it,' but at last remembered that ' they *had* entered into negotiations on the subject, which as yet had been unsuccessful.' — The favorite device on the walls at Naples is a vermilion Picture of a Male and Female Soul respectively up to the waist (the waist of a *soul*) in fire, and an Angel above each, watering the sufferers from a watering-pot. This is intended to gain alms for Masses. The same populace sit for hours on the Mole, listening to rhap-sodists who recite Ariosto. I have seen I think five of them all within a hundred yards of each other, and some sets of fiddlers to boot. Yet there are few parts of the world where I have seen less laughter than there. The Miracle of Janua-rius's Blood is, on the whole, my most curious experience. The furious entreaties, shrieks and sobs, of a set of old women, yelling till the Miracle was successfully performed, are things never to be forgotten.

" I spent three weeks in this most glittering of countries, and saw most of the usual wonders, — the Pæstan Temples being to me much the most valuable. But Pompeii and all that it has yielded, especially the Fresco Paintings, have also an infinite interest. When one considers that this prodigious series of beautiful designs supplied the place of our common room-papers, — the wealth of poetic imagery among the Ancients, and the corresponding traditional variety and ele-gance of pictorial treatment, seem equally remarkable. The

Greek and Latin Books do not give one quite so fully this sort
of impression; because they afford no direct measure of the
extent of their own diffusion.   But these are ornaments from
the smaller class of decent houses in a little Country Town;
and the greater number of them, by the slightness of the execution, show very clearly that they were adapted to ordinary
taste, and done by mere artisans.   In general clearness, sym-
metry and simplicity of feeling, I cannot say that, on the
whole, the works of Raffaelle equal them; though of course
he has endless beauties such as we could not find unless in
the great original works from which these sketches at Pompeii were taken.   Yet with all my much increased reverence
for the Greeks, it seems more plain than ever that they had
hardly anything of the peculiar devotional feeling of Christianity.

" Rome, which I loved before above all the earth, now
delights me more than ever; — though at this moment there
is rain falling that would not discredit Oxford Street.   The
depth, sincerity and splendor that there once was in the semi-
paganism of the old Catholics comes out in St. Peter's and its
dependencies, almost as grandly as does Greek and Roman
Art in the Forum and the Vatican Galleries.   I wish you were
here : but, at all events, hope to see you and your Wife once
more during this summer.
                              " Yours,
                                        " John Sterling."

At Paris, where he stopped a day and night, and generally
through his whole journey from Marseilles to Havre, one thing
attended him : the prevailing epidemic of the place and year;
now gone, and nigh forgotten, as other influenzas are.   He
writes to his Father : " I have not yet met a single Frenchman, who could give me any rational explanation *why* they
were all in such a confounded rage against us.   Definite causes
of quarrel a statesman may know how to deal with, inasmuch
as the removal of them may help to settle the dispute.   But
it must be a puzzling task to negotiate about instincts; to
which class, as it seems to me, we must have recourse for an
understanding of the present abhorrence which everybody on

the other side of the Channel not only feels, but makes a point
to boast of, against the name of Britain. France is slowly
arming, especially with Steam, *en attendant* a more than possible contest, in which they reckon confidently on the eager
co-operation of the Yankees; as, *vice versa*, an American told
me that his countrymen do on that of France. One person at
Paris (M. —— whom you know) provoked me to tell him that
' England did not want another battle of Trafalgar; but if
France did, she might compel England to gratify her.' " —
After a couple of pleasant and profitable months, he was safe
home again in the first days of June; and saw Falmouth not
under gray iron skies, and whirls of March dust, but bright
with summer opulence and the roses coming out.

It was what I call his "*fifth* peregrinity;" his fifth and
last. He soon afterwards came up to London; spent a couple
of weeks, with all his old vivacity, among us here. The
Æsculapian oracles, it would appear, gave altogether cheerful
prophecy; the highest medical authority "expresses the most
decided opinion that I have gradually mended for some years;
and in truth I have not, for six or seven, been so free from
serious symptoms of illness as at present." So uncertain are
all oracles, Æsculapian and other !

During this visit, he made one new acquaintance which he
much valued; drawn thither, as I guess, by the wish to take
counsel about *Strafford*. He writes to his Clifton friend,
under date, 1*st July* 1842: "Lockhart, of the *Quarterly Review*, I made my first oral acquaintance with; and found
him as neat, clear and cutting a brain as you would expect;
but with an amount of knowledge, good nature and liberal
anti-bigotry, that would much surprise many. The tone of
his children towards him seemed to me decisive of his real
kindness. He quite agreed with me as to the threatening
seriousness of our present social perplexities, and the necessity and difficulty of doing something effectual for so satisfying the manual multitude as not to overthrow all legal
security. . . .

"Of other persons whom I saw in London," continues he,
"there are several that would much interest you, — though

I missed Tennyson, by a mere chance. . . . John Mill has
completely finished, and sent to the bookseller, his great work
on Logic; the labor of many years of a singularly subtle,
patient and comprehensive mind. It will be our chief speculative monument of this age. Mill and I could not meet above
two or three times; but it was with the openness and freshness
of school-boy friends, though our friendship only dates from
the manhood of both."

He himself was busier than ever; occupied continually with
all manner of Poetic interests. *Cœur-de-Lion,* a new and
more elaborate attempt in the mock-heroic or comico-didactic
vein, had been on hand for some time, the scope of it greatly
deepening and expanding itself since it first took hold of him;
and now, soon after the Naples journey, it rose into shape on
the wider plan; shaken up probably by this new excitement,
and indebted to Calabria, Palermo and the Mediterranean scenes
for much of the vesture it had. With this, which opened
higher hopes for him than any of his previous efforts, he was
now employing all his time and strength; — and continued to
do so, this being the last effort granted him among us.

Already, for some months, *Strafford* lay complete: but how
to get it from the stocks; in what method to launch it? The
step was questionable. Before going to Italy he had sent me
the Manuscript; still loyal and friendly; and willing to hear
the worst that could be said of his poetic enterprise. I had
to afflict him again, the good brave soul, with the deliberate
report that I could *not* accept this Drama as his Picture of
the Life of Strafford, or as any *Picture* of that strange Fact.
To which he answered, with an honest manfulness, in a tone
which is now pathetic enough to me, that he was much grieved
yet much obliged, and uncertain how to decide. On the other
hand, Mr. Hare wrote, warmly eulogizing. Lockhart too spoke
kindly, though taking some exceptions. It was a questionable case. On the whole, *Strafford* remained, for the present,
unlaunched; and *Cœur-de-Lion* was getting its first timbers
diligently laid down. So passed, in peaceable seclusion, in
wholesome employment and endeavor, the autumn and winter
of 1842–43. On Christmas-day, he reports to his Mother: —

"I wished to write to you yesterday; but was prevented by the important business of preparing a Tree, in the German fashion, for the children. This project answered perfectly, as it did last year; and gave them the greatest pleasure. I wish you and my Father could have been here to see their merry faces. Johnny was in the thick of the fun, and much happier than Lord Anson on capturing the galleon. We are all going on well and quietly, but with nothing very new among us. . . . The last book I have lighted on is Moffat's *Missionary Labors in South Africa;* which is worth reading. There is the best collection of lion stories in it that I have ever seen. But the man is, also, really a very good fellow; and fit for something much better than most lions are. He is very ignorant, and mistaken in some things; but has strong sense and heart; and his Narrative adds another to the many proofs of the enormous power of Christianity on rude minds. Nothing can be more chaotic, that is human at all, than the notions of these poor Blacks, even after what is called their conversion; but the effect is produced. They do adopt pantaloons, and abandon polygamy; and I suppose will soon have newspapers and literary soirées."

———◆———

CHAPTER V.

DISASTER ON DISASTER.

During all these years of struggle and wayfaring, his Father's household at Knightsbridge had stood healthful, happy, increasing in wealth, free diligence, solidity and honest prosperity: a fixed sunny islet, towards which, in all his voyagings and overclouded roamings, he could look with satisfaction, as to an ever-open port of refuge.

The elder Sterling, after many battles, had reached his field of conquest in these years; and was to be regarded as a victorious man. Wealth sufficient, increasing not diminishing, had

rewarded his labors in the *Times,* which were now in their full
flower; he had influence of a sort; went busily among busy
public men; and enjoyed, in the questionable form attached
to journalism and anonymity, a social consideration and position which were abundantly gratifying to him. A singular
figure of the epoch; and when you came to know him, which
it was easy to fail of doing if you had not eyes and candid
insight, a gallant, truly gifted, and manful figure, of his kind.
We saw much of him in this house; much of all his family;
and had grown to love them all right well, — him too, though
that was the difficult part of the feat. For in his Irish way
he played the conjurer very much, — "three hundred and
sixty-five opinions in the year upon every subject," as a wag
once said. In fact his talk, ever ingenious, emphatic and
spirited in detail, was much defective in earnestness, at least
in clear earnestness, of purport and outcome; but went tumbling as if in mere welters of explosive unreason; a volcano
heaving under vague deluges of scoriæ, ashes and imponderous
pumice-stones, you could not say in what direction, nor well
whether in any. Not till after good study did you see the
deep molten lava-flood, which simmered steadily enough, and
showed very well by and by whither *it* was bound. For I
must say of Edward Sterling, after all his daily explosive
sophistries, and fallacies of talk, he had a stubborn instinctive
sense of what was manful, strong and worthy; recognized,
with quick feeling, the charlatan under his solemnest wig;
knew as clearly as any man a pusillanimous tailor in buckram,
an ass under the lion's skin, and did with his whole heart
despise the same.

The sudden changes of doctrine in the *Times,* which failed
not to excite loud censure and indignant amazement in those
days, were first intelligible to you when you came to interpret
them as his changes. These sudden whirls from east to west
on his part, and total changes of party and articulate opinion
at a day's warning, lay in the nature of the man, and could
not be helped; products of his fiery impatience, of the combined impetuosity and limitation of an intellect, which did
nevertheless continually gravitate towards what was loyal, true

and right on all manner of subjects. These, as I define them, were the mere scoriæ and pumice wreck of a steady central lava-flood, which truly was volcanic and explosive to a strange degree, but did rest as few others on the grand fire-depths of the world. Thus, if he stormed along, ten thousand strong, in the time of the Reform Bill, indignantly denouncing Toryism and its obsolete insane pretensions ; and then if, after some experience of Whig management, he discerned that Wellington and Peel, by whatever name entitled, were the men to be depended on by England, — there lay in all this, visible enough, a deeper consistency far more important than the superficial one, so much clamored after by the vulgar. Which is the lion's-skin ; which is the real lion ? Let a man, if he is prudent, ascertain that before speaking ; — but above and beyond all things, *let* him ascertain it, and stand valiantly to it when ascertained ! In the latter essential part of the operation Edward Sterling was honorably successful to a really marked degree ; in the former, or prudential part, very much the reverse, as his history in the Journalistic department at least, was continually teaching him.

An amazingly impetuous, hasty, explosive man, this " Captain Whirlwind," as I used to call him ! Great sensibility lay in him, too ; a real sympathy, and affectionate pity and softness, which he had an over-tendency to express even by tears, — a singular sight in so leonine a man. Enemies called them maudlin and hypocritical, these tears ; but that was nowise the complete account of them. On the whole, there did conspicuously lie a dash of ostentation, a self-consciousness apt to become loud and braggart, over all he said and did and felt : this was the alloy of the man, and you had to be thankful for the abundant gold along with it.

Quizzing enough he got among us for all this, and for the singular *chiaroscuro* manner of procedure, like that of an Archimagus Cagliostro, or Kaiser Joseph Incognito, which his anonymous known-unknown thunderings in the *Times* necessitated in him ; and much we laughed, — not without explosive counter-banterings on his part ; — but, in fine, one could not do without him ; one knew him at heart for a right

brave man. "By Jove, sir!" thus he would swear to you,
with radiant face; sometimes, not often, by a deeper oath.
With persons of dignity, especially with women, to whom he
was always very gallant, he had courtly delicate manners,
verging towards the wire-drawn and elaborate; on common
occasions, he bloomed out at once into jolly familiarity of the
gracefully boisterous kind, reminding you of mess-rooms and
old Dublin days. His off-hand mode of speech was always
precise, emphatic, ingenious: his laugh, which was frequent
rather than otherwise, had a sincerity of banter, but no real
depth of sense for the ludicrous; and soon ended, if it grew
too loud, in a mere dissonant scream. He was broad, well-
built, stout of stature; had a long lowish head, sharp gray
eyes, with large strong aquiline face to match; and walked,
or sat, in an erect decisive manner. A remarkable man; and
playing, especially in those years 1830–40, a remarkable part
in the world.

For it may be said, the emphatic, big-voiced, always influential and often strongly unreasonable *Times* Newspaper was
the express emblem of Edward Sterling; he, more than any
other man or circumstance, *was* the *Times* Newspaper, and
thundered through it to the shaking of the spheres. And let
us assert withal that his and its influence, in those days, was
not ill grounded but rather well; that the loud manifold unreason, often enough vituperated and groaned over, was of the
surface mostly; that his conclusions, unreasonable, partial,
hasty as they might at first be, gravitated irresistibly towards
the right: in virtue of which grand quality indeed, the root of
all good insight in man, his *Times* oratory found acceptance
and influential audience, amid the loud whirl of an England
itself logically very stupid, and wise chiefly by instinct.

England listened to this voice, as all might observe; and
to one who knew England and it, the result was not quite a
strange one, and was honorable rather than otherwise to both
parties. A good judge of men's talents has been heard to say
of Edward Sterling: "There is not a *faculty of improvising*
equal to this in all my circle. Sterling rushes out into the
clubs, into London society, rolls about all day, copiously talk-

ing modish nonsense or sense, and listening to the like, with the multifarious miscellany of men; comes home at night; redacts it into a *Times* Leader, — and is found to have hit the essential purport of the world's immeasurable babblement that day, with an accuracy beyond all other men. This is what the multifarious Babel sound did mean to say in clear words; this, more nearly than anything else. Let the most gifted intellect, capable of writing epics, try to write such a Leader for the Morning Newspapers! No intellect but Edward Sterling's can do it. An improvising faculty without parallel in my experience." — In this "improvising faculty," much more nobly developed, as well as in other faculties and qualities with unexpectedly new and improved figure, John Sterling, to the accurate observer, showed himself very much the son of Edward.

Connected with this matter, a remarkable Note has come into my hands; honorable to the man I am writing of, and in some sort to another higher man; which, as it may now (unhappily for us all) be published without scruple, I will not withhold here. The support, by Edward Sterling and the *Times*, of Sir Robert Peel's first Ministry, and generally of Peel's statesmanship, was a conspicuous fact in its day; but the return it met with from the person chiefly interested may be considered well worth recording. The following Letter, after meandering through I know not what intricate conduits, and consultations of the Mysterious Entity whose address it bore, came to Edward Sterling as the real flesh-and-blood proprietor, and has been found among his papers. It is marked *Private:* —

"(Private) *To the Editor of the Times.*

" Whitehall, 18th April, 1835.

"Sir, — Having this day delivered into the hands of the King the Seals of Office, I can, without any imputation of an interested motive, or any impediment from scrupulous feelings of delicacy, express my deep sense of the powerful support which that Government over which I had the honor to preside received from the *Times* Newspaper.

"If I do not offer the expressions of personal gratitude, it is because I feel that such expressions would do injustice to the character of a support which was given exclusively on the highest and most independent grounds of public principle. I can say this with perfect truth, as I am addressing one whose person even is unknown to me, and who during my tenure of power studiously avoided every species of intercourse which could throw a suspicion upon the motives by which he was actuated. I should, however, be doing injustice to my own feelings, if I were to retire from Office without one word of acknowledgment; without at least assuring you of the admiration with which I witnessed, during the arduous contest in which I was engaged, the daily exhibition of that extraordinary ability to which I was indebted for a support, the more valuable because it was an impartial and discriminating support. — I have the honor to be, Sir,

"Ever your most obedient and faithful servant,
"ROBERT PEEL."

To which, with due loftiness and diplomatic gravity and brevity, there is Answer, Draught of Answer in Edward Sterling's hand, from the Mysterious Entity so honored, in the following terms:—

"*To the Right Hon. Sir Robert Peel, Bart., &c. &c. &c.*

"SIR, — It gives me sincere satisfaction to learn from the Letter with which you have honored me, bearing yesterday's date, that you estimate so highly the efforts which have been made during the last five months by the *Times* Newspaper to support the cause of rational and wholesome Government which his Majesty had intrusted to your guidance; and that you appreciate fairly the disinterested motive, of regard to the public welfare, and to that alone, through which this Journal has been prompted to pursue a policy in accordance with that of your Administration. It is, permit me to say, by such motives only, that the *Times*, ever since I have known it, has been influenced, whether in defence of the Government of the day, or in constitutional resistance to it: and indeed there exist no other motives of action for a Journalist, compatible either with the safety of the press, or with the political morality of the great bulk of its readers. — With much respect, I have the honor to be, Sir, &c. &c. &c.

"The Editor of the 'Times.'"

Of this Note I do not think there was the least whisper during Edward Sterling's lifetime ; which fact also one likes to remember of him, so ostentatious and little-reticent a man. For the rest, his loyal admiration of Sir Robert Peel, — sanctioned, and as it were almost consecrated to his mind, by the great example of the Duke of Wellington, whom he reverenced always with true hero-worship, — was not a journalistic one, but a most intimate authentic feeling, sufficiently apparent in the very heart of his mind. Among the many opinions "liable to three hundred and sixty-five changes in the course of the year," this in reference to Peel and Wellington was one which never changed, but was the same all days and hours. To which, equally genuine, and coming still oftener to light in those times, there might one other be added, one and hardly more : fixed contempt, not unmingled with detestation, for Daniel O'Connell. This latter feeling, we used often laughingly to say, was his grand political principle, the one firm centre where all else went revolving. But internally the other also was deep and constant ; and indeed these were properly his *two* centres, — poles of the same axis, negative and positive, the one presupposing the other.

O'Connell he had known in young Dublin days ; — and surely no man could well venerate another less ! It was his deliberate, unalterable opinion of the then Great O, that good would never come of him ; that only mischief, and this in huge measure, would come. That however showy, and adroit in rhetoric and management, he was a man of incurably commonplace intellect, and of no character but a hollow, blustery, pusillanimous and unsound one ; great only in maudlin patriotisms, in speciosities, astucies, — in the miserable gifts for becoming Chief *Demagogos*, Leader of a deep-sunk Populace towards *its* Lands of Promise ; which trade, in any age or

country, and especially in the Ireland of this age, our indignant friend regarded (and with reason) as an extremely ugly
one for a man. He had himself zealously advocated Catholic
Emancipation, and was not without his Irish patriotism, very
different from the Orange sort; but the "Liberator" was not
admirable to him, and grew daily less so to an extreme degree.
Truly, his scorn of the said Liberator, now riding in supreme
dominion on the wings of *blarney*, devil-ward of a surety, with
the Liberated all following and huzzaing; his fierce gusts of
wrath and abhorrence over him, — rose occasionally almost to
the sublime. We laughed often at these vehemences: — and
they were not wholly laughable; there was something very
serious, and very true, in them! This creed of Edward Sterling's would not now, in either pole of its axis, look so strange
as it then did in many quarters.

During those ten years which might be defined as the cul-
minating period of Edward Sterling's life, his house at South
Place, Knightsbridge, had worn a gay and solid aspect, as if
built at last on the high table-land of sunshine and success, the
region of storms and dark weather now all victoriously traversed and lying safe below. Health, work, wages, whatever is
needful to a man, he had, in rich measure; and a frank stout
heart to guide the same: he lived in such style as pleased
him; drove his own chariot up and down (himself often acting as Jehu, and reminding you a little of *Times* thunder even
in driving); consorted, after a fashion, with the powerful of
the world; saw in due vicissitude a miscellany of social faces
round him, — pleasant parties, which he liked well enough to
garnish by a lord; "Irish lord, if no better might be," as the
banter went. For the rest, he loved men of worth and intellect, and recognized them well, whatever their title: this was
his own patent of worth which Nature had given him; a central light in the man, which illuminated into a kind of beauty,
serious or humorous, all the artificialities he had accumulated
on the surface of him. So rolled his days, not quietly, yet
prosperously, in manifold commerce with men. At one in
the morning, when all had vanished into sleep, his lamp was

kindled in his library; and there, twice or thrice a week, for a three-hours' space, he launched his bolts, which next morning were to shake the high places of the world.

John's relation to his Father, when one saw John here, was altogether frank, joyful and amiable: he ignored the *Times* thunder for most part, coldly taking the Anonymous for nonextant; spoke of it floutingly, if he spoke at all: indeed a pleasant half-bantering dialect was the common one between Father and Son; and they, especially with the gentle, simplehearted, just-minded Mother for treble-voice between them, made a very pretty glee-harmony together.

So had it lasted, ever since poor John's voyagings began; his Father's house standing always as a fixed sunny islet with safe harbor for him. So it could not always last. This sunny islet was now also to break and go down: so many firm islets, fixed pillars in his fluctuating world, pillar after pillar, were to break and go down; till swiftly all, so to speak, were sunk in the dark waters, and he with them! Our little History is now hastening to a close.

In the beginning of 1843 news reached us that Sterling had, in his too reckless way, encountered a dangerous accident: maids, in the room where he was, were lifting a heavy table; he, seeing them in difficulty, had snatched at the burden; heaved it away, — but had broken a blood-vessel by the business; and was now, after extensive hemorrhage, lying dangerously ill. The doctors hoped the worst was over; but the case was evidently serious. In the same days, too, his Mother had been seized here by some painful disease, which from its continuance grew alarming. Sad omens for Edward Sterling, who by this time had as good as ceased writing or working in the *Times*, having comfortably winded up his affairs there; and was looking forward to a freer idle life befitting his advanced years henceforth. Fatal eclipse had fallen over that household of his; never to be lifted off again till all darkened into night.

By dint of watchful nursing, John Sterling got on foot once more: but his Mother did not recover, quite the contrary.

Her case too grew very questionable. Disease of the heart,
said the medical men at last; not immediately, not perhaps
for a length of years, dangerous to life, said they; but without
hope of cure. The poor lady suffered much; and, though
affecting hope always, grew weaker and weaker. John ran
up to Town in March; I saw him, on the morrow or next day
after, in his own room at Knightsbridge: he had caught fresh
cold overnight, the servant having left his window up, but
I was charged to say nothing of it, not to flutter the already
troubled house: he was going home again that very day, and
nothing ill would come of it. We understood the family at
Falmouth, his Wife being now near her confinement again,
could at any rate comport with no long absence. He was
cheerful, even rudely merry; himself pale and ill, his poor
Mother's cough audible occasionally through the wall. Very
kind, too, and gracefully affectionate; but I observed a certain grimness in his mood of mind, and under his light laughter lay something unusual, something stern, as if already
dimmed in the coming shadows of Fate. "Yes, yes, you are
a good man: but I understand they mean to appoint you to
Rhadamanthus's post, which has been vacant for some time;
and you will see how you like that!" This was one of the
things he said; a strange effulgence of wild drollery flashing
through the ice of earnest pain and sorrow. He looked paler
than usual: almost for the first time, I had myself a twinge
of misgiving as to his own health; for hitherto I had been
used to blame as much as pity his fits of dangerous illness,
and would often angrily remonstrate with him that he might
have excellent health, would he but take reasonable care of
himself, and learn the art of sitting still. Alas, as if he *could*
learn it; as if Nature had not laid her ban on him even there,
and said in smiles and frowns manifoldly, "No, that thou
shalt not learn!"

He went that day; he never saw his good true Mother
more. Very shortly afterwards, in spite of doctors' prophe-
cies, and affectionate illusions, she grew alarmingly and soon
hopelessly worse. Here are his last two Letters to her: —

" To Mrs. Sterling, Knightsbridge, London.

"FALMOUTH, 8th April, 1843.

" DEAREST MOTHER, — I could do you no good, but it would be the greatest comfort to me if I could be near you. Nothing would detain me but Susan's condition. I feel that until her confinement is over, I ought to remain here, — unless you wished me to go to you; in which case she would be the first to send me off. Happily she is doing as well as possible, and seems even to gain strength every day. She sends her love to you.

" The children are all doing well. I rode with Edward to-day through some of the pleasant lanes in the neighborhood; and was delighted, as I have often been at the same season, to see the primroses under every hedge. It is pleasant to think that the Maker of them can make other flowers for the gardens of his other mansions. We have here a softness in the air, a smoothness of the clouds, and a mild sunshine, that combine in lovely peace with the first green of spring and the mellow whiteness of the sails upon the quiet sea. The whole aspect of the world is full of a quiet harmony, that influences even one's bodily frame, and seems to make one's very limbs aware of something living, good and immortal in all around us. Knowing how you suffer, and how weak you are, anything is a blessing to me that helps me to rise out of confusion and grief into the sense of God and joy. I could not indeed but feel how much happier I should have been, this morning, had you been with me, and delighting as you would have done in all the little as well as the large beauty of the world. But it was still a satisfaction to feel how much I owe to you of the power of perceiving meaning, reality and sweetness in all healthful life. And thus I could fancy that you were still near me ; and that I could see you, as I have so often seen you, looking with earnest eyes at wayside flowers.

" I would rather not have written what must recall your thoughts to your present sufferings : but, dear Mother, I wrote only what I felt; and perhaps you would rather have it so, than that I should try to find other topics. I still hope to be with you before long. Meanwhile and always, God bless you, is the prayer of

> "Your affectionate son,
>
>> "JOHN STERLING."

To the same.

"FALMOUTH, 12th April, 1843.

"DEAREST MOTHER, — I have just received my Father's Letter; which gives me at least the comfort of believing that you do not suffer very much pain. That your mind has remained so clear and strong, is an infinite blessing.

"I do not know anything in the world that would make up to me at all for wanting the recollection of the days I spent with you lately, when I was amazed at the freshness and life of all your thoughts. It brought back far-distant years, in the strangest, most peaceful way. I felt myself walking with you in Greenwich Park, and on the seashore at Sandgate; almost even I seemed a baby, with you bending over me. Dear Mother, there is surely something uniting us that cannot perish. I seem so sure of a love which shall last and reunite us, that even the remembrance, painful as that is, of all my own follies and ill tempers, cannot shake this faith. When I think of you, and know how you feel towards me, and have felt for every moment of almost forty years, it would be too dark to believe that we shall never meet again. It was from you that I first learnt to think, to feel, to imagine, to believe; and these powers, which cannot be extinguished, will one day enter anew into communion with you. I have bought it very dear by the prospect of losing you in this world, — but since you have been so ill, everything has seemed to me holier, loftier and more lasting, more full of hope and final joy.

"It would be a very great happiness to see you once more even here; but I do not know if that will be granted to me. But for Susan's state, I should not hesitate an instant; as it is, my duty seems to be to remain, and I have no right to repine. There is no sacrifice that she would not make for me, and it would be too cruel to endanger her by mere anxiety on my account. Nothing can exceed her sympathy with my sorrow. But she cannot know, no one can, the recollections of all you have been and done for me; which now are the most sacred and deepest, as well as most beautiful, thoughts that abide with me. May God bless you, dearest Mother. It is much to believe that He feels for you all that you have ever felt for your children.

"JOHN STERLING."

A day or two after this, "on Good Friday, 1843," his Wife got happily through her confinement, bringing him, he writes, "a stout little girl, who and the Mother are doing as well as possible." The little girl still lives and does well; but for the Mother there was another lot. Till the Monday following she too did altogether well, he affectionately watching her; but in the course of that day, some change for the worse was noticed, though nothing to alarm either the doctors or him; he watched by her bedside all night, still without alarm; but sent again in the morning, Tuesday morning, for the doctors, — who did not seem able to make much of the symptoms. She appeared weak and low, but made no particular complaint. The London post meanwhile was announced; Sterling went into another room to learn what tidings of his Mother it brought him. Returning speedily with a face which in vain strove to be calm, his Wife asked, How at Knightsbridge? "My Mother is dead," answered Sterling; "died on Sunday: She is gone." "Poor old man!" murmured the other, thinking of old Edward Sterling now left alone in the world; and these were her own last words: in two hours more she too was dead. In two hours Mother and Wife were suddenly both snatched away from him.

"It came with awful suddenness!" writes he to his Clifton friend. "Still for a short time I had my Susan: but I soon saw that the medical men were in terror; and almost within half an hour of that fatal Knightsbridge news, I began to suspect our own pressing danger. I received her last breath upon my lips. Her mind was much sunk, and her perceptions slow; but a few minutes before the last, she must have caught the idea of dissolution; and signed that I should kiss her. She

faltered painfully, 'Yes! yes!' — returned with fervency the
pressure of my lips; and in a few moments her eyes began
to fix, her pulse to cease. She too is gone from me!" It was
Tuesday morning, April 18th, 1843. His Mother had died on
the Sunday before.

He had loved his excellent kind Mother, as he ought and
well might: in that good heart, in all the wanderings of his
own, there had ever been a shrine of warm pity, of mother's
love and blessed soft affections for him; and now it was closed
in the Eternities forevermore. His poor Life-partner too, his
other self, who had faithfully attended him so long in all his
pilgrimings, cheerily footing the heavy tortuous ways along
with him, can follow him no farther; sinks now at his side:
"The rest of your pilgrimings alone, O Friend, — adieu, adieu!"
She too is forever hidden from his eyes; and he stands, on the
sudden, very solitary amid the tumult of fallen and falling
things. "My little baby girl is doing well; poor little wreck
cast upon the sea-beach of life. My children require me
tenfold now. What I shall do, is all confusion and darkness."

The younger Mrs. Sterling was a true good woman; loyal-
hearted, willing to do well, and struggling wonderfully to do
it amid her languors and infirmities; rescuing, in many ways,
with beautiful female heroism and adroitness, what of fertil-
ity their uncertain, wandering, unfertile way of life still left
possible, and cheerily making the most of it. A genial, pious
and harmonious fund of character was in her; and withal an
indolent, half-unconscious force of intellect, and justness and
delicacy of perception, which the casual acquaintance scarcely
gave her credit for. Sterling much respected her decision in
matters literary; often altering and modifying where her feeling clearly went against him; and in verses especially trusting
to her ear, which was excellent, while he knew his own to be
worth little. I remember her melodious rich plaintive tone of
voice; and an exceedingly bright smile which she sometimes
had, effulgent with sunny gayety and true humor, among other
fine qualities.

Sterling has lost much in these two hours; how much that has long been can never again be for him! Twice in one morning, so to speak, has a mighty wind smitten the corners of his house; and much lies in dismal ruins round him.

———◆———

CHAPTER VI.

VENTNOR: DEATH.

In this sudden avalanche of sorrows Sterling, weak and worn as we have seen, bore up manfully, and with pious valor fronted what had come upon him. He was not a man to yield to vain wailings, or make repinings at the unalterable: here was enough to be long mourned over; but here, for the moment, was very much imperatively requiring to be done. That evening, he called his children round him; spoke words of religious admonition and affection to them; said, "He must now be a Mother as well as Father to them." On the evening of the funeral, writes Mr. Hare, he bade them good-night, adding these words, "If I am taken from you, God will take care of you." He had six children left to his charge, two of them infants; and a dark outlook ahead of them and him. The good Mrs. Maurice, the children's young Aunt, present at this time and often afterwards till all ended, was a great consolation.

Falmouth, it may be supposed, had grown a sorrowful place to him, peopled with haggard memories in his weak state; and now again, as had been usual with him, change of place suggested itself as a desirable alleviation; — and indeed, in some sort, as a necessity. He has "friends here," he admits to himself, "whose kindness is beyond all price, all description;" but his little children, if anything befell him, have no relative within two hundred miles. He is now sole watcher over them; and his very life is so precarious; nay, at any rate, it would appear, he has to leave Falmouth every spring, or run the hazard of worse. Once more, what is to be done? Once more, — and now, as it turned out, for the last time.

A still gentler climate, greater proximity to London, where his Brother Anthony now was and most of his friends and interests were : these considerations recommended Ventnor, in the beautiful Southeastern corner of the Isle of Wight; where on inquiry an eligible house was found for sale. The house and its surrounding piece of ground, improvable both, were purchased; he removed thither in June of this year 1843; and set about improvements and adjustments on a frank scale. By the decease of his Mother, he had become rich in money; his share of the West-India properties having now fallen to him, which, added to his former incomings, made a revenue he could consider ample and abundant. Falmouth friends looked lovingly towards him, promising occasional visits; old Herst-monceux, which he often spoke of revisiting but never did, was not far off; and London, with all its resources and remem-brances, was now again accessible. He resumed his work; and had hopes of again achieving something.

The Poem of *Cœur-de-Lion* has been already mentioned, and the wider form and aim it had got since he first took it in hand. It was above a year before the date of these tragedies and changes, that he had sent me a Canto, or couple of Cantos, of *Cœur-de-Lion;* loyally again demanding my opinion, harsh as it had often been on that side. This time I felt right glad to answer in another tone : " That here was real felicity and ingenuity, on the prescribed conditions; a decisively rhythmic quality in this composition; thought and phraseology actually *dancing,* after a sort. What the plan and scope of the Work might be, he had not said, and I could not judge; but here was a light opulence of airy fancy, picturesque conception, vigorous delineation, all marching on as with cheerful drum and fife, if without more rich and complicated forms of melody : if a man *would* write in metre, this sure enough was the way to try doing it." For such encouragement from that stinted quarter, Sterling, I doubt not, was very thankful; and of course it might co-operate with the inspirations from his Naples Tour to further him a little in this his now chief task in the way of Poetry; a thought which, among my many almost pathetic remembrances of contradictions to his Poetic tendency, is pleasant for me.

But, on the whole, it was no matter. With or without encouragement, he was resolute to persevere in Poetry, and did persevere. When I think now of his modest, quiet steadfastness in this business of Poetry; how, in spite of friend and foe, he silently persisted, without wavering, in the form of utterance he had chosen for himself; and to what length he carried it, and vindicated himself against us all; — his character comes out in a new light to me, with more of a certain central inflexibility and noble silent resolution than I had elsewhere noticed in it. This summer, moved by natural feelings, which were sanctioned, too, and in a sort sanctified to him, by the remembered counsel of his late Wife, he printed the *Tragedy of Strafford*. But there was in the public no contradiction to the hard vote I had given about it: the little Book fell dead-born; and Sterling had again to take his disappointment; — which it must be owned he cheerfully did; and, resolute to try it again and ever again, went along with his *Cœur-de-Lion*, as if the public had been all with him. An honorable capacity to stand single against the whole world; such as all men need, from time to time! After all, who knows whether, in his overclouded, broken, flighty way of life, incapable of long hard drudgery, and so shut out from the solid forms of Prose, this Poetic Form, which he could well learn as he could all forms, was not the suitablest for him?

This work of *Cœur-de-Lion* he prosecuted steadfastly in his new home; and indeed employed on it henceforth all the available days that were left him in this world. As was already said, he did not live to complete it; but some eight Cantos, three or four of which I know to possess high worth, were finished, before Death intervened, and there he had to leave it. Perhaps it will yet be given to the public; and in that case be better received than the others were, by men of judgment; and serve to put Sterling's Poetic pretensions on a much truer footing. I can say, that to readers who do prefer a poetic diet, this ought to be welcome: if you can

contrive to love the thing which is still called "poetry" in
these days, here is a decidedly superior article in that
kind, — richer than one of a hundred that you smilingly
consume.

In this same month of June, 1843, while the house at
Ventnor was getting ready, Sterling was again in London
for a few days. Of course at Knightsbridge, now fallen under
such sad change, many private matters needed to be settled
by his Father and Brother and him. Captain Anthony, now
minded to remove with his family to London and quit the
military way of life, had agreed to purchase the big family
house, which he still occupies; the old man, now rid of that
encumbrance, retired to a smaller establishment of his own;
came ultimately to be Anthony's guest, and spent his last
days so. He was much lamed and broken, the half of his
old life suddenly torn away; — and other losses, which he
yet knew not of, lay close ahead of him. In a year or two,
the rugged old man, borne down by these pressures, quite
gave way; sank into paralytic and other infirmities; and was
released from life's sorrows, under his son Anthony's roof,
in the fall of 1847. — The house in Knightsbridge was, at the
time we now speak of, empty except of servants; Anthony
having returned to Dublin, I suppose to conclude his affairs
there, prior to removal. John lodged in a Hotel.

We had our fair share of his company in this visit, as in all
the past ones; but the intercourse, I recollect, was dim and
broken, a disastrous shadow hanging over it, not to be cleared
away by effort. Two American gentlemen, acquaintances also
of mine, had been recommended to him, by Emerson most
likely: one morning Sterling appeared here with a strenuous
proposal that we should come to Knightsbridge, and dine
with him and them. Objections, general dissuasions were
not wanting: The empty dark house, such needless trouble,
and the like; — but he answered in his quizzing way, "Nature
herself prompts you, when a stranger comes, to give him a
dinner. There are servants yonder; it is all easy; come;
both of you are bound to come." And accordingly we went.
I remember it as one of the saddest dinners; though Sterling

talked copiously, and our friends, Theodore Parker one of
them, were pleasant and distinguished men. All was so
haggard in one's memory, and half consciously in one's anticipations; sad, as if one had been dining in a ruin, in the
crypt of a mausoleum. Our conversation was waste and
logical, I forget quite on what, not joyful and harmoniously
effusive: Sterling's silent sadness was painfully apparent
through the bright mask he had bound himself to wear.
Withal one could notice now, as on his last visit, a certain
sternness of mood, unknown in better days; as if strange
gorgon-faces of earnest Destiny were more and more rising
round him, and the time for sport were past. He looked
always hurried, abrupt, even beyond wont; and indeed was,
I suppose, overwhelmed in details of business.

One evening, I remember, he came down hither, design-
ing to have a freer talk with us. We were all sad enough;
and strove rather to avoid speaking of what might make us
sadder. Before any true talk had been got into, an interruption occurred, some unwelcome arrival; Sterling abruptly
rose; gave me the signal to rise; and we unpolitely walked
away, adjourning to his Hotel, which I recollect was in the
Strand, near Hungerford Market; some ancient comfortable
quaint-looking place, off the street; where, in a good warm
queer old room, the remainder of our colloquy was duly finished. We spoke of Cromwell, among other things which I
have now forgotten; on which subject Sterling was trenchant,
positive, and in some essential points wrong, — as I said I
would convince him some day. "Well, well!" answered he,
with a shake of the head. — We parted before long; bedtime
for invalids being come: he escorted me down certain car-
peted backstairs, and would not be forbidden: we took leave
under the dim skies; — and alas, little as I then dreamt of it,
this, so far as I can calculate, must have been the last time
I ever saw him in the world. Softly as a common evening,
the last of the evenings had passed away, and no other would
come for me forevermore.

Through the summer he was occupied with fitting up his
new residence, selecting governesses, servants; earnestly en-

deavoring to set his house in order, on the new footing it
had now assumed. Extensive improvements in his garden
and grounds, in which he took due interest to the last, were
also going on. His Brother, and Mr. Maurice his brother-in-
law, — especially Mrs. Maurice the kind sister, faithfully
endeavoring to be as a mother to her poor little nieces, —
were occasionally with him. All hours available for labor on
his literary tasks, he employed, almost exclusively I believe,
on *Cœur-de-Lion;* with what energy, the progress he had
made in that Work, and in the art of Poetic composition
generally, amid so many sore impediments, best testifies. I
perceive, his life in general lay heavier on him than it had
done before; his mood of mind is grown more sombre; —
indeed the very solitude of this Ventnor as a place, not to
speak of other solitudes, must have been new and depressing.
But he admits no hypochondria, now or ever; occasionally,
though rarely, even flashes of a kind of wild gayety break
through. He works steadily at his task, with all the strength
left him; endures the past as he may, and makes gallant
front against the world. "I am going on quietly here, rather
than happily," writes he to his friend Newman; "sometimes
quite helpless, not from distinct illness, but from sad thoughts
and a ghastly dreaminess. The heart is gone out of my life.
My children, however, are doing well; and the place is cheerful and mild."

From Letters of this period I might select some melancholy enough; but will prefer to give the following one
(nearly the last I can give), as indicative of a less usual
temper: —

"*To Thomas Carlyle, Esq., Chelsea, London.*

"VENTNOR, 7th December, 1843.

"MY DEAR CARLYLE, — My Irish Newspaper was *not* meant
as a hint that I wanted a Letter. It contained an absurd long
Advertisement, — some project for regenerating human knowledge, &c. &c.; to which I prefixed my private mark (a blot),
thinking that you might be pleased to know of a fellow-laborer
somewhere in Tipperary.

" Your Letter, like the Scriptural oil, — (they had no patent lamps then, and used the best oil, 7s. per gallon), — has made my face to shine. There is but one person in the world, I shall not tell you who, from whom a Letter would give me so much pleasure. It would be nearly as good at Pekin, in the centre of the most enlightened Mandarins; but here at Ventnor, where there are few Mandarins and no enlightenment, — fountains in the wilderness, even were they miraculous, are nothing compared with your handwriting. Yet it is sad that you should be so melancholy. I often think that though Mercury was the pleasanter fellow, and probably the happier, Saturn was the greater god; — rather cannibal or so, but one excuses it in him, as in some other heroes one knows of.

" It is, as you say, your destiny to write about Cromwell: and you will make a book of him, at which the ears of our grandchildren will tingle; — and as one may hope that the ears of human nature will be growing longer and longer, the tingling will be proportionably greater than we are accustomed to. Do what you can, I fear there will be little gain from the Royalists. There is something very small about the biggest of them that I have ever fallen in with, unless you count old Hobbes a Royalist.

" Curious to see that you have them exactly preserved in the Country Gentlemen of our day; while of the Puritans not a trace remains except in History. Squirism had already, in that day, become the *caput mortuum* that it is now; and has therefore, like other mummies, been able to last. What was opposed to it was the Life of Puritanism, — then on the point of disappearing; and it too has left its mummy at Exeter Hall on the platform and elsewhere. One must go back to the Middle Ages to see Squirism as rampant and vivacious as Biblicism was in the Seventeenth Century: and I suppose our modern Country Gentlemen are about as near to what the old Knights and Barons were who fought the Crusades, as our modern Evangelicals to the fellows who sought the Lord by the light of their own pistol-shots.

" Those same Crusades are now pleasant matter for me.

You remember, or perhaps you do not, a thing I once sent you about Cœur-de-Lion. Long since, I settled to make the Cantos you saw part of a larger Book; and worked at it, last autumn and winter, till I had a bad illness. I am now at work on it again; and go full sail, like *my* hero. There are six Cantos done, roughly, besides what you saw. I have struck out most of the absurdest couplets, and given the whole a higher though still sportive tone. It is becoming a kind of *Odyssey*, with a laughing and Christian Achilles for hero. One may manage to wrap, in that chivalrous brocade, many things belonging to our Time, and capable of interesting it. The thing is not bad; but will require great labor. Only it is labor that I thoroughly like; and which keeps the maggots out of one's brain, until their time.

"I have never spoken to you, never been able to speak to you, of the change in my life, — almost as great, one fancies, as one's own death. Even now, although it seems as if I had so much to say, I cannot. If one could imagine —. . . But it is no use; I cannot write wisely on this matter. I suppose no human being was ever devoted to another more entirely than she; and that makes the change not less but more bearable. It seems as if she could not be gone quite; and that indeed is my faith.

"Mr. James, your New-England friend, was here only for a few days; I saw him several times, and liked him. They went, on the 24th of last month, back to London, — or so purposed, — because there is no pavement here for him to walk on. I want to know where he is, and thought I should be able to learn from you. I gave him a Note for Mill, who perhaps may have seen him. I think this is all at present from,

"Yours,

"John Sterling."

Of his health, all this while, we had heard little definite; and understood that he was very quiet and careful; in virtue of which grand improvement we vaguely considered all others would follow. Once let him learn well to be *slow* as the com-

mon run of men are, would not all be safe and well? Nor
through the winter, or the cold spring months, did bad news
reach us; perhaps less news of any kind than had been usual,
which seemed to indicate a still and wholesome way of life
and work. Not till "April 4th, 1844," did the new alarm
occur: again on some slight accident, the breaking of a blood-
vessel; again prostration under dangerous sickness, from which
this time he never rose.

There had been so many sudden fallings and happy risings
again in our poor Sterling's late course of health, we had
grown so accustomed to mingle blame of his impetuosity with
pity for his sad overthrows, we did not for many weeks quite
realize to ourselves the stern fact that here at length had the
peculiar fall come upon us, — the last of all these falls! This
brittle life, which had so often held together and victoriously
rallied under pressures and collisions, could not rally always,
and must one time be shivered. It was not till the summer
came and no improvement; and not even then wthout lin-
gering glimmers of hope against hope, that I fairly had to
own what had now come, what was now day by day sternly
advancing with the steadiness of Time.

From the first, the doctors spoke despondently; and Sterling himself felt well that there was no longer any chance
of life. He had often said so, in his former illnesses, and
thought so, yet always till now with some tacit grain of
counter-hope; he had never clearly felt so as now: Here *is*
the end; the great change is now here! — Seeing how it was,
then, he earnestly gathered all his strength to do this last act
of his tragedy, as he had striven to do the others, in a pious
and manful manner. As I believe we can say he did; few
men in any time *more* piously or manfully. For about six
months he sat looking steadfastly, at all moments, into the eyes
of Death; he too who had eyes to *see* Death and the Terrors
and Eternities; and surely it was with perfect courage and
piety, and valiant simplicity of heart, that he bore himself, and
did and thought and suffered, in this trying predicament, more
terrible than the usual death of men. All strength left to him
he still employed in working: day by day the end came nearer,

but day by day also some new portion of his adjustments was completed, by some small stage his task was nearer done. His domestic and other affairs, of all sorts, he settled to the last item. Of his own Papers he saved a few, giving brief pertinent directions about them; great quantities, among which a certain Autobiography begun some years ago at Clifton, he ruthlessly burnt, judging that the best. To his friends he left messages, memorials of books: I have a *Gough's Camden*, and other relics, which came to me in that way, and are among my sacred possessions. The very Letters of his friends he sorted and returned; had each friend's Letters made into a packet, sealed with black, and duly addressed for delivery when the time should come.

At an early period of his illness, all visitors had of course been excluded, except his most intimate ones: before long, so soon as the end became apparent, he took leave even of his Father, to avoid excitements and intolerable emotions; and except his Brother and the Maurices, who were generally about him coming and going, none were admitted. This latter form of life, I think, continued for above three months. Men were still working about his grounds, of whom he took some charge; needful works, great and small, let them not pause on account of him. He still rose from bed; had still some portion of his day which he could spend in his Library. Besides business there, he read a good deal, — earnest books; the Bible, most earnest of books, his chief favorite. He still even wrote a good deal. To his eldest Boy, now Mr. Newman's ward, who had been removed to the Maurices' since the beginning of this illness, he addressed, every day or two, sometimes daily, for eight or nine weeks, a Letter, of general paternal advice and exhortation; interspersing sparingly, now and then, such notices of his own feelings and condition as could be addressed to a boy. These Letters, I have lately read: they give, beyond any he has written, a noble image of the intrinsic Sterling; — the same face we had long known; but painted now as on the azure of Eternity, serene, victorious, divinely sad; the dusts and extraneous disfigurements imprinted on it by the world, now washed away. One little

Excerpt, not the best, but the fittest for its neighborhood here, will be welcome to the reader: —

" *To Master Edward C. Sterling, London.*

"Hillside, Ventnor, 29th June, 1844.

"My dear Boy, — We have been going on here as quietly as possible, with no event that I know of. There is nothing except books to occupy me. But you may suppose that my thoughts often move towards you, and that I fancy what you may be doing in the great City, — the greatest on the Earth, — where I spent so many years of my life. I first saw London when I was between eight and nine years old, and then lived in or near it for the whole of the next ten, and more there than anywhere else for seven years longer. Since then I have hardly ever been a year without seeing the place, and have often lived in it for a considerable time. There I grew from childhood to be a man. My little Brothers and Sisters, and since, my Mother, died and are buried there. There I first saw your Mamma, and was there married. It seems as if, in some strange way, London were a part of Me or I of London. I think of it often, not as full of noise and dust and confusion, but as something silent, grand and everlasting.

"When I fancy how you are walking in the same streets, and moving along the same river, that I used to watch so intently, as if in a dream, when younger than you are, — I could gladly burst into tears, not of grief, but with a feeling that there is no name for. Everything is so wonderful, great and holy, so sad and yet not bitter, so full of Death and so bordering on Heaven. Can you understand anything of this? If you can, you will begin to know what a serious matter our Life is; how unworthy and stupid it is to trifle it away without heed; what a wretched, insignificant, worthless creature any one comes to be, who does not as soon as possible bend his whole strength, as in stringing a stiff bow, to doing whatever task lies first before him. . . .

"We have a mist here to-day from the sea. It reminds me of that which I used to see from my house in St. Vincent, rolling over the great volcano and the mountains round it. I used to look at it from our windows with your Mamma, and you a little baby in her arms.

"This Letter is not so well written as I could wish, but I hope you will be able to read it.

"Your affectionate Papa,

"JOHN STERLING."

These Letters go from June 9th to August 2d, at which latter date vacation-time arrived, and the Boy returned to him. The Letters are preserved; and surely well worth preserving.

In this manner he wore the slow doomed months away. Day after day his little period of Library went on waning, shrinking into less and less; but I think it never altogether ended till the general end came. — For courage, for active audacity we had all known Sterling; but such a fund of mild stoicism, of devout patience and heroic composure, we did not hitherto know in him. His sufferings, his sorrows, all his unutterabilities in this slow agony, he held right manfully down; marched loyally, as at the bidding of the Eternal, into the dread Kingdoms, and no voice of weakness was heard from him. Poor noble Sterling, he had struggled so high and gained so little here! But this also he did gain, to be a brave man; and it was much.

Summer passed into Autumn: Sterling's earthly businesses, to the last detail of them, were now all as good as done: his strength too was wearing to its end, his daily turn in the Library shrunk now to a span. He had to hold himself as if in readiness for the great voyage at any moment. One other Letter I must give; not quite the last message I had from Sterling, but the last that can be inserted here: a brief Letter, fit to be forever memorable to the receiver of it: —

"*To Thomas Carlyle, Esq., Chelsea, London.*

"HILLSIDE, VENTNOR, 10th August, 1844.

MY DEAR CARLYLE, — For the first time for many months it seems possible to send you a few words; merely, however, for Remembrance and Farewell. On higher matters there is nothing to say. I tread the common road into the great dark-ness, without any thought of fear, and with very much of hope. Certainty indeed I have none. With regard to You and Me I cannot begin to write; having nothing for it but to keep shut the lid of those secrets with all the iron weights that are in my power. Towards me it is still more true than towards England that no man has been and done like you. Heaven bless you! If I can lend a hand when THERE, that will not be wanting. It is all very strange, but not one hun-dredth part so sad as it seems to the standers-by.

"Your Wife knows my mind towards her, and will believe it without asseverations.

"Yours to the last,
"JOHN STERLING."

It was a bright Sunday morning when this letter came to me: if in the great Cathedral of Immensity I did no worship that day, the fault surely was my own. Sterling affectionately refused to see me; which also was kind and wise. And four days before his death, there are some stanzas of verse for me, written as if in star-fire and immortal tears; which are among my sacred possessions, to be kept for myself alone.

His business with the world was done; the one business now to await silently what may lie in other grander worlds. "God is great," he was wont to say: "God is great." The Maurices were now constantly near him; Mrs. Maurice assiduously watching over him. On the evening of Wednesday the 18th of September, his Brother, as he did every two or three days, came down; found him in the old temper, weak in strength but not very sensibly weaker; they talked calmly together for an hour; then Anthony left his bedside, and retired for the night, not expecting any change. But suddenly, about eleven o'clock, there came a summons and alarm: hurrying to his Brother's room, he found his Brother dying; and in a short while more the faint last struggle was ended, and all those struggles and strenuous often-foiled endeavors of eight-and-thirty years lay hushed in death.

CHAPTER VII.

CONCLUSION.

STERLING was of rather slim but well-boned wiry figure, perhaps an inch or two from six feet in height; of blonde complexion, without color, yet not pale or sickly; dark-blonde hair, copious enough, which he usually wore short. The general aspect of him indicated freedom, perfect spontaneity, with a certain careless natural grace. In his apparel, you could notice, he affected dim colors, easy shapes; cleanly always, yet even in this not fastidious or conspicuous: he sat or stood, oftenest, in loose sloping postures; walked with long strides, body carelessly bent, head flung eagerly forward, right hand perhaps grasping a cane, and rather by the middle to swing it, than by the end to use it otherwise. An attitude of frank, cheerful impetuosity, of hopeful speed and alacrity; which indeed his physiognomy, on all sides of it, offered as the chief expression. Alacrity, velocity, joyous ardor, dwelt in the eyes too, which were of brownish gray, full of bright kindly life, rapid and frank rather than deep or strong. A smile, half of kindly impatience, half of real mirth, often sat on his face. The head was long; high over the vertex; in the brow, of fair breadth, but not high for such a man.

In the voice, which was of good tenor sort, rapid and strikingly distinct, powerful too, and except in some of the higher notes harmonious, there was a clear-ringing *metallic* tone, — which I often thought was wonderfully physiognomic. A certain splendor, beautiful, but not the deepest or the softest, which I could call a splendor as of burnished metal, — fiery valor of heart, swift decisive insight and utterance, then a turn for brilliant elegance, also for ostentation, rashness, &c. &c., — in short, a flash as of clear-glancing sharp-cutting steel, lay in the whole nature of the man, in his heart and in his intellect,

marking alike the excellence and the limits of them both.
His laugh, which on light occasions was ready and frequent,
had in it no great depth of gayety, or sense for the ludicrous
in men or things; you might call it rather a good smile become
vocal than a deep real laugh: with his whole man I never saw
him laugh. A clear sense of the humorous he had, as of most
other things; but in himself little or no true humor;— nor
did he attempt that side of things. To call him deficient
in sympathy would seem strange, him whose radiances and
resonances went thrilling over all the world, and kept him in
brotherly contact with all: but I may say his sympathies dwelt
rather with the high and sublime than with the low or ludicrous; and were, in any field, rather light, wide and lively,
than deep, abiding or great.

There is no Portrait of him which tolerably resembles. The
miniature Medallion, of which Mr. Hare has given an Engraving, offers us, with no great truth in physical details, one, and
not the best, superficial expression of his face, as if that with
vacuity had been what the face contained; and even that Mr.
Hare's engraver has disfigured into the nearly or the utterly
irrecognizable. Two Pencil-sketches, which no artist could
approve of, hasty sketches done in some social hour, one by
his friend Spedding, one by Banim the Novelist, whom he
slightly knew and had been kind to, tell a much truer story so
far as they go: of these his Brother has engravings; but these
also I must suppress as inadequate for strangers.

Nor in the way of Spiritual Portraiture does there, after so
much writing and excerpting, anything of importance remain
for me to say. John Sterling and his Life in this world were
— such as has been already said. In purity of character, in
the so-called moralities, in all manner of proprieties of conduct, so as tea-tables and other human tribunals rule them, he
might be defined as perfect, according to the world's pattern:
in these outward tangible respects the world's criticism of him
must have been praise and that only. An honorable man, and
good citizen; discharging, with unblamable correctness, all
functions and duties laid on him by the customs (*mores*) of

the society he lived in, — with correctness and something more. In all these particulars, a man perfectly *moral,* or of approved virtue according to the rules.

Nay in the far more essential tacit virtues, which are not marked on stone tables, or so apt to be insisted on by human creatures over tea or elsewhere, — in clear and perfect fidelity to Truth wherever found, in childlike and soldier-like, pious and valiant loyalty to the Highest, and what of good and evil that might send him, — he excelled among good men. The joys and the sorrows of his lot he took with true simplicity and acquiescence. Like a true son, not like a miserable muti-nous rebel, he comported himself in this Universe. Extremity of distress — and surely his fervid temper had enough of con-tradiction in this world — could not tempt him into impatience at any time. By no chance did you ever hear from him a whisper of those mean repinings, miserable arraignings and questionings of the Eternal Power, such as weak souls even well disposed will sometimes give way to in the pressure of their despair; to the like of this he never yielded, or showed the least tendency to yield; — which surely was well on his part. For the Eternal Power, I still remark, will not answer the like of this, but silently and terribly accounts it impious, blasphemous and damnable, and now as heretofore will visit it as such. Not a rebel but a son, I said; willing to suffer when Heaven said, Thou shalt; — and withal, what is perhaps rarer in such a combination, willing to rejoice also, and right cheerily taking the good that was sent, whensoever or in what-ever form it came.

A pious soul we may justly call him; devoutly submissive to the will of the Supreme in all things: the highest and sole essential form which Religion can assume in man, and without which all forms of religion are a mockery and a delusion in man. Doubtless, in so clear and filial a heart there must have dwelt the perennial feeling of silent worship; which silent feeling, as we have seen, he was eager enough to express by all good ways of utterance; zealously adopting such appointed forms and creeds as the dignitaries of the World had fixed upon and solemnly named recommendable; prostrating his

heart in such Church, by such accredited rituals and seemingly
fit or half-fit methods, as his poor time and country had to offer
him, — not rejecting the said methods till they stood convicted
of palpable *un*fitness, and then doing it right gently withal,
rather letting them drop as pitiably dead for him, than angrily
hurling them out of doors as needing to be killed. By few
Englishmen of his epoch had the thing called Church of England been more loyally appealed to as a spiritual mother.

And yet, as I said before, it may be questioned whether
piety, what we call devotion or worship, was the principle
deepest in him. In spite of his Coleridge discipleship, and
his once headlong operations following thereon, I used to
judge that his piety was prompt and pure rather than great
or intense ; that, on the whole, religious devotion was not the
deepest element of him. His reverence was ardent and just,
ever ready for the thing or man that deserved revering, or
seemed to deserve it : but he was of too joyful, light and
hoping a nature to go to the depths of that feeling, much
more to dwell perennially in it. He had no fear in his composition ; terror and awe did not blend with his respect of anything. In no scene or epoch could he have been a Church
Saint, a fanatic enthusiast, or have worn out his life in passive martyrdom, sitting patient in his grim coal-mine, looking
at the "three ells" of Heaven high overhead there. In sorrow he would not dwell; all sorrow he swiftly subdued, and
shook away from him. How could you have made an Indian
Fakir of the Greek Apollo, "whose bright eye lends brightness, and never yet saw a shadow"? — I should say, not religious reverence, rather artistic admiration was the essential
character of him : a fact connected with all other facts in the
physiognomy of his life and self, and giving a tragic enough
character to much of the history he had among us.

Poor Sterling, he was by nature appointed for a Poet, then,
— a Poet after his sort, or recognizer and delineator of the
Beautiful; and not for a Priest at all ? Striving towards the
sunny heights, out of such a level and through such an element as ours in these days is, he had strange aberrations
appointed him, and painful wanderings amid the miserable

gaslights, bog-fires, dancing meteors and putrid phosphorescences which form the guidance of a young human soul at
present! Not till after trying all manner of sublimely illuminated places, and finding that the basis of them was putridity,
artificial gas and quaking bog, did he, when his strength was
all done, discover his true sacred hill, and passionately climb
thither while life was fast ebbing! — A tragic history, as all
histories are; yet a gallant, brave and noble one, as not many
are. It is what, to a radiant son of the Muses, and bright
messenger of the harmonious Wisdoms, this poor world — if
he himself have not strength enough, and *inertia* enough, and
amid his harmonious eloquences silence enough — has provided at present. Many a high-striving, too hasty soul, seeking
guidance towards eternal excellence from the official Black-
artists, and successful Professors of political, ecclesiastical,
philosophical, commercial, general and particular Legerdemain, will recognize his own history in this image of a fellow-
pilgrim's.

Over-haste was Sterling's continual fault; over-haste, and
want of the due strength, — alas, mere want of the due *inertia*
chiefly; which is so common a gift for most part; and proves
so inexorably needful withal! But he was good and generous
and true; joyful where there was joy, patient and silent where
endurance was required of him; shook innumerable sorrows,
and thick-crowding forms of pain, gallantly away from him;
fared frankly forward, and with scrupulous care to tread on no
one's toes. True, above all, one may call him; a man of perfect veracity in thought, word and deed. Integrity towards
all men, — nay integrity had ripened with him into chivalrous
generosity; there was no guile or baseness anywhere found
in him. Transparent as crystal; he could not hide anything
sinister, if such there had been to hide. A more perfectly
transparent soul I have never known. It was beautiful, to
read all those interior movements; the little shades of affec-
tations, ostentations; transient spurts of anger, which never
grew to the length of settled spleen: all so naïve, so childlike,
the very faults grew beautiful to you.

And so he played his part among us, and has now ended it:

in this first half of the Nineteenth Century, such was the shape of human destinies the world and he made out between them. He sleeps now, in the little burying-ground of Bonchurch; bright, ever-young in the memory of others that must grow old; and was honorably released from his toils before the hottest of the day.

All that remains, in palpable shape, of John Sterling's activities in this world are those Two poor Volumes; scattered fragments gathered from the general waste of forgotten ephemera by the piety of a friend : an inconsiderable memorial; not pretending to have achieved greatness; only disclosing, mournfully, to the more observant, that a promise of greatness was there.   Like other such lives, like all lives, this is a tragedy; high hopes, noble efforts; under thickening difficulties and impediments, ever-new nobleness of valiant effort; — and the result death, with conquests by no means corresponding. A life which cannot challenge the world's attention; yet which does modestly solicit it, and perhaps on clear study will be found to reward it.

On good evidence let the world understand that here was a remarkable soul born into it; who, more than others, sensible to its influences, took intensely into him such tint and shape of feature as the world had to offer there and then; fashioning himself eagerly by whatsoever of noble presented itself; participating ardently in the world's battle, and suffering deeply in its bewilderments; — whose Life-pilgrimage accordingly is an emblem, unusually significant, of the world's own during those years of his. A man of infinite susceptivity; who caught everywhere, more than others, the color of the element he lived in, the infection of all that was or appeared honorable, beautiful and manful in the tendencies of his Time; — whose history therefore is, beyond others, emblematic of that of his Time.

In Sterling's Writings and Actions, were they capable of being well read, we consider that there is for all true hearts, and especially for young noble seekers, and strivers towards what is highest, a mirror in which some shadow of themselves and of their immeasurably complex arena will profitably present itself. Here also is one encompassed and struggling even as they now are. This man also had said to himself, not in mere Catechism-words, but with all his instincts, and the question thrilled in every nerve of him, and pulsed in every drop of his blood: "What is the chief end of man? Behold, I too would live and work as beseems a denizen of this Universe, a child of the Highest God. By what means is a noble life still possible for me here? Ye Heavens and thou Earth, oh, how?" — The history of this long-continued prayer and endeavor, lasting in various figures for near forty years, may now and for some time coming have something to say to men!

Nay, what of men or of the world? Here, visible to myself, for some while, was a brilliant human presence, distinguishable, honorable and lovable amid the dim common populations; among the million little beautiful, once more a beautiful human soul: whom I, among others, recognized and lovingly walked with, while the years and the hours were. Sitting now by his tomb in thoughtful mood, the new times bring a new duty for me. "Why write the Life of Sterling?" I imagine I had a commission higher than the world's, the dictate of Nature herself, to do what is now done. *Sic prosit.*

LATTER-DAY PAMPHLETS.

———•———

[February 1, 1850.]

NO. I.   THE PRESENT TIME.

THE Present Time, youngest-born of Eternity, child and heir of all the Past Times with their good and evil, and parent of all the Future, is ever a "New Era" to the thinking man; and comes with new questions and significance, however commonplace it look: to know *it*, and what it bids us do, is ever the sum of knowledge for all of us. This new Day, sent us out of Heaven, this also has its heavenly omens; — amid the bustling trivialities and loud empty noises, its silent monitions, which if we cannot read and obey, it will not be well with us! No; — nor is there any sin more fearfully avenged on men and Nations than that same, which indeed includes and presupposes all manner of sins: the sin which our old pious fathers called "judicial blindness;" — which we, with our light habits, may still call misinterpretation of the Time that now is; disloyalty to its real meanings and monitions, stupid disregard of these, stupid adherence active or passive to the counterfeits and mere current semblances of these. This is true of all times and days.

But in the days that are now passing over us, even fools are arrested to ask the meaning of them; few of the generations of men have seen more impressive days. Days of endless calamity, disruption, dislocation, confusion worse confounded: if they are not days of endless hope too, then they are days of utter despair. For it is not a small hope that will suffice, the ruin being clearly, either in action or in prospect, universal. There must be a new world, if there is to be any world at all! That human things in our Europe can ever return to the old sorry routine, and proceed with any steadiness or continuance there; this small hope is not now a tenable one. These days of universal death must be days of universal newbirth, if the ruin is not to be total and final! It is a Time to make the dullest man consider; and ask himself, Whence *he* came? Whither he is bound? — A veritable "New Era," to the foolish as well as to the wise.

Not long ago, the world saw, with thoughtless joy which might have been very thoughtful joy, a real miracle not heretofore considered possible or conceivable in the world, — a Reforming Pope. A simple pious creature, a good countrypriest, invested unexpectedly with the tiara, takes up the New Testament, declares that this henceforth shall be his rule of governing. No more finesse, chicanery, hypocrisy, or false or foul dealing of any kind: God's truth shall be spoken, God's justice shall be done, on the throne called of St. Peter: an honest Pope, Papa, or Father of Christendom, shall preside there. And such a throne of St. Peter; and such a Christendom, for an honest Papa to preside in! The European populations everywhere hailed the omen; with shouting and rejoicing, leading articles and tar-barrels; thinking people listened with astonishment, — not with sorrow if they were faithful or wise; with awe rather as at the heralding of death, and with a joy as of victory beyond death! Something pious, grand and as if awful in that joy, revealing once more the Presence of a Divine Justice in this world. For, to such men it was very clear how this poor devoted Pope would prosper, with his New Testament in his hand. An alarming business, that of governing in the throne of St. Peter by the rule of veracity! By the rule of veracity, the so-called throne of St. Peter was openly declared, above three hundred years ago, to be a falsity, a huge mistake, a pestilent dead carcass, which this Sun was weary of. More than three hundred years ago, the throne of St. Peter received peremptory judicial notice to quit; authentic order, registered in Heaven's chancery and since legible in the hearts of all brave men, to take itself away, — to begone, and let us have no more to do with *it* and its delusions and impious deliriums; — and it has been sitting every day since, it may depend upon it, at its own peril withal, and will have to pay exact damages yet for every day it has so sat. Law of veracity? What this Popedom had to do by the law of veracity, was to give up its own foul galvanic life, an offence to gods and men; honestly to die, and get itself buried.

Far from this was the thing the poor Pope undertook in regard to it; — and yet, on the whole, it was essentially this too. "Reforming Pope?" said one of our acquaintance, often in those weeks, "Was there ever such a miracle? About to break up that huge imposthume too, by 'curing' it? Turgot and Necker were nothing to this. God is great; and when a scandal is to end, brings some devoted man to take charge of it in hope, not in despair!" — But cannot he reform? asked many simple persons; — to whom our friend in grim banter would reply: "Reform a Popedom, — hardly. A wretched old kettle, ruined from top to bottom, and consisting mainly now of foul *grime* and *rust:* stop the holes of it, as your antecessors have been doing, with temporary putty, it may hang together yet a while; begin to hammer at it, solder at it, to what you call mend and rectify it, — it will fall to sherds, as sure as rust is rust; go all into nameless dissolution, — and the fat in the fire will be a thing worth looking at, poor Pope!" — So accordingly it has proved. The poor Pope, amid felicitations and tar-barrels of various kinds, went on joyfully for a season : but he had awakened, he as no other man could do, the sleeping elements; mothers of the whirlwinds, conflagrations, earthquakes. Questions not very soluble at present, were even sages and heroes set to solve them, began everywhere with new emphasis to be asked. Questions which all official men wished, and almost hoped, to postpone till Doomsday. Doomsday itself *had* come; that was the terrible truth!

For, sure enough, if once the law of veracity be acknowledged as the rule for human things, there will not anywhere be want of work for the reformer; in very few places do

human things adhere quite closely to that law! Here was
the Papa of Christendom proclaiming that such was actually
the case; — whereupon all over Christendom such results as we
have seen. The Sicilians, I think, were the first notable body
that set about applying this new strange rule sanctioned by
the general Father; they said to themselves, We do not by the
law of veracity belong to Naples and these Neapolitan Officials; we will, by favor of Heaven and the Pope, be free of
these. Fighting ensued; insurrection, fiercely maintained in
the Sicilian Cities; with much bloodshed, much tumult and
loud noise, vociferation extending through all newspapers and
countries. The effect of this, carried abroad by newspapers
and rumor, was great in all places; greatest perhaps in Paris,
which for sixty years past has been the City of Insurrections.
The French People had plumed themselves on being, whatever
else they were not, at least the chosen "soldiers of liberty,"
who took the lead of all creatures in that pursuit, at least;
and had become, as their orators, editors and littérateurs diligently taught them, a People whose bayonets were sacred,
a kind of Messiah People, saving a blind world in its own
despite, and earning for themselves a terrestrial and even
celestial glory very considerable indeed. And here were the
wretched down-trodden populations of Sicily risen to rival
them, and threatening to take the trade out of their hand.

No doubt of it, this hearing continually of the very Pope's
glory as a Reformer, of the very Sicilians fighting divinely
for liberty behind barricades, — must have bitterly aggravated
the feeling of every Frenchman, as he looked around him, at
home, on a Louis-Philippism which had become the scorn of
all the world. "*Ichabod;* is the glory departing from us?
Under the sun is nothing baser, by all accounts and evidences,
than the system of repression and corruption, of shameless
dishonesty and unbelief in anything but human baseness, that
we now live under. The Italians, the very Pope, have become
apostles of liberty, and France is — what is France!" — We
know what France suddenly became in the end of February
next; and by a clear enough genealogy, we can trace a considerable share in that event to the good simple Pope with the

New Testament in his hand. An outbreak, or at least a radical change and even inversion of affairs hardly to be achieved without an outbreak, everybody felt was inevitable in France: but it had been universally expected that France would as usual take the initiative in that matter; and had there been no reforming Pope, no insurrectionary Sicily, France had certainly not broken out then and so, but only afterwards and otherwise. The French explosion, not anticipated by the cunningest men there on the spot scrutinizing it, burst up unlimited, complete, defying computation or control.

Close following which, as if by sympathetic subterranean electricities, all Europe exploded, boundless, uncontrollable; and we had the year 1848, one of the most singular, disastrous, amazing, and, on the whole, humiliating years the European world ever saw. Not since the irruption of the Northern Barbarians has there been the like. Everywhere immeasurable Democracy rose monstrous, loud, blatant, inarticulate as the voice of Chaos. Everywhere the Official holy-of-holies was scandalously laid bare to dogs and the profane:—Enter, all the world, see what kind of Official holy it is. Kings everywhere, and reigning persons, stared in sudden horror, the voice of the whole world bellowing in their ear, "Begone, ye imbecile hypocrites, histrios not heroes! Off with you, off!"— and, what was peculiar and notable in this year for the first time, the Kings all made haste to go, as if exclaiming, "We *are* poor histrios, we sure enough;—did you want heroes? Don't kill us; we couldn't help it!" Not one of them turned round, and stood upon his Kingship, as upon a right he could afford to die for, or to risk his skin upon; by no manner of means. That, I say, is the alarming peculiarity at present. Democracy, on this new occasion, finds all Kings *conscious* that they are but Play-actors. The miserable mortals, enacting their High Life Below Stairs, with faith only that this Universe may perhaps be all a phantasm and hypocrisis,—the truculent Constable of the Destinies suddenly enters: "Scandalous Phantasms, what do *you* here? Are 'solemnly constituted Impostors' the proper Kings of men? Did you think the Life of Man was a grimacing dance of apes? To be led always by the squeak of your paltry fiddle ? Ye miserable, this Universe is not an upholstery Puppet-play, but a terrible God's Fact; and you, I think, — had not you better begone!" They fled precipitately, some of them with what we may call an exquisite ignominy, — in terror of the treadmill or worse. And everywhere the people, or the populace, take their own government upon themselves; and open "kinglessness," what we call *anarchy*, — how happy if it be anarchy *plus* a street-constable! — is everywhere the order of the day. Such was the history, from Baltic to Mediterranean, in Italy, France, Prussia, Austria, from end to end of Europe, in those March days of 1848. Since the destruction of the old Roman Empire by inroad of the Northern Barbarians, I have known nothing similar.

And so, then, there remained no King in Europe; no King except the Public Haranguer, haranguing on barrel-head, in leading article; or getting himself aggregated into a National Parliament to harangue. And for about four months all France, and to a great degree all Europe, rough-ridden by every species of delirium, except happily the murderous for most part, was a weltering mob, presided over by M. de Lamartine, at the Hôtel-de-Ville; a most eloquent fair-spoken literary gentlenan, whom thoughtless persons took for a prophet, priest and heaven-sent evangelist, and whom a wise Yankee friend of mine discerned to be properly "the first stump-orator in the world, standing too on the highest stump, — for the time." A sorrowful spectacle to men of reflection, during the time he lasted, that poor M. de Lamartine; with nothing in him but melodious wind and *soft sawder*, which he and others took for something divine and not diabolic! Sad enough; the eloquent latest impersonation of Chaos-come-again; able to talk for itself, and declare persuasively that *it* is Cosmos! However, you have but to wait a little, in such cases; all balloons do and must give up their gas in the pressure of things, and are collapsed in a sufficiently wretched manner before long.

And so in City after City, street-barricades are piled, and truculent, more or less murderous insurrection begins; populace after populace rises, King after King capitulates or absconds; and from end to end of Europe Democracy has blazed up explosive, much higher, more irresistible and less resisted than ever before; testifying too sadiy on what a bottomless volcano, or universal powder-mine of most inflammable mutinous chaotic elements, separated from us by a thin earth-rind, Society with all its arrangements and acquirements everywhere, in the present epoch, rests! The kind of persons who excite or give signal to such revolutions — students, young men of letters, advocates, editors, hot inexperienced enthusiasts, or fierce and justly bankrupt desperadoes, acting everywhere on the discontent of the millions and blowing it intc flame, — might give rise to reflections as to the character of our epoch. Never till now did young men, and almost children, take such a command in human affairs. A changed time since the word *Senior* (Seigneur, or *Elder*) was first devised to signify "lord," or superior; — as in all languages of men we find it to have been! Not an honorable document this either, as to the spiritual condition of our epoch. In times when men love wisdom, the old man will ever be venerable, and be venerated, and reckoned noble: in times that love something else than wisdom, and indeed have little or no wisdom, and see little or none to love, the old man will cease to be venerated; — and looking more closely, also, you will find that in fact he has ceased to be venerable, and has begun to be contemptible; a foolish *boy* still, a boy without the graces, generosities and opulent strength of young boys. In these days, what of *lordship* or leadership is still to be done, the youth must do it, not the mature or aged man; the mature man, hardened into sceptical egoism, knows no monition but that of his own frigid cautions, avarices, mean timidities; and can lead no-whither towards an object that even seems noble. But to return.

This mad state of matters will of course before long allay itself, as it has everywhere begun to do; the ordinary necessities of men's daily existence cannot comport with it, and these, whatever else is cast aside, will have their way. Some remounting — very temporary remounting — of the old machine, under new colors and altered forms, will probably ensue soon in most countries: the old histrionic Kings will be admitted

back under conditions, under "Constitutions," with national
Parliaments, or the like fashionable adjuncts; and everywhere
the old daily life will try to begin again. But there is now
no hope that such arrangements can be permanent; that they
can be other than poor temporary makeshifts, which, if they try
to fancy and make themselves permanent, will be displaced
by new explosions recurring more speedily than last time. In
such baleful oscillation, afloat as amid raging bottomless eddies
and conflicting sea-currents, not steadfast as on fixed foundations, must European Society continue swaying, now disas-
trously tumbling, then painfully readjusting itself, at ever
shorter intervals, — till once the *new* rock-basis does come
:o light, and the weltering deluges of mutiny, and of need to
mutiny, abate again !

For universal *Democracy*, whatever we may think of it, has
declared itself as an inevitable fact of the days in which we
live; and he who has any chance to instruct, or lead, in his
days, must begin by admitting that: new street-barricades, and
new anarchies, still more scandalous if still less sanguinary,
must return and again return, till governing persons everywhere
know and admit that. Democracy, it may be said everywhere,
is here: — for sixty years now, ever since the grand or *First*
French Revolution, that fact has been terribly announced to
all the world; in message after message, some of them very
terrible indeed; and now at last all the world ought really
to believe it. That the world does believe it; that even
Kings now as good as believe it, and know, or with just terror
surmise, that they are but temporary phantasm Play-actors,
and that Democracy is the grand, alarming, imminent and
indisputable Reality : this, among the scandalous phases we
witnessed in the last two years, is a phasis full of hope :
a sign that we are advancing closer and closer to the very
Problem itself, which it will behoove us to solve or die; —
that all fighting and campaigning and coalitioning in regard
to the *existence* of the Problem, is hopeless and superfluous
henceforth. The gods have appointed it *so ;* no Pitt, nor
body of Pitts or mortal creatures can appoint it otherwise.
Democracy, sure enough, is here; one knows not how long it

will keep hidden underground even in Russia; — and here in England, though we object to it resolutely in the form of street-barricades and insurrectionary pikes, and decidedly will not open doors to it on those terms, the tramp of its million feet is on all streets and thoroughfares, the sound of its bewildered thousand-fold voice is in all writings and speakings, in all thinkings and modes and activities of men: the soul that does not now, with hope or terror, discern *it*, is not the one we address on this occasion.

What *is* Democracy; this huge inevitable Product of the Destinies, which is everywhere the portion of our Europe in these latter days? There lies the question for us. Whence comes it, this universal big black Democracy; whither tends it; what is the meaning of it? A meaning it must have, or it would not be here. If we can find the right meaning of it, we may, wisely submitting or wisely resisting and controlling, still hope to live in the midst of it; if we cannot find the right meaning, if we find only the wrong or no meaning in it, to live will not be possible! — The whole social wisdom of the Present Time is summoned, in the name of the Giver of Wisdom, to make clear to itself, and lay deeply to heart with an eye to strenuous valiant practice and effort, what the meaning of this universal revolt of the European Populations, which calls itself Democracy, and decides to continue permanent, may be.

Certainly it is a drama full of action, event fast following event; in which curiosity finds endless scope, and there are interests at stake, enough to rivet the attention of all men, simple and wise. Whereat the idle multitude lift up their voices, gratulating, celebrating sky-high; in rhyme and prose announcement, more than plentiful, that *now* the New Era, and long-expected Year One of Perfect Human Felicity has come. Glorious and immortal people, sublime French citizens, heroic barricades; triumph of civil and religious liberty — O Heaven! one of the inevitablest private miseries, to an earnest man in such circumstances, is this multitudinous efflux of oratory and psalmody, from the universal foolish human throat; drowning for the moment all reflection whatsoever, except the sorrowful one that you are fallen in an evil, heavy-laden, long-eared age, and must resignedly bear your part in the same. The front wall of your wretched old crazy dwelling, long denounced by you to no purpose, having at last fairly folded itself over, and fallen prostrate into the street, the floors, as may happen, will still hang on by the mere beamends, and coherency of old carpentry, though in a sloping direction, and depend there till certain poor rusty nails and worm-eaten dovetailings give way: — but is it cheering, in such circumstances, that the whole household burst forth into celebrating the new joys of light and ventilation, liberty and picturesqueness of position, and thank God that now they have got a house to their mind? My dear household, cease singing and psalmodying; lay aside your fiddles, take out your work-implements, if you have any; for I can say with confidence the laws of gravitation are still active, and rusty nails, worm-eaten dovetailings, and secret coherency of old carpentry, are not the best basis for a household! — In the lanes of Irish cities, I have heard say, the wretched people are sometimes found living, and perilously boiling their potatoes, on such swing-floors and inclined planes hanging on by the joist-ends; but I did not hear that they sang very much in celebration of such lodging. No, they slid gently about, sat near the back wall, and perilously boiled their potatoes, in silence for most part! —

High shouts of exultation, in every dialect, by every vehicle of speech and writing, rise from far and near over this last avatar of Democracy in 1848: and yet, to wise minds, the first aspect it presents seems rather to be one of boundless misery and sorrow. What can be more miserable than this universal hunting out of the high dignitaries, solemn functionaries, and potent, grave and reverend signiors of the world; this stormful rising-up of the inarticulate dumb masses everywhere, against those who pretended to be speaking for them and guiding them? These guides, then, were mere blind men only pretending to see? These rulers were not ruling at all; they had merely got on the attributes and clothes of rulers, and were surreptitiously drawing the wages, while the work remained undone? The Kings were Sham-Kings, play-acting as at Drury Lane; — and what were the people withal that took them for real?

It is probably the hugest disclosure of *falsity* in human things that was ever at one time made. These reverend Dignitaries that sat amid their far-shining symbols and long-sounding long-admitted professions, were mere Impostors, then? Not a true thing they were doing, but a false thing. The story they told men was a cunningly devised fable; the gospels they preached to them were *not* an account of man's real position in this world, but an incoherent fabrication, of dead ghosts and unborn shadows, of traditions, cants, indolences, cowardices, — a falsity of falsities, which at last *ceases* to stick together. Wilfully and against their will, these high units of mankind were cheats, then; and the low millions who believed in them were dupes, — a kind of *inverse* cheats, too, or they would not have believed in them so long. A universal *Bankruptcy of Imposture;* that may be the brief definition of it. Imposture everywhere declared once more to be contrary to Nature; nobody will change its word into an act any farther : — fallen insolvent; unable to keep its head up by these false pretences, or make its pot boil any more for the present! A more scandalous phenomenon, wide as Europe, never afflicted the face of the sun. Bankruptcy everywhere; foul ignominy, and the abomination of desolation, in all high places : odious to look upon, as the carnage of a battle-field on the morrow morning; — a massacre not of the innocents; we cannot call it a massacre of the innocents; but a universal tumbling of Impostors and of Impostures into the street! —

Such a spectacle, can we call it joyful? There is a joy in it, to the wise man too; yes, but a joy full of awe, and as it were sadder than any sorrow, — like the vision of immortality, unattainable except through death and the grave! And yet who would not, in his heart of hearts, feel piously thankful that Imposture has fallen bankrupt? By all means let it fall bankrupt; in the name of God let it do so, with whatever misery to itself and to all of us. Imposture, be it known then, — known it must and shall be, — is hateful, unendurable to God and man. Let it understand this everywhere; and swiftly make ready for departure, wherever it yet lingers; and let it learn never to return, if possible! The eternal voices, very audibly again, are speaking to proclaim this message, from side to side of the world. Not a very cheering message, but a very indispensable one.

Alas, it is sad enough that Anarchy is here; that we are not permitted to regret its being here, — for who that had, for this divine Universe, an eye which was human at all, could wish that Shams of any kind, especially that Sham-Kings should continue? No: at all costs, it is to be prayed by all men that Shams may *cease.* Good Heavens, to what depths have we got, when this to many a man seems strange! Yet strange to many a man it does seem; and to many a solid Englishman, wholesomely digesting his pudding among what are called the cultivated classes, it seems strange exceedingly; a mad ignorant notion, quite heterodox, and big with mere ruin. He has been used to decent forms long since fallen empty of meaning, to plausible modes, solemnities grown ceremonial, — what you in your iconoclast humor call shams, — all his life long; never heard that there was any harm in them, that there was any getting on without them. Did not cotton spin itself, beef grow, and groceries and spiceries come in from the East and the West, quite comfortably by the side of shams? Kings reigned, what they were pleased to call reigning; lawyers pleaded, bishops preached, and honorable members perorated; and to crown the whole, as if it were all real and no sham there, did not scrip continue salable, and the banker pay in bullion, or paper with a metallic basis? "The greatest sham, I have always thought, is he that would destroy shams."

Even so. To such depth have *I*, the poor knowing person of this epoch, got; — almost below the level of lowest humanity, and down towards the state of apehood and oxhood! For never till in quite recent generations was such a scandalous blasphemy quietly set forth among the sons of Adam; never before did the creature called man believe generally in his heart that lies were the rule in this Earth; that in deliberate long-established lying could there be help or salvation for him, could there be at length other than hindrance and destruction for him. O Heavyside, my solid friend, this is the sorrow of sorrows: what on earth can become of us till this accursed enchantment, the general summary and consecration of delusions, be cast forth from the heart and life of one and all! Cast forth it will be; it must, or we are tending, at all moments, — whitherward I do not like to name. Alas, and the casting of it out, to what heights and what depths will it lead us, in the sad universe mostly of lies and shams and hollow phantasms (grown very ghastly now), in which, as in a safe home, we have lived this century or two! To heights and depths of social and individual *divorce* from delusions, — of "reform" in right sacred earnest, of indispensable amendment, and stern sorrowful abrogation and order to depart, — such as cannot well be spoken at present ; as dare scarcely be thought at present; which nevertheless are very inevitable, and perhaps rather imminent several of them! Truly we have a heavy task of work before us; and there is a pressing call that we should seriously begin upon it, before it tumble into an inextricable mass, in which there will be no working, but only suffering and hopelessly perishing ! —

Or perhaps Democracy, which we announce as now come, will itself manage it ? Democracy, once modelled into suffrages, furnished with ballot-boxes and such like, will itself accomplish the salutary universal change from Delusive to Real, and make a new blessed world of us by and by ? — To the great mass of men, I am aware, the matter presents itself quite on this hopeful side. Democracy they consider to *be* a kind of "Government." The old model, formed long since, and brought to perfection in England now two hundred years ago, has proclaimed itself to all Nations as the new healing for every woe: "Set up a Parliament," the Nations everywhere say, when the old King is detected to be a Sham-King, and hunted out or not; "set up a Parliament; let us have suffrages, universal suffrages ; and all either at once or by due degrees will be right, and a real Millennium come !" **Such is** their way of construing the matter.

Such, alas, is by no means my way of construing the matter; if it were, I should have had the happiness of remaining silent, and been without call to speak here. It is because the contrary of all this is deeply manifest to me, and appears to be forgotten by multitudes of my contemporaries, that I have had to undertake addressing a word to them. The contrary of all this; — and the farther I look into the roots of all this, the more hateful, ruinous and dismal does the state of mind all this could have originated in appear to me. To examine this recipe of a Parliament, how fit it is for governing Nations, nay how fit it may now be, in these new times, for governing England itself where we are used to it so long: this, too, is an alarming inquiry, to which all thinking men, and good citizens of their country, who have an ear for the small still voices and eternal intimations, across the temporary clamors and loud blaring proclamations, are now solemnly invited. Invited by the rigorous fact itself; which will one day, and that perhaps soon, demand practical decision or redecision of it from us, — with enormous penalty if we decide it wrong! I think we shall all have to consider this question, one day; better perhaps now than later, when the leisure may be less. If a Parliament, with suffrages and universal or any conceivable kind of suffrages, *is* the method, then certainly let us set about discovering the kind of suffrages, and rest no moment till we have got them. But it is possible a Parliament may not be the method! Possible the inveterate notions of the English People may have settled it as the method, and the Everlasting Laws of Nature may have settled it as not the method! Not the whole method; nor the method at all, if taken as the whole? If a Parliament with never such suffrages is *not* the method settled by this latter authority, then it will urgently behoove us to become aware of that fact, and to quit such method; — we may depend upon it, however unanimous *we* be, every step taken in that direction will, by the Eternal Law of things, be a step *from* improvement, not towards it.

Not towards it, I say, if so! Unanimity of voting, — that will do nothing for us if *so*. Your ship cannot double Cape

Horn by its excellent plans of voting. The ship may vote this and that, above decks and below, in the most harmonious exquisitely constitutional manner : the ship, to get round Cape Horn, will find a set of conditions already voted for, and fixed with adamantine rigor by the ancient Elemental Powers, who are entirely careless how you vote. If you can, by voting or without voting, ascertain these conditions, and valiantly conform to them, you will get round the Cape : if you cannot, — the ruffian Winds will blow you ever back again; the inexorable Icebergs, dumb privy-councillors from Chaos, will nudge you with most chaotic " admonition;" you will be flung half frozen on the Patagonian cliffs, or admonished into shivers by your iceberg councillors, and sent sheer down to Davy Jones, and will never get round Cape Horn at all! Unanimity on board ship; — yes indeed, the ship's crew may be very unanimous, which doubtless, for the time being, will be very comfortable to the ship's crew, and to their Phantasm Captain if they have one : but if the tack they unanimously steer upon is guiding them into the belly of the Abyss, it will not profit them much! — Ships accordingly do not use the ballot-box at all ; and they reject the Phantasm species of Captains : one wishes much some other Entities — since all entities lie under the same rigorous set of laws — could be brought to show as much wisdom, and sense at least of self-preservation, the *first* command of Nature. Phantasm Captains with unanimous votings : this is considered to be all the law and all the prophets, at present.

If a man could shake out of his mind the universal noise of political doctors in this generation and in the last generation or two, and consider the matter face to face, with his own sincere intelligence looking at it, I venture to say he would find this a very extraordinary method of navigating, whether in the Straits of Magellan or the undiscovered Sea of Time. To prosper in this world, to gain felicity, victory and improvement, either for a man or a nation, there is but one thing requisite, That the man or nation can discern what the true regulations of the Universe are in regard to him and his pursuit, and can faithfully and steadfastly follow these. These

will lead him to victory; whoever it may be that sets him in
the way of these, — were it Russian Autocrat, Chartist Parliament, Grand Lama, Force of Public Opinion, Archbishop of
Canterbury, M'Croudy the Seraphic Doctor with his Last-
evangel of Political Economy, — sets him in the sure way
to please the Author of this Universe, and is his friend of
friends. And again, whoever does the contrary is, for a like
reason, his enemy of enemies. This may be taken as fixed.

And now by what method ascertain the monition of the
gods in regard to our affairs? How decipher, with best
fidelity, the eternal regulation of the Universe; and read,
from amid such confused embroilments of human clamor and
folly, what the real Divine Message to us is? A divine message, or eternal regulation of the Universe, there verily is,
in regard to every conceivable procedure and affair of man :
faithfully following this, said procedure or affair will prosper,
and have the whole Universe to second it, and carry it, across
the fluctuating contradictions, towards a victorious goal; not
following this, mistaking this, disregarding this, destruction
and wreck are certain for every affair. How find it? All
the world answers me, "Count heads; ask Universal Suffrage, by the ballot-boxes, and that will tell." Universal
Suffrage, ballot-boxes, count of heads? Well, — I perceive
we have got into strange spiritual latitudes indeed. Within
the last half-century or so, either the Universe or else the
heads of men must have altered very much. Half a century ago, and down from Father Adam's time till then, the
Universe, wherever I could hear tell of it, was wont to be of
somewhat abstruse nature; by no means carrying its secret
written on its face, legible to every passer-by; on the contrary, obstinately hiding its secret from all foolish, slavish,
wicked, insincere persons, and partially disclosing it to the
wise and noble-minded alone, whose number was not the
majority in my time!

Or perhaps the chief end of man being now, in these improved epochs, to make money and spend it, his interests in
the Universe have become amazingly simplified of late; capable of being voted on with effect by almost anybody? "To

buy in the cheapest market, and sell in the dearest:" truly if that is the summary of his social duties, and the final divine message he has to follow, we may trust him extensively to vote upon that. But if it is *not*, and never was, or can be? If the Universe will not carry on its divine bosom any commonwealth of mortals that have no higher aim, — being still "a Temple and Hall of Doom," not a mere Weaving-shop and Cattle-pen? If the unfathomable Universe has decided to *reject* Human Beavers pretending to be Men; and will abolish, pretty rapidly perhaps, in hideous mud-deluges, their "markets" and them, unless they think of it? — In that case it were better to think of it: and the Democracies and Universal Suffrages, I can observe, will require to modify themselves a good deal!

Historically speaking, I believe there was no Nation that could subsist upon Democracy. Of ancient Republics, and *Demoi* and *Populi*, we have heard much; but it is now pretty well admitted to be nothing to our purpose; — a universal-suffrage republic, or a general-suffrage one, or any but a most-limited-suffrage one, never came to light, or dreamed of doing so, in ancient times. When the mass of the population were slaves, and the voters intrinsically a kind of *kings*, or men born to rule others; when the voters were *real* "aristocrats" and manageable dependents of such, — then doubtless voting, and confused jumbling of talk and intrigue, might, without immediate destruction, or the need of a Cavaignac to intervene with cannon and sweep the streets clear of it, go on; and beautiful developments of manhood might be possible beside it, for a season. Beside it; or even, if you will, by means of it, and in virtue of it, though that is by no means so certain as is often supposed. Alas, no: the reflective constitutional mind has misgivings as to the origin of old Greek and Roman nobleness; and indeed knows not how this or any other human nobleness could well be "originated," or brought to pass, by voting or without voting, in this world, except by the grace of God very mainly; — and remembers, with a sigh, that of the Seven Sages themselves no fewer than three were bits of Despotic Kings, Τύραννοι, "Tyrants" so called (such being greatly wanted there); and that the other four were very far from Red Republicans, if of any political faith whatever! We may quit the Ancient Classical concern, and leave it to College-clubs and speculative debating-societies, in these late days.

Of the various French Republics that have been tried, or that are still on trial, — of these also it is not needful to say any word. But there is one modern instance of Democracy nearly perfect, the Republic of the United States, which has actually subsisted for threescore years or more, with immense success as is affirmed; to which many still appeal, as to a sign of hope for all nations, and a " Model Republic." Is not America an instance in point? Why should not all Nations subsist and flourish on Democracy, as America does?

Of America it would ill beseem any Englishman, and me perhaps as little as another, to speak unkindly, to speak *unpatriotically*, if any of us even felt so. Sure enough, America is a great, and in many respects a blessed and hopeful phenomenon. Sure enough, these hardy millions of Anglo-Saxon men prove themselves worthy of their genealogy; and, with the axe and plough and hammer, if not yet with any much finer kind of implements, are triumphantly clearing out wide spaces, seedfields for the sustenance and refuge of mankind, arenas for the future history of the world; doing, in their day and generation, a creditable and cheering feat under the sun. But as to a Model Republic, or a model anything, the wise among themselves know too well that there is nothing to be said. Nay the title hitherto to be a Commonwealth or Nation at all, among the ἔθνη of the world, is, strictly considered, still a thing they are but striving for, and indeed have not yet done much towards attaining. Their Constitution, such as it may be, was made here, not there; went over with them from the Old-Puritan English workshop ready-made. Deduct what they carried with them from England ready-made, — their common English Language, and that same Constitution, or rather elixir of constitutions, their inveterate and now, as it were, inborn reverence for the Constable's Staff; two quite immense attainments, which England had to spend much blood, and valiant sweat of brow and brain, for centuries long, in achieving;—and what new elements of polity or nationhood, what noble new phasis of human arrangement, or social device worthy of Prometheus or of Epimetheus, yet comes to light in America? Cotton crops and Indian corn and dollars come to light; and half a world of untilled land, where populations that respect the constable can live, for the present *without* Government: this comes to light; and the profound sorrow of all nobler hearts, here uttering itself as silent patient unspeakable ennui, there coming out as vague elegiac wailings, that there is still next to nothing more. " Anarchy *plus* a street-constable : " that also is anarchic to me, and other than quite lovely !

I foresee, too, that, long before the waste lands are full, the very street-constable, on these poor terms, will have become impossible : without the waste lands, as here in our Europe, I do not see how he could continue possible many weeks. Cease to brag to me of America, and its model institutions and constitutions. To men in their sleep there is nothing granted in this world : nothing, or as good as nothing, to men that sit idly *caucusing* and ballot-boxing on the graves of their heroic ancestors, saying, "It is well, it is well!" Corn and bacon are granted: not a very sublime boon, on such conditions; a boon moreover which, on such conditions, cannot last ! No: America too will have to strain its energies, in quite other fashion than this; to crack its sinews, and all but break its heart, as the rest of us have had to do, in thousand-fold wrestle with the Pythons and mud-demons, before it can become a habitation for the gods. America's battle is yet to fight; and we, sorrowful though nothing doubting, will wish her strength for it. New Spiritual Pythons, plenty of them; enormous Megatherions, as ugly as were ever born of mud, loom huge and hideous out of the twilight Future on America; and she will have her own agony, and her own victory, but on other terms than she is yet quite aware of. Hitherto she but ploughs and hammers, in a very successful manner; hitherto, in spite of her "roast-goose with apple sauce," she is not much. "Roast-goose with apple-sauce for the poorest workingman:" well, surely that is something,—

thanks to your respect for the street-constable, and to your
continents of fertile waste land; — but that, even if it could
continue, is by no means enough; that is not even an instal-
ment towards what will be required of you. My friend, brag
not yet of our American cousins! Their quantity of cotton,
dollars, industry and resources, I believe to be almost unspeakable ; but I can by no means worship the like of these.
What great human soul, what great thought, what great noble
thing that one could worship, or loyally admire, has yet been
produced there ? None : the American cousins have yet done
none of these things. "What they have done ?" growls
Smelfungus, tired of the subject: "They have doubled their
population every twenty years. They have begotten, with a
rapidity beyond recorded example, Eighteen Millions of the
greatest *bores* ever seen in this world before, — that hitherto
is their feat in History!" — And so we leave them, for the
present; and cannot predict the success of Democracy, on this
side of the Atlantic, from their example.

Alas, on this side of the Atlantic and on that, Democracy,
we apprehend, is forever impossible! So much, with certainty
of loud astonished contradiction from all manner of men at
present, but with sure appeal to the Law of Nature and the
ever-abiding Fact, may be suggested and asserted once more.
The Universe itself is a Monarchy and Hierarchy; large liberty of "voting" there, all manner of choice, utmost free-will,
but with conditions inexorable and immeasurable annexed to
every exercise of the same. A most free commonwealth of
"voters;" but with Eternal Justice to preside over it, Eternal Justice enforced by Almighty Power! This is the model
of "constitutions;" this : nor in any Nation where there has
not yet (in some supportable and withal some constantly
increasing degree) been confided to the *Noblest*, with his select
series of *Nobler*, the divine everlasting duty of directing and
controlling the Ignoble, has the "Kingdom of God," which we
all pray for, "come," nor can "His will" even *tend* to be "done
on Earth as it is in Heaven" till then. My Christian friends,
and indeed my Sham-Christian and Anti-Christian, and all
manner of men, are invited to reflect on this. They will find

it to be the truth of the case. The Noble in the high place, the Ignoble in the low; that is, in all times and in all countries, the Almighty Maker's Law.

To raise the Sham-Noblest, and solemnly consecrate *him* by whatever method, new-devised, or slavishly adhered to from old wont, this, little as we may regard it, is, in all times and countries, a practical blasphemy, and Nature will in nowise forget it. Alas, there lies the origin, the fatal necessity, of modern Democracy everywhere. It is the Noblest, not the Sham-Noblest; it is God-Almighty's Noble, not the Court-Tailor's Noble, nor the Able-Editor's Noble, that must, in some approximate degree, be raised to the supreme place; he and not a counterfeit, — under penalties! Penalties deep as death, and at length terrible as hell-on-earth, my constitutional friend! — Will the ballot-box raise the Noblest to the chief place; does any sane man deliberately believe such a thing? That nevertheless is the indispensable result, attain it how we may: if that is attained, all is attained; if not that, nothing. He that cannot believe the ballot-box to be attaining it, will be comparatively indifferent to the ballot-box. Excellent for keeping the ship's crew at peace under their Phantasm Captain; but unserviceable, under such, for getting round Cape Horn. Alas, that there should be human beings requiring to have these things argued of, at this late time of day!

I say, it is the everlasting privilege of the foolish to be governed by the wise; to be guided in the right path by those who know it better than they. This is the first "right of man;" compared with which all other rights are as nothing, — mere superfluities, corollaries which will follow of their own accord out of this; if they be not contradictions to this, and less than nothing! To the wise it is not a privilege; far other indeed. Doubtless, as bringing preservation to their country, it implies preservation of themselves withal; but intrinsically it is the harshest duty a wise man, if he be indeed wise, has laid to his hand. A duty which he would fain enough shirk; which accordingly, in these sad times of doubt and cowardly sloth, he has long everywhere been endeavoring to reduce to its minimum, and has in fact in most cases nearly escaped altogether. It is an ungoverned world; a world which we flatter ourselves will henceforth need no governing. On the dust of our heroic ancestors we too sit ballot-boxing, saying to one another, It is well, it is well! By inheritance of their noble struggles, we have been permitted to sit slothful so long. By noble toil, not by shallow laughter and vain talk, they made this English Existence from a savage forest into an arable inhabitable field for us; and we, idly dreaming it would grow spontaneous crops forever, — find it now in a too questionable state; peremptorily requiring real labor and agriculture again. Real "agriculture" is not pleasant; much pleasanter to reap and winnow (with ballot-box or otherwise) than to plough!

Who would govern that can get along without governing? He that is fittest for it, is of all men the unwillingest unless constrained. By multifarious devices we have been endeavoring to dispense with governing; and by very superficial speculations, of *laissez-faire*, supply-and-demand, &c. &c. to persuade ourselves that it is best so. The Real Captain, unless it be some Captain of mechanical Industry hired by Mammon, where is he in these days? Most likely, in silence, in sad isolation somewhere, in remote obscurity; trying if, in an evil ungoverned time, he cannot at least govern himself. The Real Captain undiscoverable; the Phantasm Captain everywhere very conspicuous: — it is thought Phantasm Captains, aided by ballot-boxes, are the true method, after all. They are much the pleasantest for the time being! And so no *Dux* or Duke of any sort, in any province of our affairs, now *leads:* the Duke's Bailiff *leads*, what little leading is required for getting in the rents; and the Duke merely rides in the state-coach. It is everywhere so: and now at last we see a world all rushing towards strange consummations, because it is and has long been so!

———

I do not suppose any reader of mine, or many persons in England at all, have much faith in Fraternity, Equality and the Revolutionary Millenniums preached by the French

Prophets in this age : but there are many movements here too which tend inevitably in the like direction ; and good men, who would stand aghast at Red Republic and its adjuncts, seem to me travelling at full speed towards that or a similar goal ! Certainly the notion everywhere prevails among us too, and preaches itself abroad in every dialect, uncontradicted anywhere so far as I can hear, That the grand panacea for social woes is what we call "enfranchisement," "emancipation;" or, translated into practical language, the cutting asunder of human relations, wherever they are found grievous, as is like to be pretty universally the case at the rate we have been going for some generations past. Let us all be "free" of one another ; we shall then be happy. Free, without bond or connection except that of cash-payment; fair day's wages for the fair day's work; bargained for by voluntary contract, and law of supply-and-demand : this is thought to be the true solution of all difficulties and injustices that have occurred between man and man.

To rectify the relation that exists between two men, is there no method, then, but that of ending it ? The old relation has become unsuitable, obsolete, perhaps unjust; it imperatively requires to be amended ; and the remedy is, Abolish it, let there henceforth be no relation at all. From the "Sacrament of Marriage" downwards, human beings used to be manifoldly related, one to another, and each to all; and there was no relation among human beings, just or unjust, that had not its grievances and difficulties, its necessities on both sides to bear and forbear. But henceforth, be it known, we have changed all that, by favor of Heaven : "the voluntary principle" has come up, which will itself do the business for us ; and now let a new Sacrament, that of *Divorce*, which we call emancipation, and spout of on our platforms, be universally the order of the day ! — Have men considered whither all this is tending, and what it certainly enough betokens ? Cut every human relation which has anywhere grown uneasy sheer asunder ; reduce whatsoever was compulsory to voluntary, whatsoever was permanent among us to the condition of nomadic : — in other words, loosen by assiduous wedges in every joint, the whole fabric of social existence, stone from stone : till at last, all now being loose enough, it can, as we already see in most countries, be overset by sudden outburst of revolutionary rage ; and, lying as mere mountains of anarchic rubbish, solicit you to sing Fraternity, &c., over it, and to rejoice in the new remarkable era of human progress we have arrived at.

Certainly Emancipation proceeds with rapid strides among as, this good while ; and has got to such a length as might give rise to reflections in men of a serious turn. West-Indian Blacks are emancipated, and it appears refuse to work : Irish Whites have long been entirely emancipated ; and nobody asks them to work, or on condition of finding them potatoes (which, of course, is indispensable), permits them to work. — Among speculative persons, a question has sometimes risen : In the progress of Emancipation, are we to look for a time when all the Horses also are to be emancipated, and brought to the supply-and-demand principle ? Horses too have "motives ; " are acted on by hunger, fear, hope, love of oats, terror of platted leather ; nay they have vanity, ambition, emulation, thankfulness, vindictiveness ; some rude outline of all our human spiritualities, — a rude resemblance to us in mind and intelligence, even as they have in bodily frame. The Horse, poor dumb four-footed fellow, he too has his private feelings, his affections, gratitudes ; and deserves good usage ; no human master, without crime, shall treat him unjustly either, or recklessly lay on the whip where it is not needed : — I am sure if I could make him "happy," I should be willing to grant a small vote (in addition to the late twenty millions) for that object !

Him too you occasionally tyrannize over ; and with bad result to yourselves, among others ; using the leather in a tyrannous unnecessary manner ; withholding, or scantily furnishing, the oats and ventilated stabling that are due. Rugged horse-subduers, one fears they are a little tyrannous at times. "Am I not a horse, and *half*-brother ? " — To remedy which, so far as remediable, fancy — the horses all "emancipated ; " restored to their primeval right of property in the grass of this Globe : turned out to graze in an independent supply-and-demand manner! So long as grass lasts, I dare say they are very happy, or think themselves so. And Farmer Hodge sallying forth, on a dry spring morning, with a sieve of oats in his hand, and agony of eager expectation in his heart, is he happy? Help me to plough this day, Black Dobbin: oats in full measure if thou wilt. "Hlunh, No — thank!" snorts Black Dobbin; he prefers glorious liberty and the grass. Bay Darby, wilt not thou perhaps? "Hlunh!" — Gray Joan, then, my beautiful broad-bottomed mare, — O Heaven, she too answers Hlunh! Not a quadruped of them will plough a stroke for me. Corncrops are *ended* in this world! — For the sake, if not of Hodge, then of Hodge's horses, one prays this benevolent practice might now cease, and a new and better one try to begin. Small kindness to Hodge's horses to emancipate them! The fate of all emancipated horses is, sooner or later, inevitable. To have in this habitable Earth no grass to eat, — in Black Jamaica gradually none, as in White Connemara already none; — to roam aimless, wasting the seedfields of the world; and be hunted home to Chaos, by the due watch-dogs and due helldogs, with such horrors of forsaken wretchedness as were never seen before! These things are not sport; they are terribly true, in this country at this hour.

Between our Black West Indies and our White Ireland, between these two extremes of lazy refusal to work, and of famishing inability to find any work, what a world have we made of it, with our fierce Mammon-worships, and our benevolent philanderings, and idle godless nonsenses of one kind and another! Supply-and-demand, Leave-it-alone, Voluntary Principle, Time will mend it: — till British industrial existence seems fast becoming one huge poison-swamp of reeking pestilence physical and moral; a hideous *living* Golgotha of souls and bodies buried alive; such a Curtius' gulf, communicating with the Nether Deeps, as the Sun never saw till now. These scenes, which the *Morning Chronicle* is bringing home to all minds of men, — thanks to it for a service such as Newspapers have seldom done, — ought to excite unspeakable reflections in every mind. Thirty thousand outcast Needlewomen working themselves swiftly to death; three million Paupers rotting in forced idleness, *helping* said Needlewomen to die: these are but items in the sad ledger of despair.

Thirty thousand wretched women, sunk in that putrefying well of abominations; they have oozed in upon London, from the universal Stygian quagmire of British industrial life; are accumulated in the *well* of the concern, to that extent. British charity is smitten to the heart, at the laying bare of such a scene; passionately undertakes, by enormous subscription of money, or by other enormous effort, to redress that individual horror; as I and all men hope it may. But, alas, what next? This general well and cesspool once baled clean out to-day, will begin before night to fill itself anew. The universal Stygian quagmire is still there; opulent in women ready to be ruined, and in men ready. Towards the same sad cesspool will these waste currents of human ruin ooze and gravitate as heretofore; except in draining the universal quagmire itself there is no remedy. "And for that, what is the method?" cry many in an angry manner. To whom, for the present, I answer only, "Not 'emancipation,' it would seem, my friends; not the cutting loose of human ties, something far the reverse of that!"

Many things have been written about shirtmaking; but here perhaps is the saddest thing of all, not written anywhere till now, that I know of. Shirts by the thirty thousand are made at twopence-halfpenny each; and in the mean while no needlewoman, distressed or other, can be procured in London by any housewife to give, for fair wages, fair help in sewing. Ask any thrifty house-mother, high or low, and she will answer. In high houses and in low, there is the same answer: no *real* needlewoman, "distressed" or other, has been found attainable in any of the houses I frequent. Imaginary needlewomen, who demand considerable wages, and have a deepish appetite for beer and viands, I hear of everywhere; but their sewing proves too often a distracted puckering and botching; not sewing, only the fallacious hope of it, a fond imagination of the mind. Good sempstresses are to be hired in every village; and in London, with its famishing thirty thousand, not at all, or hardly. — Is not No-government beautiful in human business? To such length has the Leave-alone principle carried it, by way of organizing labor, in this affair of shirt-making. Let us hope the Leave-alone principle has now got its apotheosis; and taken wing towards higher regions than ours, to deal henceforth with a class of affairs more appropriate for it!

Reader, did you ever hear of "Constituted Anarchy"? Anarchy; the choking, sweltering, deadly and killing rule of No-rule; the consecration of cupidity, and braying folly, and dim stupidity and baseness, in most of the affairs of men? Slop-shirts attainable three halfpence cheaper, by the ruin of living bodies and immortal souls? Solemn Bishops and high Dignitaries, *our* divine "Pillars of Fire by night," debating meanwhile, with their largest wigs and gravest look, upon something they call "prevenient grace"? Alas, our noble men of genius, Heaven's *real* messengers to us, they also rendered nearly futile by the wasteful time;—preappointed they everywhere, and assiduously trained by all their pedagogues and monitors, to "rise in Parliament," to compose orations, write books, or in short speak *words*, for the approval of reviewers; instead of doing real kingly *work* to be approved of by the gods! Our "Government," a highly "responsible" one; responsible to no God that I can hear of, but to the twenty-seven million *gods* of the shilling gallery. A Government tumbling and drifting on the whirlpools and mud-deluges, floating atop in a conspicuous manner, no-whither,—like the carcass of a drowned ass. Authentic *Chaos* come up into this sunny Cosmos again; and all men singing *Gloria in excelsis* to it. In spirituals and temporals, in field and workshop, from Manchester to Dorsetshire, from Lambeth Palace to the Lanes of Whitechapel, wherever men meet and toil and traffic together,—Anarchy, Anarchy; and only the street-constable (though with ever-increasing difficulty) still maintaining himself in the middle of it; that so, for one thing, this blessed exchange of slop-shirts for the souls of women may transact itself in a peaceable manner!—I, for my part, do profess myself in eternal opposition to this, and discern well that universal Ruin has us in the wind, unless we can get out of this.

My friend Crabbe, in a late number of his *Intermittent Radiator*, pertinently enough exclaims : —

"When shall we have done with all this of British Liberty, Voluntary Principle, Dangers of Centralization, and the like ? It is really getting too bad. For British Liberty, it seems, the people cannot be taught to read. British Liberty, shuddering to interfere with the rights of capital, takes six or eight millions of money annually to feed the idle laborer whom it dare not employ. For British Liberty we live over poisonous cesspools, gully-drains, and detestable abominations ; and omnipotent London cannot sweep the dirt out of itself. British Liberty produces — what ? Floods of Hansard Debates every year, and apparently little else at present. If these are the results of British Liberty, I, for one, move we should lay it on the shelf a little, and look out for something other and farther. We have achieved British Liberty hundreds of years ago ; and are fast growing, on the strength of it, one of the most absurd populations the Sun, among his great Museum of Absurdities, looks down upon at present."

Curious enough : the model of the world just now is England and her Constitution; all Nations striving towards it : poor France swimming these last sixty years in seas of horrid dissolution and confusion, resolute to attain this blessedness of free voting, or to die in chase of it. Prussia too, solid Germany itself, has all broken out into crackling of musketry, loud pamphleteering and Frankfort parliamenting and palavering; Germany too will scale the sacred mountains, how steep soever, and, by talisman of ballot-box, inhabit a political Elysium henceforth. All the Nations have that one hope. Very notable, and rather sad to the humane on-looker. For it is sadly conjectured, all the Nations labor somewhat under a mistake as to England, and the causes of her freedom and her prosperous cotton-spinning; and have much misread the nature of her Parliament, and the effect of ballot-boxes and universal suffrages there.

What if it were because the English Parliament was from the first, and is only just now ceasing to be, a Council of actual

Rulers, real Governing Persons (called Peers, Mitred Abbots, Lords, Knights of the Shire, or howsoever called), actually *ruling* each his section of the country, — and possessing (it must be said) in the lump, or when assembled as a Council, uncommon patience, devoutness, probity, discretion and good fortune, — that the said Parliament ever came to be good for much? In that case it will not be easy to "imitate" the English Parliament; and the ballot-box and suffrage will be the mere bow of Robin Hood, which it is given to very few to bend, or shoot with to any perfection. And if the Peers become mere big Capitalists, Railway Directors, gigantic Hucksters, Kings of Scrip, *without* lordly quality, or other virtue except cash; and the Mitred Abbots change to mere Able-Editors, masters of Parliamentary Eloquence, Doctors of Political Economy, and such like; and all *have* to be elected by a universal-suffrage ballot-box, — I do not see how the English Parliament itself will long continue sea-worthy! Nay, I find England in her own big dumb heart, wherever you come upon her in a silent meditative hour, begins to have dreadful misgivings about it.

The model of the world, then, is at once unattainable by the world, and not much worth attaining? England, as I read the omens, is now called a second time to "show the Nations how to live;" for by her Parliament, as chief governing entity, I fear she is not long for this world! Poor England must herself again, in these new strange times, the old methods being quite worn out, "learn how to live." That now is the terrible problem for England, as for all the Nations; and she alone of all, not *yet* sunk into open Anarchy, but left with time for repentance and amendment; she, wealthiest of all in material resource, in spiritual energy, in ancient loyalty to law, and in the qualities that yield such loyalty, — she perhaps alone of all may be able, with huge travail, and the strain of all her faculties, to accomplish some solution. She will have to try it, she has now to try it; she must accomplish it, or perish from her place in the world!

England, as I persuade myself, still contains in it many *kings;* possesses, as old Rome did, many men not needing

"election" to command, but eternally elected for it by the
Maker Himself. England's one hope is in these, just now.
They are among the silent, I believe; mostly far away from
platforms and public palaverings; not speaking forth the image
of their nobleness in transitory words, but imprinting it, each
on his own little section of the world, in silent facts, in modest
valiant actions, that will endure forevermore. They must sit
silent no longer. They are summoned to assert themselves;
to act forth, and articulately vindicate, in the teeth of howling
multitudes, of a world too justly *maddened* into all manner
of delirious clamors, what of wisdom they derive from God.
England, and the Eternal Voices, summon them; poor England
never so needed them as now. Up, be doing everywhere: the
hour of crisis has verily come! In all sections of English life,
the god-made *king* is needed; is pressingly demanded in most;
in some, cannot longer, without peril as of conflagration, be
dispensed with. He, wheresoever he finds himself, can say,
"Here too am I wanted; here is the kingdom I have to subju-
gate, and introduce God's Laws into, — God's Laws, instead of
Mammon's and M'Croudy's and the Old Anarch's! Here is
my work, here or nowhere." — Are there many such, who will
answer to the call, in England? It turns on that, whether
England, rapidly crumbling in these very years and months,
shall go down to the Abyss as her neighbors have all done, or
survive to new grander destinies *without* solution of continuity!
Probably the chief question of the world at present.

The true "commander" and king; he who knows for himself the divine Appointments of this Universe, the Eternal
Laws ordained by God the Maker, in conforming to which lies
victory and felicity, in departing from which lies, and forever
must lie, sorrow and defeat, for each and all of the Posterity
of Adam in every time and every place; he who has sworn
fealty to these, and dare alone against the world assert these,
and dare not with the whole world at his back deflect from
these; — he, I know too well, is a rare man. Difficult to discover; not quite discoverable, I apprehend, by manœuvring
of ballot-boxes, and riddling of the popular clamor according
to the most approved methods. He is not sold at any shop I

know of, — though sometimes, as at the sign of the Ballot-box, he is advertised for sale. Difficult indeed to discover: and not very much assisted, or encouraged in late times, to discover *himself;* — which, I think, might be a kind of help? Encouraged rather, and commanded in all ways, if he be wise, to *hide* himself, and give place to the windy Counterfeit of himself; such as the universal suffrages can recognize, such as loves the most sweet voices of the universal suffrages! — O Peter, what becomes of such a People; what can become?

Did you never hear, with the mind's ear as well, that fateful Hebrew Prophecy, I think the fatefulest of all, which sounds daily through the streets, "Ou' clo! Ou' clo!" — A certain People, once upon a time, clamorously voted by overwhelming majority, "Not *he;* Barabbas, not he! *Him,* and what he is, and what he deserves, we know well enough: a reviler of the Chief Priests and sacred Chancery wigs; a seditious Heretic, physical-force Chartist, and enemy of his country and man-kind: To the gallows and the cross with him! Barabbas is our man; Barabbas, we are for Barabbas!" They got Ba-rabbas: — have you well considered what a fund of purblind obduracy, of opaque *flunkyism* grown truculent and transcen-dent; what an eye for the phylacteries, and want of eye for the eternal noblenesses; sordid loyalty to the prosperous Sem-blances, and high-treason against the Supreme Fact, such a vote betokens in these natures? For it was the consummation of a long series of such; they and their fathers had long kept voting so. A singular People; who could both produce such divine men, and then could so stone and crucify them; a Peo-ple terrible from the beginning! — Well, they got Barabbas; and they got, of course, such guidance as Barabbas and the like of him could give them; and, of course, they stumbled ever downwards and devilwards, in their truculent stiffnecked way; and — and, at this hour, after eighteen centuries of sad fortune, they prophetically sing "Ou' clo!" in all the cities of the world. Might the world, at this late hour, but take note of them, and understand their song a little!

Yes, there are some things the universal suffrage can decide, — and about these it will be exceedingly useful to consult the

universal suffrage : but in regard to most things of importance,
and in regard to the choice of men especially, there is (astonishing as it may seem) next to no capability on the part of
universal suffrage. — I request all candid persons, who have
never so little originality of mind, and every man has a little,
to consider this. If true, it involves such a change in our
now fashionable modes of procedure as fills me with astonishment and alarm. *If* popular suffrage is not the way of ascertaining what the Laws of the Universe are, and who it is that
will best guide us in the way of these, — then woe is to us if
we do not take another method. Delolme on the British Constitution will not save us; deaf will the Parcæ be to votes
of the House, to leading articles, constitutional philosophies.
The other method — alas, it involves a stopping short, or vital
change of direction, in the glorious career which all Europe,
with shouts heaven-high, is now galloping along : and that,
happen when it may, will, to many of us, be probably a rather
surprising business !

One thing I do know, and can again assert with great
confidence, supported by the whole Universe, and by some
two hundred generations of men, who have left us some
record of themselves there, That the few Wise will have, by
one method or another, to take command of the innumerable
Foolish ; that they must be got to take it ; — and that, in fact,
since Wisdom, which means also Valor and heroic Nobleness,
is alone strong in this world, and one wise man is stronger
than all men unwise, they can be got. That they must take
it ; and having taken, must keep it, and do their God's Message in it, and defend the same, at their life's peril, against all
men and devils. This I do clearly believe to be the backbone
of all Future Society, as it has been of all Past ; and that
without it, there is no Society possible in the world. And
what a business *this* will be, before it end in some degree of
victory again, and whether the time for shouts of triumph
and tremendous cheers upon it is yet come, or not yet by a
great way, I perceive too well ! A business to make us all
very serious indeed. A business not to be accomplished but
by noble manhood, and devout all-daring, all-enduring loyalty

to Heaven, such as fatally *sleeps* at present, — such as is not *dead* at present either, unless the gods have doomed this world of theirs to die! A business which long centuries of faithful travail and heroic agony, on the part of all the noble that are born to us, will not end; and which to us, of this "tremendous cheering" century, it were blessedness very great to see successfully begun. Begun, tried by all manner of methods, if there is one wise Statesman or man left among us, it verily must be; — begun, successfully or unsuccessfully, we do hope to see it!

In all European countries, especially in England, one class of Captains and commanders of men, recognizable as the beginning of a new real and not imaginary "Aristocracy," has already in some measure developed itself: the Captains of Industry; — happily the class who above all, or at least first of all, are wanted in this time. In the doing of material work, we have already men among us that can command bodies of men. And surely, on the other hand, there is no lack of men needing to be commanded: the sad class of brother-men whom we had to describe as "Hodge's emancipated horses," reduced to roving famine, — this too has in all countries developed itself; and, in fatal geometrical progression, is ever more developing itself, with a rapidity which alarms every one. On this ground, if not on all manner of other grounds, it may be truly said, the "Organization of Labor" (*not* organizable by the mad methods tried hitherto) is the universal vital Problem of the world.

To bring these hordes of outcast captainless soldiers under due captaincy? This is really the question of questions; on the answer to which turns, among other things, the fate of all Governments, constitutional and other, — the possibility of their continuing to exist, or the impossibility. Captainless, uncommanded, these wretched outcast "soldiers," since they cannot starve, must needs become banditti, street-barricaders, — destroyers of every Government that *cannot* put them under captains, and send them upon enterprises, and in short render

life human to them. Our English plan of Poor Laws, which
we once piqued ourselves upon as sovereign, is evidently fast
breaking down. Ireland, now admitted into the Idle Workhouse, is rapidly bursting it in pieces. That never was a
" human " destiny for any honest son of Adam; nowhere but
in England could it have lasted at all; and now, with Ireland
sharer in it, and the fulness of time come, it is as good as
ended. Alas, yes. Here in Connemara, your crazy Ship of
the State, otherwise dreadfully rotten in many of its timbers I believe, has sprung a leak: spite of all hands at the
pump, the water is rising; the Ship, I perceive, will founder,
if you cannot stop this leak !

To bring these Captainless under due captaincy ? The
anxious thoughts of all men that do think are turned upon
that question; and their efforts, though as yet blindly and
to no purpose, under the multifarious impediments and ob-
scurations, all point thitherward. Isolated men, and their
vague efforts, cannot do it. Government everywhere is called
upon, — in England as loudly as elsewhere, — to give the initiative. A new strange task of these new epochs; which
no Government, never so "constitutional," can escape from
undertaking. For it is vitally necessary to the existence of
Society itself; it must be undertaken, and succeeded in too,
or worse will follow, — and, as we already see in Irish Connaught and some other places, will follow soon. To whatever
thing still calls itself by the name of Government, were it
never so constitutional and impeded by official impossibilities,
all men will naturally look for help, and direction what to
do, in this extremity. If help or direction is not given; if
the thing called Government merely drift and tumble to and
fro, no-whither, on the popular vortexes, like some carcass of
a drowned ass, constitutionally put " at the top of affairs," —
popular indignation will infallibly accumulate upon it; one
day, the popular lightning, descending forked and horrible from
the black air, will annihilate said supreme carcass, and smite
it home to its native ooze again ! — Your Lordship, this is too
true, though irreverently spoken: indeed one knows not how
to speak of it; and to me it is infinitely sad and miserable,

spoken or not!—Unless perhaps the Voluntary Principle will still help us through? Perhaps this Irish leak, in such a rotten distressed condition of the Ship, with all the crew so anxious about it, will be kind enough to stop of itself?—

Dismiss that hope, your Lordship! Let all real and imaginary Governors of England, at the pass we have arrived at, dismiss forever that fallacious fatal solace to their do-nothingism: of itself, too clearly, the leak will never stop; by human skill and energy it must be stopped, or there is nothing but the sea-bottom for us all! A Chief Governor of England really ought to recognize his situation; to discern that, doing nothing, and merely drifting to and fro, in however constitutional a manner, he is a squanderer of precious moments, moments that perhaps are priceless; a truly alarming Chief Governor. Surely, to a Chief Governor of England, worthy of that high name,—surely to him, as to every living man, in every conceivable situation short of the Kingdom of the Dead, —there is *something* possible; some plan of action other than that of standing mildly, with crossed arms, till he and we—sink? Complex as his situation is, he, of all Governors now extant among these distracted Nations, has, as I compute, by far the greatest possibilities. The Captains, actual or potential, are there, and the million Captainless: and such resources for bringing them together as no other has. To these outcast soldiers of his, unregimented roving banditti for the present, or unworking workhouse prisoners who are almost uglier than banditti; to these floods of Irish Beggars, Able-bodied Paupers, and nomadic Lackalls, now stagnating or roaming everywhere, drowning the face of the world (too truly) into an untenantable swamp and Stygian quagmire, has the Chief Governor of this country no word whatever to say? Nothing but "Rate in aid," "Time will mend it," "Necessary business of the Session;" and "After me the Deluge"? A Chief Governor that can front his Irish difficulty, and steadily contemplate the horoscope of Irish and British Pauperism, and whitherward it is leading him and us, in this humor, must be a— What shall we call such a Chief Governor? Alas, in spite of old use and wont,—little other than a tolerated Sole-

cism, growing daily more intolerable! He decidedly ought
to have some word to say on this matter, — to be incessantly
occupied in getting something which he could practically say!
— Perhaps to the following, or a much finer effect?

*Speech of the British Prime-Minister to the floods of Irish and
other Beggars, the able-bodied Lackalls, nomadic or stationary,
and the general assembly, outdoor and indoor, of the Pauper
Populations of these Realms.*

"Vagrant Lackalls, foolish most of you, criminal many of
you, miserable all; the sight of you fills me with astonishment
and despair. What to do with you I know not; long have I
been meditating, and it is hard to tell. Here are some three
millions of you, as I count: so many of you fallen sheer over
into the abysses of open Beggary; and, fearful to think, every
new unit that falls is *loading* so much more the chain that
drags the others over. On the edge of the precipice hang
uncounted millions; increasing, I am told, at the rate of 1200
a day. They hang there on the giddy edge, poor souls, cramp-
ing themselves down, holding on with all their strength; but
falling, falling one after another; and the chain is getting
heavy, so that ever more fall; and who at last will stand?
What to do with you? The question, What to do with you?
especially since the potato died, is like to break my heart!

"One thing, after much meditating, I have at last discovered, and now know for some time back: That you cannot
be left to roam abroad in this unguided manner, stumbling
over the precipices, and loading ever heavier the fatal *chain*
upon those who might be able to stand; that this of locking
you up in temporary Idle Workhouses, when you stumble, and
subsisting you on Indian meal, till you can sally forth again
on fresh roamings, and fresh stumblings, and ultimate descent
to the devil; — that this is *not* the plan; and that it never
was, or could out of England have been supposed to be, much
as I have prided myself upon it!

"Vagrant Lackalls, I at last perceive, all this that has been sung and spoken, for a long while, about enfranchisement, emancipation, freedom, suffrage, civil and religious liberty over the world, is little other than sad temporary jargon, brought upon us by a stern necessity, — but now ordered by a sterner to take itself away again a little. Sad temporary jargon, I say: made up of sense and nonsense, — sense in small quantities, and nonsense in very large; — and, if taken for the whole or permanent truth of human things, it is no better than fatal infinite nonsense eternally *untrue*. All men, I think, will soon have to quit this, to consider this as a thing pretty well achieved; and to look out towards another thing much more needing achievement at the time that now is.

"All men will have to quit it, I believe. But to you, my indigent friends, the time for quitting it has palpably arrived! To talk of glorious self-government, of suffrages and hustings, and the fight of freedom and such like, is a vain thing in your case. By all human definitions and conceptions of the said fight of freedom, you for your part have lost it, and can fight no more. Glorious self-government is a glory not for you, — not for Hodge's emancipated horses, nor you. No; I say, No. You, for your part, have tried it, and *failed*. Left to walk your own road, the will-o'-wisps beguiled you, your short sight could not descry the pitfalls; the deadly tumult and press has whirled you hither and thither, regardless of your struggles and your shrieks; and here at last you lie; fallen flat into the ditch, drowning there and dying, unless the others that are still standing please to pick you up. The others that still stand have their own difficulties, I can tell you! — But you, by imperfect energy and redundant appetite, by doing too little work and drinking too much beer, you (I bid you observe) have proved that you cannot do it! You lie there plainly in the ditch. And I am to pick you up again, on these mad terms; help you ever again, as with our best heart's-blood, to do what, once for all, the gods have made impossible? To load the fatal *chain* with your perpetual staggerings and sprawlings; and ever again load it, till we all lie sprawling? My indigent incompetent friends, I will not! Know that, whoever may be 'sons of freedom,' you for your part are not and cannot be such. Not 'free' you, I think, whoever may be free. You palpably are fallen captive, — *caitiff*, as they once named it : — you do, silently but eloquently, demand, in the name of mercy itself, that some genuine command be taken of you.

"Yes, my indigent incompetent friends; some genuine practical command. Such, — if I rightly interpret those mad Chartisms, Repeal Agitations, Red Republics, and other delirious inarticulate howlings and bellowings which all the populations of the world now utter, evidently cries of pain on their and your part, — is the demand which you, Captives, make of all men that are not Captive, but are still Free. Free men, — alas, had you ever any notion who the free men were, who the not-free, the incapable of freedom! The free men, if you could have understood it, they are the wise men; the patient, self-denying, valiant; the Noblès of the World; who can discern the Law of this Universe, what it is, and piously *obey* it; these, in late sad times, having cast you loose, you are fallen captive to greedy sons of profit-and-loss; to bad and ever to worse; and at length to Beer and the Devil. Algiers, Brazil or Dahomey hold nothing in them so authentically *slave* as you are, my indigent incompetent friends!

" Good Heavens, and I have to raise some eight or nine millions annually, six for England itself, and to wreck the morals of my working population beyond all money's worth, to keep the life from going out of *you :* a small service to you, as I many times bitterly repeat! Alas, yes; before high Heaven I must declare it such. I think the old Spartans, who would have killed you instead, had shown more 'humanity,' more of manhood, than I thus do ! More humanity, I say, more of *man*hood, and of sense for what the dignity of man demands imperatively of you and of me and of us all. We call it charity, beneficence, and other fine names, this brutish Workhouse Scheme of ours; and it is but sluggish heartlessness, and insincerity, and cowardly lowness of soul. Not 'humanity' or manhood, I think; perhaps *ape*hood rather, — paltry imitancy, from the teeth outward, of what our heart never felt nor *our* understanding ever saw ; dim indolent adherence to extraneous hearsays and extinct traditions; traditions now really about extinct; not living now to almost any of us, and still haunting with their spectralities and gibbering *ghosts* (in a truly baleful manner) almost all of us! Making this our struggling 'Twelfth Hour of the Night' inexpressibly hideous! —

"But as for you, my indigent incompetent friends, I have to repeat with sorrow, but with perfect clearness, what is plainly undeniable, and is even clamorous to get itself admitted, that you are of the nature of *slaves*, — or if you prefer the word, of *nomadic, and now even vagrant and vagabond, servants that can find no master on those terms ;* which seems to me a much uglier word. Emancipation? You have been 'emancipated' with a vengeance! Foolish souls, I say the whole world cannot emancipate you. Fealty to ignorant Unruliness, to gluttonous sluggish Improvidence, to the Beer-pot and the Devil, who is there that can emancipate a man in that predicament? Not a whole Reform Bill, a whole French Revolution executed for his behoof alone : nothing but God the Maker can emancipate him, by making him anew.

"To forward which glorious consummation, will it not be well, O indigent friends, that you, fallen flat there, shall henceforth learn to take advice of others as to the methods of standing? Plainly I let you know, and all the world and the worlds know, that I for my part mean it so. Not as glorious unfortunate sons of freedom, but as recognized captives, as unfortunate fallen brothers requiring that I should command you, and if need were, control and compel you, can there henceforth be a relation between us. Ask me not for Indian meal; you shall be compelled to earn it first ; know that on other terms I will not give you any. Before Heaven and Earth, and God the Maker of us all, I declare it is a scandal to see *such* a life kept in you, by the sweat and heart's-blood of your brothers ; and that, if we cannot mend it, death were preferable! Go to, we must get out of this unutterable coil of nonsenses, constitutional, philanthropical, &c., in which (surely without mutual hatred, if with less of 'love' than is supposed) we are all strangling one another! Your want of wants, I say, is that you be *commanded* in this world, not being able to command yourselves. Know therefore that it shall be so with you. Nomadism, I give you notice, has ended; needful permanency, soldier-like obedience, and the opportunity and the necessity of hard steady labor for your living, have begun. Know that the Idle Workhouse is shut against you henceforth; you cannot enter there at will, nor leave at will;— you shall enter a quite other Refuge, under conditions strict as soldiering, and not leave till I have done with you. He that prefers the glorious (or perhaps even the rebellious *in*glorious) 'career of freedom,' let him prove that he can travel there, and be the master of himself; and right good speed to him. He who has proved that he cannot travel there or be the master of himself, — let him, in the name of all the gods, become a servant, and accept the just rules of servitude!

"Arise, enlist in my Irish, my Scotch and English 'Regiments of the New Era,' —which I have been concocting, day and night, during these three Grouse-seasons (taking earnest incessant counsel, with all manner of Industrial Notabilities and men of insight, on the matter), and have now brought to a kind of preparation for incipiency, thank Heaven! Enlist there, ye poor wandering banditti; obey, work, suffer, abstain, as all of us have had to do: so shall you be useful in God's creation, so shall you be helped to gain a manful living for yourselves; not otherwise than so. Industrial Regiments — [*Here numerous persons, with big wigs many of them, and austere aspect, whom I take to be Professors of the Dismal Science, start up in an agitated vehement manner: but the Premier resolutely beckons them down again*] — Regiments not to fight the French or others, who are peaceable enough towards us; but to fight the Bogs and Wildernesses at home and abroad, and to chain the Devils of the Pit which are walking too openly among us.

"Work, for you? Work, surely, is not quite undiscoverable in an Earth so wide as ours, if we will take the right methods for it! Indigent friends, we will adopt this new relation (which is *old* as the world); this will lead us towards such. Rigorous conditions, not to be violated on either side, lie in this relation; conditions planted there by God Himself; which woe will betide us if we do not discover, gradually more and more discover, and conform to! Industrial Colonels, Work-masters, Task-masters, Life-commanders, equitable as Rhada-manthus and inflexible as he: such, I perceive, you do need; and such, you being once put under law as soldiers are, will be discoverable for you. I perceive, with boundless alarm, that I shall have to set about discovering such, — I, since I am at the top of affairs, with all men looking to me. Alas, it is my new task in this New Era; and God knows, I too, little other than a red-tape Talking-machine, and unhappy Bag of Parliamentary Eloquence hitherto, am far behind with it! But street-barricades rise everywhere: the hour of Fate has come. In Connemara there has sprung a leak, since the potato died; Connaught, if it were not for Treasury-grants and rates-in-aid, would have to recur to Cannibalism even now, and Human Society would cease to pretend that it existed there. Done this thing must be. Alas, I perceive that if I cannot do it, then surely I shall die, and perhaps shall not have Christian burial! But I already raise near upon Ten Millions for feed-ing you in idleness, my nomadic friends; work, under due regulations, I really might try to get of — [*Here arises inde-scribable uproar, no longer repressible, from all manner of Econo-mists, Emancipationists, Constitutionalists, and miscellaneous Professors of the Dismal Science, pretty numerously scattered about; and cries of "Private enterprise," "Rights of Capital," "Voluntary Principle," "Doctrines of the British Constitution," swollen by the general assenting hum of all the world, quite drown the Chief Minister for a while. He, with invincible reso-lution, persists; obtains hearing again:*]

"Respectable Professors of the Dismal Science, soft you a little. Alas, I know what you would say. For my sins, I have read much in those inimitable volumes of yours, — really I should think, some barrowfuls of them in my time, — and, in these last forty years of theory and practice, have pretty well seized what of Divine Message you were sent with to me. Perhaps as small a message, give me leave to say, as ever there was such a noise made about before. Trust me, I have not forgotten it, shall never forget it. Those Laws of the Shop-till are indisputable to me; and practically useful in certain departments of the Universe, as the multiplication-table itself. Once I even tried to sail through the Immensities with them, and to front the big coming Eternities with them; but I found it would not do. As the Supreme Rule of Statesmanship, or Government of Men, — since this Universe is not wholly a Shop, — no. You rejoice in my improved tariffs, free-trade movements and the like, on every hand; for which be thankful, and even sing litanies if you choose. But here at last, in the Idle-Workhouse movement, — unexampled yet on Earth or in the waters under the Earth, — I am fairly brought to a stand; and have had to make reflections, of the most alarming, and indeed awful, and as it were religious nature! Professors of the Dismal Science, I perceive that the length of your tether is now pretty well run; and that I must request you to talk a little lower in future. By the side of the shop-till, — see, your small 'Law of God' is hung up, along with the multiplication-table itself. But beyond and above the shop-till, allow me to say, you shall as good as hold your peace. Respectable Professors, I perceive it is not now the Gigantic Hucksters, but it is the Immortal Gods, yes they, in their terror and their beauty, in their wrath and their beneficence, that are coming into play in the affairs of this world! Soft you a little. Do not you interrupt me, but try to understand and help me! —

— "Work, was I saying? My indigent unguided friends, I should think some work might be discoverable for you. Enlist, stand drill; become, from a nomadic Banditti of Idleness, Soldiers of Industry! I will lead you to the Irish Bogs, to the vacant desolations of Connaught now falling into Cannibalism, to mistilled Connaught, to ditto Munster, Leinster, Ulster, I will lead you: to the English fox-covers, furze-grown Commons, New Forests, Salisbury Plains: likewise to the Scotch Hill-sides, and bare rushy slopes, which as yet feed only sheep, — moist uplands, thousands of square miles in extent, which are destined yet to grow green crops, and fresh butter and milk and beef without limit (wherein no 'Foreigner can compete with us'), were the Glasgow sewers once opened on them, and you with your Colonels carried thither   In the

Three Kingdoms, or in the Forty Colonies, depend upon it, you shall be led to your work!

"To each of you I will then say: Here is work for you; strike into it with manlike, soldier-like obedience and heartiness, according to the methods here prescribed, — wages follow for you without difficulty; all manner of just remuneration, and at length emancipation itself follows. Refuse to strike' into it; shirk the heavy labor, disobey the rules, — I will admonish and endeavor to incite you; if in vain, I will flog you; if still in vain, I will at last shoot you, — and make God's Earth, and the forlorn-hope in God's Battle, free of you. Understand it, I advise you! The Organization of Labor" — [*Left speaking*, says our reporter.]

"Left speaking:" alas, that he should have to "speak" so much! There are things that should be done, not spoken; that till the doing of them is begun, cannot well be spoken. He may have to "speak" seven years yet, before a spade be struck into the Bog of Allen; and then perhaps it will be too late! —

You perceive, my friends, we have actually got into the "New Era" there has been such prophesying of: here we all are, arrived at last; — and it is by no means the land flowing with milk and honey we were led to expect! Very much the reverse. A terrible *new* country this: no neighbors in it yet, that I can see, but irrational flabby monsters (philanthropic and other) of the giant species; hyenas, laughing hyenas, predatory wolves; probably *devils*, blue (or perhaps blue-and-yellow) devils, as St. Guthlac found in Croyland long ago. A huge untrodden haggard country, the "chaotic battle-field of Frost and Fire;" a country of savage glaciers, granite mountains, of foul jungles, unhewed forests, quaking bogs; — which we shall have our own ados to make arable and habitable, I think! We must stick by it, however; — of all enterprises the impossiblest is that of getting out of *it*, and shifting into another. To work, then, one and all; hands to work!

[March 1, 1850.]

No. II. MODEL PRISONS.

THE deranged condition of our affairs is a universal topic among men at present; and the heavy miseries pressing, in their rudest shape, on the great dumb inarticulate class, and from this, by a sure law, spreading upwards, in a less palpable but not less certain and perhaps still more fatal shape on all classes to the very highest, are admitted everywhere to be great, increasing and now almost unendurable. How to diminish them. — this is every man's question. For in fact they do imperatively need diminution; and unless they can be diminished, there are many other things that cannot very long continue to exist beside them. A serious question indeed, How to diminish them!

Among the articulate classes, as they may be called, there are two ways of proceeding in regard to this. One large body of the intelligent and influential, busied mainly in personal affairs, accepts the social iniquities, or whatever you may call them, and the miseries consequent thereupon; accepts them, admits them to be extremely miserable, pronounces them entirely inevitable, incurable except by Heaven, and eats its pudding with as little thought of them as possible. Not a very noble class of citizens these; not a very hopeful or salutary method of dealing with social iniquities this of theirs, however it may answer in respect to themselves and their personal affairs! But now there is the select small minority, in whom some sentiment of public spirit and human pity still survives, among whom, or not anywhere, the Good Cause may expect to find soldiers and servants : their method of proceeding, in these times, is also very strange. They embark in the "philanthropic movement;" they calculate that the miseries of the world can be cured by bringing the philanthropic movement to bear on them. To universal public misery, and universal neglect of the clearest public duties, let private charity superadd itself: there will thus be some balance restored, and maintained again; thus, — or by what conceivable method? On these terms they, for their part, embark in the sacred cause; resolute to cure a world's woes by rose-water; desperately bent on trying to the uttermost that mild method. It seems not to have struck these good men that no world, or thing here below, ever fell into misery, without having first fallen into folly, into sin against the Supreme Ruler of it, by adopting as a law of conduct what was not a law, but the reverse of one; and that, till its folly, till its sin be cast out of it, there is not the smallest hope of its misery going, — that not for all the charity and rose-water in the world will its misery try to go till then!

This is a sad error; all the sadder as it is the error chiefly of the more humane and noble-minded of our generation; among whom, as we said, or elsewhere not at all, the cause of real Reform must expect its servants. At present, and for a long while past, whatsoever young soul awoke in England with some disposition towards generosity and social heroism, or at lowest with some intimation of the beauty of such a disposition,— he, in whom the poor world might have looked for a Reformer, and valiant mender of its foul ways, was almost sure to become a Philanthropist, reforming merely by this rose-water method. To admit that the world's ways are foul, and not the ways of God the Maker, but of Satan the Destroyer, many of them, and that they must be mended or we all die; that if huge misery prevails, huge cowardice, falsity, disloyalty, universal Injustice high and low, have still longer prevailed, and must straightway try to cease prevailing: this is what no visible reformer has yet thought of doing. All so-called "reforms" hitherto are grounded either on openly admitted egoism (cheap bread to the cotton-spinner, voting to those that have no vote, and the like), which does not point towards very celestial developments of the Reform movement; or else upon this of remedying social injustices by indiscriminate contributions of philanthropy, a method surely still more unpromising. Such contributions, being indiscriminate, are but a new injustice ; these will never lead to reform, or abolition of injustice, whatever else they lead to !

Not by that method shall we "get round Cape Horn," by never such unanimity of voting, under the most approved Phantasm Captains ! It is miserable to see. Having, as it were, quite lost our way round Cape Horn, and being sorely "admonished" by the Iceberg and other dumb councillors, the pilots, — instead of taking to their sextants, and asking with a seriousness unknown for a long while, What the Laws of wind and water, and of Earth and of Heaven are, — decide that now, in these new circumstances, they will, to the worthy and unworthy, serve out a double allowance of grog. In this way they hope to do it, — by steering on the old wrong tack, and serving out more and more copiously what little *aqua vitæ* may be still on board ! Philanthropy, emancipation, and pity for human calamity is very beautiful ; but the deep oblivion of the Law of Right and Wrong ; this " indiscriminate mashing up of Right and Wrong into a patent treacle " of the Philanthropic movement, is by no means beautiful ; this, on the contrary, is altogether ugly and alarming.

Truly if there be not something inarticulate among us, not yet uttered but pressing towards utterance, which is much wiser than anything we have lately articulated or brought into word or action, our outlooks are rather lamentable. The great majority of the powerful and active-minded, sunk in egoistic scepticisms, busied in chase of lucre, pleasure, and mere vulgar objects, looking with indifference on the world's woes, and passing carelessly by on the other side ; and the select minority, of whom better might have been expected, bending all their strength to cure them by methods which can only make bad worse, and in the end render cure hopeless. A blind loquacious pruriency of indiscriminate Philanthropism substituting itself, with much self-laudation, for the silent divinely awful sense of Right and Wrong ; — testifying too clearly that here is no longer a divine sense of Right and Wrong ; that, in the smoke of this universal, and alas inevitable and indispensable revolutionary fire, and burning up of worn-out rags of which the world is full, our life-atmosphere has (for the time) become one vile London fog, and the eternal loadstars are gone out for us! Gone out;—yet very visible if you can get above the fog; still there in their place, and quite the same as they always were! To whoever does still know of loadstars, the proceedings, which expand themselves daily, of these sublime philanthropic associations, and "universal sluggard-and-scoundrel protection-societies," are a perpetual affliction. With their emancipations and abolition principles, and reigns of brotherhood and new methods of love, they have done great things in the White and in the Black World, during late years; and are preparing for greater.

In the interest of human reform, if there is ever to be any reform, and return to prosperity or to the possibility of prospering, it is urgent that the nonsense of all this (and it is mostly nonsense, but not quite) should be sent about its business straightway, and forbidden to deceive the well-meaning souls among us any more. Reform, if we will understand that divine word, cannot begin till then. One day, I do know, this, as is the doom of all nonsense, will be drummed out of the world, with due placard stuck on its back, and the populace flinging dead cats at it: but whether soon or not, is by no means so certain. I rather guess, *not* at present, not quite soon. Fraternity, in other countries, has gone on, till it found itself unexpectedly manipulating guillotines by its chosen Robespierres, and become a fraternity like Cain's. Much to its amazement! For in fact it is not all nonsense; there is an infinitesimal fraction of sense in it withal; which is so difficult to disengage;—which must be disengaged, and laid hold of, before Fraternity can vanish.

But to our subject,—the Model Prison, and the strange theory of life now in action there. That, for the present, is my share in the wide adventure of Philanthropism; the world's share, and how and when it is to be liquidated and ended, rests with the Supreme Destinies.

Several months ago, some friends took me with them to see one of the London Prisons; a Prison of the exemplary or

model kind. An immense circuit of buildings; cut out, girt
with a high ring-wall, from the lanes and streets of the
quarter, which is a dim and crowded one. Gateway as to a
fortified place; then a spacious court, like the square of a
city; broad staircases, passages to interior courts; fronts of
stately architecture all round. It lodges some thousand or
twelve hundred prisoners, besides the officers of the establishment. Surely one of the most perfect buildings, within the
compass of London. We looked at the apartments, sleeping-
cells, dining-rooms, working-rooms, general courts or special
and private: excellent all, the ne-plus-ultra of human care and
ingenuity; in my life I never saw so clean a building; probably no Duke in England lives in a mansion of such perfect
and thorough cleanness.

The bread, the cocoa, soup, meat, all the various sorts of
food, in their respective cooking-places, we tasted: found them
of excellence superlative. The prisoners sat at work, light
work, picking oakum, and the like, in airy apartments with
glass roofs, of agreeable temperature and perfect ventilation;
silent, or at least conversing only by secret signs: others were
out, taking their hour of promenade in clean flagged courts:
methodic composure, cleanliness, peace, substantial wholesome
comfort reigned everywhere supreme. The women in other
apartments, some notable murderesses among them, all in the
like state of methodic composure and substantial wholesome
comfort, sat sewing: in long ranges of wash-houses, drying-
houses and whatever pertains to the getting-up of clean linen,
were certain others, with all conceivable mechanical further-
ances, not too arduously working. The notable murderesses
were, though with great precautions of privacy, pointed out
to us; and we were requested not to look openly at them, or
seem to notice them at all, as it was found to "cherish their
vanity" when visitors looked at them. Schools too were
there; intelligent teachers of both sexes, studiously instruct-
ing the still ignorant of these thieves.

From an inner upper room or gallery, we looked down
into a range of private courts, where certain Chartist Notabilities were undergoing their term. Chartist Notability

First struck me very much; I had seen him about a year before, by involuntary accident and much to my disgust, magnetizing a silly young person; and had noted well the unlovely voracious look of him, his thick oily skin, his heavy dull-burning eyes, his greedy mouth, the dusky potent insatiable *animalism* that looked out of every feature of him: a fellow adequate to animal-magnetize most things, I did suppose; — and here was the post I now found him arrived at. Next neighbor to him was Notability Second, a philosophic or literary Chartist; walking rapidly to and fro in his private court, a clean, high-walled place; the world and its cares quite excluded, for some months to come: master of his own time and spiritual resources to, as I supposed, a really enviable extent. What "literary man" to an equal extent! I fancied I, for my own part, so left with paper and ink, and all taxes and botherations shut out from me, could have written such a Book as no reader will here ever get of me. Never, O reader, never here in a mere house with taxes and botherations. Here, alas, one has to snatch one's poor Book, bit by bit, as from a conflagration; and to think and live, comparatively, as if the house were not one's own, but mainly the world's and the devil's. Notability Second might have filled one with envy.

The Captain of the place, a gentleman of ancient Military or Royal-Navy habits, was one of the most perfect governors; professionally and by nature zealous for cleanliness, punctuality, good order of every kind; a humane heart and yet a strong one; soft of speech and manner, yet with an inflexible rigor of command, so far as his limits went: "iron hand in a velvet glove," as Napoleon defined it. A man of real worth, challenging at once love and respect: the light of those mild bright eyes seemed to permeate the place as with an all-pervading vigilance, and kindly yet victorious illumination; in the soft definite voice it was as if Nature herself were promulgating her orders, gentlest mildest orders, which however, in the end, there would be no disobeying, which in the end there would be no living without fulfilment of. A true "*aristos*," and commander of men. A man worthy to

have commanded and guided forward, in good ways, twelve
hundred of the best common-people in London or the world:
he was here, for many years past, giving all his care and
faculty to command, and guide forward in such ways as there
were, twelve hundred of the worst. I looked with considerable admiration on this gentleman; and with considerable
astonishment, the reverse of admiration, on the work he had
here been set upon.

This excellent Captain was too old a Commander to complain of anything; indeed he struggled visibly the other way,
to find in his own mind that all here was best; but I could
sufficiently discern that, in his natural instincts, if not mounting up to the region of his thoughts, there was a continual
protest going on against much of it; that nature and all his
inarticulate persuasion (however much forbidden to articulate
itself) taught him the futility and unfeasibility of the system
followed here. The Visiting Magistrates, he gently regretted
rather than complained, had lately taken his tread-wheel from
him, men were just now pulling it down; and how he was
henceforth to enforce discipline on these bad subjects, was
much a difficulty with him. "They cared for nothing but the
tread-wheel, and for having their rations cut short:" of the
two sole penalties, hard work and occasional hunger, there
remained now only one, and that by no means the better one,
as he thought. The "sympathy" of visitors, too, their "pity"
for his interesting scoundrel-subjects, though he tried to like
it, was evidently no joy to this practical mind. Pity, yes: —
but pity for the scoundrel-species? For those who will not
have pity on themselves, and will force the Universe and the
Laws of Nature to have no "pity" on them? Meseems I
could discover fitter objects of pity!

In fact it was too clear, this excellent man had got a field
for his faculties which, in several respects, was by no means
the suitable one. To drill twelve hundred scoundrels by "the
method of kindness," and of abolishing your very tread-
wheel, — how could any commander rejoice to have such a
work cut out for him? You had but to look in the faces
of these twelve hundred, and despair, for most part, of ever

"commanding" them at all. Miserable distorted blockheads, the generality; ape-faces, imp-faces, angry dog-faces, heavy sullen ox-faces; degraded underfoot perverse creatures, sons of *in*docility, greedy mutinous darkness, and in one word, of STUPIDITY, which is the general mother of such. Stupidity intellectual and stupidity moral (for the one always means the other, as you will, with surprise or not, discover if you look) had borne this progeny: base-natured beings, on whom in the course of a maleficent subterranean life of London Scoundrelism, the Genius of Darkness (called Satan, Devil, and other names) had now visibly impressed his seal, and had marked them out as soldiers of Chaos and of him, — appointed to serve in *his* Regiments, First of the line, Second ditto, and so on in their order. Him, you could perceive, they would serve; but not easily another than him. These were the subjects whom our brave Captain and Prison-Governor was appointed to command, and reclaim to *other* service, by "the method of love," with a tread-wheel abolished.

Hopeless forevermore such a project. These abject, ape, wolf, ox, imp and other diabolic-animal specimens of humanity, who of the very gods could ever have commanded them by love? A collar round the neck, and a cart-whip flourished over the back; these, in a just and steady human hand, were what the gods would have appointed them; and now when, by long misconduct and neglect, they had sworn themselves into the Devil's regiments of the line, and got the seal of Chaos impressed on their visage, it was very doubtful whether even these would be of avail for the unfortunate commander of twelve hundred men! By "love," without hope except of peaceably teasing oakum, or fear except of a temporary loss of dinner, he was to guide these men, and wisely constrain them, — whitherward? No-whither: that was his goal, if you will think well of it; that was a second fundamental falsity in his problem. False in the warp and false in the woof, thought one of us; about as false a problem as any I have seen a good man set upon lately! To guide scoundrels by "love;" that is a false woof, I take it, a method that will not hold together; hardly for the flower of men will love alone do; and for the

. sediment and scoundrelism of men it has not even a chance to
do. And then to guide any class of men, scoundrel or other,
No-whither, which was this poor Captain's problem, in this
Prison with oakum for its one element of hope or outlook, how
can that prosper by "love" or by any conceivable method?
That is a warp wholly false. Out of which false warp, or
originally false condition to start from, combined and daily
woven into by your false woof, or methods of "love" and
such like, there arises for our poor Captain the falsest of
problems, and for a man of his faculty the unfairest of situations. His problem was, not to command good men to do
something, but bad men to do (with superficial disguises)
nothing.

On the whole, what a beautiful Establishment here fitted up
for the accommodation of the scoundrel-world, male and female! As I said, no Duke in England is, for all rational
purposes which a human being can or ought to aim at, lodged,
fed, tended, taken care of, with such perfection. Of poor
craftsmen that pay rates and taxes from their day's wages, of
the dim millions that toil and moil continually under the sun,
we know what is the lodging and the tending. Of the Johnsons, Goldsmiths, lodged in their squalid garrets; working
often enough amid famine, darkness, tumult, dust and desolation, what work *they* have to do:— of these as of "spiritual
backwoodsmen," understood to be preappointed to such a life,
and like the pigs to killing, "quite used to it," I say nothing.
But of Dukes, which Duke, I could ask, has cocoa, soup, meat,
and food in general made ready, so fit for keeping him in
health, in ability to do and to enjoy? Which Duke has a
house so thoroughly clean, pure and airy; lives in an element
so wholesome, and perfectly adapted to the uses of soul and
body as this same, which is provided here for the Devil's
regiments of the line? No Duke that I have ever known.
Dukes are waited on by deleterious French cooks, by perfunc-
tory grooms of the chambers, and expensive crowds of eye-
servants, more imaginary than real: while here, Science, Human
Intellect and Beneficence have searched and sat studious, eager

to do their very best; they have chosen a real Artist in Governing to see their best, in all details of it, done. Happy regiments of the line, what soldier to any earthly or celestial Power has such a lodging and attendance as you here? No soldier or servant direct or indirect of God or of man, in this England at present. Joy to you, regiments of the line. Your Master, I am told, has his Elect, and professes to be "Prince of the Kingdoms of this World;" and truly I see he has power to do a good turn to those he loves, in England at least. Shall we say, May *he*, may the Devil give you good of it, ye Elect of Scoundrelism? I will rather pass by, uttering no prayer at all; musing rather in silence on the singular "worship of God," or practical "reverence done to Human Worth" (which is the outcome and essence of all real "worship" whatsoever) among the Posterity of Adam at this day.

For all round this beautiful Establishment, or Oasis of Purity, intended for the Devil's regiments of the line, lay continents of dingy poor and dirty dwellings, where the unfortunate not *yet* enlisted into that Force were struggling manifoldly, — in their workshops, in their marble-yards and timber-yards and tan-yards, in their close cellars, cobbler-stalls, hungry garrets, and poor dark trade-shops with red-herrings and tobacco-pipes crossed in the window, — to keep the Devil out-of-doors, and *not* enlist with him. And it was by a tax on these that the Barracks for the regiments of the line were kept up. Visiting Magistrates, impelled by Exeter Hall, by Able-Editors, and the Philanthropic Movement of the Age, had given orders to that effect. Rates on the poor servant of God and of her Majesty, who still serves both in his way, painfully selling red-herrings; rates on him and his red-herrings to boil right soup for the Devil's declared Elect! Never in my travels, in any age or clime, had I fallen in with such Visiting Magistrates before. Reserved they, I should suppose, for these ultimate or penultimate ages of the world, rich in all prodigies, political, spiritual, — ages surely with such a length of ears as was never paralleled before.

If I had a commonwealth to reform or to govern, certainly it should not be the Devil's regiments of the time that I would

first of all concentrate my attention on! With them I should
be apt so make rather brief work; to them one would apply
the besom, try to sweep *them* with some rapidity into the
dust-bin, and well out of one's road, I should rather say. Fill
your thrashing-floor with docks, ragweeds, mugworths, and ply
your flail upon them, — that is not the method to obtain sacks
of wheat. Away, you; begone swiftly, *ye* regiments of the
line: in the name of God and of His poor struggling servants,
sore put to it to live in these bad days, I mean to rid myself
of you with some degree of brevity. To feed you in palaces,
to hire captains and schoolmasters and the choicest spiritual
and material artificers to expend their industries on you, —
No, by the Eternal! I have quite other work for that class
of artists ; Seven-and-twenty Millions of neglected mortals
who have not yet quite declared for the Devil. Mark it, my
diabolic friends, I mean to lay leather on the backs of you,
collars round the necks of you; and will teach you, after the
example of the gods, that this world is *not* your inheritance,
or glad to see you in it. You, ye diabolic canaille, what has a
Governor much to do with you? You, I think, he will rather
swiftly dismiss from his thoughts, — which have the whole
celestial and terrestrial for their scope, and not the subterranean of scoundreldom alone. You, I consider, he will sweep
pretty rapidly into some Norfolk Island, into some special
Convict Colony or remote domestic Moorland, into some
stone-walled Silent-System, under hard drill-sergeants, just as
Rhadamanthus, and inflexible as he, and there leave you to
reap what you have sown; he meanwhile turning his endeavors to the thousand-fold immeasurable interests of men and
gods, — dismissing the one extremely contemptible interest of
scoundrels ; sweeping that into the cesspool, tumbling that
over London Bridge, in a very brief manner, if needful! Who
are you, ye thriftless sweepings of Creation, that we should
forever be pestered with you? Have we no work to do but
drilling Devil's regiments of the line?

If I had schoolmasters, my benevolent friend, do you imagine
I would set them on teaching a set of unteachables, who as
you perceive have already made up their mind that black *is*

white, — that the Devil namely is the advantageous Master to serve in this world? My esteemed Benefactor of Humanity, it shall be far from me. Minds open to that particular conviction are not the material I like to work upon. When once my schoolmasters have gone over all the other classes of society from top to bottom; and have no other soul to try with teaching, all being thoroughly taught, — I will then send them to operate on *these* regiments of the line: then, and, assure yourself, never till then. The truth is, I am sick of scoundreldom, my esteemed Benefactor; it always was detestable to me; and here where I find it lodged in palaces and waited on by the benevolent of the world, it is more detestable, not to say insufferable to me than ever.

Of Beneficence, Benevolence, and the people that come together to talk on platforms and subscribe five pounds, I will say nothing here; indeed there is not room here for the twentieth part of what were to be said of them. The beneficence, benevolence, and sublime virtue which issues in eloquent talk reported in the Newspapers, with the subscription of five pounds, and the feeling that one is a good citizen and ornament to society, — concerning this, there were a great many unexpected remarks to be made; but let this one, for the present occasion, suffice : —

My sublime benevolent friends, don't you perceive, for one thing, that here is a shockingly unfruitful investment for your capital of Benevolence; precisely the *worst*, indeed, which human ingenuity could select for you? "Laws are unjust, temptations great," &c. &c.: alas, I know it, and mourn for it, and passionately call on all men to help in altering it. But according to every hypothesis as to the law, and the temptations and pressures towards vice, here are the individuals who, of all the society, have yielded to said pressure. These are of the worst substance for enduring pressure! The others yet stand and make resistance to temptation, to the law's injustice; under all the perversities and strangling impediments there are, the rest of the society still keep their feet, and struggle forward, marching under the banner of *Cosmos*, of God and Human Virtue; these select Few, as I explain to you, are

they who have fallen to *Chaos*, and are sworn into certain
regiments of the line. A superior proclivity to Chaos is declared in these, by the very fact of their being here! Of all
the generation we live in, these are the worst stuff. These,
I say, are the Elixir of the Infatuated among living mortals:
if you want the *worst* investment for your Benevolence, here
you accurately have it. O my surprising friends! Nowhere
so as here can you be certain that a given quantity of wise
teaching bestowed, of benevolent trouble taken, will yield
zero, or the net *minimum* of return. It is sowing of your
wheat upon Irish quagmires ; laboriously harrowing it in
upon the sand of the seashore. O my astonishing benevolent
friends !

Yonder, in those dingy habitations, and shops of red her-
ring and tobacco-pipes, where men have not yet quite declared
for the Devil; there, I say, is land: here is mere sea-beach.
Thither go with your benevolence, thither to those dingy
caverns of the poor ; and there instruct and drill and manage,
there where some fruit may come from it. And, above all
and inclusive of all, cannot you go to those Solemn human
Shams, Phantasm Captains, and Supreme Quacks that ride
prosperously in every thoroughfare ; and with severe benevolence, ask them, What they are doing here ? They are the
men whom it would behoove you to drill a little, and tie to
the halberts in a benevolent manner, if you could ! "We cannot," say you? Yes, my friends, to a certain extent you can.
By many well-known active methods, and by all manner of
passive methods, you can. Strive thitherward, I advise you ;
thither, with whatever social effort there may lie in you !
The well-head and "consecrated" thrice-accursed chief fountain of all those waters of bitterness, — it is they, those Solemn
Shams and Supreme Quacks of yours, little as they or you
imagine it ! Them, with severe benevolence, put a stop to ;
them send to their Father, far from the sight of the true and
just, — if you would ever see a just world here !

What sort of reformers and workers are you, that work only
on the rotten material ? That never think of meddling with
the material while it continues sound ; that stress it and strain

it with new rates and assessments, till once it has given way and declared itself rotten; whereupon you snatch greedily at it, and say, Now let us try to do some good upon it! You mistake in every way, my friends: the fact is, you fancy yourselves men of virtue, benevolence, what not; and you are not even men of sincerity and honest sense. I grieve to say it; but it is true. Good from you, and your operations, is not to be expected. You may go down!

Howard is a beautiful Philanthropist, eulogized by Burke, and in most men's minds a sort of beatified individual. How glorious, having finished off one's affairs in Bedfordshire, or in fact finding them very dull, inane, and worthy of being quitted and got away from, to set out on a cruise over the Jails first of Britain; then, finding that answer, over the Jails of the habitable Globe! "A voyage of discovery, a circumnavigation of charity; to collate distresses, to gauge wretchedness, to take the dimensions of human misery:" — really it is very fine. Captain Cook's voyage for the Terra Australis, Ross's, Franklin's for the ditto Borealis: men make various cruises and voyages in this world, — for want of money, want of work, and one or the other want, — which are attended with their difficulties too, and do *not* make the cruiser a demigod. On the whole, I have myself nothing but respect, comparatively speaking, for the dull solid Howard, and his "benevolence," and other impulses that set him cruising; Heaven had grown weary of Jail-fevers, and other the like *un*just penalties inflicted upon scoundrels, — for scoundrels too, and even the very Devil, should not have *more* than their due; — and Heaven, in its opulence, created a man to make an end of that. Created him; disgusted him with the grocer business; tried him with Calvinism, rural ennui, and sore bereavement in his Bedfordshire retreat; — and, in short, at last got him set to his work, and in a condition to achieve it. For which I am thankful to Heaven; and do also, with doffed hat, humbly salute John Howard. A practical solid man, if a dull and even dreary; "carries his weighing-scales in his pocket:" when your jailer answers, "The prisoner's allowance of food is so and so; and we observe it sacredly; here, for example, is a ration."—"Hey! A ration this?" and solid John suddenly produces his weighing-scales; weighs it, marks down in his tablets what the actual quantity of it is. That is the art and manner of the man. A man full of English accuracy; English veracity, solidity, simplicity; by whom this universal Jail-commission, not to be paid for in money but far otherwise, is set about, with all the slow energy, the patience, practicality, sedulity and sagacity common to the best English commissioners paid in money and not expressly otherwise.

For it is the glory of England that she has a turn for fidelity in practical work; that sham-workers, though very numerous, are rarer than elsewhere; that a man who undertakes work for you will still, in various provinces of our affairs, do it, instead of merely seeming to do it. John Howard, without pay in money, *did* this of the Jail-fever, as other Englishmen do work, in a truly workmanlike manner: his distinction was that he did it without money. He had not £500 or £5,000 a year of salary for it; but lived merely on his Bedfordshire estates, and as Snigsby irreverently expresses it, "by chewing his own cud." And, sure enough, if any man might chew the cud of placid reflections, solid Howard, a mournful man otherwise, might at intervals indulge a little in that luxury. No money-salary had he for his work; he had merely the income of his properties, and what he could derive from within. Is this such a sublime distinction, then? Well, let it pass at its value. There have been benefactors of mankind who had more need of money than he, and got none too. Milton, it is known, did his *Paradise Lost* at the easy rate of five pounds. Kepler worked out the secret of the Heavenly Motions in a dreadfully painful manner; "going over the calculations sixty times;" and having not only no public money, but no private either; and, in fact, writing almanacs for his bread-and-water, while he did this of the Heavenly Motions; having no Bedfordshire estates; nothing but a pension of £18 (which they would not pay him), the valuable faculty of writing almanacs, and at length the invaluable one of dying, when the Heavenly bodies were vanquished, and battle's conflagration had collapsed into cold dark ashes, and the starvation reached too high a pitch for the poor man.

Howard is not the only benefactor that has worked without money for us; there have been some more, — and will be, I hope! For the Destinies are opulent; and send here and there a man into the world to do work, for which they do not mean to pay him in money. And they smite him beneficently with sore afflictions, and blight his world all into grim frozen ruins round him, — and can make a wandering Exile of their Dante, and not a soft-bedded Podestà of Florence, if they wish to get a *Divine Comedy* out of him. Nay that rather is their way, when they have worthy work for such a man; they scourge him manifoldly to the due pitch, sometimes nearly of despair, that he may search desperately for his work, and find it; they urge him on still with beneficent stripes when needful, as is constantly the case between whiles; and, in fact, have privately decided to reward him with beneficent death by and by, and not with money at all. O my benevolent friend, I honor Howard very much; but it is on this side idolatry a long way, not to an infinite, but to a decidedly finite extent! And you, — put not the modest noble Howard, a truly modest man, to the blush, by forcing these reflections on us!

Cholera Doctors, hired to dive into black dens of infection and despair, they, rushing about all day from lane to lane, with their life in their hand, are found to do their function; which is a much more rugged one than Howard's. Or what say we, Cholera Doctors? Ragged losels gathered by beat of drum from the overcrowded streets of cities, and drilled a little and dressed in red, do not they stand fire in an uncensurable manner; and handsomely give their life, if needful, at the rate of a shilling per day? Human virtue, if we went down to the roots of it, is not so rare. The materials of human virtue are everywhere abundant as the light of the sun: raw materials, — O woe, and loss, and scandal thrice and threefold, that they so seldom are elaborated, and built into a result! that they lie yet unelaborated, and stagnant in the souls of wide-spread dreary millions, fermenting, festering; and issue at last as energetic vice instead of strong practical virtue! A Mrs. Manning "dying game," — alas, is not that the foiled potentiality of a kind of heroine too? Not a heroic Judith, not a mother of the Gracchi now, but a hideous murderess, fit to be the mother of hyenas! To such extent can potentialities be foiled. Education, kingship, command, — where is it, whither has it fled? Woe a thousand times, that this, which is the task of all kings, captains, priests, public speakers, land-owners, book-writers, mill-owners, and persons possessing or pretending to possess authority among mankind, — is left neglected among them all; and instead of it so little done but protocolling, black-or-white surplicing, partridge-shooting, parliamentary eloquence and popular twaddle-literature; with such results as we see! —

Howard abated the Jail-fever; but it seems to me he has been the innocent cause of a far more distressing fever which rages high just now; what we may call the Benevolent-Platform Fever. Howard is to be regarded as the unlucky fountain of that tumultuous frothy ocean-tide of benevolent sentimentality, "abolition of punishment," all-absorbing "prison-discipline," and general morbid sympathy, instead of hearty hatred, for scoundrels; which is threatening to drown human society as in deluges, and leave, instead of an "edifice of society" fit for the habitation of men, a continent of fetid ooze inhabitable only by mud-gods and creatures that walk upon their belly. Few things more distress a thinking soul at this time.

Most sick am I, O friends, of this sugary disastrous jargon of philanthropy, the reign of love, new era of universal brotherhood, and not Paradise to the Well-deserving but Paradise to All-and-sundry, which possesses the benighted minds of men and women in our day. My friends, I think you are much mistaken about Paradise! "No Paradise for anybody: he that cannot do without Paradise, go his ways:" suppose you tried that for a while! I reckon that the safer version. — Unhappy sugary brethren, this is all untrue, this other; contrary to the fact; not a tatter of it will hang together in the wind and weather of fact. In brotherhood with the base and foolish I, for one, do not mean to live. Not in brotherhood with them was life hitherto worth much to me; in pity, in hope not yet quite swallowed of disgust, — otherwise in enmity that must last through eternity, in unappeasable aversion shall I have to live with these! Brotherhood? No, be the thought far from me. They are Adam's children, — alas yes, I well remember that, and never shall forget it; hence this rage and sorrow. But they have gone over to the dragons; they have quitted the Father's house, and set up with the Old Serpent: till they return, how can they be brothers? They are enemies, deadly to themselves and to me and to you, till then; till then, while hope yet lasts, I will treat them as brothers fallen insane; — when hope has ended, with tears grown sacred and wrath grown sacred, I will cut them off in the name of God! It is at my peril if I do not. With the servant of Satan I dare not continue in partnership. Him I must put away, resolutely and forever; "lest," as it is written, "I become partaker of his plagues."

Beautiful Black Peasantry, who have fallen idle and have got the Devil at your elbow; interesting White Felonry, who are not idle, but have enlisted into the Devil's regiments of the line, — know that my benevolence for you is comparatively trifling! What I have of that divine feeling is due to others, not to you. A "universal Sluggard-and-Scoundrel Protection Society" is not the one I mean to institute in these times, where so much wants protection, and is sinking to sad issues for want of it! The scoundrel needs no protection. The scoundrel that *will* hasten to the gallows, why not rather clear the way for him! Better he reach *his* goal and outgate by the natural proclivity, than be so expensively dammed up and detained, poisoning everything as he stagnates and meanders along, to arrive at last a hundred times fouler, and swollen a hundred times bigger! Benevolent men should reflect on this. — And you Quashee, my pumpkin, — (not a bad fellow either, this poor Quashee, when tolerably guided!) — idle Quashee, I say you must get the Devil *sent away* from your elbow, my poor dark friend! In this world there will be no existence for you otherwise. No, not as the brother of your folly will I live beside you. Please to withdraw out of my way, if I am not to contradict your folly, and amend it, and put it in the stocks if it will not amend. By the Eternal Maker, it is on that footing alone that you and I can live together! And if you had respectable traditions dated from beyond Magna Charta, or from beyond the Deluge, to the contrary, and written sheepskins that would thatch the face of the world, — behold I, for one individual, do not believe said respectable traditions, nor regard said written sheepskins except as things which *you*, till you grow wiser, will believe. Adieu, Quashee; I will wish you better guidance than you have had of late.

On the whole, what a reflection is it that we cannot bestow on an unworthy man any particle of our benevolence, our patronage, or whatever resource is ours, — without withdrawing it, it and all that will grow of it, from one worthy, to whom it of right belongs! We cannot, I say; impossible; it is the eternal law of things. Incompetent Duncan M'Pastehorn, the hapless incompetent mortal to whom I· give the cobbling of my boots, — and cannot find in my heart to refuse it, the poor drunken wretch having a wife and ten children; he *withdraws* the job from sober, plainly competent, and meritorious Mr. Sparrowbill, generally short of work too; discourages Sparrowbill; teaches him that he too may as well drink and loiter and bungle; that this is not a scene for merit and demerit at all, but for dupery, and whining flattery, and incompetent cobbling of every description; — clearly tending to the ruin of poor Sparrowbill! What harm had Sparrowbill done me that I should so help to ruin him? And I could n't *save* the insalvable M'Pastehorn; I merely yielded him, for insufficient work, here and there a half-crown, — which he oftenest drank. And now Sparrowbill also is drinking!

Justice, Justice : woe betides us everywhere when, for this reason or for that, we fail to do justice! No beneficence, benevolence, or other virtuous contribution will make good the want. And in what a rate of terrible geometrical progression, far beyond *our* poor computation, any act of Injustice once done by us grows; rooting itself ever anew, spreading ever anew, like a banyan-tree, — blasting all life under it, for it is a poison-tree! There is but one thing needed for the world; but that one is indispensable. Justice, Justice, in the name of Heaven; give us Justice, and we live; give us only counterfeits of it, or succedanea for it, and we die!

Oh, this universal syllabub of philanthropic twaddle! My friend, it is very sad, now when Christianity is as good as extinct in all hearts, to meet this ghastly Phantasm of Christianity parading through almost all. "I will clean your foul thoroughfares, and make your Devil's-cloaca of a world into a garden of Heaven," jabbers this Phantasm, itself a phosphorescence and unclean! The worst, it is written, comes from corruption of the best: — Semitic forms now lying putrescent, dead and still unburied, this phosphorescence rises. I say sometimes, such a blockhead Idol, and miserable *White* Mumbo-jumbo, fashioned out of deciduous sticks and cast clothes, out of extinct cants and modern sentimentalisms, as that which they sing litanies to at Exeter Hall and extensively elsewhere, was perhaps never set up by human folly before. Unhappy creatures, that is not the Maker of the Universe, not that, — look one moment at the Universe, and see! That is a paltry Phantasm, engendered in your own sick brain; whoever follows that as a Reality will fall into the ditch.

Reform, reform, all men see and feel, is imperatively needed. Reform must either be got, and speedily, or else we die: and nearly all the men that speak, instruct us, saying, "Have you quite done your interesting Negroes in the Sugar Islands? Rush to the Jails, then, O ye reformers; snatch up the interesting scoundrel-population there, to them be nursing-fathers and nursing-mothers. And oh, wash, and dress, and teach, and recover to the service of Heaven these poor lost souls: *so*, we assure you, will society attain the needful reform, and life be still possible in this world." Thus sing the oracles everywhere; nearly all the men that speak, — though we doubt not, there are, as usual, immense majorities consciously or unconsciously wiser who hold their tongue.

But except this of whitewashing the scoundrel-population, one sees little "reform" going on. There is perhaps some endeavor to do a little scavengering; and, as the all-including point, to cheapen the terrible cost of Government: but neither of these enterprises makes progress, owing to impediments.

"Whitewash your scoundrel-population; sweep out your abominable gutters (if not in the name of God, ye brutish slatterns, then in the name of Cholera and the Royal College of Surgeons): do these two things; — and observe, much cheaper if you please!" — Well, here surely is an Evangel of Freedom, and real Program of a new Era. What surliest misanthrope would not find this world lovely, were these things done: scoundrels whitewashed; some degree of scavengering upon the gutters; and at a cheap rate, thirdly? That surely is an occasion on which, if ever on any, the Genius of Reform may pipe all hands! — Poor old Genius of Reform; bedrid this good while; with little but broken ballot-boxes, and tattered stripes of Benthamee Constitutions lying round him; and on the walls mere shadows of clothing-colonels, rates-in-aid, poor-law unions, defunct potato and the Irish difficulty, — he does not seem long for this world, piping to that effect?

Not the least disgusting feature of this Gospel according to the Platform is its reference to religion, and even to the Christian Religion, as an authority and mandate for what it does. Christian Religion? Does the Christian or any religion prescribe love of scoundrels, then? I hope it prescribes a healthy hatred of scoundrels; — otherwise what am I, in Heaven's name, to make of it? Me, for one, it will not serve as a religion on those strange terms. Just hatred of scoundrels, I say; fixed, irreconcilable, inexorable enmity to the enemies of God: this, and not love for them, and incessant whitewashing, and dressing and cockering of them, must, if you look into it, be the backbone of any human religion whatsoever. Christian Religion! In what words can I address you, ye unfortunates, sunk in the slushy ooze till the worship of mud-serpents, and unutterable Pythons and poisonous slimy monstrosities, seems to you the worship of God? This is the rotten carcass of Christianity; this mal-odorous phosphorescence of *post-mortem* sentimentalism. O Heavens, from the Christianity of Oliver Cromwell, wrestling in grim fight with Satan and his incarnate Blackguardisms, Hypocrisies, Injustices, and legion of human and infernal angels, to that of eloquent Mr. Hesperus Fiddlestring denouncing capital punishments, and inculcating the benevolence on platforms, what a road have we travelled!

A foolish stump-orator, perorating on his platform mere benevolences, seems a pleasant object to many persons; a harmless or insignificant one to almost all. Look at him, however; scan him till you discern the nature of him, he is not pleasant, but ugly and perilous. That beautiful speech of his takes captive every long ear, and kindles into quasi-sacred enthusiasm the minds of not a few; but it is quite in the teeth of the everlasting facts of this Universe, and will come only to mischief for every party concerned. Consider that little spouting wretch. Within the paltry skin of him, it is too probable, he holds few human virtues, beyond those essential for digesting victual: envious, cowardly, vain, splenetic hungry soul; what heroism, in word or thought or action, will you ever get from the like of him? He, in his necessity, has taken into the benevolent line; warms the cold vacuity of his inner man to some extent, in a comfortable manner, not by silently doing some virtue of his own, but by fiercely recommending hearsay pseudo-virtues and respectable benevolences to other people. Do you call that a good trade? Long-eared fellow-creatures, more or less resembling himself, answer, "Hear, hear! Live Fiddlestring forever!" Wherefrom follow Abolition Congresses, Odes to the Gallows; — perhaps some dirty little Bill, getting itself debated next Session in Parliament, to waste certain nights of our legislative Year, and cause skipping in our Morning Newspaper, till the abortion can be emptied out again and sent fairly floating down the gutters.

Not with entire approbation do I, for one, look on that eloquent individual. Wise benevolence, if it had authority, would order that individual, I believe, to find some other trade: "Eloquent individual, pleading here against the Laws of Nature, — for many reasons, I bid thee close that mouth of thine. Enough of balderdash these long-eared have now drunk. Depart thou; *do* some benevolent work; at lowest, be silent. Disappear, I say; away, and jargon no more in that manner, lest a worst thing befall thee." *Exeat* Fiddlestring! — Beneficent men are not they who appear on platforms, pleading against the Almighty Maker's Laws; these are the maleficent men, whose lips it is pity that some authority cannot straightway shut. Pandora's Box is not more baleful than the gifts these eloquent benefactors are pressing on us. Close your pedler's pack, my friend; swift, away with it! Pernicious, fraught with mere woe and sugary poison is that kind of benevolence and beneficence.

Truly, one of the saddest sights in these times is that of poor creatures, on platforms, in parliaments and other situations, making and unmaking "Laws;" in whose soul, full of mere vacant hearsay and windy babble, is and was no image of Heaven's Law; whom it never struck that Heaven had a Law, or that the Earth — could not have what kind of Law you pleased! Human Statute-books, accordingly, are growing horrible to think of. An impiety and poisonous futility every Law of them that is so made; all Nature is against it; it will and can do nothing but mischief wheresoever it shows itself in Nature: and such Laws lie now like an incubus over this Earth, so innumerable are they. How long, O Lord, how long!— O ye Eternities, Divine Silences, do you dwell no more, then, in the hearts of the noble and the true; and is there no inspiration of the Almighty any more vouchsafed us? The inspiration of the Morning Newspapers — alas, we have had enough of that, and are arrived at the gates of death by means of that!

"Really, one of the most difficult questions this we have in these times, What to do with our criminals?" blandly observed a certain Law-dignitary, in my hearing once, taking the cigar from his mouth, and pensively smiling over a group of us under the summer beech-tree, as Favonius carried off the tobacco-smoke; and the group said nothing, only smiled and nodded, answering by new tobacco-clouds. "What to do with our criminals?" asked the official Law-dignitary again, as if entirely at a loss. — "I suppose," said one ancient figure not engaged in smoking, "the plan would be to treat them according to the real law of the case; to make the Law of England, in respect of them, correspond to the Law of the Universe. Criminals, I suppose, would prove manageable in that way: if we could do approximately as God Almighty does towards them; in a word, if we could try to do Justice towards them." — "I'll thank you for a definition of Justice?" sneered the official person in a cheerily scornful and triumphant manner, backed by a slight laugh from the honorable company; which irritated the other speaker. — "Well, I have no pocket definition of Justice," said he, "to give your Lordship. It has not quite been my trade to look for such a definition; I could rather fancy it had been your Lordship's trade, sitting on your high place this long while. But one thing I can tell you: Justice always *is*, whether we define it or not. Everything done, suffered or proposed, in Parliament or out of it, *is* either just or else unjust; either is accepted by the gods and eternal facts, or is rejected by them. Your Lordship and I, with or without definition, do a little know Justice, I will hope; if we don't both know it and do it, we are hourly travelling down towards — Heavens, must I name such a place! That is the place we are bound to, with all our trading-pack, and the small or extensive budgets of human business laid on us; and there, if we *don't know* Justice, we, and all our budgets and Acts of Parliament, shall find lodging when the day is done!" — The official person, a polite man otherwise, grinned as he best could some semblance of a laugh, mirthful as that of the ass eating thistles, and ended in "Hah, oh, ah!" —

Indeed, it is wonderful to hear what account we at present give ourselves of the punishment of criminals. No "revenge" — O Heavens, no; all preachers on Sunday strictly forbid that; and even (at least on Sundays) prescribe the contrary of that. It is for the sake of "example," that you punish; to "protect

society" and its purse and skin; to deter the innocent from
falling into crime; and especially withal, for the purpose of
improving the poor criminal himself, — or at lowest, of hanging and ending him, that he may not grow worse. For the
poor criminal is to be "improved" if possible : against him
no "revenge" even on week-days; nothing but love for him,
and pity and help; poor fellow, is he not miserable enough?
Very miserable, — though much less so than the Master of
him, called Satan, is understood (on Sundays) to have long
deservedly been!

My friends, will you permit me to say that all this, to one
poor judgment among your number, is the mournfulest twaddle
that human tongues could shake from them; that it has no
solid foundation in the nature of things; and to a healthy
human heart no credibility whatever. Permit me to say, only
to hearts long drowned in dead Tradition, and for themselves
neither believing nor disbelieving, could this seem credible.
Think, and ask yourselves, in spite of all this preaching and
perorating from the teeth outward! Hearts that are quite
strangers to eternal Fact, and acquainted only at all hours
with temporary Semblances parading about in a prosperous
and persuasive condition; hearts that from their first appearance in this world have breathed since birth, in all spiritual
matters, which means in all matters not pecuniary, the poisonous atmosphere of universal Cant, could believe such a thing.
Cant moral, Cant religious, Cant political; an atmosphere
which envelops all things for us unfortunates, and has long
done; which goes beyond the Zenith and below the Nadir for
us, and has as good as choked the spiritual life out of all of
us, — God pity such wretches, with little or nothing *real* about
them but their purse and their abdominal department! Hearts,
alas, which everywhere except in the metallurgic and cotton-
spinning provinces, have communed with no Reality, or awful
Presence of a Fact, godlike or diabolic, in this Universe or
this unfathomable Life at all. Hunger-stricken asphyxied
hearts, which have nourished themselves on what they call
religions, Christian religions. Good Heaven, once more fancy
the Christian religion of Oliver Cromwell; or of some noble

Christian man, whom you yourself may have been blessed enough, once, long since, in your life, to know! These are not *untrue* religions; they are the putrescences and foul residues of religions that are extinct, that have plainly to every honest nostril been dead some time, and the remains of which — O ye eternal Heavens, will the nostril never be delivered from them! — Such hearts, when they get upon platforms, and into questions not involving money, can "believe" many things! —

I take the liberty of asserting that there is one valid reason, and only one, for either punishing a man or rewarding him in this world; one reason, which ancient piety could well define: That you may do the will and commandment of God with regard to him; that you may do justice to him. This is your one true aim in respect of him; aim thitherward, with all your heart and all your strength and all your soul; thitherward, and not elsewhither at all! This aim is true, and will carry you to all earthly heights and benefits, and beyond the stars and Heavens. All other aims are purblind, illegitimate, untrue; and will never carry you beyond the shop-counter, nay very soon will prove themselves incapable of maintaining you even there. Find out what the Law of God is with regard to a man; make that your human law, or I say it will be ill with you, and not well! If you love your thief or murderer, if Nature and eternal Fact love him, then do as you are now doing. But if Nature and Fact do *not* love him? If they have set inexorable penalties upon him, and planted natural wrath against him in every god-created human heart, — then I advise you, cease, and change your hand.

Reward and punishment? Alas, alas, I must say you reward and punish pretty much alike! Your dignities, peerages, promotions, your kingships, your brazen statues erected in capital and county towns to our select demigods of *your* selecting, testify loudly enough what kind of heroes and hero-worshippers you are. Woe to the People that no longer venerates, as the emblem of God himself, the aspect of Human Worth; that no longer knows what human worth and unworth is! Sure as the Decrees of the Eternal, that People cannot come to good. By a course too clear, by a necessity too evident, that People

will come into the hands of the unworthy; and either turn
on its bad career, or stagger downwards to ruin and abolition.
Does the Hebrew People prophetically sing " Ou' clo' ! " in all
thoroughfares, these eighteen hundred years in vain ?

To reward men according to their worth : alas, the perfection of this, we know, amounts to the millennium ! Neither
is perfect punishment, according to the like rule, to be attained, — nor even, by a legislator of these chaotic days, to be
too zealously attempted. But when he does attempt it, — yes,
when he summons out the Society to sit deliberative on this
matter, and consult the oracles upon it, and solemnly settle it
in the name of God ; then, if never before, he should try to
be a little in the right in settling it ! — In regard to reward
of merit, I do not bethink me of any attempt whatever, worth
calling an attempt, on the part of modern Governments ; which
surely is an immense oversight on their part, and will one day
be seen to have been an altogether fatal one. But as to the
punishment of crime, happily this cannot be quite neglected.
When men have a purse and a skin, they seek salvation at
least for these ; and the Four Pleas of the Crown are a thing
that must and will be attended to. By punishment, capital
or other, by treadmilling and blind rigor, or by whitewashing
and blind laxity, the extremely disagreeable offences of theft
and murder must be kept down within limits.

And so you take criminal caitiffs, murderers, and the like,
and hang them on gibbets "for an example to deter others."
Whereupon arise friends of humanity, and object. With very
great reason, as I consider, if _your_ hypothesis be correct. What
right have you to hang any poor creature " for an example " ?
He can turn round upon you and say, " Why make an ' example ' of me, a merely ill-situated, pitiable man ? Have you
no more respect for misfortune ? Misfortune, I have been
told, is sacred. And yet you hang me, now I am fallen into
your hands ; choke the life out of me, for an example ! Again
I ask, Why make an example of _me_, for your own convenience
alone ? " — All " revenge " being out of the question, it seems
to me the caitiff is unanswerable ; and he and the philanthropic
platforms have the logic all on their side.

The one answer to him is : " Caitiff, we hate thee ; and discern for some six thousand years now, that we are called upon by the whole Universe to do it. Not with a diabolic but with a divine hatred. God himself, we have always understood, 'hates sin,' with a most authentic, celestial, and eternal hatred. A hatred, a hostility inexorable, unappeasable, which blasts the scoundrel, and all scoundrels ultimately, into black annihilation and disappearance from the sum of things. The path of it as the path of a flaming sword : he that has eyes may see it, walking inexorable, divinely beautiful and divinely terrible, through the chaotic gulf of Human History, and everywhere burning, as with unquenchable fire, the false and death-worthy from the true and life-worthy ; making all Human History, and the Biography of every man, a God's Cosmos in place of a Devil's Chaos. So is it, in the end ; even so, to every man who is a man, and not a mutinous beast, and has eyes to see. To thee, caitiff, these things were and are, quite incredible ; to us they are too awfully certain, — the Eternal Law of this Universe, whether thou and others will believe it or disbelieve. We, not to be partakers in thy destructive adventure of *defying* God and all the Universe, dare not allow thee to continue longer among us. As a palpable deserter from the ranks where all men, at their eternal peril, are bound to be : palpable deserter, taken with the red hand fighting thus against the whole Universe and its Laws, we — send thee back into the whole Universe, solemnly expel thee from our community ; and will, in the name of God, not with joy and exultation, but with sorrow stern as thy own, hang thee on Wednesday next, and so end."

Other ground on which to deliberately slay a disarmed fellow-man I can see none. Example, effects upon the public mind, effects upon this and upon that : all this is mere appendage and accident ; of all this I make no attempt to keep account, — sensible that no arithmetic will or can keep account of it ; that its "effects," on this hand and on that, transcend all calculation. One thing, if I can calculate it, will include all, and produce beneficial effects beyond calculation, and no ill effect at all, anywhere or at any time : What the Law of the

Universe, or Law of God, *is* with regard to this caitiff? That, by all sacred research and consideration, I will try to find out; to that I will come as near as human means admit; that shall be my exemplar and "example;" all men shall through me see that, and be profited *beyond* calculation by seeing it.

What this Law of the Universe, or Law made by God, is? Men at one time read it in their Bible. In many Bibles, Books, and authentic symbols and monitions of Nature and the World (of Fact, that is, and of Human Speech, or Wise Interpretation of Fact), there are still clear indications towards it. Most important it is, for this and for some other reasons, that men do, in some way, get to see it a little! And if no man could now see it by any Bible, there is written in the heart of every man an authentic copy of it direct from Heaven itself: there, if he have learnt to decipher Heaven's writing, and can read the sacred oracles (a sad case for him if he altogether cannot), every born man may still find some copy of it.

"Revenge," my friends! revenge, and the natural hatred of scoundrels, and the ineradicable tendency to *revancher* oneself upon them, and pay them what they have merited: this is forevermore intrinsically a correct, and even a divine feeling in the mind of every man. Only the excess of it is diabolic; the essence I say is manlike, and even godlike, — a monition sent to poor man by the Maker himself. Thou, poor reader, in spite of all this melancholy twaddle, and blotting out of Heaven's sunlight by mountains of horsehair and officiality, hast still a human heart. If, in returning to thy poor peaceable dwelling-place, after an honest hard day's work, thou wert to find, for example, a brutal scoundrel who for lucre or other object of his, had slaughtered the life that was dearest to thee; thy true wife, for example, thy true old mother, swimming in her blood; the human scoundrel, or two-legged wolf, standing over such a tragedy: I hope a man would have so much divine rage in his heart as to snatch the nearest weapon, and put a conclusion upon said human wolf, for one! A palpable messenger of Satan, that one; accredited by all the Devils, to be put an end to by all the children of God. The soul of every god-created man flames wholly into one divine blaze of sacred wrath at sight of such a Devil's-messenger; authentic first-hand monition from the Eternal Maker himself as to what is next to be done. Do it, or be thyself an ally of Devil's-messengers; a sheep for two-legged human wolves, well deserving to be eaten, as thou soon wilt be!

My humane friends, I perceive this same sacred glow of divine wrath, or authentic monition at first hand from God himself, to be the foundation for all Criminal Law, and Official horsehair-and-bombazine procedure against Scoundrels in this world. This first-hand gospel from the Eternities, imparted to every mortal, this is still, and will forever be, your sanction and commission for the punishment of human scoundrels. See well how you will translate this message from Heaven and the Eternities into a form suitable to this World and its Times. Let not violence, haste, blind impetuous impulse, preside in executing it; the injured man, invincibly liable to fall into these, shall not himself execute it: the whole world, in person of a Minister appointed for that end, and surrounded with the due solemnities and caveats, with bailiffs, apparitors, advocates, and the hushed expectation of all men, shall do it, as under the eye of God who made all men. How it shall be done? this is ever a vast question, involving immense considerations. Thus Edmund Burke saw, in the Two Houses of Parliament, with King, Constitution, and all manner of Civil-Lists, and Chancellors' wigs and Exchequer budgets, only the "method of getting twelve just men put into a jury-box:" that, in Burke's view, was the summary of what they were all meant for. How the judge will do it? Yes, indeed: — but let him see well that he does do it: for it is a thing that must by no means be left undone! A sacred gospel from the Highest: not to be smothered under horsehair and bombazine, or drowned in platform froth, or in any wise omitted or neglected, without the most alarming penalties to all concerned!

Neglect to treat the hero as hero, the penalties — which are inevitable too, and terrible to think of, as your Hebrew friends can tell you — may be some time in coming; they will only gradually come. Not all at once will your thirty thousand Needlewomen, your three million Paupers, your Connaught fallen into potential Cannibalism, and other fine consequences of the practice, come to light; — though come to light they will; and "Ou' clo'!" itself may be in store for you, if you per sist steadily enough. But neglect to treat even your declared scoundrel as scoundrel, this is the last consummation of the process, the drop by which the cup runs over; the penalties of this, most alarming, extensive, and such as you little dream of, will straightway very rapidly come. Dim oblivion of Right and Wrong, among the masses of your population, will come; doubts as to Right and Wrong, indistinct notion that Right and Wrong are not eternal, but accidental, and settled by uncertain votings and talkings, will come. Prurient influenza of Platform Benevolence, and "Paradise to All-and-sundry," will come. In the general putrescence of your "religions," as you call them, a strange new religion, named of Universal Love, with Sacraments mainly of *Divorce*, with Balzac, Sue and Company for Evangelists, and Madame Sand for Virgin, will come, — and results fast following therefrom which will astonish you very much!

"The terrible anarchies of these years," says Crabbe, in his *Radiator*, "are brought upon us by a necessity too visible. By the crime of Kings, — alas, yes; but by that of Peoples too. Not by the crime of one class, but by the fatal obscuration, and all but obliteration of the sense of Right and Wrong in the minds and practices of every class. What a scene in the drama of Universal History, this of ours! A world-wide loud bellow and bray of universal Misery; *lowing*, with crushed maddened heart, its inarticulate prayer to Heaven: — very pardonable to me, and in some of its transcendent developments, as in the grand French Revolution, most respectable and ever-memorable. For Injustice reigns everywhere; and this murderous struggle for what they call 'Fraternity,' and so forth, has a spice of eternal sense in it, though so terribly disfigured! Amalgam of sense and nonsense; eternal sense by the grain, and temporary nonsense by the square mile: as is the habit with poor sons of men. Which pardonable amalgam, however, if it be taken as the pure final sense, I must warn you and all creatures, is unpardonable, criminal, and fatal nonsense; — with which I, for one, will take care not to concern myself!

"*Dogs should not be taught to eat leather*, says the old adage: no; — and where, by general fault and error, and the inevitable nemesis of things, the universal kennel is set to diet upon *leather;* and from its keepers, its 'Liberal Premiers,' or whatever their title is, will accept or expect nothing else, and calls it by the pleasant name of progress, reform, emancipation, abolition-principles, and the like, — I consider the fate of said kennel and of said keepers to be a thing settled. Red republic in Phrygian nightcap, organization of labor *à la* Louis Blanc; street-barricades, and then murderous cannon-volleys *à la* Cavaignac and Windischgrätz, follow out of one another, as grapes, must, new wine, and sour all-splitting vinegar do: — vinegar is but *vin-aigre*, or the self-same 'wine' grown *sharp!* If, moreover, I find the Worship of Human Nobleness abolished in any country, and a *new* astonishing Phallus-Worship, with universal Balzac-Sand melodies and litanies in treble and in bass, established in its stead, what can I compute but that Nature, in horrible throes, will repugn against such substitution, — that, in short, the astonishing new Phallus-Worship, with its finer sensibilities of the heart, and 'great satisfying loves,' with its sacred kiss of peace for scoundrel and hero alike, with its all-embracing Brotherhood, and universal Sacrament of Divorce, will have to take itself away again!"

The Ancient Germans, it appears, had no scruple about public executions; on the contrary, they thought the just gods themselves might fitly preside over these; that these were a solemn and highest act of worship, if justly done. When a German man had done a crime deserving death, they, in solemn general assembly of the tribe, doomed him, and considered that Fate and all Nature had from the beginning doomed him, to die with ignominy. Certain crimes there were of a supreme nature; him that had perpetrated one of these, they believed to have declared himself a prince of scoundrels. Him once convicted they laid hold of, nothing doubting; —

bore him, after judgment, to the deepest convenient Peat-bog; plunged him in there, drove an oaken frame down over him, solemnly in the name of gods and men: "There, prince of scoundrels, that is what we have had to think of thee, on clear acquaintance; our grim good-night to thee is that! In the name of all the gods lie there, and be our partnership with thee dissolved henceforth. It will be better for us, we imagine!"

My friends, after all this beautiful whitewash and humanity and prison-discipline; and such blubbering and whimpering, and soft Litany to divine and also to quite other sorts of Pity, as we have had for a century now, — give me leave to admonish you that that of the Ancient Germans too was a thing inexpressibly necessary to keep in mind. If that is not kept in mind, the universal Litany to Pity is a mere universal nuisance, and torpid blasphemy against the gods. I do not much respect it, that purblind blubbering and litanying, as it is seen at present; and the litanying over scoundrels I go the length of disrespecting, and in some cases even of detesting. Yes, my friends, scoundrel is scoundrel: that remains forever a fact; and there exists not in the earth whitewash that can make the scoundrel a friend of this Universe; he remains an enemy if you spent your life in whitewashing him. He won't whitewash; this one won't. The one method clearly is, That, after fair trial, you dissolve partnership with him; send him, in the name of Heaven, whither *he* is striving all this while, and have done with him. And, in a time like this, I would advise you, see likewise that you be speedy about it! For there is immense work, and of a far hopefuler sort, to be done *elsewhere*.

Alas, alas, to see once the "prince of scoundrels," the Supreme Scoundrel, him whom of all men the gods liked *worst*, solemnly laid hold of, and hung upon the gallows in sight of the people; what a lesson to all the people! Sermons might be preached; the Son of Thunder and the Mouth of Gold might turn their periods now with some hope; for here, in the most impressive way, is a divine sermon *acted*. Didactic as no spoken sermon could be. Didactic, devotional too; — in awed solemnity, a recognition that Eternal Justice rules the world; that at the call of this, human pity shall fall silent, and man be stern as his Master and Mandatory is! — Understand too that except upon a basis of even such rigor, sorrowful, silent, inexorable as that of Destiny and Doom, there is no true pity possible. The pity that proves so possible and plentiful without that basis, is mere *ignavia* and cowardly effeminacy; maudlin laxity of heart, grounded on blinkard dimness of head — contemptible as a drunkard's tears.

To see our Supreme Scoundrel hung upon the gallows, alas, that is far from us just now! There is a *worst* man in England, too, — curious to think of, — whom it would be inexpressibly advantageous to lay hold of, and hang, the first of all. But we do not know him with the least certainty, the least approach even to a guess, — such buzzards and dullards and poor children of the Dusk are we, in spite of our Statistics, Unshackled Presses, and Torches of Knowledge; — not eagles soaring sunward, not brothers of the lightnings and the radiances we; a dim horn-eyed, owl-population, intent mainly on the catching of mice! Alas, the supreme scoundrel, alike with the supreme hero, is very far from being known. Nor have we the smallest apparatus for dealing with either of them, if he were known. Our supreme scoundrel sits, I conjecture, well-cushioned, in high places, at this time; rolls softly through the world, and lives a prosperous gentleman; instead of sinking him in peat-bogs, we mount the brazen image of him on high columns: such is the world's temporary judgment about its supreme scoundrels; a mad world, my masters. To get the supreme scoundrel always accurately the first hanged, — this, which presupposes that the supreme hero were always the first promoted, this were precisely the millennium itself, clear evidence that the millennium had come: alas, we must forbear hope of this. Much water will run by before we see this.

And yet to quit all aim towards it; to go blindly floundering along, wrapt up in clouds of horsehair, bombazine, and sheepskin officiality, oblivious that there exists such an aim:

this is indeed fatal. In every human law there must either exist such an aim, or else the law is not a human but a diabolic one. Diabolic, I say : no quantity of bombazine, or lawyers' wigs, three-readings, and solemn trumpeting and bow-wowing in high places or in low, can hide from me its frightful infernal tendency ; — bound, and sinking at all moments gradually to Gehenna, this "law ;" and dragging down much with it ! " To decree *injustice* by a *law :* " inspired Prophets have long since seen, what every clear soul may still see, that of all Anarchies and Devil-worships there is none like this; that this is the "Throne of Iniquity" set up in the name of the Highest, the human Apotheosis of Anarchy itself. " *Quiet* Anarchy," you exultingly say ? Yes; quiet Anarchy, which the longer it sits "quiet" will have the frightfuler account to settle at last. For every doit of the account, as I often say, will have to be settled one day, as sure as God lives. Principal, and compound interest rigorously computed; and the interest is at a terrible rate per cent in these cases ! Alas, the aspect of certain beatified Anarchies, sitting "quiet;" and of others in a state of infernal explosion for sixty years back: this, the one view our Europe offers at present, makes these days very sad. —

My unfortunate philanthropic friends, it is this long-continued oblivion of the soul of law that has reduced the Criminal Question to such a pass among us. Many other things have come, and are coming, for the same sad reason, to a pass ! Not the supreme scoundrel have our laws aimed at ; but, in an uncertain fitful manner, at the inferior or lowest scoundrel, who robs shop-tills and puts the skin of mankind in danger. How can Parliament get through the Criminal Question ? Parliament, oblivious of Heavenly Law, will find itself in hopeless *reductio ad absurdum* in regard to innumerable other questions, — in regard to all questions whatsoever by and by. There will be no existence possible for Parliament on these current terms. Parliament, in its law-makings, must really try to attain some vision again of what Heaven's Laws are. A thing not easy to do; a thing requiring sad sincerity of heart, reverence, pious earnestness, valiant manful wisdom; —

qualities not overabundant in Parliament just now, nor out of
it, I fear.

Adieu, my friends. My anger against you is gone; my sad
reflections on you, and on the depths to which you and I and
all of us are sunk in these strange times, are not to be uttered
at present. You would have saved the Sarawak Pirates, then?
The Almighty Maker is wroth that the Sarawak cut-throats,
with their poisoned spears, are away? What must his wrath
be that the thirty thousand Needlewomen are still here, and
the question of "prevenient grace" not yet settled! O my
friends, in sad earnest, sad and deadly earnest, there much
needs that God would mend all this, and that we should help
him to mend it! — And don't you think, for one thing, "Farmer
Hodge's horses" in the Sugar Islands are pretty well "emancipated" now? My clear opinion farther is, we had better
quit the Scoundrel-province of Reform; better close that under
hatches, in some rapid summary manner, and go elsewhither
with our Reform efforts. A whole world, for want of Reform,
is drowning and sinking; threatening to swamp itself into a
Stygian quagmire, uninhabitable by any noble-minded man.
Let us to the well-heads, I say; to the chief fountains of these
waters of bitterness; and there strike home and dig! To
puddle in the embouchures and drowned outskirts, and ulterior
and ultimate *issues* and cloacas of the affair: what profit can
there be in that? Nothing to be saved there; nothing to be
fished up there, except, with endless peril and spread of pestilence, a miscellany of broken waifs and dead dogs! In the
name of Heaven, quit that!

[April 1, 1850.]

No. III. DOWNING STREET.

FROM all corners of the wide British Dominion there rises
one complaint against the ineffectuality of what are nicknamed
our "red-tape" establishments, our Government Offices, Colo-

nial Office, Foreign Office and the others, in Downing Street
and the neighborhood. To me individually these branches of
human business are little known; but every British citizen
and reflective passer-by has occasion to wonder much, and inquire earnestly, concerning them. To all men it is evident
that the social interests of one hundred and fifty Millions of
us depend on the mysterious industry there carried on; and
likewise that the dissatisfaction with it is great, universal,
and continually increasing in intensity, — in fact, mounting,
we might say, to the pitch of settled despair.

Every colony, every agent for a matter colonial, has his
tragic tale to tell you of his sad experiences in the Colonial
Office; what blind obstructions, fatal indolences, pedantries,
stupidities, on the right and on the left, he had to do battle
with; what a world-wide jungle of red-tape, inhabited by doleful creatures, deaf or nearly so to human reason or entreaty,
he had entered on; and how he paused in amazement, almost
in despair; passionately appealed now to this doleful creature,
now to that, and to the dead red-tape jungle, and to the living
Universe itself, and to the Voices and to the Silences; — and,
on the whole, found that it was an adventure, in sorrowful
fact, equal to the fabulous ones by old knights-errant against
dragons and wizards in enchanted wildernesses and waste
howling solitudes; not achievable except by nearly super-
human exercise of all the four cardinal virtues, and unexpected favor of the special blessing of Heaven. His adventure
achieved or found unachievable, he has returned with experiences new to him in the affairs of men. What this Colonial
Office, inhabiting the head of Downing Street, really *was*, and
had to do, or try doing, in God's practical Earth, he could not
by any means precisely get to know; believes that it does
not itself in the least precisely know. Believes that nobody
knows; — that it is a mystery, a kind of Heathen myth; —
and stranger than any piece of the old mythological Pantheon;
for *it* practically presides over the destinies of many millions
of living men.

Such is his report of the Colonial Office: and if we oftener
hear such a report of that than we do of the Home Office,

Foreign Office or the rest, — the reason probably is, that Colonies excite more attention at present than any of our other interests. The Forty Colonies, it appears, are all pretty like rebelling just now; and are to be pacified with constitutions;— luckier constitutions, let us hope, than some late ones have been. Loyal Canada, for instance, had to quench a rebellion the other year; and this year, in virtue of its constitution, it is called upon to pay the rebels their damages; which surely is a rather surprising result, however constitutional!— Men have rents and moneys dependent in the Colonies; Emigration schemes, Black Emancipations, New-Zealand and other schemes; and feel and publish more emphatically what their Downing-Street woes in these respects have been.

Were the state of poor *sallow* English ploughers and weavers, what we may call the Sallow or Yellow Emancipation interest, as much an object with Exeter-Hall Philanthropists as that of the Black blockheads now all emancipated, and going at large without work, or need of working, in West-India clover (and fattening very much in it, one delights to hear), — then perhaps the Home Office, its huge virtual task better understood, and its small actual performance better seen into, might be found still more deficient, and behind the wants of the age, than the Colonial itself is.

How it stands with the Foreign Office, again, one still less knows. Seizures of Sapienza, and the like sudden appearances of Britain in the character of Hercules-Harlequin, waving, with big bully-voice, her huge sword-of-sharpness over field-mice, and in the air making horrid circles (horrid catherine-wheels and death-disks of metallic terror from said huge sword), to see how they will like it, — do from time to time astonish the world, in a not pleasant manner. Hercules-Harlequin, the Attorney Triumphant, the World's Busybody: none of these are parts this Nation has a turn for; she, if you consulted her, would rather *not* play these parts, but another! Seizures of Sapienza, correspondences with Sotomayor, remonstrances to Otho King of Athens, fleets hanging by their anchor in behalf of the Majesty of Portugal; and in short the whole, or at present very nearly the whole, of that industry of protocolling, diplomatizing, remonstrating, admonishing, and "having the honor to be," — has sunk justly in public estimation to a very low figure.

For in fact, it is reasonably asked, What vital interest has England in any cause now deciding itself in foreign parts? Once there was a Papistry and Protestantism, important as life eternal and death eternal; more lately there was an interest of Civil Order and Horrors of the French Revolution, important at least as rent-roll and preservation of the game; but now what is there? No cause in which any god or man of this British Nation can be thought to be concerned. Sham-kingship, now recognized and even self-recognized everywhere to be sham, wrestles and struggles with mere ballot-box Anarchy: not a pleasant spectacle to British minds. Both parties in the wrestle professing earnest wishes of peace to us, what have we to do with it except answer earnestly, "Peace, yes certainly," and mind our affairs elsewhere. The British Nation has no concern with that indispensable sorrowful and shameful wrestle now going on everywhere in foreign parts. The British Nation already, by self-experience centuries old, understands all that; was lucky enough to transact the greater part of that, in noble ancient ages, while the wrestle had not yet become a shameful one, but on *both* sides of it there was wisdom, virtue, heroic nobleness fruitful to all time, — thrice-lucky British Nation! The British Nation, I say, has nothing to learn there; has now quite another set of lessons to learn, far ahead of what is going on there. Sad example there, of what the issue is, and how inevitable and how imminent, might admonish the British Nation to be speedy with its new lessons; to bestir itself, as men in peril of conflagration do, with the neighboring houses all on fire! To obtain, for its own very pressing behoof, if by possibility it could, some real Captaincy instead of an imaginary one: to remove resolutely, and replace by a better sort, its own peculiar species of teaching and guiding histrios of various name, who here too are numerous exceedingly, and much in need of gentle removal, while the play is still good, and the comedy has not yet become *tragic ;* — and to be a little swift about it withal; and so to escape the otherwise inevitable evil day! This Britain might learn: but she does not need a protocolling establishment, with much "having the honor to be," to teach it her.

No : — she has in fact certain cottons, hardwares and such like to sell in foreign parts, and certain wines, Portugal oranges, Baltic tar and other products to buy; and does need, I suppose, some kind of Consul, or accredited agent, accessible to British voyagers, here and there, in the chief cities of the Continent: through which functionary, or through the penny-post, if she had any specific message to foreign courts, it would be easy and proper to transmit the same. Special message-carriers, to be still called Ambassadors, if the name gratified them, could be sent when occasion great enough demanded; not sent when it did not. But for all purposes of a resident ambassador, I hear persons extensively and well acquainted among our foreign embassies at this date declare, That a well-selected *Times* reporter or "own correspondent" ordered to reside in foreign capitals, and keep his eyes open, and (though sparingly) his pen going, would in reality be much more effective; — and surely we see well, he would come a good deal cheaper! Considerably cheaper in expense of money; and in expense of falsity and grimacing hypocrisy (of which no human arithmetic can count the ultimate *cost*) incalculably cheaper! If this is the fact, why not treat it as such? If this is so in any measure, we had better in that measure admit it to be so! The time, I believe, has come for asking with considerable severity, How far is it so? Nay there are men now current in political society, men of weight though also of wit, who have been heard to say, " That there was but one reform for the Foreign Office, — to set a live coal under it," and with, of course, a fire-brigade which could prevent the undue spread of the devouring element into neighboring houses, let that reform it! In such odor is the Foreign Office too, if it were not that the Public, oppressed and nearly stifled with a mere infinitude of bad odors, neglects this one, — in fact, being able nearly always to avoid the street where it is, *escapes* this one, and (except a passing curse, once in the quarter or so) as good as forgets the existence of it.

Such, from sad personal experience and credited prevailing rumor, is the exoteric public conviction about these sublime establishments in Downing Street and the neighborhood, — the esoteric mysteries of which are indeed still held sacred by the initiated, but believed by the world to be mere Dalai-Lama pills, manufactured let not refined lips hint how, and quite *un*salvatory to mankind. Every one may remark what a hope animates the eyes of any circle, when it is reported or even confidently asserted, that Sir Robert Peel has in his mind privately resolved to go, one day, into that stable of King Augeas, which appalls human hearts, so rich is it, high-piled with the droppings of two hundred years; and Hercules-like to load a thousand night-wagons from it, and turn running water into it, and swash and shovel at it, and never leave it till the antique pavement, and real basis of the matter, show itself clean again! In any intelligent circle such a rumor, like the first break of day to men in darkness, enlightens all eyes; and each says devoutly, "*Faxitis*, O ye righteous Powers that have pity on us! All England grateful, with kindling looks, will rise in the rear of him, and from its deepest heart bid him good speed!"

For it is universally felt that some *esoteric* man, well acquainted with the mysteries and properties good and evil of the administrative stable, is the fittest to reform it, nay can alone reform it otherwise than by sheer violence and destruction, which is a way we would avoid; that in fact Sir Robert Peel is, at present, the one likely or possible man to reform it. And secondly it is felt that "reform" in that Downing-Street department of affairs is precisely the reform which were worth all others; that those administrative establishments in Downing Street are really the Government of this huge ungoverned Empire; that to clean out the dead pedantries, unveracities, indolent somnolent impotences, and accumulated dung-mountains there, is the beginning of all practical good whatsoever. Yes, get down once again to the actual *pavement* of that; ascertain what the thing is, and was before dung accumulated in it; and what it should and may, and must, for the life's sake of this Empire, henceforth become: here clearly lies the heart of the whole matter.

Political reform, if this be not reformed, is naught and a mere mockery.

What England wants, and will require to have, or sink in nameless anarchies, is not a Reformed Parliament, meaning thereby a Parliament elected according to the six or the four or any other number of "points" and cunningly devised improvements in hustings mechanism, but a Reformed Executive or Sovereign Body of Rulers and Administrators, — some improved method, innumerable improvements in our poor blind methods, of getting hold of these. Not a better Talking-Apparatus, the best conceivable Talking-Apparatus would do very little for us at present; — but an infinitely better Acting-Apparatus, the benefits of which would be invaluable now and henceforth. The practical question puts itself with ever-increasing stringency to all English minds: Can we, by no industry, energy, utmost expenditure of human ingenuity, and passionate invocation of the Heavens and Earth, get to attain some twelve or ten or six men to manage the affairs of this nation in Downing Street and the chief posts elsewhere, who are abler for the work than those we have been used to, this long while? For it is really a heroic work, and cannot be done by histrios, and dexterous talkers having the honor to be: it is a heavy and appalling work; and, at the starting of it especially, will require Herculean men; such mountains of pedant exuviæ and obscene owl-droppings have accumulated in those regions, long the habitation of doleful creatures; the old *pavements*, the natural facts and real essential functions of those establishments, have not been seen by eyes for these two hundred years last past! Herculean men acquainted with the virtues of running water, and with the divine necessity of getting down to the clear pavements and old veracities; who tremble before no amount of pedant exuviæ, no loudest shrieking of doleful creatures; who tremble only to live, themselves, like inane phantasms, and to leave their life as a paltry *contribution* to the guano mountains, and not as a divine eternal protest against them!

These are the kind of men we want; these, the nearest possible approximation to these, are the men we must find and have, or go bankrupt altogether; for the concern as it is will evidently not hold long together. How true is this of Crabbe: "Men sit in Parliament eighty-three hours per week, debating about many things. Men sit in Downing Street, doing protocols, Syrian treaties, Greek questions, Portuguese, Spanish, French, Egyptian and Æthiopian questions; dexterously writing despatches, and having the honor to be. Not a question of them is at all pressing in comparison with the English question. Pacifico the miraculous Gibraltar Jew has been hustled by some populace in Greece: upon him let the British Lion drop, very rapidly indeed, a constitutional tear. Radetzky is said to be advancing upon Milan;—I am sorry to hear it, and perhaps it does deserve a despatch, or friendly letter, once and away: but the Irish Giant, named of Despair, is advancing upon London itself, laying waste all English cities, towns and villages; that is the interesting Government despatch of the day! I notice him in Piccadilly, blue-visaged, thatched in rags, a blue child on each arm; hunger-driven, wide-mouthed, seeking whom he may devour: he, missioned by the just Heavens, too truly and too sadly their 'divine missionary' come at last in *this* authoritative manner, will throw us all into Doubting Castle, I perceive! That is the phenomenon worth protocolling about, and writing despatches upon, and thinking of with all one's faculty day and night, if one wishes to have the honor to be — anything but a Phantasm Governor of England just now! I entreat your Lordship's all but undivided attention to that Domestic Irish Giant, named of Despair, for a great many years to come. Prophecy of him there has long been; but now by the rot of the potato (blessed be the just gods, who send us either swift death or some beginning of cure at last!), he is here in person, and there is no denying him, or disregarding him any more; and woe to the public watchman that ignores *him*, and sees Pacifico the Gibraltar Jew instead!"

What these strange Entities in Downing Street intrinsically are; who made them, why they were made; how they do their function ; and what their function, so huge in appearance, may in net-result amount to, — is probably known to no mortal. The unofficial mind passes by in dark wonder; not pretending to know. The official mind must not blab; — the official mind, restricted to its own square foot of territory in the vast labyrinth, is probably itself dark, and unable to blab. We see the outcome; the mechanism we do not see. How the tailors clip and sew, in that sublime sweating establishment of theirs, we know not : that the coat they bring us out is the sorrowfulest fantastic mockery of a coat, a mere intricate artistic network of traditions and formalities, an embroiled reticulation made of web-listings and superannuated thrums and tatters, endurable to no grown Nation as a coat, is mournfully clear ! —

Two kinds of fundamental error are supposable in such a set of Offices ; these two, acting and reacting, are the vice of all inefficient Offices whatever. *First,* that the work, such as it may be, is ill done in these establishments. That it is delayed, neglected, slurred over, committed to hands that cannot do it well; that, in a word, the questions sent thither are not wisely handled, but unwisely ; not decided truly and rapidly, but with delays and wrong at last : which is the principal character, and the infallible result, of an insufficient Intellect being set to decide them. Or *second,* what is still fataler, the work done there may itself be quite the wrong kind of work. Not the kind of supervision and direction which Colonies, and other such interests, Home or Foreign, do by the nature of them require from the Central Government; not that, but a quite other kind ! The Sotomayor correspondence, for example, is considered by many persons not to be mismanaged merely, but to be a thing which should never have been managed at all; a quite superfluous concern, which and the like of which the British Government has almost no call to get into, at this new epoch of time. And not Sotomayor only, nor Sapienza only, in regard to that Foreign Office, but innumerable other things, if our witty friend of the "live coal" have reason in him ! Of the Colonial Office, too, it is urged that the questions they decide and operate upon are, in very great part, questions which they never should have meddled with, but almost all of which should have been decided in the Colonies themselves, — Mother Country or Colonial Office reserving its energy for a quite other class of objects, which are terribly neglected just now.

These are the two vices that beset Government Offices; both of them originating in insufficient Intellect, — that sad insufficiency from which, directly or indirectly, all evil whatsoever springs! And these two vices act and react, so that where the one is, the other is sure to be; and each encouraging the growth of the other, both (if some cleaning of the Augeas stable have not intervened for a long while) will be found in frightful development. You cannot have your work well done, if the work be not of a right kind, if it be not work prescribed by the law of Nature as well as by the rules of the office. Laziness, which lies in wait round all human labor-offices, will in that case infallibly leak in, and vitiate the doing of the work. The work is but idle; if the doing of it will but pass, what need of more? The essential problem, as the rules of office prescribe it for you, if Nature and Fact say nothing, is that your work be got to pass; if the work itself is worth nothing, or little or an uncertain quantity, what more can gods or men require of it, or, above all, can I who am the doer of it require, but that it be got to pass?

And now enters another fatal effect, the mother of ever-new mischiefs, which renders well-doing or improvement impossible, and drives bad everywhere continually into worse. The work being what we see, a stupid subaltern will do as well as a gifted one; the essential point is, that he be a quiet one, and do not bother me who have the driving of him. Nay, for this latter object, is not a certain height of intelligence even dangerous? I want no mettled Arab horse, with his flashing glances, arched neck and elastic step, to draw my wretched sand-cart through the streets; a broken, grass-fed galloway, Irish garron, or painful ass with nothing in the belly of him but patience and furze, will do it safelier for me, if more slowly. Nay I myself, am I the worse for being of a feeble order of intelligence; what the irreverent speculative world calls barren, red-tapish, limited, and even intrinsically dark and small, and if it must be said, stupid ? — To such a climax does it come in all Government and other Offices, where Human Stupidity has once introduced itself (as it will every-where do), and no Scavenger God intervenes. The work, at first of some worth, is ill done, and becomes of less worth and of ever less, and finally of none : the worthless work can now *afford* to be ill done ; and Human Stupidity, at a double geometrical ratio, with frightful expansion grows and accumu-lates, — towards the unendurable.

The reforming Hercules, Sir Robert Peel or whoever he is to be, that enters Downing Street, will ask himself this ques-tion first of all, What work *is* now necessary, not in form and by traditionary use -and wont, but in very fact, for the vital interests of the British Nation, to be done here ? The second question, How to get it well done, and to keep the best hands doing it well, will be greatly simplified by a good answer to that. Oh for an eye that could see in those hideous mazes, and a heart that could dare and do ! Strenuous faithful scrutiny, not of what is *thought* to be what in the red-tape regions, but of what really is what in the realms of Fact and Nature her-self ; deep-seeing, wise and courageous eyes, that could look through innumerable cobweb veils, and detect what fact or no-fact lies at heart of them, — how invaluable these ! For, alas, it is long since such eyes were much in the habit of looking steadfastly at any department of our affairs; and poor com-monplace creatures, helping themselves along, in the way of makeshift, from year to year, in such an element, do wonder-ful works indeed. Such creatures, like moles, are safe only underground, and their engineerings there become very dæda-lean. In fact, such unfortunate persons have no resource but to become what we call Pedants; to ensconce themselves in a safe world of habitudes, of applicable or inapplicable tradi-tions; not coveting, rather avoiding the general daylight of common-sense, as very extraneous to them and their proced-ure ; by long persistence in which course they become Com-pleted Pedants, hidebound, impenetrable, able to *defy* the hostile extraneous element : an alarming kind of men. Such

men, left to themselves for a century or two, in any Colonial,
Foreign, or other Office, will make a terrible affair of it!

For the one enemy we have in this Universe is Stupidity,
Darkness of Mind; of which darkness, again, there are many
sources, every *sin* a source, and probably self-conceit the chief
source. Darkness of mind, in every kind and variety, does to
a really tragic extent abound: but of all the kinds of darkness, surely the Pedant darkness, which asserts and believes
itself to be *light*, is the most formidable to mankind! For
empires or for individuals there is but one class of men to
be trembled at; and that is the Stupid Class, the class that
cannot see, who alas are they mainly that will not see. A
class of mortals under which as administrators, kings, priests,
diplomatists, &c., the interests of mankind in every European
country have sunk overloaded, as under universal nightmare,
near to extinction; and indeed are at this moment convul-
sively writhing, decided either to throw off the unblessed
superincumbent nightmare, or roll themselves and it to the
Abyss. Vain to reform Parliament, to invent ballot-boxes,
to reform this or that; the real Administration, practical
Management of the Commonwealth, goes all awry; choked up
with long-accumulated pedantries, so that your appointed workers have been reduced to work as moles; and it is one vast
boring and counter-boring, on the part of eyeless persons irreverently called stupid; and a dædalean bewilderment, writing
"impossible" on all efforts or proposals, supervenes.

───────

The State itself, not in Downing Street alone but in every
department of it, has altered much from what it was in past
times; and it will again have to alter very much, to alter I
think from top to bottom, if it means to continue existing
in the times that are now coming and come!

The State, left to shape itself by dim pedantries and traditions, without distinctness of conviction, or purpose beyond
that of helping itself over the difficulty of the hour, has
become, instead of a luminous vitality permeating with its
light all provinces of our affairs, a most monstrous agglome-

rate of inanities, as little adapted for the actual wants of a modern community as the worst citizen need wish. The thing it is doing is by no means the thing we want to have done. What we want! Let the dullest British man endeavor to raise in his mind this question, and ask himself in sincerity what the British Nation wants at this time. Is it to have, with endless jargoning, debating, motioning and counter-motioning, a settlement effected between the Honorable Mr. This and the Honorable Mr. That, as to their respective pretensions to ride the high horse? Really it is unimportant which of them ride it. Going upon past experience long continued now, I should say with brevity, "Either of them — Neither of them." If our Government is to be a No-Government, what is the matter who administers it? Fling an orange-skin into St. James's Street; let the man it hits be your man. He, if you breed him a little to it, and tie the duc official bladders to his ankles, will do as well as another this sublime problem of balancing himself upon the vortexes, with the long loaded-pole in his hands; and will, with straddling painful gestures, float hither and thither, walking the waters in that singular manner for a little while, as well as his foregoers did, till he also capsize, and be left floating feet uppermost; after which you choose another.

What an immense pother, by parliamenting and palavering in all corners of your empire, to decide such a question as that! I say, if that is the function, almost any human creature can learn to discharge it: fling out your orange-skin again; and save an incalculable labor, and an emission of nonsense and falsity, and electioneering beer and bribery and balderdash, which is terrible to think of, in deciding. Your National Parliament, in so far as it has only that question to decide, may be considered as an enormous National Palaver existing mainly for imaginary purposes; and certain, in these days of abbreviated labor, to get itself sent home again to its partridge-shootings, fox-huntings, and above all, to its rat-catchings, if it could but understand the time of day, and know (as our indignant Crabbe remarks) that "the *real* Nimrod of this era, who alone does any good to the era, is the rat-catcher!"

The notion that any Government is or can be a No-Government, without the deadliest peril to all noble interests of the Commonwealth, and by degrees slower or swifter to all ignoble ones also, and to the very gully-drains, and thief lodging-houses, and Mosaic sweating establishments, and at last without destruction to such No-Government itself, — was never my notion; and I hope it will soon cease altogether to be the world's or to be anybody's. But if it be the correct notion, as the world seems at present to flatter itself, I point out improvements and abbreviations. Dismiss your National Palaver; make the *Times* Newspaper your National Palaver, which needs no beer-barrels or hustings, and is *cheaper* in expense of money and of falsity a thousand and a million fold; have an economical red-tape drilling establishment (it were easier to devise such a thing than a right *Modern University*); — and fling out your orange-skin among the graduates, when you want a new Premier.

A mighty question indeed! Who shall be Premier, and take in hand the "rudder of government," otherwise called the "spigot of taxation;" shall it be the Honorable Felix Parvulus, or the Right Honorable Felicissimus Zero? By our electioneerings and Hansard Debatings, and ever-enduring tempest of jargon that goes on everywhere, we manage to settle that; to have it declared, with no bloodshed except insignificant blood from the nose in hustings-time, but with immense beershed and inkshed and explosion of nonsense, which darkens all the air, that the Right Honorable Zero is to be the man. That we firmly settle; Zero, all shivering with rapture and with terror, mounts into the high saddle; cramps himself on, with knees, heels, hands and feet; and the horse gallops — whither it lists. That the Right Honorable Zero should attempt controlling the horse — Alas, alas, he, sticking on with beak and claws, is too happy if the horse will only gallop any-whither, and not throw him. Measure, polity, plan or scheme of public good or evil, is not in the head of Felicissimus; except, if he could but devise it, some measure that would please his horse for the moment, and encourage him to go with softer paces, godward or devilward

as it might be, and save Felicissimus's leather, which is fast
wearing. This is what we call a Government in England, for
nearly two centuries now.

I wish Felicissimus were saddle-sick forever and a day ! He
is a dreadful object, however much we are used to him. If the
horse had not been bred and broken in, for a thousand years,
by real riders and horse-subduers, perhaps the best and bravest
the world ever saw, what would have become of Felicissimus
and him long since ? This horse, by second-nature, religiously
respects all fences ; gallops, if never so madly, on the highways alone ; — seems to me, of late, like a desperate Sleswick
thunder-horse who had lost his way, galloping in the labyrinthic
lanes of a woody flat country ; passionate to reach his goal ;
unable to reach it, because in the flat leafy lanes there is no
outlook whatever, and in the bridle there is no guidance whatever. So he gallops stormfully along, thinking it is forward
and forward ; and alas, it is only round and round, out of
one old lane into the other ; — nay (according to some) " he
mistakes *his own footprints*, which of course grow ever more
numerous, for the sign of a more and more frequented road ; "
and his despair is hourly increasing. My impression is, he
is certain soon, such is the growth of his necessity and his
despair, to — plunge *across* the fence, into an opener survey of
the country ; and to sweep Felicissimus off his back, and comb
him away very tragically in the process ! Poor Sleswicker, I
wish you were better ridden. I perceive it lies in the Fates
you must now either be better ridden, or else not long at all.
This plunging in the heavy labyrinth of over-shaded lanes,
with one's stomach getting empty, one's Ireland falling into
cannibalism, and no vestige of a goal either visible or possible,
cannot last.

Colonial Offices, Foreign, Home and other Offices, got together under these strange circumstances, cannot well be expected to be the best that human ingenuity could devise ; the
wonder rather is to see them so good as they are. Who made
them, ask me not. Made they clearly were ; for we see them
here in a concrete condition, writing despatches, and drawing

salary with a view to buy pudding. But how those Offices in Downing Street were made; who made them, or for what kind of objects they were made, would be hard to say at present. Dim visions and phantasmagories gathered from the Books of Horace Walpole, Memoirs of Bubb Doddington, Memoirs of my Lady Sundon, Lord Fanny Hervey, and innumerable others, rise on us, beckoning fantastically towards, not an answer, but some conceivable intimations of an answer, and proclaiming very legibly the old text, "*Quam parvâ sapientiâ,*" in respect of this hard-working much-subduing British Nation; — giving rise to endless reflections in a thinking Englishman of this day. Alas, it is ever so : each generation has its task, and does it better or worse ; greatly neglecting what is not immediately its task. Our poor grandfathers, so busy conquering Indias, founding Colonies, inventing spinning-jennies, kindling Lancashires and Bromwichams, took no thought about the government of all that; left it all to be governed by Lord Fanny and the Hanover Succession, or how the gods pleased. And now we the poor grandchildren find that it will not stick together on these terms any longer ; that our sad, dangerous and sore task is to discover some government for this big world which has been conquered to us ; that the red-tape Offices in Downing Street are near the end of their rope ; that if we can get nothing better, in the way of government, it is all over with our world and us. How the Downing-Street Offices originated, and what the meaning of them was or is, let Dryasdust, when in some lucid moment the whim takes him, instruct us. Enough for us to know and see clearly, with urgent practical inference derived from such insight, That they were not made for us or for our objects at all ; that the devouring Irish Giant is here, and that he cannot be fed with red-tape, and will eat us if we cannot feed him.

On the whole, let us say Felicissimus made them ; — or rather it was the predecessors of Felicissimus, who were not so dreadfully hunted, sticking to the wild and ever more desperate Sleswicker in the leafy labyrinth of lanes, as he now is. He, I think, will never make anything ; but be combed off by the elm-boughs, and left sprawling in the ditch. But in past

time, this and the other heavy-laden red-tape soul had withal
a glow of patriotism in him; now and then, in his whirling
element, a gleam of human ingenuity, some eye towards business that must be done. At all events, for him and every one,
Parliament needed to be persuaded that business was done.
By the contributions of many such heavy-laden souls, driven
on by necessity outward and inward, these singular Establishments are here. Contributions — who knows how far back
they go, far beyond the reign of George the Second, or perhaps
the reign of William Conqueror. Noble and genuine some of
them were, many of them were, I need not doubt: for there is
no human edifice that stands long but has got itself planted,
here and there, upon the basis of fact; and being built, in
many respects, according to the laws of statics: no standing
edifice, especially no edifice of State, but has had the wise and
brave at work in it, contributing their lives to it; and is
"cemented," whether it know the fact or not, "by the blood
of heroes!" None; not even the Foreign Office, Home Office,
still less the National Palaver itself. William Conqueror, I
find, must have had a first-rate Home Office, for his share.
The *Domesday Book*, done in four years, and done as it is, with
such an admirable brevity, explicitness and completeness, testifies emphatically what kind of under-secretaries and officials
William had. Silent officials and secretaries, I suppose; not
wasting themselves in parliamentary talk; reserving all their
intelligence for silent survey of the huge dumb fact, silent
consideration how they might compass the mastery of that.
Happy secretaries, happy William!

But indeed nobody knows what inarticulate traditions, rem-
nants of old wisdom, priceless though quite anonymous, survive in many modern things that still have life in them. Ben
Brace, with his taciturnities, and rugged stoical ways, with
his tarry breeches, stiff as plank-breeches, I perceive is still a
kind of *Lod-brog* (Loaded-breeks) in more senses than one;
and derives, little conscious of it, many of his excellences from
the old Sea-kings and Saxon Pirates themselves; and how
many Blakes and Nelsons since have contributed to Ben!
"Things are not so false always as they seem," said a certain

Professor to me once : " of this you will find instances in every country, and in your England more than any — and I hope will draw lessons from them. An English Seventy-four, if you look merely at the articulate law and methods of it, is one of the impossiblest entities. The captain is appointed not by pre-eminent merit in sailorship, but by parliamentary connection ; the men [this was spoken some years ago] are got by impress-ment ; a press-gang goes out, knocks men down on the streets of sea-towns, and drags them on board, — if the ship were to be stranded, I have heard they would nearly all run ashore and desert. Can anything be more unreasonable than a Seventy-four ? Articulately almost nothing. But it has inarticulate traditions, ancient methods and habitudes in it, stoicisms, noblenesses, *true* rules both of sailing and of conduct ; enough to keep it afloat on Nature's veridical bosom, after all. See ; if you bid it sail to the end of the world, it will lift anchor, go, and arrive. The raging oceans do not beat it back ; it too, as well as the raging oceans, has a relationship to Nature, and it does not sink, but under the due conditions is borne along. If it meet with hurricanes, it rides them out ; if it meet an Ene-my's ship, it shivers it to powder ; and in short, it holds on its way, and to a wonderful extent *does* what it means and pretends to do. Assure yourself, my friend, there is an immense fund of truth somewhere or other stowed in that Seventy-four."

More important than the past history of these Offices in Downing Street, is the question of their future history ; the question, How they are to be got mended! Truly an immense problem, inclusive of all others whatsoever; which demands to be attacked, and incessantly persisted in, by all good citi-zens, as the grand problem of Society, and the one thing need-ful for the Commonwealth ! A problem in which all men, with all their wisdoms and all their virtues, faithfully and continually co-operating at it, will never have done *enough,* and will still only be struggling *towards* perfection in it. In which some men can do much ; — in which every man can do some-thing. Every man, and thou my present Reader canst do this:

Be thyself a man abler to be governed; more reverencing the divine faculty of governing, more sacredly detesting the diabolical semblance of said faculty in self and others; so shalt thou, if not govern, yet actually according to thy strength assist in real governing. And know always, and even lay to heart with a quite unusual solemnity, with a seriousness altogether of a religious nature, that as "Human Stupidity" is verily the accursed parent of all this mischief, so Human Intelligence alone, to which and to which only is victory and blessedness appointed here below, will or can cure it. If we knew this as devoutly as we ought to do, the evil, and all other evils were curable;— alas, if we had from of old known this, as all men made in God's image ought to do, the evil never would have been! Perhaps few Nations have ever known it less than we, for a good while back, have done. Hence these sorrows.

What a People are the poor Thibet idolaters, compared with us and our "religions," which issue in the worship of King Hudson as our Dalai-Lama! They, across such hulls of abject ignorance, have seen into the heart of the matter; we, with our torches of knowledge everywhere brandishing themselves, and such a human enlightenment as never was before, have quite missed it. Reverence for Human Worth, earnest devout search for it and encouragement of it, loyal furtherance and obedience to it : this, I say, is the outcome and essence of all true "religions," and was and ever will be. We have not known this. No; loud as our tongues sometimes go in that direction, we have no true reverence for Human Intelligence, for Human Worth and Wisdom : none, or too little, — and I pray for a restoration of such reverence, as for the change from Stygian darkness to Heavenly light, as for the return of life to poor sick moribund Society and all its interests. Human Intelligence means little for most of us but Beaver Contrivance, which produces spinning-mules, cheap cotton, and large fortunes. Wisdom, unless it give us railway scrip, is not wise.

True nevertheless it forever remains that Intellect is the real object of reverence, and of devout prayer, and zealous wish and pursuit, among the sons of men; and even, well understood, the one object. It is the Inspiration of the Almighty that giveth men understanding. For it must be repeated, and ever again repeated till poor mortals get to discern it, and awake from their baleful paralysis, and degradation under foul enchantments, That a man of Intellect, of real and not sham Intellect, is by the nature of him likewise inevitably a man of nobleness, a man of courage, rectitude, pious strength; who, even *because* he is and has been loyal to the Laws of this Universe, is initiated into *discernment* of the same; to this hour a Missioned of Heaven; whom if men follow, it will be well with them; whom if men do not follow, it will not be well. Human Intellect, if you consider it well, is the exact summary of Human *Worth ;* and the essence of all worth-ships and worships is reverence for that same. This much surprises you, friend Peter; but I assure you it is the fact; — and I would advise you to consider it, and to try if you too do not gradually find it so. With me it has long been an article, not of "faith" only, but of settled insight, of conviction as to what the ordainments of the Maker in this Universe are. Ah, could you and the rest of us but get to know it, and everywhere religiously act upon it, — as our *Fortieth* Article, which includes all the other Thirty-nine, and without which the Thirty-nine are good for almost nothing, — there might then be some hope for us ! In this world there is but one appalling creature : the Stupid man *considered* to be the Missioned of Heaven, and followed by men. He is our King, men say, he ; — and they follow him, through straight or winding courses, I for one know well whitherward.

Abler men in Downing Street, abler men to govern us : yes, that, sure enough, would gradually remove the dung-mountains, however high they are; that would be the way, nor is there any other way, to remedy whatsoever has gone wrong in Downing Street and in the wide regions, spiritual and temporal, which Downing Street presides over ! For the Able Man, meet him where you may, is definable as the born enemy of Falsity and Anarchy, and the born soldier of Truth and Order: into what absurdest element soever you put him, he is there to make it a little less absurd, to fight continually with it till it become a little sane and human again. Peace on other terms he, for his part, cannot make with it; not he, while he continues *able*, or possessed of real intellect and not imaginary. There is but one man fraught with blessings for this world, fated to diminish and successively abolish the curses of the world; and it is he. For him make search, him reverence and follow; know that to find *him* or miss him, means victory or defeat for you, in all Downing Streets, and establishments and enterprises here below. — I leave your Lordship to judge whether this has been our practice hitherto; and would humbly inquire what your Lordship thinks is likely to be the consequence of continuing to neglect this. It ought to have been our practice; ought, in all places and all times, to be the practice in this world; so says the fixed law of things forevermore: — and it must cease to be *not* the practice, your Lordship; and cannot too speedily do so I think! —

Much has been done in the way of reforming Parliament in late years; but that of itself seems to avail nothing, or almost less. The men that sit in Downing Street, governing us, are not abler men since the Reform Bill than were those before it. Precisely the same kind of men; obedient formerly to Tory traditions, obedient now to Whig ditto and popular clamors. Respectable men of office: respectably commonplace in faculty, — while the situation is becoming terribly original! Rendering their outlooks, and ours, more ominous every day.

Indisputably enough the meaning of all reform-movement, electing and electioneering, of popular agitation, parliamentary eloquence, and all political effort whatsoever, is that you may get the ten Ablest Men in England put to preside over your ten principal departments of affairs. To sift and riddle the Nation, so that you might extricate and sift out the true ten gold grains, or ablest men, and of these make your Governors or Public Officers; leaving the dross and common sandy or silty material safely aside, as the thing to be governed, not to govern; certainly all ballot-boxes, caucuses, Kennington-Common meetings, Parliamentary debatings, Red Republics, Russian Despotisms, and constitutional or unconstitutional methods of society among mankind, are intended to achieve this one end; and some of them, it will be owned, achieve it very ill!—If you have got your gold grains, if the men you have got are actually the ablest, then rejoice; with whatever astonishment, accept your Ten, and thank the gods; under this Ten your destruction will at least be milder than under another. But if you have *not* got them, if you are very far from having got them, then do not rejoice at all, then *lament* very much; then admit that your sublime political constitutions and contrivances do not prove themselves sublime, but ridiculous and contemptible; that your world's wonder of a political mill, the envy of surrounding nations, does not yield you real meal; yields you only powder of millstones (called Hansard Debatings), and a detestable brown substance not unlike the grindings of dried horse-dung or prepared street-mud, which though sold under royal patent, and much recommended by the trade, is quite unfit for culinary purposes!—

But the disease at least is not mysterious, whatever the remedy be. Our disease,—alas, is it not clear as the sun, that we suffer under what is the disease of all the miserable in this world, *want of wisdom;* that in the Head there is no vision, and that thereby all the members are dark and in bonds? No vision in the head; heroism, faith, devout insight to discern what is needful, noble courage to do it, greatly defective there: not seeing eyes there, but spectacles constitutionally ground, which, to the unwary, *seem* to see. A quite fatal circumstance, had you never so many Parliaments! How is your ship to be steered by a Pilot with no *eyes* but a pair of glass ones got from the constitutional optician? He must steer by the *ear*, I think, rather than by the eye; by the shoutings he catches from the shore, or from the Parliamentary benches nearer hand:—one of the frightfulest objects to see steering in a difficult sea! Reformed Parliaments in that case, reform-leagues, outer agitations and excitements in never such abundance, cannot profit: all this is but the writhing, and painful blind convulsion of the limbs that are in bonds, that are all in dark misery till the head be delivered, till the pressure on the brain be removed.

Or perhaps there *is* now no heroic wisdom left in England; England, once the land of heroes, is itself sunk now to a dim owlery, and habitation of doleful creatures, intent only on money-making and other forms of catching mice, for whom the proper gospel is the gospel of M'Croudy, and all nobler impulses and insights are forbidden henceforth? Perhaps these present agreeable Occupants of Downing Street, such as the parliamentary mill has yielded them, are the *best* the miserable soil had grown? The most Herculean Ten Men that could be found among the English Twenty-seven Millions, are these? There *are* not, in any place, under any figure, ten diviner men among us? Well; in that case, the riddling and searching of the twenty-seven millions has been *successful*. Here are our ten divinest men; with these, unhappily not divine enough, we must even content ourselves and die in peace; what help is there? No help, no hope, in that case.

But, again, if these are *not* our divinest men, then evidently there always is hope, there always is possibility of help; and ruin never is quite inevitable, till we *have* sifted out our actually divinest ten, and set these to try their hand at governing! — That this has been achieved; that these ten men are the most Herculean souls the English population held within it, is a proposition credible to no mortal. No, thank God; low as we are sunk in many ways, this is not yet credible! Evidently the reverse of this proposition is the fact. Ten much diviner men do certainly exist. By some conceivable, not forever impossible, method and methods, ten very much diviner men could be sifted out! — Courage; let us fix our eyes on that important fact, and strive all thitherward as towards a door of hope!

Parliaments, I think, have proved too well, in late years, that they are not the remedy. It is not Parliaments, reformed or other, that will ever send Herculean men to Downing Street, to reform Downing Street for us; to diffuse therefrom a light of Heavenly Order, instead of the murk of Stygian Anarchy, over this sad world of ours. That function does not lie in the capacities of Parliament. That is the function of a

King, — if we could get such a priceless entity, which we cannot just now ! Failing which, Statesmen, or Temporary Kings, and at the very lowest one real Statesman, to shape the dim tendencies of Parliament, and guide them wisely to the goal : he, I perceive, will be a primary condition, indispensable for any progress whatsoever.

One such, perhaps, might be attained ; one such might prove discoverable among our Parliamentary populations ? That one, in such an enterprise as this of Downing Street, might be invaluable ! One noble man, at once of natural wisdom and practical experience ; one Intellect still really human, and not red-tapish, owlish and pedantical, appearing there in that dim chaos, with word of command ; to brandish Hercules-like the divine broom and shovel, and turn running water in upon the place, and say as with a fiat, "Here shall be truth, and real work, and talent to do it henceforth ; I will seek for able men to work here, as for the elixir of life to this poor place and me : " — what might not one such man effect there !

Nay one such is not to be dispensed with anywhere in the affairs of men. In every ship, I say, there must be a *seeing* pilot, not a mere hearing one ! It is evident you can never get your ship steered through the difficult straits by persons standing ashore, on this bank and that, and shouting *their* confused directions to you : " 'Ware that Colonial Sandbank ! — Starboard now, the Nigger Question ! — Larboard, lar*board,* the Suffrage Movement ! — Financial Reform, your Clothing-Colonels overboard ! The Qualification Movement, 'Ware-re-re ! — Helm-a-lee ! Bear a hand there, will you ! Hr-r-r, lubbers, imbeciles, fitter for a tailor's shopboard than a helm of Government, Hr-r-r ! " — And so the ship wriggles and tumbles, and, on the whole, goes as wind and current drive. No ship was ever steered except to destruction in that manner. I deliberately say so : no ship of a State either. If you cannot get a real pilot on board, and put the helm into his hands, your ship is as good as a wreck. One real pilot on board may save you ; all the bellowing from the banks that ever was, will not, and by the nature of things cannot. Nay your pilot will have to succeed, if he do succeed, very much in spite of said bellowing; he will hear all that, and regard very little of it, — in a patient mild-spoken wise manner, will regard all of *it* as what it is. And I never doubt but there is in Parliament itself, in spite of its vague palaverings which fill us with despair in these times, a dumb instinct of inarticulate sense and stubborn practical English insight and veracity, that would manfully support a Statesman who could take command with really manful notions of Reform, and as one deserving to be obeyed. Oh for one such; even one! More precious to us than all the bullion in the Bank, or perhaps that ever was in it, just now!

For it is Wisdom alone that can recognize wisdom : Folly or Imbecility never can; and that is the fatalest ban it labors under, dooming it to perpetual failure in all things. Failure which, in Downing Street and places of *command*, is especially accursed; cursing not one but hundreds of millions! Who is there that can recognize real intellect, and do reverence to it; and discriminate it well from sham intellect, which is so much more abundant, and deserves the reverse of reverence? He that himself has it ! — One really human Intellect, invested with command, and charged to reform Downing Street for us, would continually attract real intellect to those regions, and with a divine magnetism search it out from the modest corners where it lies hid. And every new accession of intellect to Downing Street would bring to it benefit only, and would increase such divine attraction in it, the parent of all benefit there and elsewhere !

" What method, then; by what method ?" ask many. — Method, alas ! To secure an increased supply of Human Intellect to Downing Street, there will evidently be no quite effectual " method " but that of increasing the supply of Human Intellect, otherwise definable as Human Worth, in Society generally; increasing the supply of sacred reverence for it, of loyalty to it, and of life-and-death desire and pursuit of it, among all classes, — if we but knew such a " method "! Alas, that were simply the method of making all classes Servants of Heaven; and except it be devout prayer to Heaven, I have never heard of any method! To increase the reverence for Human Intellect or God's Light, and the detestation of Human Stupidity or the Devil's Darkness, what method is there? No method, — except even this, that we should each of us "pray" for it, instead of praying for mere scrip and the like; that Heaven would please to vouchsafe us each a little of it, one by one! As perhaps Heaven, in its infinite bounty, by stern methods, gradually will? Perhaps Heaven has mercy too in these sore plagues that are oppressing us; and means to teach us reverence for Heroism and Human Intellect, by such baleful experience of what issue Imbecility and Parliamentary Eloquence lead to? Such reverence, I do hope, and even discover and observe, is silently yet extensively going on among us even in these sad years. In which small salutary fact there burns for us, in this black coil of universal baseness fast becoming universal wretchedness, an inextinguishable hope; far-off but sure, a divine "pillar of fire by night." Courage, courage! —

Meanwhile, that our one reforming Statesman may have free command of what Intellect there is among us, and room to try all means for awakening and inviting ever more of it, there has one small Project of Improvement been suggested; which finds a certain degree of favor wherever I hear it talked of, and which seems to merit much more consideration than it has yet received. Practical men themselves approve of it hitherto, so far as it goes; the one objection being that the world is not yet prepared to insist on it, — which of course the world can never be, till once the world consider it, and in the first place hear tell of it! I have, for my own part, a good opinion of this project. The old unreformed Parliament of rotten boroughs *had* one advantage; but that is hereby, in a far more fruitful and effectual manner, secured to the new.

The Proposal is, That Secretaries under and upper, that all manner of changeable or permanent servants in the Government Offices shall be selected *without* reference to their power of getting into Parliament; — that, in short, the Queen shall

have power of nominating the half-dozen or half-score Officers
of the Administration, whose presence is thought necessary in
Parliament, to official seats there, without reference to any
constituency but her own only, which of course will mean her
Prime Minister's. A very small encroachment on the present
constitution of Parliament; offering the minimum of change
in present methods, and I almost think a maximum in results
to be derived therefrom. — The Queen nominates John Thomas
(the fittest man she, much inquiring, can hear tell of in her
three kingdoms) President of the Poor-Law Board, Under
Secretary of the Colonies, Under, or perhaps even Upper Secretary of what she and her Premier find suitablest for a working head so eminent, a talent so precious; and grants him, by
her direct authority, seat and vote in Parliament so long as he
holds that office. Upper Secretaries, having more to do in
Parliament, and being so bound to be in favor there, would, I
suppose, at least till new times and habits come, be expected
to be chosen from among the *People's* Members as at present.
But whether the Prime Minister himself is, in all times, bound
to be first a People's Member; and which, or how many, of
his Secretaries and subordinates he might be allowed to take
as *Queen's* Members, my authority does not say, — perhaps
has not himself settled; the project being yet in mere outline
or foreshadow, the practical embodiment in all details to be
fixed by authorities much more competent than he. The soul
of his project is, That the Crown also have power to elect a
few members to Parliament.

From which project, however wisely it were embodied,
there could probably, at first or all at once, no great "accession of intellect" to the Government Offices ensue; though
a little might, even at first, and a little is always precious:
but in its ulterior operation, were that faithfully developed,
and wisely presided over, I fancy an immense accession of
intellect might ensue; — nay a natural ingress might thereby
be opened to all manner of accessions, and the actual flower
of whatever intellect the British Nation had might be at-
tracted towards Downing Street, and continue flowing steadily
thither! For, let us see a little what effects this simple

change carries in it the possibilities of. Here are beneficent germs, which the presence of one truly wise man as Chief Minister, steadily fostering them for even a few years, with the sacred fidelity and vigilance that would beseem him, might ripen into living practices and habitual facts, invaluable to us all.

What it is that Secretaries of State, Managers of Colonial Establishments, of Home and Foreign Government interests, have really and truly to do in Parliament, might admit of various estimate in these times. An apt debater in Parliament is by no means certain to be an able administrator of Colonies, of Home or Foreign Affairs; nay, rather quite the contrary is to be presumed of him; for in order to become a "brilliant speaker," if that is his character, considerable portions of his natural internal endowment must have gone to the surface, in order to make a shining figure there, and precisely so much the less (few men in these days know how much less!) must remain available in the internal silent state, or as faculty for thinking, for devising and acting, which latter and which alone is the function essential for him in his Secretaryship. Not to tell a good story for himself "in Parliament and to the twenty-seven millions, many of them fools;" not that, but to do good administration, to know with sure eye, and decide with just and resolute heart, what is what in the *things* committed to his charge: this and not that is the service which poor England, whatever it may think and maunder, does require and want of the Official Man in Downing Street. Given a good Official Man or Secretary, he really ought, as far as it is possible, to be left working in the silent state. No mortal can both work, and do good talking in Parliament, or out of it: the feat is impossible as that of serving two hostile masters.

Nor would I, if it could be helped, much trouble my good Secretary with addressing Parliament: needful explanations; yes, in a free country, surely; — but not to every frivolous and vexatious person, in or out of Parliament, who chooses to apply for them. There should be demands for explanation too which were reckoned frivolous and vexatious, and censured as such. These, I should say, are the *not* needful explanations: and if my poor Secretary is to be called out from his workshop to answer every one of these, — his workshop will become (what we at present see it, deservedly or not) little other than a pillory; the poor Secretary a kind of talking-machine, exposed to dead cats and rotten eggs; and the "work" got out of him or of it will, as heretofore, be very inconsiderable indeed! — Alas, on this side also, important improvements are conceivable; and will even, I imagine, get them whence we may, be found indispensable one day. The honorable gentleman whom you interrupt here, he, in his official capacity, is not an individual now, but the embodiment of a Nation; he is the "People of England" engaged in the work of Secretaryship, this one; and cannot forever afford to let the three Tailors of Tooley Street break in upon him at all hours! —

But leaving this, let us remark one thing which is very plain: That whatever be the uses and duties, real or supposed, of a Secretary in Parliament, his faculty to accomplish these is a point entirely unconnected with his ability to get elected into Parliament, and has no relation or proportion to it, and no concern with it whatever. Lord Tommy and the Honorable John are not a whit better qualified for Parliamentary duties, to say nothing of Secretary duties, than plain Tom and Jack; they are merely better qualified, as matters stand, for getting admitted to try them. Which state of matters a reforming Premier, much in want of abler men to help him, now proposes *altering*. Tom and Jack, once admitted by the Queen's writ, there is every reason to suppose will do quite as well there as Lord Tommy and the Honorable John. In Parliament quite *as* well: and elsewhere, in the other infinitely more important duties of a Government Office, which indeed are and remain the essential, vital and intrinsic duties of such a personage, is there the faintest reason to surmise that Tom and Jack, if well chosen, will fall short of Lord Tommy and the Honorable John? No shadow of a reason. Were the intrinsic genius of the men exactly equal, there is no shadow of a reason: but rather there is quite the reverse;

for Tom and Jack have been at least workers all their days,
not idlers, game-preservers and mere human clothes-horses, at
any period of their lives; and have gained a schooling *thereby*,
of which Lord Tommy and the Honorable John, unhappily
strangers to it for most part, can form no conception! Tom
and Jack have already, on this most narrow hypothesis, a
decided *superiority* of likelihood over Lord Tommy and the
Honorable John.

But the hypothesis is very narrow, and the fact is very
wide; the hypothesis counts by units, the fact by millions.
Consider how *many* Toms and Jacks there are to choose from,
well or ill! The aristocratic class from whom Members of
Parliament can be elected extends only to certain thousands;
from these you are to choose your Secretary, if a seat in
Parliament is the primary condition. But the general population is of Twenty-seven Millions; from all sections of which
you can choose, if the seat in Parliament is not to be primary.
Make it ultimate instead of primary, a last investiture instead
of a first indispensable condition, and the whole British Nation, learned, unlearned, professional, practical, speculative
and miscellaneous, is at your disposal! In the lowest broad
strata of the population, equally as in the highest and narrowest, are produced men of every kind of genius; man for man,
your chance of genius is as good among the millions as among
the units;—and class for class, what must it be! From all
classes, not from certain hundreds now but from several
millions, whatsoever man the gods had gifted with intellect
and nobleness, and power to help his country, could be
chosen: O Heavens, *could*,—if not by Tenpound Constitu-
encies and the force of beer, then by a Reforming Premier
with eyes in his head, who I think might do it quite infinitely better. Infinitely better. For ignobleness cannot, by
the nature of it, choose the noble: no, there needs a seeing
man who is himself noble, cognizant by internal experience
of the symptoms of nobleness. Shall we never think of this;
shall we never more remember this, then? It is forever true;
and Nature and Fact, however we may rattle our ballot-boxes,
do at no time forget it.

From the lowest and broadest stratum of Society, where the births are by the million, there was born, almost in our own memory, a Robert Burns; son of one who " had not capital for his poor moor-farm of Twenty Pounds a year." Robert Burns never had the smallest chance to get into Parliament, much as Robert Burns deserved, for all our sakes, to have been found there. For the man — it was not known to men purblind, sunk in their poor dim vulgar element, but might have been known to men of insight who had any loyalty or any royalty of their own — was a born king of men : full of valor, of intelligence and heroic nobleness ; fit for far other work than to break his heart among poor mean mortals, gauging beer ! Him no Tenpound Constituency chose, nor did any Reforming Premier : in the deep-sunk British Nation, overwhelmed in foggy stupor, with the loadstars all gone out for it, there was no whisper of a notion that it could be desirable to choose him, — except to come and dine with you, and in the interim to gauge. And yet heaven-born Mr. Pitt, at that period, was by no means without need of Heroic Intellect, for other purposes than gauging ! But sorrowful strangulation by red-tape, much *tighter* then than it now is when so many revolutionary earthquakes have tussled it, quite tied up the meagre Pitt ; and he said, on hearing of this Burns and his sad hampered case, " Literature will take care of itself." — " Yes, and of you too, if you don't mind it ! " answers one.

And so, like Apollo taken for a Neat-herd, and perhaps for none of the best on the Admetus establishment, this new Norse Thor had to put up with what was going ; to gauge ale, and be thankful ; pouring *his* celestial sunlight through Scottish Song-writing, — the narrowest chink ever offered to a Thunder-god before ! And the meagre Pitt, and his Dundasses and rep-tape Phantasms (growing very ghastly now to think of), did not in the least know or understand, the impious, god-forgetting mortals, that Heroic Intellects, if Heaven were pleased to send such, were the one salvation for the world and for them and all of us. No ; they " had done very well without " such ; did not see the use of such ; went along " very well " without such ; well presided over by a singular Heroic

Intellect called George the Third : and the Thunder-god, as
was rather fit of him, departed early, still in the noon of life,
somewhat weary of gauging ale ! — O Peter, what a scandalous
torpid element of yellow London fog, favorable to owls only
and their mousing operations, has blotted out the stars of
Heaven for us these several generations back, — which, I rejoice to see, is now visibly about to take itself away again, or
perhaps to be *dispelled* in a very tremendous manner !

For the sake of my Democratic friends, one other observation. Is not this Proposal the very essence of whatever truth
there is in " Democracy ; " this, that the able man be chosen,
in whatever rank he is found ? That he be searched for as
hidden treasure is ; be trained, supervised, set to the work
which he alone is fit for. All Democracy lies in this ; this, I
think, is worth all the ballot-boxes and suffrage-movements
now going. Not that the noble soul, born poor, should be set
to spout in Parliament, but that he should be set to assist in
governing men : this is our grand Democratic interest. With
this we can be saved ; without this, were there a Parliament
spouting in every parish, and Hansard Debates to stem the
Thames, we perish, — die constitutionally drowned, in mere
oceans of palaver.

All reformers, constitutional persons, and men capable of
reflection, are invited to reflect on these things. Let us brush
the cobwebs from our eyes ; let us bid the inane traditions be
silent for a moment ; and ask ourselves, like men dreadfully
intent on having it *done*, " By what method or methods can
the able men from every rank of life be gathered, as diamond-
grains from the general mass of sand : the able men, not the
sham-able ; — and set to do the work of governing, contriving,
administering and guiding for us ! " It is the question of
questions. All that Democracy ever meant lies there : the
attainment of a truer and truer *Aristocracy*, or Government
again by the *Best*.

Reformed Parliaments have lamentably failed to attain it
for us ; and I believe will and must forever fail. One true
Reforming Statesman, one noble worshipper and knower of

human intellect, with the quality of an experienced Politician too; he, backed by such a Parliament as England, once recognizing him, would loyally send, and at liberty to choose his working subalterns from all the Englishmen alive; he surely might do something? Something, by one means or another, is becoming fearfully necessary to be done! He, I think, might accomplish more for us in ten years, than the best conceivable Reformed Parliament, and utmost extension of the suffrage, in twice or ten times ten.

What is extremely important too, you could try this method with safety; extension of the suffrage you cannot so try. With even an approximately heroic Prime Minister, you could get nothing but good from prescribing to him thus, to choose the fittest man, under penalties; to choose, not the fittest of the four or the three men that were in Parliament, but the fittest from the whole Twenty-seven Millions that he could hear of, — at his peril. Nothing but good from this. From extension of the suffrage, some think, you might get quite other than good. From extension of the suffrage, till it became a universal counting of heads, one sees not in the least what wisdom could be extracted. A Parliament of the Paris pattern, such as we see just now, might be extracted: and from that? Solution into universal slush; drownage of all interests divine and human, in a Noah's-Deluge of Parliamentary eloquence, — such as we hope our sins, heavy and manifold though they are, have *not* yet quite deserved!

Who, then, is to be the Reforming Statesman, and begin the noble work for us? He is the preliminary; one such; with him we may prosecute the enterprise to length after length; without him we cannot stir in it at all. A true *king*, temporary king, that dare undertake the government of Britain, on condition of beginning in sacred earnest to " reform " it, not at this or that extremity, but at the heart and centre. That will expurgate Downing Street, and the practical Administration of our Affairs; clear out its accumulated mountains of pedantries and cobwebs; bid the Pedants and the Dullards depart,

bid the Gifted and the Seeing enter and inhabit. So that
henceforth there be Heavenly light there, instead of Stygian
dusk; that God's vivifying light instead of Satan's deadening
and killing dusk, may radiate therefrom, and visit with healing all regions of this British Empire, which now writhes
through every limb of it, in dire agony as if of death! The
enterprise is great, the enterprise may be called formidable
and even awful; but there is none nobler among the sublunary affairs of mankind just now. Nay tacitly it is the enterprise of every man who undertakes to be British Premier in
these times; — and I cannot esteem him an enviable Premier
who, because the engagement is *tacit,* flatters himself that it
does not exist! "Show it me in the bond," he says. Your
Lordship, it actually exists: and I think you will see it yet, in
another kind of "bond" than that sheepskin one!

But truly, in any time, what a strange feeling, enough to
alarm a very big Lordship, this: that he, of the size he is, has
got to the apex of English affairs! Smallest wrens, we know,
by training and the aid of machinery, are capable of many
things. For this world abounds in miraculous combinations,
far transcending anything they do at Drury Lane in the melo-
dramatic way. A world which, as solid as it looks, is made
all of aerial and even of spiritual stuff; permeated all by incalculable sleeping forces and electricities; and liable to go
off, at any time, into the hugest developments, upon a scratch
thoughtfully or thoughtlessly given on the right point: — Nay,
for every one of us, could not the sputter of a poor pistol-shot
shrivel the Immensities together like a burnt scroll, and make
the Heavens and the Earth pass away with a great noise? Smallest wrens, and canary-birds of some dexterity, can be trained
to handle lucifer-matches; and have, before now, fired off whole
powder-magazines and parks of artillery. Perhaps *without*
much astonishment to the canary-bird. The canary-bird can
hold only its own quantity of astonishment; and may possibly
enough retain *its* presence of mind, were even Doomsday to
come. It is on this principle that I explain to myself the
equanimity of some men and Premiers whom we have known.

This and the other Premier seems to take it with perfect coolness. And yet, I say, what a strange feeling, to find himself Chief Governor of England; girding on, upon his moderately sized new soul, the old battle-harness of an Oliver Cromwell, an Edward Longshanks, a William Conqueror. " I, then, am the Ablest of English attainable Men ? This English People, which has spread itself over all lands and seas, and achieved such works in the ages, — which has done America, India, the Lancashire Cotton-trade, Bromwicham Iron-trade, Newton's Principia, Shakspeare's Dramas, and the British Constitution, — the apex of all its intelligences and mighty instincts and dumb longings: it is I ? William Conqueror's big gifts, and Edward's and Elizabeth's; Oliver's lightning soul, noble as Sinai and the thunders of the Lord: these are mine, I begin to perceive, — to a certain extent. These heroisms have I, — though rather shy of exhibiting them. These; and something withal of the huge beaver-faculty of our Arkwrights, Brindleys ; touches too of the phœnix-melodies and *sunny* heroisms of our Shakspeares, of our Singers, Sages and inspired Thinkers; all this is in me, I will hope, — though rather shy of exhibiting it on common occasions. The Pattern Englishman, raised by solemn acclamation upon the bucklers of the English People, and saluted with universal ' God save THEE ! ' — has now the honor to announce himself. After fifteen hundred years of constitutional study as to methods of raising on the bucklers, which is the operation of operations, the English People, surely pretty well skilled in it by this time, has raised — the remarkable individual now addressing you. The best-combined sample of whatsoever divine qualities are in this big People, the consummate flower of all that they have done and been, the ultimate product of the Destinies, and English man of men, arrived at last in the fulness of time, is — who think you ? Ye worlds, the Ithuriel javelin by which, with all these heroisms and accumulated energies old and new, the English People means to smite and pierce, is this poor tailor's-bodkin, hardly adequate to bore an eylet-hole, who now has the honor to " — Good Heavens, if it were not that men generally are very much of the canary-bird, here are reflections sufficient to annihilate any man, almost before starting!

But to us also it ought to be a very strange reflection! This, then, is the length we have brought it to, with our constitution-ing, and ballot-boxing, and incessant talk and effort in every kind for so many centuries back; this? The golden flower of our grand alchemical projection, which has set the world in astonishment so long, and been the envy of surrounding nations, is — what we here see. To be governed by his Lord-ship, and guided through the undiscovered paths of Time by this respectable degree of human faculty. With our utmost soul's travail we could discover, by the sublimest methods eulogized by all the world, no abler Englishman than this?

Really it should make us pause upon the said sublime methods, and ask ourselves very seriously, whether, notwith-standing the eulogy of all the world, they can be other than extremely astonishing methods, that require revisal and re-consideration very much indeed! For the kind of "man" we get to govern us, all conclusions whatsoever centre there, and likewise all manner of issues flow infallibly therefrom. "Ask well, who is your Chief Governor," says one: "for around him men like to him will infallibly gather, and by degrees all the world will be made in his image." "He who is him-self a noble man, has a chance to know the nobleness of men; he who is not, has none. And as for the poor Public, — alas, is not the kind of 'man' you set upon it the liveliest symbol of its and your veracity and victory and blessedness, or un-veracity and misery and cursedness; the general summation and practical outcome of all else whatsoever in the Public and in you?"

Time was when an incompetent Governor could not be per-mitted among men. He was, and had to be, by one method or the other, clutched up from his place at the helm of affairs, and hurled down into the hold, perhaps even overboard, if he could not really steer. And we call those ages barbarous, because they shuddered to see a Phantasm at the helm of their affairs; an eyeless Pilot with constitutional spectacles, steering by the *ear* mainly? And we have changed all that:

no-government is now the best; and a tailor's foreman, who gives no trouble, is preferable to any other for governing? My friends, such truly is the current idea; but you dreadfully mistake yourselves, and the fact is not such. The fact, now beginning to disclose itself again in distressed Needlewomen, famishing Connaughts, revolting Colonies, and a general rapid advance towards Social Ruin, remains really what it always was, and will so remain!

Men have very much forgotten it at present; and only here a man and there a man begins again to bethink himself of it: but all men will gradually get reminded of it, perhaps terribly to their cost; and the sooner they all lay it to heart again, I think it will be the better. For in spite of our oblivion of it, the thing remains forever true; nor is there any Constitution or body of Constitutions, were they clothed with never such venerabilities and general acceptabilities, that avails to deliver a Nation from the consequences of forgetting it. Nature, I assure you, does forevermore remember it; and a hundred British Constitutions are but as a hundred cobwebs between her and the penalty she levies for forgetting it. Tell me what kind of man governs a People, you tell me, with much exactness, what the net sum-total of social worth in that People has for some time been. Whether *they* have loved the phylacteries or the eternal noblenesses; whether they have been struggling heavenward like eagles, brothers of the radiances, or groping owl-like with horn-eyed diligence, catching mice and balances at their banker's, — poor devils, you will see it all in that one fact. A fact long prepared beforehand; which, if it is a peaceably received one, must have been acquiesced in, judged to be " best," by the poor mousing owls, intent only to have a large balance at their banker's and keep a whole skin.

Such sordid populations, which were long blind to Heaven's light, are getting themselves burnt up rapidly, in these days, by street-insurrection and Hell-fire; — as is indeed inevitable, my esteemed M'Croudy! Light, accept the blessed light, if you will have it when Heaven vouchsafes. You refuse? You prefer Delolme on the British Constitution, the Gospel according to M'Croudy, and a good balance at your banker's?

Very well: the "light" is more and more withdrawn; and for
some time you have a general dusk, very favorable for catching
mice; and the opulent owlery is very "happy," and well-off at
its banker's; — and furthermore, by due sequence, infallible as
the foundations of the Universe and Nature's oldest law, the
light *returns* on you, condensed, this time, into *lightning*, which
there is not any skin whatever too thick for taking in!

------◆------

[April 15, 1850.]

No. IV. THE NEW DOWNING STREET.

In looking at this wreck of Governments in all European
countries, there is one consideration that suggests itself, sadly
elucidative of our modern epoch. These Governments, we may
be well assured, have gone to anarchy for this one reason inclusive of every other whatsoever, That they were not wise
enough; that the spiritual talent embarked in them, the
virtue, heroism, intellect, or by whatever other synonyms we
designate it, was not adequate, — probably had long been inadequate, and so in its dim helplessness had suffered, or perhaps
invited falsity to introduce itself; had suffered injustices, and
solecisms, and contradictions of the Divine Fact, to accumulate
in more than tolerable measure; whereupon said Governments
were overset, and declared before all creatures to be too false.

This is a reflection sad but important to the modern Governments now fallen anarchic, That they had not spiritual talent
enough. And if this is so, then surely the question, How
these Governments came to sink for *want* of intellect? is a
rather interesting one. Intellect, in some measure, is born
into every Century; and the Nineteenth flatters itself that it
is rather distinguished that way! What had become of this
celebrated Nineteenth Century's intellect? Surely some of
it existed, and was "developed" withal; — nay in the "unde-
veloped," unconscious, or inarticulate state, it is not dead; but
alive and at work, if mutely not less beneficently, some think

even more so ! And yet Governments, it would appear, could
by no means get enough of it ; almost none of it came their
way : what had become of it ?   Truly there must be something
very questionable, either in the intellect of this celebrated
Century, or in the methods Governments now have of supplying their wants from the same.   One or other of two grand
fundamental shortcomings, in regard to intellect or human
enlightenment, is very visible in this enlightened Century of
ours ; for it has now become the most anarchic of Centuries ;
that is to say, has fallen practically into such Egyptian darkness that it cannot grope its way at all !

Nay I rather think both of these shortcomings, fatal deficits
both, are chargeable upon us ; and it is the joint harvest of
both that we are now reaping, with such havoc to our affairs.
I rather guess, the intellect of the Nineteenth Century, so full
of miracle to Heavyside and others, is itself a mechanical or
beaver intellect rather than a high or eminently human one.
A dim and mean though authentic kind of intellect, this ; venerable only in defect of better.   This kind will avail but little
in the higher enterprises of human intellect, especially in that
highest enterprise of guiding men Heavenward, which, after
all, is the one real " governing " of them on this God's-Earth :
— an enterprise not to be achieved by beaver intellect, but by
other higher and highest kinds.   This is deficit *first*.   And
then *secondly*, Governments have, really to a fatal and extraordinary extent, neglected in late ages to supply themselves with
what intellect was going ; having, as was too natural in the
dim time, taken up a notion that human intellect, or even
beaver intellect, was not necessary to them at all, but that a
little of the *vulpine* sort (if attainable), supported by routine,
red-tape traditions, and tolerable parliamentary eloquence on
occasion, would very well suffice.   A most false and impious
notion ; leading to fatal lethargy on the part of Governments,
while Nature and Fact were preparing strange phenomena in
contradiction to it.

These are two very fatal deficits ; — the remedy of either of
which would be the remedy of both, could we but find it !   For
indeed they are vitally connected : one of them is sure to pro-

duce the other; and both once in action together, the advent
of darkness, certain enough to issue in anarchy by and by,
goes on with frightful acceleration. If Governments neglect
to invite what noble intellect there is, then too surely all intellect, not omnipotent to resist bad influences, will tend to
become beaverish ignoble intellect; and quitting high aims,
which seem shut up from it, will help itself forward in the
way of making money and such like; or will even sink to be
sham intellect, helping itself by methods which are not only
beaverish but vulpine, and so "ignoble" as not to have common
honesty. The Government, taking no thought to choose intellect for itself, will gradually find that there is less and less
of a good quality to choose from : thus, as in all impieties it
does, bad grows worse at a frightful *double* rate of progression;
and your impiety is twice cursed. If you are impious enough
to tolerate darkness, you will get ever more darkness to tolerate; and at that inevitable stage of the account (inevitable
in all such accounts) when actual light or else destruction is
the alternative, you will call to the Heavens and the Earth for
light, and none will come !

Certainly this evil, for one, has *not* "wrought its own cure;"
but has wrought precisely the reverse, and has been hourly
eating away what possibilities of cure there were. And so, I
fear, in spite of rumors to the contrary, it always is with evils,
with solecisms against Nature, and contradictions to the divine
fact of things : not an evil of them has ever wrought its own
cure in my experience; — but has continually grown worse and
wider and uglier, till some *good* (generally a good *man*) not
able to endure the abomination longer, rose upon it and cured
or else extinguished it. Evil Governments, divested of God's
light because they have loved darkness rather, are not like-
lier than other evils to work their own cure out of that bad
plight.

It is urgent upon all Governments to pause in this fatal
course; persisted in, the goal is fearfully evident; every
hour's persistence in it is making return more difficult. Intellect exists in all countries; and the function appointed it by
Heaven, — Governments had better not attempt to contradict

that, for they cannot! Intellect *has* to govern in this world; and will do it, if not in alliance with so-called "Governments" of red-tape and routine, then in divine hostility to such, and sometimes alas in diabolic hostility to such; and in the end, as sure as Heaven is higher than Downing Street, and the Laws of Nature are tougher than red-tape, with entire victory over them and entire ruin to them. If there is one thinking man among the Politicians of England, I consider these things extremely well worth his attention just now.

Who are available to your Offices in Downing Street? All the gifted souls, of every rank, who are born to you in this generation. These are appointed, by the true eternal "divine right" which will never become obsolete, to be your governors and administrators; and precisely as you employ them, or neglect to employ them, will your State be favored of Heaven or disfavored. This noble young soul, you can have him on either of two conditions; and on one of them, since he is here in the world, you must have him. As your ally and coadjutor; or failing that, as your natural enemy: which shall it be? I consider that every Government convicts itself of infatuation and futility, or absolves and justifies itself before God and man, according as it answers this question. With all sublunary entities, this is the question of questions. What talent is born to you? How do you employ that? The crop of spiritual talent that is born to you, of human nobleness and intellect and heroic faculty, this is infinitely more important than your crops of cotton or corn, or wine or herrings or whale-oil, which the Newspapers record with such anxiety every season. This is not quite counted by seasons, therefore the Newspapers are silent: but by generations and centuries, I assure you it becomes amazingly sensible; and surpasses, as Heaven does Earth, all the corn and wine, and whale-oil and California bullion, or any other crop you grow. If that crop cease, the other crops — please to take them also, if you are anxious about them. That once ceasing, we may shut shop; for no other crop whatever will stay with us, nor is worth having if it would.

To promote men of talent, to search and sift the whole society in every class for men of talent, and joyfully promote them, has not always been found impossible. In many forms of polity they have done it, and still do it, to a certain degree. The degree to which they succeed in doing it marks, as I have said, with very great accuracy the degree of divine and human worth that is in them, the degree of success or real ultimate victory they can expect to have in this world.—Think, for example, of the old Catholic Church, in its merely terrestrial relations to the State; and see if your reflections, and contrasts with what now is, are of an exulting character. Progress of the species has gone on as with seven-league boots, and in various directions has shot ahead amazingly, with three cheers from all the world; but in this direction, the most vital and indispensable, it has lagged terribly, and has even moved backward, till now it is quite gone out of sight in clouds of cotton-fuzz and railway-scrip, and has fallen fairly over the horizon to rearward!

In those most benighted Feudal societies, full of mere tyrannous steel Barons, and totally destitute of Tenpound Franchises and Ballot-boxes, there did nevertheless authentically preach itself everywhere this grandest of gospels, without which no other gospel can avail us much, to all souls of men, "Awake ye noble souls; here is a noble career for you!" I say, everywhere a road towards promotion, for human nobleness, lay wide open to all men. The pious soul,—which, if you reflect, will mean the ingenuous and ingenious, the gifted, intelligent and nobly-aspiring soul,—such a soul, in whatever rank of life it were born, had one path inviting it; a generous career, whereon, by human worth and valor, all earthly heights and Heaven itself were attainable. In the lowest stratum of social thraldom, nowhere was the noble soul doomed quite to choke, and die ignobly. The Church, poor old benighted creature, had at least taken care of that: the noble aspiring soul, not doomed to choke ignobly in its penuries, could at least run into the neighboring Convent, and there take refuge. Education awaited it there; strict training not only to whatever useful knowledge could be had from writing and reading, but to obedience, to pious reverence, self-restraint, annihilation of self, — really to human nobleness in many most essential respects. No questions asked about your birth, genealogy, quantity of money-capital or the like; the one question was, " Is there some human nobleness in you, or is there not ? " The poor neat-herd's son, if he were a Noble of Nature, might rise to Priesthood, to High-priesthood, to the top of this world, — and best of all, he had still high Heaven lying high enough above him, to keep his head steady, on whatever height or in whatever depth his way might lie !

A thrice-glorious arrangement, when I reflect on it ; most salutary to all high and low interests ; a truly human arrangement. You made the born noble yours, welcoming him as what he was, the Sent of Heaven : you did not force him either to die or become your enemy ; idly neglecting or suppressing him as what he was not, a thing of no worth. You accepted the blessed *light ;* and in the shape of infernal *lightning* it needed not to visit you. How, like an immense mine-shaft through the dim oppressed strata of society, this Institution of the Priesthood ran ; opening, from the lowest depths towards all heights and towards Heaven itself, a free road of egress and emergence towards virtuous nobleness, heroism and well-doing, for every born man. This we may call the living lungs and blood-circulation of those old Feudalisms. When I think of that immeasurable all-pervading lungs ; present in every corner of human society, every meanest hut a *cell* of said lungs ; inviting whatsoever noble pious soul was born there to the path that was noble for him ; and leading thereby sometimes, if he were worthy, to be the Papa of Christendom, and Commander of all Kings, — I perceive how the old Christian society continued healthy, vital, and was strong and heroic. When I contrast this with the noble aims now held out to noble souls born in remote huts, or beyond the verge of Palace-Yard ; and think of what your Lordship has done in the way of making priests and papas, — I see a society *without* lungs, fast wheezing itself to death, in horrid convulsions ; and deserving to die.

Over Europe generally in these years, I consider that the
State has died, has fairly coughed its last in street musketry,
and fallen down dead, incapable of any but *galvanic* life henceforth, — owing to this same fatal want of *lungs*, which includes
all other wants for a State.   And furthermore that it will
never come alive again, till it contrive to get such indispensable vital apparatus; the outlook toward which consummation
is very distant in most communities of Europe.   If you let it
come to death or suspended animation in States, the case is
very bad!   Vain to call in universal-suffrage parliaments at
that stage : the universal-suffrage parliaments cannot give you
any breath of life, cannot find any *wisdom* for you; by long
impiety, you have let the supply of noble human wisdom die
out; and the wisdom that now courts your universal suffrages
is beggarly human *attorneyism* or sham-wisdom, which is *not* an
insight into the Laws of God's Universe, but into the laws of
hungry Egoism and the Devil's Chicane, and can in the end
profit no community or man.

No ; the kind of heroes that come mounted on the shoulders
of the universal suffrage, and install themselves as Prime Minis-
ters and healing Statesmen by force of able editorship, do not
bid very fair to bring Nations back to the ways of God.   Eloquent high-lacquered *pinchbeck* specimens these, expert in the
arts of Belial mainly ; — fitter to be markers at some exceedingly expensive billiard-table than sacred chief-priests of men!
" Greeks of the Lower Empire ; " with a varnish of parliamentary rhetoric ; and, I suppose, this other great gift, toughness
of character, — proof that they have *persevered* in their Master's service.   Poor wretches, their industry is mob-worship,
place-worship, parliamentary intrigue, and the multiplex art of
tongue-fence : flung into that bad element, there they swim for
decades long, throttling and wrestling one another according to
their strength, — and the toughest or luckiest gets to land, and
becomes Premier.   A more entirely unbeautiful class of Premiers was never raked out of the ooze, and set on high places,
by any ingenuity of man.   Dame Dubarry's petticoat was a
better seine-net for fishing out Premiers than that.   Let all
Nations whom necessity is driving towards that method, take
warning in time !

Alas, there is, in a manner, but one Nation that can still take warning! In England alone of European Countries the State yet survives; and might help itself by better methods. In England heroic wisdom is not yet dead, and quite replaced by attorneyism: the honest beaver faculty yet abounds with us, the heroic manful faculty shows itself also to the observant eye, not dead but dangerously sleeping. I said there were many *kings* in England: if these can yet be rallied into strenuous activity, and set to govern England in Downing Street and elsewhere, which their function always is, — then England can be saved from anarchies and universal suffrages; and that Apotheosis of Attorneyism, blackest of terrestrial curses, may be spared us. If these cannot, the other issue, in such forms as may be appropriate to us, is inevitable. What escape is there? England must conform to the eternal laws of life, or England too must die!

England with the largest mass of real living interests ever intrusted to a Nation; and with a mass of extinct imaginary and quite dead interests piled upon it to the very Heavens, and encumbering it from shore to shore, — does reel and stagger ominously in these years; urged by the Divine Silences and the Eternal Laws to take practical hold of its living interests and manage them: and clutching blindly into its venerable extinct and imaginary interests, as if that were still the way to do it. England must contrive to manage its living interests, and quit its dead ones and their methods, or else depart from its place in this world. Surely England is called as no Nation ever was, to summon out its *kings,* and set them to that high work! — Huge inorganic England, nigh choked under the exuviæ of a thousand years, and blindly sprawling amid chartisms, ballot-boxes, prevenient graces, and bishops' nightmares, must, as the preliminary and commencement of organization, learn to *breathe* again, — get "lungs" for herself again, as we defined it. That is imperative upon her: she too will die, otherwise, and cough her last upon the streets some day; — how can she continue living? To enfranchise whatsoever of Wisdom is born in England, and set that to the sacred task of coercing and amending what of Folly is born in

England : Heaven's blessing is purchasable by that; by not that, only Heaven's curse is purchasable. The reform contemplated, my liberal friends perceive, is a truly radical one ; no ballot-box ever went so deep into the roots : a radical, most painful, slow and difficult, but most indispensable reform of reforms!

How short and feeble an approximation to these high ulterior results, the best Reform of Downing Street, presided over by the fittest Statesman one can imagine to exist at present, would be, is too apparent to me. A long time yet till we get our living interests put under due administration, till we get our dead interests handsomely dismissed. A long time yet till, by extensive change of habit and ways of thinking and acting, *we* get living "lungs" for ourselves ! Nevertheless, by Reform of Downing Street, we do begin to breathe : we do start in the way towards that and all high results. Nor is there visible to me any other way. Blessed enough were the way once entered on; could we, in our evil days, but see the noble enterprise begun, and fairly in progress !

What the " *New* Downing Street " can grow to, and will and must if England is to have a Downing Street beyond a few years longer, it is far from me, in my remote watch-tower, to say with precision. A Downing Street inhabited by the gifted of the intellects of England ; directing all its energies upon the real and living interests of England, and silently but incessantly, in the alembics of the place, burning up the extinct imaginary interests of England, that we may see God's sky a little plainer overhead, and have all of us a great accession of " heroic wisdom " to dispose of: such a Downing Street — to draw the plan of it, will require architects ; many successive architects and builders will be needed there. Let not editors, and remote unprofessional persons, interfere too much ! — Change in the present edifice, however, radical change, all men can discern to be inevitable ; and even, if there shall not worse swiftly follow, to be imminent. Outlines of the future edifice paint themselves against the sky (to men that still have a *sky*, and are above the miserable London fogs of the hour) ; noble elements of new State Architecture, foreshadows of a new Downing Street for the New Era that is come. These with pious hope all men can see; and it is good that all men, with whatever faculty they have, were earnestly looking thitherward; — trying to get above the fogs, that they might look thitherward!

Among practical men the idea prevails that Government can do nothing but "keep the peace." They say all higher tasks are unsafe for it, impossible for it, — and in fine not necessary for it or for us. On this footing a very feeble Downing Street might serve the turn! — I am well aware that Government, for a long time past, has taken in hand no other public task, and has professed to have no other, but that of keeping the peace. This public task, and the private one of ascertaining whether Dick or Jack was to do it, have amply filled the capabilities of Government for several generations now. Hard tasks both, it would appear. In accomplishing the first, for example, have not heaven-born Chancellors of the Exchequer had to shear us very bare; and to leave an overplus of Debt, or of fleeces shorn *before* they are grown, justly esteemed among the wonders of the world? Not a first-rate keeping of the peace, this, we begin to surmise! At least it seems strange to us.

For we, and the overwhelming majority of all our acquaintances, in this Parish and Nation and the adjacent Parishes and Nations, are profoundly conscious to ourselves of being by nature peaceable persons; following our necessary industries; without wish, interest or faintest intention to cut the skin of any mortal, to break feloniously into his industrial premises, or do any injustice to him at all. Because indeed, independent of Government, there is a thing called conscience, and we dare not. So that it cannot but appear to us, "the peace," under dexterous management, might be very much more easily kept, your Lordship; nay, we almost think, if well let alone, it would in a measure keep *itself* among such a set of persons! And how it happens that when a poor hard-working creature of us has laboriously earned sixpence, the

Government comes in, and (as some compute) says, "I will thank you for threepence of that, as per account, for getting you peace to spend the other threepence," our amazement begins to be considerable, — and I think results will follow from it by and by. Not the most dexterous keeping of the peace, your Lordship, unless it be more difficult to do than appears!

Our domestic peace, we cannot but perceive, as good as keeps itself. Here and there a select Equitable Person, appointed by the Public for that end, clad in ermine, and backed by certain companies of blue Police, is amply adequate, without immoderate outlay in money or otherwise, to keep down the few exceptional individuals of the scoundrel kind; who, we observe, by the nature of them, are always weak and inconsiderable. And as to foreign peace, really all Europe, now especially with so many railroads, public journals, printed books, penny-post, bills of exchange, and continual intercourse and mutual dependence, is more and more becoming (so to speak) one Parish; the Parishioners of which being, as we ourselves are, in immense majority peaceable hard-working people, could, if they were moderately well guided, have almost no disposition to quarrel. Their economic interests are one, "To buy in the cheapest market, and sell in the dearest;" their faith, any *religious* faith they have, is one, "To annihilate shams — by all methods, street-barricades included." Why should they quarrel? The Czar of Russia, in the Eastern parts of the Parish, may have other notions; but he knows too well he must keep them to himself. He, if he meddled with the Western parts, and attempted anywhere to crush or disturb that sacred Democratic Faith of theirs, is aware there would rise from a hundred and fifty million human throats such a *Hymn of the Marseillaise* as was never heard before; and England, France, Germany, Poland, Hungary, and the Nine Kingdoms, hurling themselves upon him in never-imagined fire of vengeance, would swiftly reduce his Russia and him to a strange situation! Wherefore he forbears, — and being a person of some sense, will long forbear. In spite of editorial prophecy, the Czar of Russia does not disturb our night's rest. And with the other parts of the

Parish our dreams and our thoughts are of anything but of fighting, or of the smallest need to fight.

For keeping of the peace, a thing highly desirable to us, we strive to be grateful to your Lordship. Intelligible to us, also, your Lordship's reluctance to get out of the old routine. But we beg to say farther, that peace by itself has no feet to stand upon, and would not suit us even if it had. Keeping of the peace is the function of a policeman, and but a small fraction of that of any Government, King or Chief of men. Are not all men bound, and the Chief of men in the name of all, to do properly this : To see, so far as human effort under pain of eternal reprobation can, God's Kingdom incessantly advancing here below, and His will done on Earth as it is in Heaven ? On Sundays your Lordship knows this well ; forget it not on week-days. I assure you it is forevermore a fact. That is the immense divine and never-ending task which is laid on every man, and with unspeakable increase of emphasis on every Government or Commonwealth of men. Your Lordship, that is the basis upon which peace and all else depends ! That basis once well lost, there is no peace capable of being kept, — the only peace that could then be kept is that of the churchyard. Your Lordship may depend on it, whatever thing takes upon it the name of Sovereign or Government in an English Nation such as this will have to get out of that old routine ; and set about keeping something very different from the peace, in these days !

Truly it is high time that same beautiful notion of No-Government should take itself away. The world is daily rushing towards wreck, while that lasts. If your Government is to be a Constituted Anarchy, what issue can it have ? Our one interest in such Government is, that it would be kind enough to cease and go its ways, *before* the inevitable arrive. The question, Who is to float atop no-whither upon the popular vortexes, and act that sorry character, "carcass of the drowned ass upon the mud-deluge"? is by no means an important one for almost anybody, — hardly even for the drowned ass himself. Such drowned ass ought to ask himself, If the function is a sublime one? For him too, though he looks sublime to the vulgar and floats atop, a private situation, down out of sight in his natural ooze, would be a luckier one.

Crabbe, speaking of constitutional philosophies, faith in the ballot-box and such like, has this indignant passage: "If any voice of deliverance or resuscitation reach us, in this our low and all but lost estate, sunk almost beyond plummet's sounding in the mud of Lethe, and oblivious of all noble objects, — it will be an intimation that we must put away all this abominable nonsense, and understand, once more, that Constituted Anarchy, with however many ballot-boxes, caucuses, and hustings beer-barrels, is a continual offence to gods and men. That to be governed by small men is not only a misfortune, but it is a curse and a sin; the effect, and alas the cause also, of all manner of curses and sins. That to profess subjection to phantasms, and pretend to accept guidance from fractional parts of tailors, is what Smelfungus in his rude dialect calls it, 'a damned *lie*,' and nothing other. A lie which, by long use and wont, we have grown accustomed to, and do not the least feel to be a lie, having spoken and done it continually everywhere for such a long time past; — but has Nature grown to accept it as a veracity, think you, my friend? Have the Parcæ fallen asleep, because you wanted to make money in the City? Nature at all moments knows well that it is a lie; and that, like all lies, it is cursed and damned from the beginning.

"Even so, ye indigent millionnaires, and miserable bankrupt populations rolling in gold, — whose note-of-hand will go to any length in Threadneedle Street, and to whom in Heaven's Bank the stern answer is, 'No effects!' Bankrupt, I say; and Californias and Eldorados will not save us. And every time we speak such lie, or do it or look it, as we have been incessantly doing, and many of us with clear consciousness, for about a hundred and fifty years now, Nature marks down the exact penalty against us. 'Debtor to so much lying: forfeiture of existing stock of worth to such extent; — approach to general damnation by so much.' Till now, as we look round us over a convulsed anarchic Europe, and at home over an anarchy not yet convulsed, but only heaving towards convulsion, and to judge by the Mosaic sweating-establishments, cannibal Connaughts and other symptoms, not far from convulsion now, we seem to have pretty much *exhausted* our accumulated stock of worth; and unless money's 'worth' and bullion at the Bank will save us, to be rubbing very close upon that ulterior bourn which I do not like to name again!

"On behalf of nearly twenty-seven millions of my fellow-countrymen, sunk deep in Lethean sleep, with mere owl-dreams of Political Economy and mice-catching, in this pacific thrice-infernal slush-element; and also of certain select thousands, and hundreds and units, awakened or beginning to awaken from it, and with horror in their hearts perceiving where they are, I beg to protest, and in the name of God to say, with poor human ink, desirous much that I had divine thunder to say it with, Awake, arise, — before you sink to death eternal! Unnamable destruction, and banishment to Houndsditch and Gehenna, lies in store for all Nations that, in angry perversity or brutal torpor and owlish blindness, neglect the eternal message of the gods, and vote for the Worse while the Better is there. Like owls they say, 'Barabbas will do; any orthodox Hebrew of the Hebrews, and peaceable believer in M'Croudy and the Faith of Leave-alone will do: the Right Honorable Minimus is well enough; he shall be our Maximus, under him it will be handy to catch mice, and Owldom shall continue a flourishing empire.'"

One thing is undeniable, and must be continually repeated till it get to be understood again: Of all constitutions, forms of government, and political methods among men, the question to be asked is even this, What kind of man do you set over us? All questions are answered in the answer to this. Another thing is worth attending to: No people or populace, with never such ballot-boxes, can select such man for you; only the man of worth can recognize worth in men; — to the commonplace man of no or of little worth, you, unless you wish to be *misled*, need not apply on such an occasion. Those poor Tenpound Franchisers of yours, they are not even in earnest; the poor sniffing sniggering Honorable Gentlemen they send to Parliament are as little so. Tenpound Franchisers full of mere beer and balderdash; Honorable Gentlemen come to Parliament as to an Almack's series of evening parties, or big cockmain (battle of all the cocks) very amusing to witness and bet upon: what can or could men in that predicament ever do for you? Nay, if they were in life-and-death earnest, what could it avail you in such a case? I tell you, a million blockheads looking authoritatively into one man of what you call genius, or noble sense, will make nothing but nonsense out of him and his qualities, and his virtues and defects, if they look till the end of time. He understands them, sees what they are; but that they should understand him, and see with rounded outline what his limits are, — this, which would mean that they are bigger than he, is forever denied them. Their one good understanding of him is that they at last should loyally say, "We do not quite understand thee; we perceive thee to be nobler and wiser and bigger than we, and will loyally follow thee."

The question therefore arises, Whether, since reform of parliament and such like have done so little in that respect, the problem might not be with some hope attacked in the direct manner? Suppose all our Institutions, and Public Methods of Procedure, to continue for the present as they are; and suppose farther a Reform Premier, and the English Nation once awakening under him to a due sense of the infinite importance, nay the vital necessity there is of getting able and abler men: — might not some heroic wisdom, and actual "ability" to do what must be done, prove discoverable to said Premier; and so the indispensable Heaven's-blessing descend to us from *above*, since none has yet sprung from below? From above we shall have to try it; the other is exhausted, — a hopeless method that! The utmost passion of the house-inmates, ignorant of masonry and architecture, cannot avail to cure the house of smoke: not if *they* vote and agitate forever, and bestir themselves to the length even of street-barricades, will the *smoke* in the least abate: how can it? Their passion exercised in such ways, till Doomsday, will avail them nothing. Let their passion rage steadily against the existing major-domos to this effect, "*Find* us men skilled in house-building, acquainted with the laws of atmospheric suction, and capable to cure smoke;" something might come of it! In the lucky circumstance of having one man of real intellect and courage to put at the head of the movement, much would come of it; — a New Downing Street, fit for the British Nation and its bitter necessities in this New Era, would come; and from that, in answer to continuous sacred fidelity and valiant toil, all good whatsoever would gradually come.

Of the Continental nuisance called "Bureaucracy," — if this should alarm any reader, — I can see no risk or possibility in England. Democracy is hot enough here, fierce enough; it is perennial, universal, clearly invincible among us henceforth. No danger it should let itself be flung in chains by sham secretaries of the Pedant species, and accept their vile Age of Pinchbeck for its Golden Age! Democracy clamors, with its Newspapers, its Parliaments, and all its twenty-seven million throats, continually in this Nation forevermore. I remark, too, that the unconscious purport of all its clamors is even this, "Find us men skilled," — *make* a New Downing Street, fit for the New Era!

Of the Foreign Office, in its reformed state, we have not much to say. Abolition of imaginary work, and replacement of it by real, is on all hands understood to be very urgent there. Large needless expenditures of money, immeasurable ditto of hypocrisy and grimace; embassies, protocols, worlds of extinct traditions, empty pedantries, foul cobwebs: — but we will by no means apply the "live coal" of our witty friend; the Foreign Office will repent, and not be driven to suicide! A truer time will come for the Continental Nations too: Authorities based on truth, and on the silent or spoken Worship of Human Nobleness, will again get themselves established there; all Sham-Authorities, and consequent Real-Anarchies based on universal suffrage and the Gospel according to George

Sand, being put away; and noble action, heroic new-developments of human faculty and industry, and blessed fruit as of Paradise getting itself conquered from the waste battle-field of the chaotic elements, will once more, there as here, begin to show themselves.

When the Continental Nations have once got to the bottom of *their* Augean Stable, and begun to have real enterprises based on the eternal facts again, our Foreign Office may again have extensive concerns with them. And at all times, and even now, there will remain the question to be sincerely put and wisely answered, What essential concern *has* the British Nation with them and their enterprises? Any concern at all, except that of handsomely keeping apart from them? If so, what are the methods of best managing it? — At present, as was said, while Red Republic but clashes with foul Bureaucracy; and Nations, sunk in blind ignavia, demand a universal-suffrage Parliament to heal their wretchedness; and wild Anarchy and Phallus-Worship struggle with Sham-Kingship and extinct or galvanized Catholicism; and in the Cave of the Winds all manner of rotten waifs and wrecks are hurled against each other, — our English interest in the controversy, however huge said controversy grow, is quite trifling; we have only in a handsome manner to say to it: "Tumble and rage along, ye rotten waifs and wrecks; clash and collide as seems fittest to you; and smite each other into annihilation at your own good pleasure. In that huge conflict, dismal but unavoidable, we, thanks to our heroic ancestors, having got so far ahead of you, have now no interest at all. Our decided notion is, the dead ought to bury their dead in such a case: and so we have the honor to be, with distinguished consideration, your entirely devoted, — FLIMNAP, SEC. FOREIGN DEPARTMENT." — I really think Flimnap, till truer times come, ought to treat much of his work in this way: cautious to give offence to his neighbors; resolute not to concern himself in any of their self-annihilating operations whatsoever.

Foreign wars are sometimes unavoidable. We ourselves, in the course of natural merchandising and laudable business, have now and then got into ambiguous situations; into quarrels which needed to be settled, and without fighting would not settle. Sugar Islands, Spice Islands, Indias, Canadas, — these, by the real decree of Heaven, were ours; and nobody would or could believe it, till it was tried by cannon law, and *so* proved. Such cases happen. In former times especially, owing very much to want of intercourse and to the consequent mutual ignorance, there did occur misunderstandings: and therefrom many foreign wars, some of them by no means unnecessary. With China, or some distant country, too unintelligent of us and too unintelligible to us, there still sometimes rises necessary occasion for a war. Nevertheless wars — misunderstandings that get to the length of arguing themselves out by sword and cannon — have, in these late generations of improved intercourse, been palpably becoming less and less necessary; have in a manner become superfluous, — if we had a little wisdom, and our Foreign Office on a good footing.

Of European wars I really hardly remember any, since Oliver Cromwell's last Protestant or Liberation war with Popish antichristian Spain some two hundred years ago, to which I for my own part could have contributed my life with any heartiness, or in fact would have subscribed money itself to any considerable amount. Dutch William, a man of some heroism, did indeed get into troubles with Louis Fourteenth; and there rested still some shadow of Protestant Interest, and question of National and individual Independence, over those wide controversies; a little money and human enthusiasm was still due to Dutch William. Illustrious Chatham also, not to speak of his Manilla ransoms and the like, did one thing: assisted Fritz of Prussia, a brave man and king (almost the only sovereign *King* I have known since Cromwell's time) like to be borne down by ignoble men and sham-kings; for this let illustrious Chatham too have a little money and human enthusiasm, — a little, by no means much. But what am I to say of heaven-born Pitt the son of Chatham? England sent forth her fleets and armies; her money into every country; money as if the heaven-born Chancellor had got a Fortunatus' purse;

as if this Island had become a volcanic fountain of gold, or
new terrestrial sun capable of radiating mere guineas. The
result of all which, what was it? Elderly men can remember
the tar-barrels burnt for success and thrice-immortal victory
in the business; and yet what result had we? The French
Revolution, a Fact decreed in the Eternal Councils, could
not be put down: the result was, that heaven-born Pitt had
actually been fighting (as the old Hebrews would have said)
against the Lord, — that the Laws of Nature were stronger
than Pitt. Of whom therefore there remains chiefly his unac-
countable radiation of guineas, for the gratitude of posterity.
Thank you for nothing, — for eight hundred millions *less* than
nothing!

Our War Offices, Admiralties, and other Fighting Establishments, are forcing themselves on everybody's attention at this
time. Bull grumbles audibly: "The money you have cost me
these five-and-thirty years, during which you have stood elabo-
rately ready to fight at any moment, without at any moment
being called to fight, is surely an astonishing sum. The National Debt itself might have been half paid by that money,
which has all gone in pipeclay and blank cartridges!" Yes,
Mr. Bull, the money can be counted in hundreds of millions;
which certainly is something: — but the "strenuously organized idleness," and what mischief that amounts to, — have you
computed it? A perpetual solecism, and blasphemy (of its
sort), set to march openly among us, dressed in scarlet! Bull,
with a more and more sulky tone, demands that such solecism
be abated; that these Fighting Establishments be as it were
disbanded, and set to do some work in the Creation, since
fighting there is now none for them. This demand is irrefragably just, is growing urgent too; and yet this demand cannot be complied with, — not yet while the State grounds itself
on unrealities, and Downing Street continues what it is.

The old Romans made their soldiers work during intervals
of war. The New Downing Street too, we may predict, will
have less and less tolerance for idleness on the part of soldiers
or others. Nay the New Downing Street, I foresee, when

once it has got its "*Industrial* Regiments" organized, will make these mainly do its fighting, what fighting there is; and so save immense sums. Or indeed, all citizens of the Commonwealth, as is the right and the interest of every free man in this world, will have themselves trained to arms; each citizen ready to defend his country with his own body and soul, — he is not worthy to have a country otherwise. In a State grounded on veracities, that would be the rule. Downing Street, if it cannot bethink itself of returning to the veracities, will have to vanish altogether!

To fight with its neighbors never was, and is now less than ever, the real trade of England. For far other objects was the English People created into this world; sent down from the Eternities, to mark with its history certain spaces in the current of sublunary Time! Essential, too, that the English People should discover what its real objects are; and resolutely follow these, resolutely refusing to follow other than these. The State will have victory so far as it can do that; so far as it cannot, defeat.

In the New Downing Street, discerning what its real functions are, and with sacred abhorrence putting away from it what its functions are *not*, we can fancy changes enough in Foreign Office, War Office, Colonial Office, Home Office! Our War-soldiers *Industrial*, first of all; doing nobler than Roman works, when fighting is not wanted of them. Seventy-fours not hanging idly by their anchors in the Tagus, or off Sapienza (one of the saddest sights under the sun), but busy, every Seventy-four of them, carrying over streams of British Industrials to the immeasurable Britain that lies beyond the sea in every zone of the world. A State grounding itself on the veracities, not on the semblances and the injustices: every citizen a soldier for it. Here would be new *real* Secretaryships and Ministries, not for foreign war and diplomacy, but for domestic peace and utility. Minister of Works; Minister of Justice, — clearing his Model Prisons of their scoundrelism; shipping his scoundrels wholly abroad, under hard and just drill-sergeants (hundreds of such stand wistfully ready for you, these thirty years, in the Rag-and-Famish Club and elsewhere !) into fertile desert countries; to make railways, — one big railway (says the Major[1]) quite across America; fit to employ all the able-bodied Scoundrels and efficient Half-pay Officers in Nature !

Lastly, — or rather *firstly*, and as the preliminary of all, — would there not be a Minister of Education? Minister charged to get this English People taught a little, at his and our peril! Minister of Education; no longer dolefully embayed amid the wreck of moribund "religions," but clear ahead of all that; steering, free and piously fearless, towards *his* divine goal under the eternal stars ! — O heaven, and are these things forever impossible, then? Not a whit. To-morrow morning they might all begin to be, and go on through blessed centuries realizing themselves, if it were not that — alas, if it were not that we are most of us insincere persons, sham talking-machines and hollow windy fools! Which it is *not* "impossible" that we should cease to be, I hope?

———

Constitutions for the Colonies are now on the anvil; the discontented Colonies are all to be cured of their miseries by Constitutions. Whether that will cure their miseries, or only operate as a Godfrey's-cordial to stop their whimpering, and in the end worsen all their miseries, may be a sad doubt to us. One thing strikes a remote spectator in these Colonial questions: the singular placidity with which the British Statesman at this time, backed by M'Croudy and the British moneyed classes, is prepared to surrender whatsoever interest Britain, as foundress of those establishments, might pretend to have in the decision. "If you want to go from us, go; we by no means want you to stay: you cost us money yearly, which is scarce; desperate quantities of trouble too: why not go, if you wish it?" Such is the humor of the British Statesman, at this time. — Men clear for rebellion, "annexation" as they call it, walk openly abroad in our American Colonies; found newspapers, hold platform palaverings. From Canada there

———

[1] Major Carmichael Smith : see his Pamphlets on this subject.

comes duly by each mail a regular statistic of Annexationism: increasing fast in this quarter, diminishing in that; — Majesty's Chief Governor seeming to take it as a perfectly open question; Majesty's Chief Governor in fact seldom appearing on the scene at all, except to receive the impact of a few rotten eggs on occasion, and then duck in again to his private contemplations. And yet one would think the Majesty's Chief Governor ought to have a kind of interest in the thing? Public liberty is carried to a great length in some portions of her Majesty's dominions. But the question, "Are we to continue subjects of her Majesty, or start rebelling against her? So many as are for rebelling, hold up your hands!" Here is a public discussion of a very extraordinary nature to be going on under the nose of a Governor of Canada. How the Governor of Canada, being a British piece of flesh and blood, and not a Canadian lumber-log of mere pine and rosin, can stand it, is not very conceivable at first view. He does it, seemingly, with the stoicism of a Zeno. It is a constitutional sight like few.

And yet an instinct deeper than the Gospel of M'Croudy teaches all men that Colonies are worth something to a country! That if, under the present Colonial Office, they are a vexation to us and themselves, some other Colonial Office can and must be contrived which shall render them a blessing; and that the remedy will be to contrive such a Colonial Office or method of administration, and by no means to cut the Colonies loose. Colonies are not to be picked off the street every day; not a Colony of them but has been bought dear, well purchased by the toil and blood of those we have the honor to be sons of; and we cannot just afford to cut them away because M'Croudy finds the present management of them cost money. The present management will indeed require to be cut away; — but as for the Colonies, we purpose through Heaven's blessing to retain them a while yet! Shame on us for unworthy sons of brave fathers if we do not. Brave fathers, by valiant blood and sweat, purchased for us, from the bounty of Heaven, rich possessions in all zones; and we, wretched imbeciles, cannot do the function of administering them? And because the accounts do not stand well in the ledger, our remedy is, not to take shame to ourselves, and repent in sackcloth and ashes, and amend our beggarly imbe-cilities and insincerities in that as in other departments of our business, but to fling the business overboard, and declare the business itself to be bad? We are a hopeful set of heirs to a big fortune! It does not suit our Manton gunneries, grouse-shootings, mousings in the City; and like spirited young gentlemen we will give it up, and let the attorneys take it?

Is there no value, then, in human things, but what can write itself down in the cash-ledger? All men know, and even M'Croudy in his inarticulate heart knows, that to men and Nations there are invaluable values which cannot be sold for money at all. George Robins is great; but he is not omnipo-tent. George Robins cannot quite sell Heaven and Earth by auction, excellent though he be at the business. Nay, if M'Croudy offered his own life for *sale* in Threadneedle Street, would anybody buy it? Not I, for one. "Nobody bids: pass on to the next lot," answers Robins. And yet to M'Croudy this unsalable lot is worth all the Universe: — nay, I believe, to us also it is worth something; good monitions, as to several things, do lie in this Professor of the dismal science; and con-siderable sums even of money, not to speak of other benefit, will yet come out of his life and him, for which nobody bids! Robins has his own field where he reigns triumphant; but to that we will restrict him with iron limits; and neither Colonies nor the lives of Professors, nor other such invaluable objects shall come under his hammer.

Bad state of the ledger will demonstrate that your way of dealing with your Colonies is absurd, and urgently in want of reform; but to demonstrate that the Empire itself must be dismembered to bring the ledger straight? Oh never. Some-thing else than the ledger must intervene to do that. Why does not England repudiate Ireland, and insist on the "Repeal," instead of prohibiting it under death-penalties? Ireland has never been a paying speculation yet, nor is it like soon to be! Why does not Middlesex repudiate Surrey, and Chelsea Kensington, and each county and each parish, and in the end

each individual set up for himself and his cash-box, repudiating
the other and his, because their mutual interests have got into
an irritating course ? They must change the course, seek till
they discover a soothing one ; that is the remedy, when limbs
of the same body come to irritate one another. Because the
paltry tatter of a garment, reticulated for you out of thrums
and listings in Downing Street, ties foot and hand together in
an intolerable manner, will you relieve yourself by cutting off
the hand or the foot ? You will cut off the paltry tatter of a
pretended body-coat, I think, and fling that to the nettles ; and
imperatively require one that fits your size better.

Miserabler theory than that of money on the ledger being
the primary rule for Empires, or for any higher entity than
City owls and their mice-catching, cannot well be propounded.
And I would by no means advise Felicissimus, ill at ease on
his high-trotting and now justly impatient Sleswicker, to let
the poor horse in its desperation go in that direction for a
momentary solace. If by lumber-log Governors, by Godfrey's-
cordial Constitutions or otherwise, he contrived to cut off the
Colonies or any real right the big British Empire has in her
Colonies, both he and the British Empire will bitterly repent
it one day ! The Sleswicker, relieved in ledger for a moment,
will find that it is wounded in heart and honor forever ; and
the turning of its wild forehoofs upon Felicissimus as he lies
in the ditch combed off, is not a thing I like to think of !
Britain, whether it be known to Felicissimus or not, has other
tasks appointed her in God's Universe than the making of
money ; and woe will betide her if she forget those other
withal. Tasks, colonial and domestic, which are of an eternally
divine nature, and compared with which all money, and all
that is procurable by money, are in strict arithmetic an im-
ponderable quantity, have been assigned this Nation ; and
they also at last are coming upon her again, clamorous, abstruse,
inevitable, much to her bewilderment just now !

This poor Nation, painfully dark about said tasks and the
way of doing them, means to keep its Colonies nevertheless,
as things which somehow or other must have a value, were
it better seen into. They are portions of the general Earth,

where the children of Britain now dwell; where the gods have
so far sanctioned their endeavor, as to say that they have a
right to dwell. England will not readily admit that her own
children are worth nothing but to be flung out of doors! England looking on her Colonies can say: "Here are lands and
seas, spice-lands, corn-lands, timber-lands, overarched by zodiacs
and stars, clasped by many-sounding seas; wide spaces of the
Maker's building, fit for the cradle yet of mighty Nations and
their Sciences and Heroisms. Fertile continents still inhabited
by wild beasts are mine, into which all the distressed populations of Europe might pour themselves, and make at once
an Old World and a New World human. By the eternal fiat
of the gods, this must yet one day be; this, by all the Divine
Silences that rule this Universe, silent to fools, eloquent and
awful to the hearts of the wise, is incessantly at this moment,
and at all moments, commanded to begin to be. Unspeakable
deliverance, and new destiny of thousand-fold expanded manfulness for all men, dawns out of the Future here. To me
has fallen the godlike task of initiating all that: of me and
of my Colonies, the abstruse Future asks, Are you wise enough
for so sublime a destiny? Are you too foolish?"

That you ask advice of whatever wisdom is to be had in
the Colony, and even take note of what *un*wisdom is in it,
and record that too as an existing fact, will certainly be very
advantageous. But I suspect the kind of Parliament that
will suit a Colony is much of a secret just now! Mr. Wake-
field, a democratic man in all fibres of him, and acquainted
with Colonial Socialities as few are, judges that the franchise
for your Colonial Parliament should be decidedly select, and
advises a high money-qualification; as there is in all Colonies a fluctuating migratory mass, not destitute of money, but
very much so of loyalty, permanency, or civic availability; —
whom it is extremely advantageous *not* to consult on what
you are about attempting for the Colony or Mother Country.
This I can well believe; — and also that a "high money-
qualification," in the present sad state of human affairs, might
be some help to you in selecting; though whether even that

would quite certainly bring "wisdom," the one thing indispensable, is much a question with me. It might help, it might help! And if by any means you could (which you cannot) exclude the Fourth Estate, and indicate decisively that Wise Advice was the thing wanted here, and Parliamentary Eloquence was not the thing wanted anywhere just now, — there might really some light of experience and human foresight, and a truly valuable benefit, be found for you in such assemblies.

And there is one thing, too apt to be forgotten, which it much behooves us to remember : In the Colonies, as everywhere else in this world, the vital point is not who decides, but what is decided on! That measures tending really to the best advantage temporal and spiritual of the Colony be adopted, and strenuously put in execution; there lies the grand interest of every good citizen British and Colonial. Such measures, whosoever have originated and prescribed them, will gradually be sanctioned by all men and gods; and clamors of every kind in reference to them may safely to a great extent be neglected, as clamorous merely, and sure to be transient. Colonial Governor, Colonial Parliament, whoever or whatever does an injustice, or resolves on an *un*wisdom, he is the pernicious object, however parliamentary he be!

I have known things done, in this or the other Colony, in the most parliamentary way before now, which carried written on the brow of them sad symptoms of eternal reprobation ; not to be mistaken, had you painted an inch thick. In Montreal, for example, at this moment, standing amid the ruins of the "Elgin Marbles" (as they call the burnt walls of the Parliament House there), what rational British soul but is forced to institute the mournfulest constitutional reflection ? Some years ago the Canadas, probably not without materials for discontent, and blown upon by skilful artists, blazed up into crackling of musketry, open flame of rebellion ; a thing smacking of the gallows in all countries that pretend to have any "Government." Which flame of rebellion, had there been no loyal population to fling themselves upon it at peril of their life, might have ended we know not how. It ended speedily, in the good way; Canada got a Godfrey's-cordial Constitution; and for the moment all was varnished into some kind of feasibility again. A most poor feasibility; momentary, not lasting, nor like to be of profit to Canada! For this year, the Canadian most constitutional Parliament, such a congeries of persons as one can imagine, decides that the aforesaid flame of rebellion shall not only be forgotten as per bargain, but that — the loyal population, who flung their lives upon it and quenched it in the nick of time, shall pay the rebels their damages! Of this, I believe, on sadly conclusive evidence, there is no doubt whatever. Such, when you wash off the constitutional pigments, is the Death's-head that discloses itself. I can only say, if all the Parliaments in the world were to vote that such a thing was just, I should feel painfully constrained to answer, at my peril, "No, by the Eternal, never!" And I would recommend any British Governor who might come across that Business, there or here, to overhaul it again. What the meaning of a Governor, if he is not to overhaul and control such things, may be, I cannot conjecture. A Canadian Lumber-log may as well be made Governor. *He* might have some cast-metal hand or shoulder-crank (a thing easily contrivable in Birmingham) for signing his name to Acts of the Colonial Parliament; he would be a "native of the country" too, with popularity on that score if on no other; — he is your man, if you really want a Log Governor! —

I perceive therefore that, besides choosing Parliaments never so well, the New Colonial Office will have another thing to do: Contrive to send out a new kind of Governors to the Colonies. This will be the mainspring of the business; without this the business will not go at all. An experienced, wise and valiant British man, to represent the Imperial Interest; he, with such a speaking or silent Collective Wisdom as he can gather round him in the Colony, will evidently be the condition of all good between the Mother Country and it. If you can find such a man, your point is gained; if you cannot, lost. By him and his Collective Wisdom all manner of *true* relations, mutual interests and duties such as they do exist in fact between Mother Country and Colony, can be gradually devel-

oped into practical methods and results; and all manner of true
and noble successes, and veracities in the way of governing,
be won.   Choose well your Governor; — not from this or that
poor section of the Aristocracy, military, naval, or red-tapist;
wherever there are born kings of men, you had better seek
them out, and breed them to this work.   All sections of the
British Population will be open to you : and, on the whole,
you must succeed in finding a man *fit*.   And having found
him, I would farther recommend you to keep him some time !
It would be a great improvement to end this present *nomadism* of Colonial Governors.   Give your Governor due power ;
and let him know withal that he is wedded to his enterprise,
and having once well learned it, shall continue with it; that
it is not a Canadian Lumber-log you want there, to tumble
upon the vortexes and sign its name by a Birmingham shoulder-crank, but a Governor of Men; who, you mean, shall
fairly gird himself to his enterprise, and fail with it and
conquer with it, and as it were live and die with it : he will
have much to learn ; and having once learned it, will stay,
and turn his knowledge to account.

From this kind of Governor, were you once in the way of
finding him with moderate certainty, from him and his Collective Wisdom, all good whatsoever might be anticipated.
And surely, were the Colonies once enfranchised from red-
tape, and the poor Mother Country once enfranchised from
it; were our idle Seventy-fours all busy carrying out streams
of British Industrials, and those Scoundrel Regiments all
working, under divine drill-sergeants, at the grand Atlantic
and Pacific Junction Railway, — poor Britain and her poor
Colonies might find that they *had* true relations to each
other : that the Imperial *Mother* and her constitutionally obedient Daughters were not a red-tape fiction, provoking bitter
mockery as at present, but a blessed God's-Fact destined to
fill half the world with its fruits one day !

But undoubtedly our grand primary concern is the Home
Office, and its Irish Giant named of Despair.   When the

Home Office begins dealing with this Irish Giant, which it is
vitally urgent for us the Home Office should straightway do,
it will find its duties enlarged to a most unexpected extent,
and, as it were, altered from top to bottom. A changed time
now when the question is, What to do with three millions of
paupers (come upon you for food, since you have no work for
them) increasing at a frightful rate per day ? Home Office,
Parliament, King, Constitution will find that they have now,
if they will continue in this world long, got a quite immense
new question and continually recurring set of questions. That
huge question of the Irish Giant, with his Scotch and English
Giant-Progeny advancing open-mouthed upon us, will, as I
calculate, change from top to bottom not the Home Office
only but all manner of Offices and Institutions whatsoever,
and gradually the structure of Society itself. I perceive, it
will make us a new Society, if we are to continue a Society
at all. For the alternative is not, Stay where we are, or
change ? But Change, with new wise effort fit for the new
time, to true and wider nobler National Life; or Change,
by indolent folding of the arms, as we are now doing, in horrible anarchies and convulsions to Dissolution, to National
Death, or Suspended-animation ? Suspended-animation itself
is a frightful possibility for Britain: this Anarchy whither
all Europe has preceded us, where all Europe is now weltering, would suit us as ill as any ! The question for the British Nation is : Can we work our course pacifically, on firm
land, into the New Era; or must it be, for us too, as for all
the others, through black abysses of Anarchy, hardly escaping, if we do with all our struggles escape, the jaws of eternal
Death ?

For Pauperism, though it now absorbs its high figure of
millions annually, is by no means a question of money only,
but of infinitely higher and greater than all conceivable
money. If our Chancellor of the Exchequer had a Fortunatus' purse, and miraculous sacks of Indian meal that would
stand scooping from forever, — I say, even on these terms Pauperism could not be endured ; and it would vitally concern all
British Citizens to abate Pauperism, and never rest till they

had ended it again. Pauperism is the general leakage through every joint of the ship that it is rotten. Were all men doing their duty, or even seriously trying to do it, there would be no Pauper. Were the pretended Captains of the world at all in the habit of commanding; were the pretended Teachers of the world at all in the habit of teaching, — of admonishing said Captains among others, and with sacred zeal apprising them to what *place* such neglect was leading, — how could Pauperism exist ? Pauperism would lie far over the horizon; we should be lamenting and denouncing quite inferior sins of men, which were only tending afar off towards Pauperism. A true Captaincy; a true Teachership, either making all men and Captains know and devoutly recognize the eternal law of things, or else breaking its own heart, and going about with sackcloth round its loins, in testimony of continual sorrow and protest, and prophecy of God's vengeance upon such a course of things : either of these divine equipments would have saved us ; and it is because we have neither of them that we are come to such a pass !

We may depend upon it, where there is a Pauper, there is a sin; to make one Pauper there go many sins. Pauperism is our Social Sin grown manifest ; developed from the state of a spiritual ignobleness, a practical impropriety and base oblivion of duty, to an affair of the ledger. Here is not now an unheeded sin against God ; here is a concrete ugly hulk of Beggary demanding that you should buy Indian meal for it. Men of reflection have long looked with a horror for which there was no response in the idle public, upon Pauperism ; but the quantity of meal it demands has now awakened men of no reflection to consider it. Pauperism is the poisonous dripping from all the sins, and putrid unveracities and god-forgetting greedinesses and devil-serving cants and jesuitisms, that exist among us. Not one idle Sham lounging about Creation upon false pretences, upon means which he has not earned, upon theories which he does not practise, but yields his share of Pauperism somewhere or other. His sham-work oozes down ; finds at last its issue as human Pauperism, — in a human being that by those false pretences cannot live. The Idle Workhouse, now about to burst of overfilling, what is it but the scandalous poison-tank of drainage from the universal Stygian quagmire of our affairs? Workhouse Paupers; immortal sons of Adam rotted into that scandalous condition, subterslavish, demanding that you would make slaves of them as an unattainable blessing! My friends, I perceive the quagmire must be drained, or we cannot live. And farther, I perceive, this of Pauperism is the corner where we must *begin,* — the levels all pointing thitherward, the possibilities lying all clearly there. On that Problem we shall find that innumerable things, that all things whatsoever hang. By courageous steadfast persistence in that, I can foresee Society itself regenerated. In the course of long strenuous centuries, I can see the State become what it is actually bound to be, the keystone of a most real " Organization of Labor," — and on this Earth a world of some veracity, and some heroism, once more worth living in!

The State in all European countries, and in England first of all, as I hope, will discover that its functions are now, and have long been, very wide of what the State in old pedant Downing Streets has aimed at; that the State is, for the present, not a reality but in great part a dramatic speciosity, expending its strength in practices and objects fallen many of them quite obsolete; that it must come a little nearer the true aim again, or it cannot continue in this world. The "Champion of England" cased in iron or tin, and "able to mount his horse with little assistance," — this Champion and the thousand-fold cousinry of Phantasms he has, nearly all dead now but still walking as ghosts, must positively take himself away : who can endure him, and his solemn trumpetings and obsolete gesticulations, in a Time that is full of deadly realities, coming open-mouthed upon us? At Drury Lane let him play his part, him and his thousand-fold cousinry ; and welcome, so long as any public will pay a shilling to see him : but on the solid earth, under the extremely earnest stars, we dare not palter with him, or accept his tomfooleries any more. Ridiculous they seem to some ; horrible they seem to me : all lies, if one look whence they come and whither they go, are horrible.

Alas, it will be found, I doubt, that in England more than in any country, our Public Life and our Private, our State and our Religion, and all that we do and speak (and the most even of what we *think*), is a tissue of half-truths and whole-lies ; of hypocrisies, conventionalisms, worn-out traditionary rags and cobwebs ; such a life-garment of beggarly incredible and uncredited falsities as no honest souls of Adam's Posterity were ever enveloped in before.   And we walk about in it with a stately gesture, as if it were some priestly stole or imperial mantle ; not the foulest beggar's gabardine that ever was. " No Englishman dare believe the truth," says one : " he stands, for these two hundred years, enveloped in lies of every kind ; from nadir to zenith an ocean of traditionary cant surrounds him as his life-element.   He really thinks the truth dangerous.   Poor wretch, you see him everywhere endeavoring to temper the truth by taking the falsity along with it, and welding them together ; this he calls ' safe course,' ' moderate course,' and other fine names ; there, balanced between God and the Devil, he thinks he *can* serve two masters, and that things will go well with him."

In the cotton-spinning and similar departments our English friend knows well that truth or God will have nothing to do with the Devil or falsehood, but will ravel all the web to pieces if you introduce the Devil or Non-veracity in any form into it : in this department, therefore, our English friend avoids falsehood.   But in the religious, political, social, moral, and all other spiritual departments he freely introduces falsehood, nothing doubting ; and has long done so, with a profuseness not elsewhere met with in the world.   The unhappy creature, does he not know, then, that every lie is accursed, and the parent of mere curses ?   That he must *think* the truth ; much more speak it ?   That, above all things, by the oldest law of Heaven and Earth which no man violates with impunity, he must not and shall not wag the tongue of him except to utter his thought ?   That there is not a grin or beautiful acceptable grimace he can execute upon his poor countenance, but is either an express veracity, the image of what passes within him; or else is a bit of Devil-worship which he and the rest of us will have to pay for yet? Alas, the grins he executes upon his poor *mind* (which is all tortured into St. Vitus dances, and ghastly merry-andrewisms, by the practice) are the most extraordinary this sun ever saw.

We have Puseyisms, black-and-white surplice controversies : — do not, officially and otherwise, the select of the longest heads in England sit with intense application and iron gravity, in open forum, judging of "prevenient grace"? Not a head of them suspects that it can be improper so to sit, or of the nature of treason against the Power who gave an Intellect to man; — that it can be other than the duty of a good citizen to use his god-given intellect in investigating prevenient grace, supervenient moonshine, or the color of the Bishop's nightmare, if that happened to turn up. I consider them far ahead of Cicero's Roman Augurs with their chicken-bowels : "Behold these divine chicken-bowels, O Senate and Roman People; the midriff has fallen eastward !" solemnly intimates one Augur. "By Proserpina and the triple Hecate !" exclaims the other, "I say the midriff has fallen to the west !" And they look at one another with the seriousness of men prepared to die in their opinion, — the authentic seriousness of men betting at Tattersall's, or about to receive judgment in Chancery. There is in the Englishman something great, beyond all Roman greatness, in whatever line you meet him; even as a Latter-Day Augur he seeks his fellow ! — Poor devil, I believe it is his intense love of peace, and hatred of breeding discussions which lead no-whither, that has led him into this sad practice of amalgamating true and false.

He has been at it these two hundred years; and has now carried it to a terrible length. He could n't follow Oliver Cromwell in the Puritan path heavenward, so steep was it, and beset with thorns, — and becoming uncertain withal. He much preferred, at that juncture, to go heavenward with his Charles Second and merry Nell Gwynns, and old decent formularies and good respectable aristocratic company, for escort; sore he tried, by glorious restorations, glorious revolutions and so forth, to perfect this desirable amalgam; hoped always it might be possible; — is only just now, if even now, beginning to give up the hope; and to see with wide-eyed horror that it is not at Heaven he is arriving, but at the Stygian marshes, with their thirty thousand Needlewomen, cannibal Connaughts, rivers of lamentation, continual wail of infants, and the yellow-burning gleam of a Hell-on-Earth! — Bull, my friend, you must strip that astonishing pontiff-stole, imperial mantle, or whatever you imagine it to be, which I discern to be a garment of curses, and poisoned Nessus'-shirt now at last about to take fire upon you; you must strip that off your poor body, my friend; and, were it only in a soul's suit of Utilitarian buff, and such belief as that a big loaf is better than a small one, come forth into contact with your world, under *true* professions again, and not false. You wretched man, you ought to weep for half a century on discovering what lies you have believed, and what every lie leads to and proceeds from. O my friend, no honest fellow in this Planet was ever so served by his cooks before; or has eaten such quantities and qualities of dirt as you have been made to do, for these two centuries past. Arise, my horribly maltreated yet still beloved Bull; steep yourself in running water for a long while, my friend; and begin forthwith in every conceivable direction, physical and spiritual, the long-expected *Scavenger Age.*

Many doctors have you had, my poor friend; but I perceive it is the Water-Cure alone that will help you : a complete course of *scavengerism* is the thing you need! A new and veritable heart-divorce of England from the Babylonish woman, who is Jesuitism and Unveracity, and dwells not at Rome now, but under your own nose and everywhere; whom, and her foul worship of Phantasms and Devils, poor England *had* once divorced, with a divine heroism not forgotten yet, and well worth remembering now : a clearing-out of Church and State from the unblessed host of Phantasms which have too long nestled thick there, under those astonishing "Defenders of the Faith," — Defenders of the Hypocrisies, the spiritual Vampires and obscene Nightmares, under which England lies in syncope ; — this is what you need ; and if you cannot get it, you must die, my poor friend !

Like people, like priest. Priest, King, Home Office, all manner of establishments and offices among a people bear a striking resemblance to the people itself. It is because Bull has been eating so much dirt that his Home Offices have got into such a shockingly dirty condition, — the old pavements of them quite gone out of sight and out of memory, and nothing but mountains of long-accumulated dung in which the poor cattle are sprawling and tumbling. Had his own life been pure, had his own daily conduct been grounding itself on the clear pavements or actual beliefs and veracities, would he have let his Home Offices come to such a pass ? Not in Downing Street only, but in all other thoroughfares and arenas and spiritual or physical departments of his existence, running water and Herculean scavengerism have become indispensable, unless the poor man is to choke in his own exuviæ, and die the sorrowfulest death.

If the State could once get back to the real sight of its essential function, and with religious resolution begin doing that, and putting away its multifarious imaginary functions, and indignantly casting out these as mere dung and insalubrious horror and abomination (which they are), what a promise of reform were there ! The British Home Office, surely this and its kindred Offices exist, if they will think of it, that life and work may continue possible, and may not become impossible, for British men. If honorable existence, or existence on human terms at all, have become impossible for millions of British men, how can the Home Office or any other Office long exist ? With thirty thousand Needlewomen, a Connaught fallen into potential cannibalism, and the Idle Workhouse everywhere bursting, and declaring itself an *in*humanity and stupid ruinous brutality not much longer to be tolerated among rational human creatures, it is time the State were bethinking itself.

So soon as the State attacks that tremendous cloaca of Pauperism, which will choke the world if it be not attacked, the

State will find its real functions very different indeed from what it had long supposed them! The State is a reality, and not a dramaturgy; it exists here to render existence possible, existence desirable and noble, for the State's subjects. The State, as it gets into the track of its real work, will find that same expand into whole continents of new unexpected, most blessed activity; as its dramatic functions, declared superfluous, more and more fall inert, and go rushing like huge torrents of extinct exuviæ, dung and rubbish, down to the Abyss forever. O Heaven, to see a State that knew a little why it was there, and on what ground, in this Year 1850, it could pretend to exist, in so extremely earnest a world as ours is growing! The British State, if it will be the crown and keystone of our British Social Existence, must get to recognize, with a veracity very long unknown to it, what the real objects and indispensable necessities of our Social Existence are. Good Heavens, it is not prevenient grace, or the color of the Bishop's nightmare, that is pinching us; it is the impossibility to get along any farther for mountains of accumulated dung and falsity and horror; the total closing-up of noble aims from every man, — of any aim at all, from many men, except that of rotting out in Idle Workhouses an existence below that of beasts!

Suppose the State to have fairly started its "Industrial Regiments of the New Era," which alas, are yet only beginning to be talked of, — what continents of new real work opened out, for the Home and all other Public Offices among us! Suppose the Home Office looking out, as for life and salvation, for proper men to command these "Regiments." Suppose the announcement were practically made to all British souls that the want of wants, more indispensable than any jewel in the crown, was that of men *able to command men* in ways of industrial and moral well-doing; that the State would give its very life for such men; that such men *were* the State; that the quantity of them to be found in England lamentably small at present, was the exact measure of England's worth, — what a new dawn of everlasting day for all British souls! Noble British soul, to whom the gods have given faculty and heroism, what men call genius, here at last is a career for thee. It will not be needful now to swear fealty to the Incredible, and traitorously cramp thyself into a cowardly canting play-actor in God's Universe; or, solemnly forswearing that, into a mutinous rebel and waste bandit in thy generation: here is an aim that is clear and credible, a course fit for a man. No need to become a tormenting and self-tormenting mutineer, banded with rebellious souls, if thou wouldst live; no need to rot in suicidal idleness; or take to platform preaching, and writing in Radical Newspapers, to pull asunder the great Falsity in which thou and all of us are choking. The great Falsity, behold it has become, in the very heart of it, a great Truth of Truths; and invites thee and all brave men to co-operate with it in transforming all the body and the joints into the noble likeness of that heart! Thrice-blessed change. The State aims, once more, with a true aim; and has loadstars in the eternal Heaven. Struggle faithfully for it; noble is *this* struggle; thou too, according to thy faculty, shalt reap in due time, if thou faint not. Thou shalt have a wise command of men, thou shalt be wisely commanded by men, — the summary of all blessedness for a social creature here below. The sore struggle, never to be relaxed, and not forgiven to any son of man, is once more a noble one; glory to the Highest, it is now once more a true and noble one, wherein a man can afford to die! Our path is now again Heavenward. Forward, with steady pace, with drawn weapons, and unconquerable hearts, in the name of God that made us all! —

Wise obedience and wise command, I foresee that the regimenting of Pauper Banditti into Soldiers of Industry is but the beginning of this blessed process, which will extend to the topmost heights of our Society; and, in the course of generations, make us all once more a Governed Commonwealth, and *Civitas Dei*, if it please God! Waste-land Industrials succeeding, other kinds of Industry, as cloth-making, shoe-making, plough-making, spade-making, house-building, — in the end, all kinds of Industry whatsoever, will be found capable of regimenting. Mill-operatives, all manner of free operatives, as yet unregimented, nomadic under private masters, they, seeing such example and its blessedness, will say: "Masters, you must regiment us a little; make our interests with you permanent a little, instead of temporary and nomadic; we will enlist with the State otherwise!" This will go on, on the one hand, while the State-operation goes on, on the other: thus will all Masters of Workmen, private Captains of Industry, be forced to incessantly co-operate with the State and its public Captains; they regimenting in their way, the State in its way, with ever-widening field; till their fields *meet* (so to speak) and coalesce, and there be no unregimented worker, or such only as are fit to remain unregimented, any more. — O my friends, I clearly perceive this horrible cloaca of Pauperism, wearing nearly bottomless now, is the point where we must begin. Here, in this plainly unendurable portion of the general quagmire, the lowest point of all, and hateful even to M'Croudy, must our main drain begin: steadily prosecuting that, tearing that along with Herculean labor and divine fidelity, we shall gradually drain the entire Stygian swamp, and make it all once more a fruitful field!

For the State, I perceive, looking out with right sacred earnestness for persons able to command, will straightway also come upon the question: "What kind of schools and seminaries, and teaching and also preaching establishments have I, for the training of young souls to take command and to yield obedience? Wise command, wise obedience: the capability of these two is the net measure of culture, and human virtue, in every man; all good lies in the possession of these two capabilities; all evil, wretchedness and ill-success in the want of these. He is a good man that can command and obey; he that cannot is a bad. If my teachers and my preachers, with their seminaries, high schools and cathedrals, do train men to these gifts, the thing they are teaching and preaching must be true; if they do not, not true!"

The State, once brought to its veracities by the thumb-screw in this manner, what *will* it think of these same seminaries and cathedrals! I foresee that our Etons and Oxfords with their nonsense-verses, college-logics, and broken crumbs of mere *speech*, — which is not even English or Teutonic speech, but old Grecian and Italian speech, dead and buried and much lying out of our way these two thousand years last past, — will be found a most astonishing seminary for the training of young English souls to take command in human Industries, and act a valiant part under the sun ! The State does not want vocables, but manly wisdoms and virtues : the State, does it want parliamentary orators, first of all, and men capable of writing books ? What a rag-fair of extinct monkeries, high-piled here in the very shrine of our existence, fit to smite the generations with atrophy and beggarly paralysis, — as we see it do ! The Minister of Education will not want for work, I think, in the New Downing Street !

How it will go with Souls'-Overseers, and what the *new* kind will be, we do not prophesy just now. Clear it is, however, that the last finish of the State's efforts, in this operation of regimenting, will be to get the *true* Souls'-Overseers set over men's souls, to regiment, as the consummate flower of all, and constitute into some Sacred Corporation, bearing authority and dignity in their generation, the Chosen of the Wise, of the Spiritual and Devout-minded, the Reverent who deserve rever-ence, who are as the Salt of the Earth ; — that not till this is done can the State consider its edifice to have reached the first story, to be safe for a moment, to be other than an arch without the keystones, and supported hitherto on mere wood. How will this be done ? Ask not ; let the second or the third generation after this begin to ask ! Alas, wise men do exist, born duly into the world in every current generation ; but the getting of *them* regimented is the highest pitch of human Polity, and the feat of all feats in political engineering : — im-possible for us, in this poor age, as the building of St. Paul's would be for Canadian Beavers, acquainted only with the architecture of fish-dams, and with no trowel but their tail.

Literature, the strange entity so called, — that indeed is here. If Literature continue to be the haven of expatriated spiritualisms, and have its Johnsons, Goethes and *true* Arch-bishops of the World, to show for itself as heretofore, there may be hope in Literature. If Literature dwindle, as is prob-able, into mere merry-andrewism, windy twaddle, and feats of spiritual legerdemain, analogous to rope-dancing, opera-dancing, and street-fiddling with a hat carried round for halfpence or for guineas, there will be no hope in Literature. What if our next set of Souls'-Overseers were to be *silent* ones very mainly? — Alas, alas, why gaze into the blessed continents and delectable mountains of a Future based on *truth*, while as yet we struggle far down, nigh suffocated in a slough of lies, uncertain whether or how we shall be able to climb at all!

Who will begin the long steep journey with us; who of living statesmen will snatch the standard, and say, like a hero on the forlorn-hope for his country, Forward! Or is there none; no one that can and dare? And our lot too, then, is Anarchy by barricade or ballot-box, and Social Death? — We will not think so.

Whether Sir Robert Peel will undertake the Reform of Downing Street for us, or any Ministry or Reform farther, is not known. He, they say, is getting old, does himself recoil from it, and shudder at it; which is possible enough. The clubs and coteries appear to have settled that he surely will not; that this melancholy wriggling seesaw of red-tape Trojans and Protectionist Greeks must continue its course till — what *can* happen, my friends, if this go on continuing?

And yet, perhaps, England has by no means so settled it. Quit the clubs and coteries, you do not hear two rational men speak long together upon politics, without pointing their inquiries towards this man. A Minister that will attack the Augeas Stable of Downing Street, and begin producing a real Management, no longer an imaginary one, of our affairs; *he*, or else in few years Chartist Parliament and the Deluge come: that seems the alternative. As I read the omens, there was no man in my time more authentically called to a post of difficulty, of danger, and of honor than this man. The enterprise is ready for him, if he is ready for it. He has but to lift his finger in this enterprise, and whatsoever is wise and manful in England will rally round him. If the faculty and heart for it be in him, he, strangely and almost tragically if we look upon

his history, is to have leave to try it; he now, at the eleventh
hour, has the opportunity for such a feat in reform as has not,
in these late generations, been attempted by all our reformers
put together.

As for Protectionist jargon, who in these earnest days would
occupy many moments of his time with that? "A Costermonger in this street," says Crabbe, "finding lately that his
rope of onions, which he hoped would have brought a shilling,
was to go for only sevenpence henceforth, burst forth into
lamentation, execration and the most pathetic tears. Throw-
ing up the window, I perceived the other costermongers preparing impatiently to pack this one out of their company as a
disgrace to it, if he would not hold his peace and take the
market-rate for his onions. I looked better at this Costermonger. To my astonished imagination, a star-and-garter
dawned upon the dim figure of the man; and I perceived that
here was no Costermonger to be expelled with ignominy, but
a sublime goddess-born Ducal Individual, whom I forbear to
name at this moment! What an omen; — nay to my astonished imagination, there dawned still fataler omens. Surely,
of all human trades ever heard of, the trade of Owning Land in
England ought *not* to bully us for drink-money just now!"

"Hansard's Debates," continues Crabbe farther on, "present
many inconsistencies of speech; lamentable unveracities uttered in Parliament, by one and indeed by all; in which sad
list Sir Robert Peel stands for his share among others. Unveracities not a few were spoken in Parliament: in fact, to one
with a sense of what is called God's truth, it seemed all one
unveracity, a talking from the teeth outward, not as the con-
victions but as the expediencies and inward astucities directed;
and, in the sense of God's *truth*, I have heard no true word
uttered in Parliament at all. Most lamentable unveracities
continually *spoken* in Parliament, by almost every one that
had to open his mouth there. But the largest veracity ever
done in Parliament in our time, as we all know, was of this
man's doing; — and that, you will find, is a very considerable
item in the calculation!"

Yes, and I believe England in her dumb way remembers that

too. And "the Traitor Peel" can very well afford to let innumerable Ducal Costermongers, parliamentary Adventurers, and lineal representatives of the Impenitent Thief, say all their say about him, and do all their do. With a virtual England at his back, and an actual eternal sky above him, there is not much in the total net-amount of that. When the master of the horse rides abroad, many dogs in the village bark; but he pursues his journey all the same.

———◆———

[May 1, 1850.]

No. V.   STUMP–ORATOR.

It lies deep in our habits, confirmed by all manner of educational and other arrangements for several centuries back, to consider human talent as best of all evincing itself by the faculty of eloquent speech. Our earliest schoolmasters teach us, as the one gift of culture they have, the art of spelling and pronouncing, the rules of correct speech; rhetorics, logics follow, sublime mysteries of grammar, whereby we may not only speak but write. And onward to the last of our schoolmasters in the highest university, it is still intrinsically grammar, under various figures grammar. To speak in various languages, on various things, but on all of them to speak, and appropriately deliver ourselves by tongue or pen, — this is the sublime goal towards which all manner of beneficent preceptors and learned professors, from the lowest hornbook upwards, are continually urging and guiding us. Preceptor or professor, looking over his miraculous seedplot, seminary as he well calls it, or crop of young human souls, watches with attentive view one organ of his delightful little seedlings growing to be men, — the tongue. He hopes we shall all get to speak yet, if it please Heaven. "Some of you shall be book-writers, eloquent review-writers, and astonish mankind, my young friends: others in white neckcloths shall do sermons by Blair and Lindley Murray, nay by Jeremy Taylor

and judicious Hooker, and be priests to guide men heavenward by skilfully brandished handkerchief and the torch of
rhetoric.   For others there is Parliament and the election
beer-barrel, and a course that leads men very high indeed ;
these shall shake the senate-house, the Morning Newspapers,
shake the very spheres, and by dexterous wagging of the tongue
disenthrall mankind, and lead our afflicted country and us on
the way we are to go.   The way if not where noble deeds are
done, yet where noble words are spoken, — leading us if not
to the real Home of the Gods, at least to something which shall
more or less deceptively resemble it ! "

So fares it with the son of Adam, in these bewildered epochs ;
so, from the first opening of his eyes in this world, to his last
closing of them, and departure hence.   Speak, speak, oh speak ;
— if thou have any faculty, speak it, or thou diest and it is
no faculty !   So in universities, and all manner of dames' and
other schools, of the very highest class as of the very lowest ;
and Society at large, when we enter there, confirms with all
its brilliant review-articles, successful publications, intellectual tea-circles, literary gazettes, parliamentary eloquences,
the grand lesson we had.   Other lesson in fact we have none,
in these times.   If there be a human talent, let it get into the
tongue, and make melody with that organ.   The talent that can
say nothing for itself, what is it ?   Nothing ; or a thing that
can do mere drudgeries, and at best make money by railways.

All this is deep-rooted in our habits, in our social, educational and other arrangements ; and all this, when we look at
it impartially, is astonishing.   Directly in the teeth of all this
it may be asserted that speaking is by no means the chief faculty a human being can attain to ; that his excellence therein
is by no means the best test of his general human excellence,
or availability in this world ; nay that, unless we look well, it
is liable to become the very worst test ever devised for said
availability.   The matter extends very far, down to the very
roots of the world, whither the British reader cannot conve-
niently follow me just now ; but I will venture to assert the
three following things, and invite him to consider well what
truth he can gradually find in them : —

First, that excellent speech, even speech *really* excellent, is not, and never was, the chief test of human faculty, or the measure of a man's ability, for any true function whatsoever; on the contrary, that excellent *silence* needed always to accompany excellent speech, and was and is a much rarer and more difficult gift.

Secondly, that really excellent speech — which I, being possessed of the Hebrew Bible or Book, as well as of other books in my own and foreign languages, and having occasionally heard a wise man's word among the crowd of unwise, do almost unspeakably esteem, as a human gift — is terribly apt to get confounded with its counterfeit, sham-excellent speech! And furthermore, that if really excellent human speech is among the best of human things, then sham-excellent ditto deserves to be ranked with the very worst.   False speech, — capable of becoming, as some one has said, the falsest and basest of all human things : — put the case, one were listening to *that* as to the truest and noblest!   Which, little as we are conscious of it, I take to be the sad lot of many excellent souls among us just now.   So many as admire parliamentary eloquence, divine popular literature, and such like, are dreadfully liable to it just now : and whole nations and generations seem as if getting themselves *asphyxiaed*, constitutionally into their last sleep, by means of it just now !

For alas, much as we worship speech on all hands, here is a *third* assertion which a man may venture to make, and invite considerate men to reflect upon : That in these times, and for several generations back, there has been, strictly considered, no really excellent speech at all, but sham-excellent merely ; that is to say, false or quasi-false speech getting itself admired and worshipped, instead of detested and suppressed.   A truly alarming predicament; and not the less so if we find it a quite pleasant one for the time being, and welcome the advent of *asphyxia*, as we would that of comfortable natural sleep ; — as, in so many senses, we are doing !   Surly judges there have been who did not much admire the " Bible of Modern Literature," or anything you could distil from it, in contrast with the ancient Bibles; and found that in the matter of speaking, our far best excellence, where that could be obtained, was excellent silence, which means endurance and exertion, and good *work* with lips closed; and that our tolerablest speech was of the nature of honest commonplace introduced where indispensable, which only set up for being brief and true, and could not be mistaken for excellent.

These are hard sayings for many a British reader, unconscious of any damage, nay joyfully conscious to himself of much profit, from that side of his possessions. Surely on this side, if on no other, matters stood not ill with him? The ingenuous arts had softened his manners; the parliamentary eloquences supplied him with a succedaneum for government, the popular literatures with the finer sensibilities of the heart: surely on this *wind*ward side of things the British reader was not ill off? — Unhappy British reader!

In fact, the spiritual detriment we unconsciously suffer, in every province of our affairs, from this our prostrate respect to power of speech is incalculable. For indeed it is the natural consummation of an epoch such as ours. Given a general insincerity of mind for several generations, you will certainly find the Talker established in the place of honor; and the Doer, hidden in the obscure crowd, with activity lamed, or working sorrowfully forward on paths unworthy of him. All men are devoutly prostrate, worshipping the eloquent talker; and no man knows what a scandalous idol he is. Out of whom in the mildest manner, like comfortable natural rest, comes mere asphyxia and death everlasting! Probably there is not in Nature a more distracted phantasm than your commonplace eloquent speaker, as he is found on platforms, in parliaments, on Kentucky stumps, at tavern-dinners, in windy, empty, insincere times like ours. The "excellent Stump-Orator," as our admiring Yankee friends define him, he who in any occurrent set of circumstances can start forth, mount upon his "stump," his rostrum, tribune, place in parliament, or other ready elevation, and pour forth from him his appropriate "excellent speech," his interpretation of the said circumstances, in such manner as poor windy mortals round him shall cry bravo to, — he is not an artist I can much admire, as matters go! Alas, he is in general merely the windiest mortal of them all; and is admired for being so, into the bargain. Not a windy blockhead there who kept silent but is better off than this excellent stump-orator. Better off, for a great many reasons; for this reason, were there no other: the silent one is *not* admired; the silent suspects, perhaps partly admits, that he is a kind of blockhead, from which salutary self-knowledge the excellent stump-orator is debarred. A mouthpiece of Chaos to poor benighted mortals that lend ear to him as to a voice from Cosmos, this excellent stump-orator fills me with amazement. Not empty these musical wind-utterances of his; they are big with prophecy; they announce, too audibly to me, that the end of many things is drawing nigh!

Let the British reader consider it a little; he too is not a little interested in it. Nay he, and the European reader in general, but he chiefly in these days, will require to consider it a great deal, — and to take important steps in consequence by and by, if I mistake not. And in the mean while, sunk as he himself is in that bad element, and like a jaundiced man struggling to discriminate yellow colors, — he will have to meditate long before he in any measure get the immense meanings of the thing brought home to him; and discern, with astonishment, alarm, and almost terror and despair, towards what fatal issues, in our Collective Wisdom and elsewhere, this notion of talent meaning eloquent speech, so obstinately entertained this long while, has been leading us! Whosoever shall look well into origins and issues, will find this of eloquence and the part it now plays in our affairs, to be one of the gravest phenomena; and the excellent stump-orator of these days to be not only a ridiculous but still more a highly tragical personage. While the many listen to him, the few are used to pass rapidly, with some gust of scornful laughter, some growl of impatient malediction; but he deserves from this latter class a much more serious attention.

In the old Ages, when Universities and Schools were first instituted, this function of the schoolmaster, to teach mere speaking, was the natural one. In those healthy times, guided by silent instincts and the monition of Nature, men had from of old been used to teach themselves what it was essential to learn, by the one sure method of learning anything, practical apprenticeship to it. This was the rule for all classes; as it now is the rule, unluckily, for only one class. The Working Man as yet sought only to know his craft; and educated himself sufficiently by ploughing and hammering, under the conditions given, and in fit relation to the persons given : a course of education, then as now and ever, really opulent in manful culture and instruction to him; teaching him many solid virtues, and most indubitably useful knowledges; developing in him valuable faculties not a few both to do and to endure, — among which the faculty of elaborate grammatical utterance, seeing he had so little of extraordinary to utter, or to learn from spoken or written utterances, was not bargained for; the grammar of Nature, which he learned from his mother, being still amply sufficient for him. This was, as it still is, the grand education of the Working Man.

As for the Priest, though his trade was clearly of a reading and speaking nature, he knew also in those veracious times that grammar, if needful, was by no means the one thing needful, or the chief thing. By far the chief thing needful, and indeed the one thing then as now, was, That there should be in him the feeling and the practice of reverence to God and to men; that in his life's core there should dwell, spoken or silent, a ray of pious wisdom fit for illuminating dark human destinies; — not so much that he should possess the art of speech, as that he should have something to speak ! And for that latter requisite the Priest also trained himself by apprenticeship, by actual attempt to practise, by manifold long-continued trial, of a devout and painful nature, such as his superiors prescribed to him. This, when once judged satisfactory, procured him ordination; and his grammar-learning, in the good times of priesthood, was very much of a parergon with him, as indeed in all times it is intrinsically quite insignificant in comparison.

The young Noble again, for whom grammar schoolmasters

were first hired and high seminaries founded, he too without these, or above and over these, had from immemorial time been used to learn his business by apprenticeship. The young Noble, before the schoolmaster as after him, went apprentice to some elder noble; entered himself as page with some distinguished earl or duke; and here, serving upwards from step to step, under wise monition, learned his chivalries, his practice of arms and of courtesies, his baronial duties and manners, and what it would beseem him to do and to be in the world, — by practical attempt of his own, and example of one whose life was a daily concrete pattern for him. To such a one, already filled with intellectual substance, and possessing what we may call the practical gold-bullion of human culture, it was an obvious improvement that he should be taught to speak it out of him on occasion; that he should carry a spiritual bank-note producible on demand for what of "gold-bullion" he had, not so negotiable otherwise, stored in the cellars of his mind. A man, with wisdom, insight and heroic worth already acquired for him, naturally demanded of the schoolmaster this one new faculty, the faculty of uttering in fit words what he had. A valuable superaddition of faculty : — and yet we are to remember it was scarcely a new faculty; it was but the tangible sign of what other faculties the man had in the silent state: and many a rugged inarticulate chief of men, I can believe, was most enviably "educated," who had not a Book on his premises; whose signature, a true sign-*manual*, was the stamp of his iron hand duly inked and clapt upon the parchment; and whose speech in Parliament, like the growl of lions, did indeed convey his meaning, but would have torn Lindley Murray's nerves to pieces! To such a one the schoolmaster adjusted himself very naturally in that manner; as a man wanted for teaching grammatical utterance; the thing to utter being already there. The thing to utter, here was the grand point! And perhaps this is the reason why among earnest nations, as among the Romans for example, the craft of the schoolmaster was held in little regard; for indeed as mere teacher of grammar, of ciphering on the abacus and such like, how did he differ much from the dancing-master or fencing-master, or deserve much regard? — Such was the rule in the ancient healthy times.

Can it be doubtful that this is still the rule of human education; that the human creature needs first of all to be educated not that he may speak, but that he may have something weighty and valuable to say! If speech is the bank-note for an inward capital of culture, of insight and noble human worth, then speech is precious, and the art of speech shall be honored. But if there *is* no inward capital; if speech represent no real culture of the mind, but an imaginary culture; no bullion, but the fatal and now almost hopeless deficit of such? Alas, alas, said bank-note is then a *forged* one; passing freely current in the market; but bringing damages to the receiver, to the payer, and to all the world, which are in sad truth infallible, and of amount incalculable. Few think of it at present; but the truth remains forever so. In parliaments and other loud assemblages, your eloquent talk, *dis*united from Nature and her facts, is taken as wisdom and the correct image of said facts: but Nature well knows what it is, Nature will not have it as such, and will reject your forged note one day, with huge costs. The foolish traders in the market pass it freely, nothing doubting, and rejoice in the dexterous execution of the piece : and so it circulates from hand to hand, and from class to class; gravitating ever downwards towards the *practical* class; till at last it reaches some poor *working* hand, who can pass it no farther, but must take it to the bank to get bread with it, and there the answer is, "Unhappy caitiff, this note is forged. It does not mean performance and reality, in parliaments and elsewhere, for thy behoof; it means fallacious semblance of performance; and thou, poor dupe, art thrown into the stocks on offering it here!"

Alas, alas, looking abroad over Irish difficulties, Mosaic sweating-establishments, French barricades, and an anarchic Europe, is it not as if all the populations of the world were rising or had risen into incendiary madness; unable longer to endure such an avalanche of forgeries, and of penalties in consequence, as had accumulated upon them? The speaker is "excellent;" the notes he does are beautiful? Beautifully fit for the market, yes; *he* is an excellent artist in his business; — and the more excellent he is, the more is my desire to lay him by the heels, and fling *him* into the treadmill, that I might save the poor sweating tailors, French Sansculottes, and Irish Sanspotatoes from bearing the smart!

For the smart must be borne; some one must bear it, as sure as God lives. Every word of man is either a note or a forged note: — have these eternal skies forgotten to be in earnest, think you, because men go grinning like enchanted apes? Foolish souls, this now as of old is the unalterable law of your existence. If you know the truth and do it, the Universe itself seconds you, bears you on to sure victory everywhere: — and, observe, to sure defeat everywhere if you do *not* do the truth. And alas, if you *know* only the eloquent fallacious semblance of the truth, what chance is there of your ever doing it? You will do something very different from *it*, I think! — He who well considers, will find this same "art of speech," as we moderns have it, to be a truly astonishing product of the Ages; and the longer he considers it, the more astonishing and alarming. I reckon it the saddest of all the curses that now lie heavy on us. With horror and amazement, one perceives that this much-celebrated "art," so diligently practised in all corners of the world just now, is the chief destroyer of whatever good is born to us (softly, swiftly shutting up all nascent good, as if under exhausted glass receivers, there to choke and die); and the grand parent manufactory of evil to us, — as it were, the last finishing and varnishing workshop of all the Devil's ware that circulates under the sun. No Devil's sham is fit for the market till it have been polished and enamelled here; this is the general assaying-house for such, where the artists examine and answer, "Fit for the market; not fit!" Words will not express what mischiefs the misuse of words has done, and is doing, in these heavy-laden generations.

Do you want a man *not* to practise what he believes, then encourage him to keep often speaking it in words. Every time he speaks it, the tendency to do it will grow less. His empty speech of what he believes, will be a weariness and an affliction to the wise man. But do you wish his empty speech of what he believes, to become farther an insincere speech of what he does not believe? Celebrate to him his gift of speech; assure him that he shall rise in Parliament by means of it, and achieve great things without any performance; that eloquent speech, whether performed or not, is admirable. My friends, eloquent unperformed speech, in Parliament or elsewhere, is horrible! The eloquent man that delivers, in Parliament or elsewhere, a beautiful speech, and will perform nothing of it, but leaves it as if already performed, — what can you make of that man? He has enrolled himself among the *Ignes Fatui* and Children of the Wind; means to serve, as beautifully illuminated Chinese Lantern, in that corps henceforth. I think, the serviceable thing you could do to that man, if permissible, would be a severe one: To *clip off* a bit of his eloquent tongue by way of penance and warning; another bit, if he again spoke without performing; and so again, till you had clipt the whole tongue away from him, — and were delivered, you and he, from at least one miserable mockery: "There, eloquent friend, see now in silence if there be any redeeming deed in thee; of blasphemous wind-eloquence, at least, we shall have no more!" How many pretty men have gone this road, escorted by the beautifulest marching music from all the "public organs;" and have found at last that it ended — where? It is the *broad* road, that leads direct to Limbo and the Kingdom of the Inane. Gifted men, and once valiant nations, and as it were the whole world with one accord, are marching thither, in melodious triumph, all the drums and hautboys giving out their cheerfulest *Ça-ira*. It is the universal humor of the world just now. My friends, I am very sure you will *arrive*, unless you halt!—

Considered as the last finish of education, or of human culture, worth and acquirement, the art of speech is noble, and even divine; it is like the kindling of a Heaven's light to *show* us what a glorious world exists, and has perfected itself, in a man. But if no world exist in the man; if nothing but continents of empty vapor, of greedy self-conceits, commonplace hearsays, and indistinct loomings of a sordid *chaos* exist in him, what will be the use of "light" to show us that? Better a thousand times that such a man do not speak; but keep his empty vapor and his sordid chaos to himself, hidden to the utmost from all beholders. To look on that, can be good for no human beholder; to look away from that, must be good. And if, by delusive semblances of rhetoric, logic, first-class degrees, and the aid of elocution-masters and parliamentary reporters, the poor proprietor of said chaos should be led to persuade himself, and get others persuaded, — which it is the nature of his sad task to do, and which, in certain eras of the world, it is fatally possible to do, — that this is a *cosmos* which he owns; that *he,* being so perfect in tongue-exercise and full of college-honors, is an "educated" man, and pearl of great price in his generation; that round him, and his parliament emulously listening to him, as round some divine apple of gold set in a picture of silver, all the world should gather to adore: what is likely to become of him and the gathering world? An apple of Sodom set in the clusters of Gomorrah: that, little as he suspects it, is the definition of the poor chaotically eloquent man, with his emulous parliament and miserable adoring world! — Considered as the whole of education, or human culture, which it now is in our modern manners; all apprenticeship except to mere handicraft having fallen obsolete, and the "educated man" being with us emphatically and exclusively the man that can speak well with tongue or pen, and astonish men by the quantities of speech he has *heard* ("tremendous *reader,*" "walking encyclopædia," and such like), — the Art of Speech is probably definable in that case as the short summary of all the Black Arts put together.

————

But the Schoolmaster is secondary, an effect rather than a cause in this matter: what the Schoolmaster with his universities shall manage or attempt to teach will be ruled by what the Society with its practical industries is continually demanding that men should learn. We spoke once of vital *lungs* for

Society: and in fact this question always rises as the alpha and omega of social questions, What methods the Society has of summoning aloft into the high places, for its help and governance, the wisdom that is born to it in all places, and of course is born chiefly in the more populous or lower places? For this, if you will consider it, expresses the ultimate available result, and net sum-total, of all the efforts, struggles and confused activities that go on in the Society; and determines whether they are true and wise efforts, certain to be victorious, or false and foolish, certain to be futile, and to fall captive and caitiff. How do men rise in your Society? In all Societies, Turkey included, and I suppose Dahomey included, men do rise; but the question of questions always is, What kind of men? Men of noble gifts, or men of ignoble? It is the one or the other; and a life-and-death inquiry which! For in all places and all times, little as you may heed it, Nature most silently but most inexorably demands that it be the one and *not* the other. And you need not try to palm an ignoble sham upon her, and call it noble; for she is a judge. And her penalties, as quiet as she looks, are terrible: amounting to world-earthquakes, to anarchy and death everlasting; and admit of no appeal! —

Surely England still flatters herself that she has *lungs;* that she can still breathe a little? Or is it that the poor creature, driven into mere blind industrialisms; and as it were, gone pearl-diving this long while many fathoms deep, and tearing up the oyster-beds so as never creature did before, hardly knows, — so busy in the belly of the oyster chaos, where is no thought of "breathing," — whether she has lungs or not? Nations of a robust habit, and fine deep chest, can sometimes take in a deal of breath *before* diving; and live long, in the muddy deeps, without new breath: but they too come to need it at last, and will die if they cannot get it!

To the gifted soul that is born in England, what is the career, then, that will carry him, amid noble Olympic dust, up to the immortal gods? For his country's sake, that it may not lose the service he was born capable of doing it; for his own sake, that his life be not choked and perverted, and his light from **Heaven** be not changed into lightning from the Other Place, — it is essential that there be such a career. The country that can offer no career in that case, is a doomed country ; nay it is already a dead country : it has secured the ban of Heaven upon it; will not have Heaven's light, will have the Other Place's lightning ; and may consider itself as appointed to expire, in frightful coughings of street musketry or otherwise, on a set day, and to be in the eye of law dead. In no country is there not some career, inviting to it either the noble Hero, or the tough Greek of the Lower Empire : which of the two do your careers invite ? There is no question more important. The kind of careers you offer in countries still living, determines with perfect exactness the kind of the life that is in them, — whether it is natural blessed life, or galvanic accursed ditto, and likewise what degree of strength is in the same.

Our English careers to born genius are twofold. There is the silent or unlearned career of the Industrialisms, which are very many among us ; and there is the articulate or learned career of the three professions, Medicine, Law (under which we may include Politics), and the Church. Your born genius, therefore, will first have to ask himself, Whether he can hold his tongue or cannot ? True, all human talent, especially all deep talent, is a talent to *do*, and is intrinsically of silent nature ; inaudible, like the Sphere Harmonies and Eternal Melodies, of which it is an incarnated fraction. All real talent, I fancy, would much rather, if it listened only to Nature's monitions, express itself in rhythmic facts than in melodious words, which latter at best, where they are good for anything, are only a feeble echo and shadow or foreshadow of the former. But talents differ much in this of power to be silent ; and circumstances, of position, opportunity and such like, modify them still more ; — and Nature's monitions, oftenest quite drowned in foreign hearsays, are by no means the only ones listened to in deciding ! — The Industrialisms are all of silent nature ; and some of them are heroic and eminently human ; others, again, we may call unheroic, not eminently human : *beaverish* rather, but still honest ; some are even *vul pine,* altogether inhuman and dishonest. Your born genius must make his choice.

If a soul is born with divine intelligence, and has its lips touched with hallowed fire, in consecration for high enterprises under the sun, this young soul will find the question asked of him by England every hour and moment: "Canst thou turn thy human intelligence into the beaver sort, and make honest contrivance, and accumulation of capital by it? If so, do it; and avoid the vulpine kind, which I don't recommend. Honest triumphs in engineering and machinery await thee; scrip awaits thee, commercial successes, kingship in the counting-room, on the stock-exchange; — thou shalt be the envy of surrounding flunkies, and collect into a heap more gold than a dray-horse can draw." — "Gold, so much gold?" answers the ingenuous soul, with visions of the envy of surrounding flunkies dawning on him; and in very many cases decides that he will contract himself into beaverism, and with such a horse-draught of gold, emblem of a never-imagined success in beaver heroism, strike the surrounding flunkies yellow.

This is our common course; this is in some sort open to every creature, what we call the beaver career; perhaps more open in England, taking in America too, than it ever was in any country before. And, truly, good consequences follow out of it: who can be blind to them? Half of a most excellent and opulent result is realized to us in this way; baleful only when it sets up (as too often now) for being the whole result. A half-result which will be blessed and heavenly so soon as the other half is had, — namely wisdom to guide the first half. Let us honor all honest human power of contrivance in its degree. The beaver intellect, so long as it steadfastly refuses to be vulpine, and answers the tempter pointing out short routes to it with an honest "No, no," is truly respectable to me; and many a highflying speaker and singer whom I have known, has appeared to me much less of a developed man than certain of my mill-owning, agricultural, commercial, mechanical, or otherwise industrial friends, who have held their peace all their days and gone on in the silent state. If a man *can* keep his intellect silent, and make it even into honest beaverism, several very manful moralities, in danger of wreck on other courses, may comport well with that, and give it a genuine and partly human character; and I will tell him, in these days he may do far worse with himself and his intellect than change it into beaverism, and make honest money with it. If indeed he could become a *heroic* industrial, and have a life "eminently human"! But that is not easy at present. Probably some ninety-nine out of every hundred of our gifted souls, who have to seek a career for themselves, go this beaver road. Whereby the first half-result, national wealth namely, is plentifully realized; and only the second half, or wisdom to guide it, is dreadfully behindhand.

But now if the gifted soul be not of taciturn nature, be of vivid, impatient, rapidly productive nature, and aspire much to give itself sensible utterance, — I find that, in this case, the field it has in England is narrow to an extreme; is perhaps narrower than ever offered itself, for the like object, in this world before. Parliament, Church, Law: let the young vivid soul turn whither he will for a career, he finds among variable conditions one condition invariable, and extremely surprising, That the proof of excellence is to be done by the tongue. For heroism that will not speak, but only act, there is no account kept: — The English Nation does not need that silent kind, then, but only the talking kind? Most astonishing. Of all the organs a man has, there is none held in account, it would appear, but the tongue he uses for talking. Premiership, woolsack, mitre, and quasi-crown: all is attainable if you can talk with due ability. Everywhere your proof-shot is to be a well-fired volley of talk. Contrive to talk well, you will get to Heaven, the modern Heaven of the English. Do not talk well, only work well, and heroically hold your peace, you have no chance whatever to get thither; with your utmost industry you may get to Threadneedle Street, and accumulate more gold than a dray-horse can draw. Is not this a very wonderful arrangement?

I have heard of races done by mortals tied in sacks; of human competitors, high aspirants, climbing heavenward on the soaped pole; seizing the soaped pig; and clutching with deft fist, at full gallop, the fated goose tied aloft by its foot; — which feats do prove agility, toughness and other useful faculties in man: but this of dexterous talk is probably as strange a competition as any. And the question rises, Whether certain of these other feats, or perhaps an alternation of all of them, relieved now and then by a bout of grinning through the collar, might not be profitably substituted for the solitary proof-feat of talk, now getting rather monotonous by its long continuance? Alas, Mr. Bull, I do find it is all little other than a proof of toughness, which is a quality I respect, with more or less expenditure of falsity and astucity superadded, which I entirely condemn. Toughness *plus* astucity : — perhaps a simple wooden mast set up in Palace-Yard, well soaped and duly presided over, might be the honester method? Such a method as this by trial of talk, for filling your chief offices in Church and State, was perhaps never heard of in the solar system before. You are quite used to it, my poor friend; and nearly dead by the consequences of it: but in the other Planets, as in other epochs of your own Planet it would have done had you proposed it, the thing awakens incredulous amazement, world-wide Olympic laughter, which ends in tempestuous hootings, in tears and horror! My friend, if you can, as heretofore this good while, find nobody to take care of your affairs but the expertest talker, it is all over with your affairs and you. Talk never yet could guide any man's or nation's affairs; nor will it yours, except towards the *Limbus Patrum,* where all talk, except a very select kind of it, lodges at last.

Medicine, guarded too by preliminary impediments, and frightful medusa-heads of quackery, which deter many generous souls from entering, is of the *half*-articulate professions, and does not much invite the ardent kinds of ambition. The intellect required for medicine might be wholly human, and indeed should by all rules be, — the profession of the Human Healer being radically a sacred one and connected with the highest priesthoods, or rather being itself the outcome and acme of all priesthoods, and divinest conquests of intellect here below. As will appear one day, when men take off their old monastic and ecclesiastic spectacles, and look with eyes again! In essence the Physician's task is always heroic, eminently human: but in practice most unluckily at present we find it too become in good part *beaverish ;* yielding a money-result alone. And what of it is not beaverish, — does not that too go mainly to ingenious talking, publishing of yourself, ingratiating of yourself; a partly human exercise or waste of intellect, and alas a partly vulpine ditto; — making the once sacred 'Ιατρὸs, or Human Healer, more impossible for us than ever!

Angry basilisks watch at the gates of Law and Church just now; and strike a sad damp into the nobler of the young aspirants. Hard bonds are offered you to sign; as it were, a solemn engagement to constitute yourself an impostor, before ever entering; to declare your belief in incredibilities, — your determination, in short, to take Chaos for Cosmos, and Satan for the Lord of things, if he come with money in his pockets, and horsehair and bombazine decently wrapt about him. Fatal preliminaries, which deter many an ingenuous young soul, and send him back from the threshold, and I hope will deter ever more. But if you do enter, the condition is well known: "Talk; who can talk best here? His shall be the mouth of gold, and the purse of gold; and with my μίτρα (once the head-dress of unfortunate females, I am told) shall his sacred temples be begirt."

Ingenuous souls, unless forced to it, do now much shudder at the threshold of both these careers, and not a few desperately turn back into the wilderness rather, to front a very rude fortune, and be devoured by wild beasts as is likeliest. But as to Parliament, again, and its eligibility if attainable, there is yet no question anywhere; the ingenuous soul, if possessed of money-capital enough, is predestined by the parental and all manner of monitors to that career of talk; and accepts it with alacrity and clearness of heart, doubtful only whether he shall be *able* to make a speech. Courage, my brave young fellow. If you can climb a soaped pole of any kind, you will certainly be able to make a speech. All mortals have a tongue; and carry on some jumble, if not of thought, yet of stuff which they could talk. The weakest of animals has got a cry in it, and can give voice before dying. If you are tough enough, bent upon it desperately enough, I engage you shall make a speech; — but whether that will be the way to Heaven for you, I do not engage.

These, then, are our two careers for genius: mute Industrialism, which can seldom become very human, but remains beaverish mainly : and the three Professions named learned, — that is to say, able to talk. For the heroic or higher kinds of human intellect, in the silent state, there is not the smallest inquiry anywhere; apparently a thing not wanted in this country at present. What the supply may be, I cannot inform M'Croudy; but the market-demand, he may himself see, is *nil*. These are our three professions that require human intellect in part or whole, not able to do with mere beaverish; and such a part does the gift of talk play in one and all of them. Whatsoever is not beaverish seems to go forth in the shape of talk. To such length is human intellect wasted or suppressed in this world!

If the young aspirant is not rich enough for Parliament, and is deterred by the basilisks or otherwise from entering on Law or Church, and cannot altogether reduce his human intellect to the beaverish condition, or satisfy himself with the prospect of making money, — what becomes of him in such case, which is naturally the case of very many, and ever of more? In such case there remains but one outlet for him, and notably enough that too is a talking one: the outlet of Literature, of trying to write Books. Since, owing to preliminary basilisks, want of cash, or superiority to cash, he cannot mount aloft by eloquent talking, let him try it by dexterous eloquent writing. Here happily, having three fingess, and capital to buy a quire of paper, he can try it to all lengths and in spite of all mortals : in this career there is happily no public impediment that can turn him back; nothing but private starvation — which is itself a *finis* or kind of goal — can pretend to hinder a British man from prosecuting Literature to the very utmost, and wringing the final secret from her: "A

talent is in thee; No talent is in thee." To the British subject who fancies genius may be lodged in him, this liberty
remains; and truly it is, if well computed, almost the only
one he has.

A crowded portal this of Literature, accordingly! The
haven of expatriated spiritualisms, and alas also of expatriated
vanities and prurient imbecilities: here do the windy aspirations, foiled activities, foolish ambitions, and frustrate human
energies reduced to the vocable condition, fly as to the one
refuge left; and the Republic of Letters increases in population at a faster rate than even the Republic of America. The
strangest regiment in her Majesty's service, this of the Soldiers
of Literature: — would your Lordship much like to march
through Coventry with them? The immortal gods are there
(quite irrecognizable under these disguises), and also the lowest
broken valets; — an extremely miscellaneous regiment. In
fact the regiment, superficially viewed, looks like an immeasurable motley flood of discharged play-actors, funambulists, false
prophets, drunken ballad-singers; and marches not as a regiment, but as a boundless canaille, — without drill, uniform,
captaincy or billet; with huge *over*-proportion of drummers;
you would say, a regiment gone wholly to the drum, with
hardly a good musket to be seen in it, — more a canaille than
a regiment. Canaille of all the loud-sounding levities, and
general winnowings of Chaos, marching through the world in
a most ominous manner; proclaiming, audibly if you have
ears: "Twelfth hour of the Night; ancient graves yawning;
pale clammy Puseyisms screeching in their winding-sheets;
owls busy in the City regions; many goblins abroad! Awake
ye living; dream no more; arise to judgment! Chaos and
Gehenna are broken loose; the Devil with his Bedlams must
be flung in chains again, and the Last of the Days is about
to dawn!" Such is Literature to the reflective soul at this
moment.

But what now concerns us most is the circumstance that
here too the demand is, Vocables, still vocables. In all appointed courses of activity and paved careers for human
genius, and in this unpaved, unappointed, broadest career of

Literature, broad way that leadeth to destruction for so many, the one duty laid upon you is still, Talk, talk. Talk well with pen or tongue, and it shall be well with you; do not talk well, it shall be ill with you. To wag the tongue with dexterous acceptability, there is for human worth and faculty, in our England of the Nineteenth Century, that one method of emergence and no other. Silence, you would say, means annihilation for the Englishman of the Nineteenth Century. The worth that has not spoken itself, is not; or is potentially only, and as if it were not. Vox is the God of this Universe. If you have human intellect, it avails nothing unless you either make it into beaverism, or talk with it. Make it into beaverism, and gather money; or else make talk with it, and gather what you can. Such is everywhere the demand for talk among us: to which, of course, the supply is proportionate.

From dinners up to woolsacks and divine mitres, here in England, much may be gathered by talk; without talk, of the human sort nothing. Is Society become wholly a bag of wind, then, ballasted by guineas? Are our interests in it as a sounding brass and a tinkling cymbal? — In Army or Navy, when unhappily we have war on hand, there is, almost against our will, some kind of demand for certain of the silent talents. But in peace, that too passes into mere demand of the ostentations, of the pipeclays and the blank cartridges; and, — except that Naval men are occasionally, on long voyages, forced to hold their tongue, and converse with the dumb elements, and illimitable oceans, that moan and rave there without you and within you, which is a great advantage to the Naval man, — our poor United Services have to make conversational windbags and ostentational paper-lanterns of themselves, or do worse, even as the others.

My friends, must I assert, then, what surely all men know, though all men seem to have forgotten it, That in the learned professions as in the unlearned, and in human things throughout, in every place and in every time, the true function of intellect is *not* that of talking, but of understanding and discerning with a view to performing! An intellect may easily talk too much, and perform too little. Gradually, if it get into the noxious habit of talk, there will less and less perform-ance come of it, talk being so delightfully handy in compari-son with work; and at last there will no work, or thought of work, be got from it at all. Talk, except as the preparation for work, is worth almost nothing; — sometimes it is worth infinitely less than nothing; and becomes, little conscious of playing such a fatal part, the general summary of pretentious nothingnesses, and the chief of all the curses the Posterity of Adam are liable to in this sublunary world! Would you dis-cover the Atropos of Human Virtue; the sure Destroyer, "by painless extinction," of Human Veracities, Performances, and Capabilities to perform or to be veracious, — it is this, you have it here.

Unwise talk is matchless in unwisdom. Unwise work, if it but persist, is everywhere struggling towards correction, and restoration to health; for it is still in contact with Nature, and all Nature incessantly contradicts it, and will heal it or annihilate it: not so with unwise talk, which addresses itself, regardless of veridical Nature, to the universal suffrages; and can if it be dexterous, find harbor there till all the suffrages are bankrupt and gone to Houndsditch, Nature not interfering with her protest till then. False speech, definable as the acme of unwise speech, is capable, as we already said, of be-coming the falsest of all things. Falsest of all things: — and whither will the general deluge of that, in Parliament and Synagogue, in Book and Broadside, carry you and your affairs, my friend, when once they are embarked on it as now?

———

Parliament, *Parliamentum*, is by express appointment the Talking Apparatus; yet not in Parliament either is the essen-tial function, by any means, talk. Not to speak your opinion well, but to have a good and just opinion worth speaking, — for every Parliament, as for every man, this latter is the point. Contrive to have a true opinion, you will get it told in some way, better or worse; and it will be a blessing to all creatures. Have a false opinion, and tell it with the tongue of Angels,

what can that profit? The better you *tell* it, the worse it
will be!

In Parliament and out of Parliament, and everywhere in
this Universe, your one salvation is, That you can discern
with just insight, and follow with noble valor, what the law of
the case before you is, what the appointment of the Maker in
regard to it has been. Get this out of one man, you are
saved; fail to get this out of the most August Parliament
wrapt in the sheepskins of a thousand years, you are lost, —
your Parliament, and you, and all your sheepskins are lost.
Beautiful talk is by no means the most pressing want in Parliament! We have had some reasonable modicum of talk in
Parliament! What talk has done for us in Parliament, and is
now doing, the dullest of us at length begins to see!

Much has been said of Parliament's breeding men to business.; of the training an Official Man gets in this school of
argument and talk. He is here inured to patience, tolerance;
sees what is what in the Nation and in the Nation's Government; attains official knowledge, official courtesy and
manners; — in short, is polished at all points into official articulation, and here better than elsewhere qualifies himself to
be a Governor of men. So it is said. — Doubtless, I think, he
will see and suffer much in Parliament, and inure himself to
several things; — he will, with what eyes he has, gradually
see Parliament itself, for one thing; what a high-soaring, help-
lessly floundering, ever-babbling yet inarticulate dark dumb
Entity it is (certainly one of the strangest under the sun just
now): which doubtless, if he have in view to get measures
voted there one day, will be an important acquisition for him.
But as to breeding himself for a Doer of Work, much more for
a King, or Chief of Doers, here in this element of talk; as to
that I confess the fatalest doubts, or rather, alas, I have no
doubt! Alas, it is our fatalest misery just now, not easily
alterable, and yet urgently requiring to be altered, That no
British man can attain to be a Statesman, or Chief of *Workers,*
till he has first proved himself a Chief of *Talkers:* which
mode of trial for a Worker, is it not precisely, of all the trials
you could set him upon, the falsest and unfairest?

Nay, I doubt much you are not likely ever to meet the fittest material for a Statesman, or Chief of Workers, in such an element as that. Your Potential Chief of Workers, will he come there at all, to try whether he can talk? Your poor tenpound franchisers and electoral world generally, in love with eloquent talk, are they the likeliest to discern what man it is that has worlds of silent work in him? No. Or is such a man, even if born in the due rank for it, the likeliest to present himself, and court their most sweet voices? Again, no.

The Age that admires talk so much can have little discernment for inarticulate work, or for anything that is deep and genuine. Nobody, or hardly anybody, having in himself an earnest sense for truth, how can anybody recognize an inarticulate Veracity, or Nature-fact of any kind; a Human *Doer* especially, who is the most complex, profound, and inarticulate of all Nature's Facts? Nobody can recognize him: till once he is patented, get some public stamp of authenticity, and has been articulately proclaimed, and asserted to be a Doer. To the worshipper of talk, such a one is a sealed book. An excellent human soul, direct from Heaven, — how shall any excellence of man become recognizable to this unfortunate? Not except by announcing and placarding itself as excellent, — which, I reckon, it above other things will probably be in no great haste to do.

Wisdom, the divine message which every soul of man brings into this world; the divine prophecy of what the new man has got the new and peculiar capability to do, is intrinsically of silent nature. It cannot at once, or completely at all, be read off in words; for it is written in abstruse facts, of endowment, position, desire, opportunity, granted to the man; — interprets itself in presentiments, vague struggles, passionate endeavors; and is only legible in whole when his work is *done*. Not by the noble monitions of Nature, but by the ignoble, is a man much tempted to publish the secret of his soul in words. Words, if he have a secret, will be forever inadequate to it. Words do but disturb the real answer of fact which could be given to it; disturb, obstruct, and will in the end abolish, and render impossible, said answer. No grand Doer in this world

can be a copious speaker about his doings. William the Silent
spoke himself best in a country liberated; Oliver Cromwell
did not shine in rhetoric; Goethe, when he had but a book in
view, found that he must say nothing even of that, if it was to
succeed with him.

Then as to politeness, and breeding to business. An official
man must be bred to business; of course he must: and not for
essence only, but even for the manners of office he requires
breeding. Besides his intrinsic faculty, whatever that may be,
he must be cautious, vigilant, discreet, — above all things, he
must be reticent, patient, polite. Certain of these qualities
are by nature imposed upon men of station; and they are
trained from birth to some exercise of them: this constitutes
their one intrinsic qualification for office; — this is their one
advantage in the New Downing Street projected for this New
Era; and it will not go for much in that Institution. One
advantage, or temporary advantage; against which there are
so many counterbalances. It is the indispensable preliminary
for office, but by no means the complete outfit, — a miserable
outfit where there is nothing farther.

Will your Lordship give me leave to say that, practically,
the intrinsic qualities will presuppose these preliminaries too,
but by no means *vice versâ*. That, on the whole, if you have
got the intrinsic qualities, you have got everything, and the
preliminaries will prove attainable; but that if you have got
only the preliminaries, you have yet got nothing. A man of
real dignity will not find it impossible to bear himself in a
dignified manner; a man of real understanding and insight
will get to know, as the fruit of his very first study, what the
laws of his situation are, and will conform to these. Rough
old Samuel Johnson, blustering Boreas and rugged Arctic Bear
as he often was, defined himself, justly withal, as a polite man:
a noble manful attitude of soul is his; a clear, true and loyal
sense of what others are, and what he himself is, shines
through the rugged coating of him; comes out as grave deep
rhythmus when his King honors him, and he will not "bandy
compliments with his King;" — is traceable too in his indignant trampling down of the Chesterfield patronages, tailor-

made insolences, and contradictions of sinners ; which may be called his *revolutionary* movements, hard and peremptory by the law of them; these could not be soft like his *constitutional* ones, when men and kings took him for somewhat like the thing he was. Given a noble man, I think your Lordship may expect by and by a polite man. No " politer " man was to be found in Britain than the rustic Robert Burns : high duchesses were captivated with the chivalrous ways of the man; recognized that here was the true chivalry, and divine nobleness of bearing, — as indeed they well might, now when the Peasant God and Norse Thor had come down among them again! Chivalry this, if not as they do chivalry in Drury Lane or West-End drawing-rooms, yet as they do it in Valhalla and the General Assembly of the Gods.

For indeed, who *invented* chivalry, politeness, or anything that is noble and melodious and beautiful among us, except precisely the like of Johnson and of Burns ? The select few who in the generations of this world were wise and valiant, they, in spite of all the tremendous majority of blockheads and slothful belly-worshippers, and noisy ugly persons, have devised whatsoever is noble in the manners of man to man. I expect they will learn to be polite, your Lordship, when you give them a chance ! — Nor is it as a school of human culture, for this or for any other grace or gift, that Parliament will be found first-rate or indispensable. As experience in the river is indispensable to the ferryman, so is knowledge of his Parliament to the British Peel or Chatham ; — so was knowledge of the Œil-de-Bœuf to the French Choiseul. Where and how said river, whether Parliament with Wilkeses, or Œil-de-Bœuf with Pompadours, can be waded, boated, swum ; how the miscellaneous cargoes, " measures " so called, can be got across it, according to their kinds, and landed alive on the hither side as facts : — we have all of us our *ferries* in this world; and must know the river and its ways, or get drowned some day ! In that sense, practice in Parliament is indispensable to the British Statesman ; but not in any other sense.

A school, too, of manners and of several other things, the Parliament will doubtless be to the aspirant Statesman ; a

school better or worse; — as the Œil-de-Bœuf likewise was,
and as all scenes where men work or live are sure to be.
Especially where many men work together, the very rubbing
against one another will grind and polish off their angularities
into roundness, into "politeness" after a sort; and the official
man, place him how you may, will never want for schooling,
of extremely various kinds. A first-rate school one cannot
call this Parliament for him; — I fear to say what rate at present! In so far as it teaches him vigilance, patience, courage,
toughness of lungs or of soul, and skill in any kind of swimming, it is a good school. In so far as it forces him to speak
where Nature orders silence; and even, lest all the world
should learn his secret (which often enough would kill his
secret, and little profit the world), forces him to speak falsities, vague ambiguities, and the froth-dialect usual in Parliaments in these times, it may be considered one of the worst
schools ever devised by man; and, I think, may almost challenge the Œil-de-Bœuf to match it in badness.

Parliament will train your men to the manners required of
a statesman; but in a much less degree to the intrinsic functions of one. To these latter, it is capable of *mis*training
as nothing else can. Parliament will train you to talk; and
above all things to hear, with patience, unlimited quantities of
foolish talk. To tell a good story for yourself, and to make it
appear that you have done your work: this, especially in constitutional countries, is something; — and yet in all countries,
constitutional ones too, it is intrinsically nothing, probably
even less. For it is not the function of any mortal, in Downing Street or elsewhere here below, to wag the tongue of him,
and make it appear that he has done work; but to wag some
quite other organs of him, and to do work; there is no danger
of his work's appearing by and by. Such an accomplishment,
even in constitutional countries, I grieve to say, may become
much *less* than nothing: Have you at all computed how much
less? The human creature who has once given way to satisfying himself with "appearances," to seeking his salvation in
"appearances," the moral life of such human creature is rapidly bleeding out of him. Depend upon it, Beelzebub, Satan,

or however you may name the too authentic Genius of Eternal
Death, has got that human creature in his claws. By and by
you will have a dead parliamentary bagpipe, and your living
man fled away without return!

Such parliamentary bagpipes I myself have heard play tunes,
much to the satisfaction of the people. Every tune lies within their compass; and their mind (for they still call it *mind*)
is ready as a hurdy-gurdy on turning of the handle: "My
Lords, this question now before the House" — Ye Heavens,
O ye divine Silences, was there in the womb of Chaos, then,
such a product, liable to be evoked by human art, as that same?
While the galleries were all applausive of heart, and the Fourth
Estate looked with eyes enlightened, as if you had touched its
lips with a staff dipped in honey, — I have sat with reflections
too ghastly to be uttered. A poor human creature and learned
friend, once possessed of many fine gifts, possessed of intellect, veracity, and manful conviction on a variety of objects,
has he now lost all that; — converted all that into a glistering
phosphorescence which can show itself on the outside; while
within, all is dead, chaotic, dark; a painted sepulchre full of
dead-men's bones! Discernment, knowledge, intellect, in the
human sense of the words, this man has now none. His
opinion you do not ask on any matter: on the *matter* he has
no opinion, judgment, or insight; only on what may be said
about the matter, how it may be argued of, what tune may be
played upon it to enlighten the eyes of the Fourth Estate.

Such a soul, though to the eye he still keeps tumbling
about in the Parliamentary element, and makes "motions,"
and passes bills, for aught I know, — are we to define him as
a *living* one, or as a dead? Partridge the Almanac-Maker,
whose "publications" still regularly appear, is known to be
dead! The dog that was drowned last summer, and that floats
up and down the Thames with ebb and flood ever since, — is
it not dead? Alas, in the hot months, you meet here and
there such a floating dog; and at length, if you often use
the river steamers, get to know him by sight. "There he
is again, still astir there in his quasi-stygian element!" you
dejectedly exclaim (perhaps reading your Morning Newspaper

at the moment); and reflect, with a painful oppression of nose
and imagination, on certain completed professors of parliamentary eloquence in modern times. Dead long since, but
not resting; daily doing motions in that Westminster region
still, — daily from Vauxhall to Blackfriars, and back again;
and cannot get away at all! Daily (from Newspaper or river
steamer) you may see him at some point of his fated course,
hovering in the eddies, stranded in the ooze, or rapidly pro-
gressing with flood or ebb; and daily the odor of him is getting more intolerable : daily the condition of him appeals
more tragically to gods and men.

Nature admits no lie; most men profess to be aware of this,
but few in any measure lay it to heart. Except in the departments of mere material manipulation, it seems to be taken
practically as if this grand truth were merely a polite flourish
of rhetoric. What is a lie? The question is worth asking,
once and away, by the practical English mind.

A voluntary spoken divergence from the fact as it stands,
as it has occurred and will proceed to develop itself : this
clearly, if adopted by any man, will so far forth *mis*lead him
in all practical dealing with the fact; till he cast that statement out of him, and reject it as an unclean poisonous thing,
he can have no success in dealing with the fact. If such
spoken divergence from the truth be involuntary, we lament
it as a misfortune; and are entitled, at least the speaker of
it is, to lament it extremely as the most palpable of all mis-
fortunes, as the indubitablest losing of his way, and turning
aside from the goal instead of pressing towards it, in the race
set before him. If the divergence is voluntary, — there super-
adds itself to our sorrow a just indignation : we call the voluntary spoken divergence a lie, and justly abhor it as the
essence of human treason and baseness, the desertion of a man
to the Enemy of men against himself and his brethren. A
lost deserter; who has gone over to the Enemy, called Satan;
and cannot *but* be lost in the adventure! Such is every liar
with the tongue; and such in all nations is he, at all epochs,

considered. Men pull his nose, and kick him out of doors; and by peremptory expressive methods signify that they can and will have no trade with him. Such is spoken divergence from the fact; so fares it with the practiser of that sad art.

But have we well considered a divergence *in thought* from what is the fact? Have we considered the man whose very thought is a lie to him and to us! He too is a frightful man; repeating about this Universe on every hand what is not, and driven to repeat it; the sure herald of ruin to all that follow him, that know with *his* knowledge! And would you learn how to get a mendacious thought, there is no surer recipe than carrying a loose tongue. The lying thought, you already either have it, or will soon get it by that method. He who lies with his very tongue, *he* clearly enough has long ceased to think truly in his mind. Does he, in any sense, "think"? All his thoughts and imaginations, if they extend beyond mere beaverisms, astucities and sensualisms, are false, incomplete, perverse, untrue even to himself. He has become a false mirror of this Universe; not a small mirror only, but a crooked, bedimmed and utterly deranged one. But all loose tongues too are akin to lying ones; are insincere at the best, and go rattling with little meaning; the thought lying languid at a great distance behind them, if thought there be behind them at all. Gradually there will be none or little! How can the thought of such a man, what he calls thought, be other than false?

Alas, the palpable liar with his tongue does at least know that he is lying, and has or might have some faint vestige of remorse and chance of amendment; but the impalpable liar, whose tongue articulates mere accepted commonplaces, cants and babblement, which means only, "Admire me, call me an excellent stump-orator!" — of him what hope is there? His thought, what thought he had, lies dormant, inspired only to invent vocables and plausibilities; while the tongue goes so glib, the thought is absent, gone a wool-gathering; getting itself drugged with the applausive "Hear, hear!" — what will become of such a man? His idle thought has run all to seed, and grown false and the giver of falsities; the inner light of his mind is gone out; all his light is mere putridity and phosphorescence henceforth. Whosoever is in quest of ruin, let him with assurance follow that man; he or no one is on the right road to it.

Good Heavens, from the wisest Thought of a man to the actual truth of a Thing as it lies in Nature, there is, one would suppose, a sufficient interval! Consider it, — and what other intervals we introduce! The faithfulest, most glowing word of a man is but an imperfect image of the thought, such as it is, that dwells within him; his best word will never but with error convey his thought to other minds: and then between *his* poor thought and Nature's Fact, which is the Thought of the Eternal, there may be supposed to lie some discrepancies, some shortcomings! Speak your sincerest, think your wisest, there is still a great gulf between you and the fact. And now, do *not* speak your sincerest, and, what will inevitably follow out of that, do not think your wisest, but think only your plausiblest, your showiest for parliamentary purposes, where will you land with that guidance? — I invite the British Parliament, and all the Parliamentary and other Electors of Great Britain, to reflect on this till they have well understood it; and then to ask, each of himself, What probably the horoscopes of the British Parliament, at this epoch of World-History, may be? —

Fail, by any sin or any misfortune, to discover what the truth of the fact is, you are lost so far as that fact goes! If your thought do not image truly but do image falsely the fact, you will vainly try to work upon the fact. The fact will not obey you, the fact will silently resist you; and ever, with silent invincibility, will go on resisting you, till you do get to image it truly instead of falsely. No help for you whatever, except in attaining to a true image of the fact. Needless to vote a false image true; vote it, revote it by overwhelming majorities, by jubilant unanimities and universalities; read it thrice or three hundred times, pass acts of parliament upon it till the Statute-book can hold no more, — it helps not a whit: the thing is not so, the thing is otherwise than so; and Adam's whole Posterity, voting daily on it till the world finish, will not alter it a jot. Can the sublimest sanhedrim, constitutional parliament, or other Collective Wisdom of the world, persuade fire not to burn, sulphuric acid to be sweet milk, or the Moon to become green cheese? The fact is much the reverse:— and even the Constitutional British Parliament abstains from such arduous attempts as these latter in the voting line; and leaves the multiplication-table, the chemical, mechanical and other qualities of material substances to take their own course; being aware that voting and perorating, and reporting in Hansard, will not in the least alter any of these. Which is indisputably wise of the British Parliament.

Unfortunately the British Parliament does not, at present, quite know that *all* manner of things and relations of things, spiritual equally with material, all manner of qualities, entities, existences whatsoever, in this strange visible and invisible Universe, are equally inflexible of nature; that they will, one and all, with precisely the same obstinacy, continue to obey their own law, not our law; deaf as the adder to all charm of parliamentary eloquence, and of voting never so often repeated; silently, but inflexibly and forevermore, declining to change themselves, even as sulphuric acid declines to become sweet milk, though you vote so to the end of the world. This, it sometimes seems to me, is not quite sufficiently laid hold of by the British and other Parliaments just at present. Which surely is a great misfortune to said Parliaments! For, it would appear, the grand point, after all constitutional improvements, and such wagging of wigs in Westminster as there has been, is precisely what it was before any constitution was yet heard of, or the first official wig had budded out of nothing: namely, to ascertain what the truth of your question, in Nature, really is! Verily so. In this time and place, as in all past and in all future times and places. To-day in St. Stephen's, where constitutional, philanthropical, and other great things lie in the mortar-kit; even as on the Plain of Shinar long ago, where a certain Tower, likewise of a very philanthropic nature, indeed one of the desirablest towers I ever heard of, was to be built,—

but could n't! My friends, I do not laugh; truly I am more inclined to weep.

Get, by six hundred and fifty-eight votes, or by no vote at all, by the silent intimation of your own eyesight and understanding given you direct out of Heaven, and more sacred to you than anything earthly, and than all things earthly, — a correct image of the fact in question, as God and Nature have made it: that is the one thing needful; with that it shall be well with you in whatsoever you have to do with said fact. Get, by the sublimest constitutional methods, belauded by all the world, an *in*correct image of the fact: so shall it be other than well with you; so shall you have laud from able editors and vociferous masses of mistaken human creatures; and from the Nature's Fact, continuing quite silently the same as it was, contradiction, and that only. What else? Will Nature change, or sulphuric acid become sweet milk, for the noise of vociferous blockheads? Surely not. Nature, I assure you, has not the smallest intention of doing so.

On the contrary, Nature keeps silently a most exact Savings-bank, and official register correct to the most evanescent item, Debtor and Creditor, in respect to one and all of us; silently marks down, Creditor by such and such an unseen act of veracity and heroism; Debtor to such a loud blustery blunder, twenty-seven million strong or one unit strong, and to all acts and words and thoughts executed in consequence of that, — Debtor, Debtor, Debtor, day after day, rigorously as Fate (for this *is* Fate that is writing); and at the end of the account you will have it all to pay, my friend; there is the rub! Not the infinitesimalest fraction of a farthing but will be found marked there, for you and against you; and with the due rate of interest you will have to pay it, neatly, completely, as sure as you are alive. You will have to pay it even in money if you live: — and, poor slave, do you think there is no payment but in money? There is a payment which Nature rigorously exacts of men, and also of Nations, and this I think when her wrath is sternest, in the shape of dooming you to possess money. To possess it; to have your bloated vanities fostered into monstrosity by it, your foul passions blown into explosion by it, your heart and perhaps your very stomach ruined with intoxication by it; your poor life and all its manful activities stunned into frenzy and comatose sleep by it, — in one word, as the old Prophets said, your soul forever lost by it. Your soul; so that, through the Eternities, *you* shall have no soul, or manful trace of ever having had a soul; but only, for certain fleeting moments, shall have had a money-bag, and have given soul and heart and (frightfuler still) stomach itself in fatal exchange for the same. You wretched mortal, stumbling about in a God's Temple, and thinking it a brutal Cookery-shop! Nature, when her scorn of a slave is divinest, and blazes like the blinding lightning against his slavehood, often enough flings him a bag of money, silently saying: "That! Away; thy doom is that!" —

For no man, and for no body or biggest multitude of men, has Nature favor, if they part company with her facts and her. Excellent stump-orator; eloquent parliamentary dead-dog, making motions, passing bills; reported in the Morning News-papers, and reputed the "best speaker going"? From the Universe of Fact he has turned himself away; he is gone into partnership with the Universe of Phantasm; finds it profita-blest to deal in forged notes, while the foolish shopkeepers will accept them. Nature for such a man, and for Nations that follow such, has her patibulary forks, and prisons of death everlasting: — dost thou doubt it? Unhappy mortal, Nature otherwise were herself a Chaos and no Cosmos. Nature was not made by an Impostor; not she, I think, rife as they are! — In fact, by money or otherwise, to the uttermost frac-tion of a calculable and incalculable value, we have, each one of us, to settle the exact balance in the above-said Savings-bank, or official register kept by Nature : Creditor by the quantity of veracities we have done, Debtor by the quantity of falsities and errors; there is not, by any conceivable device, the faintest hope of escape from that issue for one of us, nor for all of us.

This used to be a well-known fact; and daily still, in certain edifices, steeple-houses, joss-houses, temples sacred or other, everywhere spread over the world, we hear some dim mumblement of an assertion that such is still, what it was always and will forever be, the fact: but meseems it has terribly fallen out of memory nevertheless; and, from Dan to Beersheba, one in vain looks out for a man that really in his heart believes it. In his heart he believes, as we perceive, that scrip will yield dividends: but that Heaven too has an office of account, and unerringly marks down, against us or for us, whatsoever thing we do or say or think, and treasures up the same in regard to every creature, — this I do not so well perceive that he believes. Poor blockhead, no: he reckons that all payment is in money, or approximately representable by money; finds money go a strange course; disbelieves the parson and his Day of Judgment; discerns not that there is any judgment except in the small or big debt court; and lives (for the present) on that strange footing in this Universe. The unhappy mortal, what is the use of his "civilizations" and his "useful knowledges," if he have forgotten that beginning of human knowledge; the earliest perception of the awakened human soul in this world; the first dictate of Heaven's inspiration to all men? I cannot account him a man any more; but only a kind of human beaver, who has acquired the art of ciphering. He lives without rushing hourly towards suicide, because his soul, with all its noble aspirations and imaginations, is sunk at the bottom of his stomach, and lies torpid there, unaspiring, unimagining, unconsidering, as if it were the vital principle of a mere *four-*footed beaver. A soul of a man, appointed for spinning cotton and making money, or, alas, for merely shooting grouse and gathering rent; to whom Eternity and Immortality, and all human Noblenesses and divine Facts that did not tell upon the stock-exchange, were meaningless fables, empty as the inarticulate wind. He will recover out of that persuasion one day, or be ground to powder, I believe! —

To such a pass, by our beaverisms and our mammonisms; by canting of "prevenient grace" everywhere, and so boarding and lodging our poor souls upon supervenient moonshine everywhere, for centuries long; by our sordid stupidities and our idle babblings; through faith in the divine Stump-Orator, and Constitutional Palaver, or august Sanhedrim of Orators, —

have men and Nations been reduced, in this sad epoch! I cannot call them happy Nations; I must call them Nations like to perish; Nations that will either begin to recover, or else soon die. Recovery is to be hoped; — yes, since there is in Nature an Almighty Beneficence, and His voice, divinely terrible, can be heard in the world-whirlwind now, even as from of old and forevermore. Recovery, or else destruction and annihilation, is very certain; and the crisis, too, comes rapidly on: but by Stump-Orator and Constitutional Palaver, however perfected, my hopes of *recovery* have long vanished. Not by them, I should imagine, but by something far the reverse of them, shall we return to truth and God! —

I tell you, the ignoble intellect cannot think the *truth*, even within its own limits, and when it seriously tries! And of the ignoble intellect that does not seriously try, and has even reached the "ignobleness" of seriously trying the reverse, and of lying with its very tongue, what are we to expect? It is frightful to consider. Sincere wise speech is but an imperfect corollary, and insignificant outer manifestation, of sincere wise thought. He whose very tongue utters falsities, what has his heart long been doing? The thought of his heart is not its wisest, not even *its* wisest; it is its foolishest; — and even of that we have a false and foolish copy. And it is Nature's Fact, or the Thought of the Eternal, which we want to arrive at in regard to the matter, — which if we do *not* arrive at, we shall not save the matter, we shall drive the matter into shipwreck!

The practice of modern Parliaments, with reporters sitting among them, and twenty-seven millions mostly fools listening to them, fills me with amazement. In regard to no *thing*, or fact as God and Nature have made it, can you get so much as the real thought of any honorable head, — even so far as *it*, the said honorable head, still has capacity of thought. What the honorable gentleman's wisest thought is or would have been, had he led from birth a life of piety and earnest veracity and heroic virtue, you, and he himself poor deep-sunk creature, vainly conjecture as from immense dim distances far in the rear of what he is led to *say*. And again,

far in the rear of what his thought is, — surely long infini-
tudes beyond all *he* could ever think, — lies the Thought of
God Almighty, the Image itself of the Fact, the thing you
are in quest of, and must find or do worse! Even his, the
honorable gentleman's, actual bewildered, falsified, vague surmise or quasi-thought, even this is not given you; but only
some falsified copy of this, such as he fancies may suit the
reporters and twenty-seven millions mostly fools. And upon
that latter you are to act; — with what success, do you expect? That is the thought you are to take for the Thought
of the Eternal Mind, — that double-distilled falsity of a block-
headism from one who is false· even as a blockhead!

Do I make myself plain to Mr. Peter's understanding?
Perhaps it will surprise him less that parliamentary eloquence
excites more wonder than admiration in me; that the fate of
countries governed by that sublime alchemy does not appear
the hopefulest just now. Not by that method, I should
apprehend, will the Heavens be scaled and the Earth vanquished; not by that, but by another.

A benevolent man once proposed to me, but without pointing out the methods how, this plan of reform for our benighted
world: To cut from one generation, whether the current one
or the next, all the tongues away, prohibiting Literature too;
and appoint at least one generation to pass its life in silence.
"There, thou one blessed generation, from the vain jargon
of babble thou art beneficently freed. Whatsoever of truth,
traditionary or original, thy own god-given intellect shall
point out to thee as true, that thou wilt go and *do*. In doing
of it there will be a verdict for thee; if a verdict of True,
thou wilt hold by it, and ever again do it; if of Untrue, thou
wilt never try it more, but be eternally delivered from it.
To do aught because the vain hearsays order thee, and the
big clamors of the sanhedrim of fools, is not thy lot, — what
worlds of misery are spared thee! Nature's voice heard in
thy own inner being, and the sacred Commandment of thy
Maker: these shall be thy guidances, thou happy tongueless
generation. What is good and beautiful thou shalt know;

not merely what is said to be so. Not to talk of thy doings, and become the envy of surrounding flunkies, but to taste of the fruit of thy doings themselves, is thine. What the Eternal Laws will sanction for thee, do; what the Froth Gospels and multitudinous long-eared Hearsays never so loudly bid, all this is already chaff for thee, — drifting rapidly along, thou knowest whitherward, on the eternal winds."

Good Heavens, if such a plan were practicable, how the chaff might be winnowed out of every man, and out of all human things; and ninety-nine hundredths of our whole big Universe, spiritual and practical, might blow itself away, as mere torrents of chaff; — whole trade-winds of chaff, many miles deep, rushing continually with the voice of whirlwinds towards a certain FIRE, which knows how to deal with it! Ninety-nine hundredths blown away; all the lies blown away, and some skeleton of a spiritual and practical Universe left standing for us which were *true:* O Heavens, is it forever impossible, then? By a generation that had no *tongue* it really might be done; but not so easily by one that had. Tongues, platforms, parliaments, and fourth-estates; unfettered presses, periodical and stationary literatures: we are nearly all gone to tongue, I think; and our fate is very questionable.

Truly, it is little known at present, and ought forthwith to become better known, what ruin to all nobleness and fruitfulness and blessedness in the genius of a poor mortal you generally bring about, by ordering him to speak, to do all things with a view to their being seen! Few good and fruitful things ever were done, or could be done, on those terms. Silence, silence; and be distant ye profane, with your jargonings and superficial babblements, when a man has anything to *do!* Eye-service, — dost thou know what that is, poor England? — eye-service is all the man can do in these sad circumstances; grows to be all he has the idea of doing, of his or any other man's ever doing, or ever having done, in any circumstances. Sad enough. Alas, it is our saddest woe of all; — too sad for being spoken of at present, while all or nearly all men consider it an imaginary sorrow on my part!

Let the young English soul, in whatever logic-shop and nonsense-verse establishment of an Eton, Oxford, Edinburgh, Halle, Salamanca, or other High Finishing-School, he may be getting his young idea taught how to speak and spout, and print sermons and review-articles, and thereby show himself and fond patrons that it *is* an idea, — lay this solemnly to heart; this is my deepest counsel to him! The idea you have once spoken, if it even were an idea, is no longer yours; it is gone from you, so much life and virtue is gone, and the vital circulations of your self and your destiny and activity are henceforth deprived of it. If you could not get it spoken, if you could still constrain it into silence, so much the richer are you. Better keep your idea while you can: let it still circulate in your blood, and there fructify; inarticulately inciting you to good activities; giving to your whole spiritual life a ruddier health. When the time does come for speaking it, you will speak it all the more concisely, the more expressively, appropriately; and if such a time should never come, have you not already acted it, and uttered it as no words can? Think of this, my young friend; for there is nothing truer, nothing more forgotten in these shabby gold-laced days. Incontinence is half of all the sins of man. And among the many kinds of that base vice, I know none baser, or at present half so fell and fatal, as that same Incontinence of Tongue. "Public speaking," "parliamentary eloquence:" it is a Moloch, before whom young souls are made to pass through the fire. They enter, weeping or rejoicing, fond parents consecrating them to the red-hot Idol, as to the Highest God: and they come out spiritually *dead*. Dead enough; to live thenceforth a galvanic life of mere Stump-Oratory; screeching and gibbering, words without wisdom, without veracity, without conviction more than skin-deep. A divine gift, that? It is a thing admired by the vulgar, and rewarded with seats in the Cabinet and other preciosities; but to the wise, it is a thing not admirable, not adorable; unmelodious rather, and ghastly and bodeful, as the speech of sheeted spectres in the streets at midnight!

Be not a Public Orator, thou brave young British man, thou that art now growing to be something: not a Stump-Orator, if thou canst help it. Appeal not to the vulgar, with its long ears and its seats in the Cabinet; not by spoken words to the vulgar; *hate* the profane vulgar, and bid it begone. Appeal by silent work, by silent suffering if there be no work, to the gods, who have nobler than seats in the Cabinet for thee! Talent for Literature, thou hast such a talent? Believe it not, be slow to believe it! To speak, or to write, Nature did not peremptorily order thee; but to work she did. And know this: there never was a talent even for real Literature, not to speak of talents lost and damned in doing sham Literature, but was primarily a talent for something infinitely better of the silent kind. Of Literature, in all ways, be shy rather than otherwise, at present! There where thou art, work, work; whatsoever thy hand findeth to do, do it, — with the hand of a man, not of a phantasm; be that thy unnoticed blessedness and exceeding great reward. Thy words, let them be few, and well-ordered. Love silence rather than speech in these tragic days, when, for very speaking, the voice of man has fallen inarticulate to man; and hearts, in this loud babbling, sit dark and dumb towards one another. Witty, — above all, oh be not witty: none of us is bound to be witty, under penalties; to be wise and true we all are, under the terriblest penalties!

Brave young friend, dear to me, and *known* too in a sense, though never seen, nor to be seen by me, — you are, what I am not, in the happy case to learn to *be* something and to *do* something, instead of eloquently talking about what has been and was done and may be! The old are what they are, and will not alter; our hope is in you. England's hope, and the world's, is that there may once more be millions such, instead of units as now. *Mactè; i fausto pede.* And may future generations, acquainted again with the silences, and once more cognizant of what is noble and faithful and divine, look back on *us* with pity and incredulous astonishment!